Automate It with Zapier

Boost your business productivity using effective workflow automation techniques

Kelly Goss

BIRMINGHAM—MUMBAI

Automate It with Zapier

Publishing Product Manager: Pavan Ramchandani
Senior Editor: Sofi Rogers
Content Development Editor: Rakhi Patel
Technical Editor: Saurabh Kadave
Copy Editor: Safis Editing
Project Coordinator: Manthan Patel
Proofreader: Safis Editing
Indexer: Manju Arsan
Production Designer: Jyoti Chauhan

First published: July 2021

Production reference: 1230721

Published by Packt Publishing Ltd.
Livery Place
35 Livery Street
Birmingham
B3 2PB, UK.

ISBN 978-1-80020-897-1

www.packt.com

To my father, Eugene, and in loving memory of my mother, Winnie, for their love, sacrifice, and wisdom. You taught me to work hard, challenge myself, and follow my dreams.

To my loving partner, Dawn, for always being present and supportive in our journey together. You are my rock.

To my mentors, David Feldman, Giuseppe Salvati, and Eric Wood, for their unwavering guidance, encouragement, clarity, and insight.

To my fellow consultants, contractors, and freelancers, who work tirelessly to help small businesses succeed and drive our economy.

To women in business, everywhere.

– Kelly Goss

Foreword

Here at Zapier, we're just some humans that think computers should do more work. This was the founding belief of our software, and today we see millions of people automating their tedious tasks with Zapier so they can spend more time on what they love.

Just like playing with Lego, Zapier will allow you to create anything. However, sometimes it is helpful to have a step-by-step guide to ensure you build what you want. That is why we are so excited about Kelly's book.

As one of our Zapier Certified Experts since 2018, Kelly Goss is at the core of what automation and process mapping can do for businesses. She makes it easy for readers to grasp the concepts of process and automation, enabling them to harness the power of Zapier for their needs. Whether businesses are just starting out or have established complex operations, this book will guide them through setting up their first "Zaps" all the way through building advanced workflows.

We appreciate how committed Kelly is to working alongside the Zapier brand and hope you enjoy her perspective on how to make automation work for you!

Cody Jones

Head of Global Partnerships & Channels at Zapier

Ensuring your processes and automations   stay current   91
                                                           Summary   92

4

Managing Your Zaps

Technical requirements   94   Zap editor   107

Keeping your Zaps organized   94   Understanding Zap statuses   109
Labeling your Zaps adequately   94   Managing your connected apps
Using folders in the Zap management   111
area   96   Sharing your connected apps   114

Managing your Zaps   100   Sharing your Zaps and folders   117
Managing your Zaps using the top   Sharing a copy of your Zap   117
navigation bar   101   Sharing Zaps and folders in your Team
Managing your Zaps from within their   or Company account   120
specific
Zap boxes   102   Summary   123
Utilizing the Zap Settings tab in the

5

Troubleshooting and Handling Zap Errors

Technical requirements   126   Understanding the Zap history page   136
                                             Understanding task statuses   141
Managing Zap error alerts   126   Viewing detailed Zap run information 143
Adjusting your email notification   Managing Zap history data   146
settings   127
Setting up an error alert workflow with   Finding help: help center,
the Zapier Manager built-in app   127   customer support, community,
                                             and experts   149
Managing app status alerts   130   Finding app-specific help in app
Monitoring the Zapier Status page   130   profiles   150
Setting up an app status alert   Utilizing the Zapier help center   150
workflow with the App Status by   Engaging with the Zapier community   151
Zapier built-in app   133   Reaching out to Zapier customer
                                             support   152
Utilizing Zap history   Hiring a Zapier Certified Expert   152
information for troubleshooting
                                     136   Summary   153

Section 2:
Customizing Your Zaps with Built-in Apps by Zapier – Functionality and Practical Uses

6
Creating Multi-Step Zaps and Using Built-In Apps

Technical requirements	158	Using apps by Zapier for communication	173
Creating Zaps with multiple action and search steps	**158**	Extracting and compiling data with apps by Zapier	174
Adding a search step using the + icon	160	Other useful apps by Zapier	174
Adding a Search step in a Choose value… field	167	Advanced apps by Zapier	175
Exercise – Creating a multi-step Zap with a search action	171	Managing your Zapier account with apps by Zapier	176
		The powerful Formatter by Zapier app	176
Introducing apps by Zapier	**171**	**Summary**	**177**
Setting run conditions and using logic with apps by Zapier	172		

7
Getting Started with Built-In Apps

Technical requirements	**180**	The Delay After Queue action event	196
Filter by Zapier – applying conditional logic to your Zaps	**180**	**Schedule by Zapier – scheduling your Zaps to run at intervals**	**198**
Setting up the Filter by Zapier app	181	The Every Hour trigger event	198
Understanding filter conditions	184	The Every Day trigger event	200
		The Every Week trigger event	201
Paths by Zapier – adding branching logic to your Zaps	**187**	The Every Month trigger event	202
Setting up the Paths by Zapier app	190	**Exercise – creating a multi-step Zap with a scheduled trigger, search action, filter, path, and delay**	**204**
Delay by Zapier – adding delays to your Zaps	**192**		
The Delay For action event	193		
The Delay Until action event	194	**Summary**	**205**

8
Built-In Communication Apps

Technical requirements   208
SMS by Zapier – sending text
messages   208
Setting up SMS by Zapier   209

Email by Zapier – sending and
receiving emails   212
The New Inbound Email trigger event   212
The Send Outbound Email action event   214
The New Read Receipt trigger event   217

SMTP by Zapier – sending
emails through mail servers   218

Setting up the SMTP by Zapier app   220
IMAP by Zapier – retrieving
emails
from mail servers   223
Setting up the IMAP by Zapier app   224
Customizing and using the New Email
trigger event   226
Customizing the New Mailbox trigger
event   226

Summary   227

9
Exploring Built-In Apps for Extracting and Compiling Data

Technical requirements   230
Email Parser by Zapier –
extracting data from emails   230
The New Email trigger event   231
The New Mailbox trigger event   237

RSS by Zapier – using RSS feed
readers   238
The New Item in Feed trigger event   239
The New Items in Multiple Feeds
trigger event   241

The Create Item in Feed action event   243
Digest by Zapier – compiling
data in digests   247
The Append Entry and Schedule Digest
action event   248
The Release Existing Digest action
event   256
The Find Digest search action event   257

Exercise – creating a multi-step
Zap with an RSS feed digest   259
Summary   260

10
Other Useful Built-In Apps by Zapier

Technical requirements   262
Zapier Chrome extension –

triggering one-off automations
from any web page   262

Setting up the Google Chrome extension on your browser 263
The New Push trigger event 264

URL Shortener by Zapier – shortening URLs in your Zaps 266
Setting up the Shorten URL action event 267

Translate by Zapier – translating text 268
The Translate Text action event 268
The Detect Language action event 270

Lead Score by Zapier – scoring and retrieving lead information 271
The Find Person and Company

Information search action event 272

Weather by Zapier – using weather conditions in your Zaps 275
The Will It Rain Today? trigger event 276
The Today's Forecast trigger event 277
The Get Current Weather search action event 278
The Tomorrow's Forecast search action event 282

Retrograde by Zapier – using astrological predictions in your Zaps 283
Setting up a Retrograde by Zapier trigger event 283

Summary 285

11
Advanced Built-In Apps by Zapier

Technical requirements 288
Webhooks by Zapier – Using webhooks in your Zaps 288
Code by Zapier – Using

JavaScript or Python code in your Zaps 291
Storage by Zapier – Saving and storing data 292
Summary 295

12
Managing Your Zapier Account with Built-In Apps

Technical requirements 298
App Status by Zapier – Getting notifications of integration incidents 298
Zapier Manager – Managing errors and account changes 299
Events for managing Zap errors and alerts 300

Events for managing app, Zaps, and folders 301
Events for Zapier account administration 311
Events for Team and Company account user management 315

Use cases 318
Summary 318

Section 3: Using the Features of the Formatter by Zapier Built-In App

13
Formatting Date and Time

Technical requirements 322

An introduction to the Formatter by Zapier built-in app 322

The basics of adjusting date and time values using Zapier 323
Using the date and time your Zap runs in fields 325

Manipulating dates and times with Formatter by Zapier 327
Using custom date formats 327
Adding or subtracting time 329
Formatting dates and times 331

Summary 334

14
Formatting Numbers

Technical requirements 336
Using Zapier to transform numerical values 336
Formatting numbers with Formatter by Zapier 337
Setting up the Numbers action event with the Format Number transform option 338

Formatting currencies with Formatter by Zapier 340
Understanding country locales and currency formatting 341
Setting up the Numbers action event with the Format Currency transform option 342

Formatting phone numbers with Formatter by Zapier 344
Setting up the Numbers action event with the Format Phone Number transform option 345

Performing mathematical operations with Formatter by Zapier 348
Setting up the Numbers action event with the Perform Math Operation transform option 348

Using spreadsheet-style formulas with Formatter by Zapier 350

Setting up the Numbers action event with the Spreadsheet-Style Formula

transform option 351

Summary 353

15

Text Formatting Functions in Zapier – Part 1

Technical requirements 356

Using Zapier to transform text values 356

Capitalizing the first letter of every word 358

Applying title case to a string of words 360

Setting up the Text action event with the Titlecase transform option 361

Converting all the characters in a string of text to uppercase 363

Converting all the characters in a string of text to lowercase 365

Pluralizing words 367

Setting up the Text action event with the Pluralize transform option 368

Finding the first position of specified text 369

Setting up the Text action event with

the Find transform option 370

Replacing characters, words, or phrases 372

Setting up the Text action event with the Replace transform option 373

Counting the number of characters in a string of text 375

Setting up the Text action event with the Length transform option 376

Counting the number of words in a string of text 377

Setting up the Text action event with the Word Count transform option 378

Removing whitespace 380

Setting up the Text action event with the Trim Whitespace transform option 380

Summary 382

16

Text Formatting Functions in Zapier – Part 2

Technical requirements 384

Converting a name into the name of a superhero 384

Setting up the Text action event with the Superhero Name transform option 385

Splitting characters or words

into segments 386

Setting up the Text action event with the Split transform option 387

Truncating text to a specified character length 389

Setting up the Text action event with

the Truncate transform option   390

Removing HTML to leave plain text   392

Setting up the Text action event with the Remove HTML transform option   393

Assigning a default value   394

Setting up the Text action event with the Default Value transform option   395

Extracting data from blocks of

text   397

Extracting an email address from a block of text   398
Extracting numbers from blocks of text 400
Extracting URLs from blocks of text   402
Extracting phone numbers from blocks of text   404

Advanced text formatting features   407

Summary   408

17
Zapier's Utilities Functions

Technical requirements   410

Introducing the Formatter by Zapier Utilities action event   410

Importing data from CSV files   411

Using lookup tables   415

Setting up the Utilities action event with the Lookup Table transform option   416

Picking data from a list   418

Setting up the Utilities action event

with the Pick from List transform option   419

Manipulating line-items   421

Understanding line-items   422
Converting text to line-items   424
Converting line-items to text   426
Using a line itemizer to create, append, or prepend line-items   429

Summary   433

Section 4:
Getting the Most Out of Zapier – Business Automation Examples

18
Automating Your Marketing Processes

Technical requirements   438

An introduction to automating your marketing processes with

Zapier   438

Understanding what marketing processes can be automated with

Zapier 439

Where to start with automating your marketing processes with Zapier 444

Automating social media marketing processes with the

Facebook Pages integration 445
Facebook Pages trigger events 446
Facebook Pages action events 447
Setting up a multi-step Zap with the Facebook Pages integration 448

Summary 453

19

Automating Your Sales Processes

Technical requirements 456

An introduction to automating your sales processes with Zapier 456
Understanding what sales processes can be automated with Zapier 457

Where to start with automating your sales processes with Zapier 463

Automating lead management

processes with CRM integrations, illustrated with Pipedrive 464
Pipedrive trigger events 465
Pipedrive action events 469
Pipedrive search action events 474
Tips for using the Pipedrive integration 477
Setting up a multi-step Zap with the Pipedrive integration 478

Summary 486

20

Automating Your Operations Processes

Technical requirements 488

An introduction to automating your operations processes with Zapier 488
Understanding what operations processes can be automated with Zapier 489

Where to start with automating your operations processes with Zapier 494

Automating online Word

document processes with the Google Docs integration 495
Google Docs trigger events 496
Google Docs action events 497
Google Docs search action events 499
Setting up a multi-step Zap with the Google Docs integration 500

Summary 512

21

Automating Your Finance and Reporting Processes

Technical requirements 514
An introduction to automating your finance processes with Zapier 515
Understanding what finance processes can be automated with Zapier 515

An introduction to automating your reporting processes with Zapier 519
Understanding what reporting processes can be automated with Zapier 520

Where to start with automating your finance and reporting processes with Zapier 523
Automating accounting processes with the Xero integration 524
Common fields in Xero trigger, action, and search action events 525
Xero trigger events 526
Xero action events 528
Xero search action events 534
Tips for using the Xero integration 536
Setting up a multi-step Zap with the Xero integration 537

Summary 547

22

Tips, Tricks, and Best Practices to Enhance Your Productivity

Technical requirements 550
Best practices for using Zapier effectively 550
Start with the basics 550
Prepare before you automate 550
Get to grips with steps, fields, and data mapping 551
Manage your Zaps effectively 551
Stay on top of your task usage 551
Set up alerts and understand how to troubleshoot 551
Understand the different built-in Zapier apps 552
Get inspired 552
Review your processes and automations regularly 552

Tips and tricks to enhance your use of Zapier 553
Trigger data not pulling through 553
Extra Fields alerts 553
Refresh fields when you make adjustments in your app 554
Improving the Zapier integration 554
Think outside of the box 555
Use the Zapier community as a resource 555

Summary 555

23

Challenge Your Problem-Solving and Zap-Building Skills

Technical requirements	558	solutions for each scenario	562
Introduction and guidance	558	Scenario 1 – one possible solution	562
Scenario 1 – novice	559	Scenario 2 – one possible solution	562
Scenario 2 – intermediate	559	Scenario 3 – one possible solution	564
Scenario 3 – advanced	560	Summary	566
Guidance on suggested		Why subscribe?	567

Other Books You May Enjoy

Index

Preface

Zapier is an emerging no-code workflow automation technology that enables organizations to connect their cloud-based/web applications and automate data transfer between them. Its built-in features and flexibility allow users to integrate thousands of business applications and create simple to complex automations to decrease the amount of time spent on repetitive tasks, therefore increasing productivity.

The purpose of this book is to teach business owners, their employees, and independent freelancers and contractors how to use Zapier for business process automation. The book takes a hands-on approach to implementation and associated problem-solving methodologies that will have you up and running and productive in no time while leveling your advanced skills. Complete with step-by-step explanations of essential concepts, expert tips, practical examples, and self-assessment challenges, you will begin by exploring how Zapier works, including an overview of strategy in problem-solving. We will teach you how to plan your automation building for best results, what the native features available in Zapier are, and the applications that connect with it, as well as how to optimally configure your workflows to automate your processes in the fewest steps. You will learn how to create advanced workflow automations from scratch and learn how to troubleshoot issues.

By the end of this book, you will be able to build your own advanced workflow automations using Zapier, addressing the key pain points encountered in many businesses with manual and repetitive tasks.

Who this book is for

If you are an owner or employee of a micro-, small- or medium-sized business and you want to learn how to increase productivity using workflow automation with Zapier, then this book will teach you how to get to grips with Zapier and use it optimally. Freelancers and contractors that provide digital process improvement, systemizing, and automation services will also find the content in this book useful to gain key skills to leverage themselves as more advanced users. This may include solution architects, process consultants, business analysts, virtual assistants, digital marketers, CRM consultants, online business managers, technical consultants, bookkeepers, and accountants. No experience with business process automation or Zapier is required to get started.

What this book covers

Chapter 1, Introduction to Business Process Automation with Zapier, initially focuses on the basic principles of business process automation with Zapier and then covers features, functionality, and key terminology used to help familiarize you with the Zapier platform.

Chapter 2, Preparing to Automate Your Processes, explores how to brainstorm your processes, simplify them and assess what can be automated. We cover the process to establish how your apps work with Zapier and explain how to use the Zapier app ecosystem directory.

Chapter 3, Building Your First Automated Workflow (Zap), dives into how best to strategize and plan your workflows ahead of working through a step-by-step process of creating your first Zap. We explore how to connect your apps to Zapier, use the Zap editor, work with different field types, and use pre-built workflows.

Chapter 4, Managing Your Zaps, takes you through the best ways to keep your Zapier account organized. We discuss how to keep your Zaps and folders organized, how to manage your connected apps, and help you to understand Zap statuses. Lastly, we cover some collaboration tips for users working in teams.

Chapter 5, Troubleshooting and Handling Zap Errors, covers typical Zap behavior and the best ways to handle and troubleshoot errors. We discuss how to set up Zaps to report on Zap issues and app status changes, how to use Zap History information effectively, and we explore the various channels of support available.

Chapter 6, Creating Multi-Step Zaps with Built-in Apps, teaches you how to set up and customize multi-step Zaps using multiple action and search steps. We also introduce you to all the built-in Apps by Zapier. You will be able to test your knowledge by building your first multi-step Zap.

Chapter 7, Getting Started with Built-in Apps, explores the most commonly used built-in Zapier apps and covers specific functions such as using conditional logic (filtering and paths) and delays in your Zaps, as well as scheduling your Zaps to run as intervals. You will be able to test your knowledge by building a multi-step Zap using some of these built-in apps.

Chapter 8, Built-In Communication Apps, introduces communication-specific built-in Zapier apps such as for sending and receiving emails and sending SMS messages.

Chapter 9, Exploring Built-In Apps for Extracting and Compiling Data, covers how to extract data from emails, use RSS feed readers in your automations, and compile data into digests. You will be able to test your knowledge by building a multi-step Zap using some of these built-in apps.

Chapter 10, Other Useful Built-In Apps by Zapier, describes how to initiate workflows from web pages, shorten URLs, translate text, score lead information, and use weather and astrological predictions in your Zaps.

Chapter 11, Advanced Built-In Apps by Zapier, briefly explores the more advanced functionality in some of the built-in Apps by Zapier, such as using webhooks and code in your Zaps, as well as saving and storing data.

Chapter 12, Managing Your Zapier Account with Built-in Apps, teaches you how to get notifications on integration issues, manage errors with your Zaps, and monitor Zapier account changes.

Chapter 13, Formatting Date and Time, introduces the versatile Formatter app and covers how to format date and time values and add or subtract time. We provide practical tips on how to use each of the date and time formatter functions.

Chapter 14, Formatting Numbers, dives into the functionality available to format numbers, phone numbers, currencies, and to use spreadsheet-type formulas and math operations.

Chapter 15, Text Formatting Functions in Zapier – Part 1, describes the extensive functionality available to format text. We cover a range of text formatting actions, such as capitalizing and pluralizing text; applying title case, uppercase, and lowercase; finding and replacing text; trimming whitespace; and counting characters and words.

Chapter 16, Text Formatting Functions in Zapier – Part 2, covers more functionality available to format text. We explore how to split and truncate text; remove HTML; assign default values; extract data such as patterns, URLs, and email addresses; and use a superhero name. We also briefly cover more advanced text manipulation features such as how to convert Markdown to HTML, URL Encode and Decode, and converting text to ASCII.

Chapter 17, Zapier's Utilities Functions, explores the Utilities functions within the Formatter app. We cover line-item creation and customization, converting text to line-items and vice versa, using lookup tables and picklists, and importing CSV files.

Chapter 18, Automating Your Marketing Processes, explores some examples of marketing processes that can be automated using Zapier. We will provide practical tips on how to get started with automating these processes. We will also cover how to automate marketing processes with Facebook Pages integration.

Chapter 19, Automating Your Sales Processes, covers some examples of sales processes that can be automated using Zapier. We will provide practical tips on how to get started with automating these processes. We will also cover how to automate sales processes with Pipedrive integration.

Chapter 20, Automating Your Operations Processes, dives into some examples of operations processes that can be automated using Zapier. We provide practical tips on how to address automating these processes. We also cover how to automate operations processes with Google Docs integration.

Chapter 21, Automating Your Finance and Reporting Processes, takes you through some examples of finance and reporting processes that can be automated using Zapier. We provide practical tips on how to tackle automating these processes. We also explore how to automate accounting processes with Xero integration.

Chapter 22, Tips, Tricks, and Best Practices to Enhance Your Productivity, focuses on best practices for utilizing Zapier effectively and builds on the tips and tricks we have presented in each chapter.

Chapter 23, Challenge Your Problem-Solving and Zap-Building Skills, presents you with three scenarios that describe a specific problem that can be solved by using Zapier. We will work through each example practically with tips being given along the way. The scenarios are classified by skill level and you will have the opportunity to test your knowledge while adapting your problem-solving and Zap-building skills.

To get the most out of this book

Each chapter in this book builds on the knowledge and information presented in the previous chapters. If you don't have experience of business process automation with Zapier, we recommend you start with *Chapter 1, An Introduction to Business Process Automation with Zapier*, and complete each chapter in the order they are presented. If you have experience with Zapier, feel free to jump to the chapters that cover topics that interest you and will further your knowledge. To get started, we recommend you sign up for a Zapier account. To work through the content and exercises in *Chapter 1, An Introduction to Business Process Automation with Zapier*, to *Chapter 5, Troubleshooting and Handling Zap Errors*, the Zapier Free plan will be suitable. From *Chapter 6, Creating Multi-Step Zaps with Built-In Apps by Zapier*, onwards, a Starter plan will be required, and for some topics, higher price plans will be necessary.

Before you start working through the content in this book, we recommend that you get access to all the Zap templates used as examples in this book, as well as the systems and process audit templates, and other supporting materials here: `https://bit.ly/3e5BUkn`.

Download the color images

We also provide a PDF file that has color images of the screenshots and diagrams used in this book. You can download it here: `https://static.packt-cdn.com/downloads/9781800208971_ColorImages.pdf`.

Conventions used

There are a number of text conventions used throughout this book.

`Code in text`: Indicates code words in text, database table names, folder names, filenames, file extensions, pathnames, dummy URLs, user input, and Twitter handles. Here is an example: "For example, we could give the digest a title of `New Sales Invoice Summary`."

Bold: Indicates a new term, an important word, or words that you see onscreen. For instance, words in menus or dialog boxes appear in **bold**. Here is an example: "Let's take a look at the different **Frequency** field options."

> **Tips or important notes**
> Appear like this.

Get in touch

Feedback from our readers is always welcome.

General feedback: If you have questions about any aspect of this book, email us at `customercare@packtpub.com` and mention the book title in the subject of your message.

Errata: Although we have taken every care to ensure the accuracy of our content, mistakes do happen. If you have found a mistake in this book, we would be grateful if you would report this to us. Please visit `www.packtpub.com/support/errata` and fill in the form.

Piracy: If you come across any illegal copies of our works in any form on the internet, we would be grateful if you would provide us with the location address or website name. Please contact us at `copyright@packt.com` with a link to the material.

If you are interested in becoming an author: If there is a topic that you have expertise in and you are interested in either writing or contributing to a book, please visit `authors.packtpub.com`.

Share Your Thoughts

Once you've read *Automate It with Zapier*, we'd love to hear your thoughts! Scan the QR code below to go straight to the Amazon review page for this book and share your feedback.

https://packt.link/r/1800208979

Your review is important to us and the tech community and will help us make sure we're delivering excellent quality content.

Section 1: Getting Started with Zapier

In this section, you will gain an understanding of the fundamentals of the Zapier platform, how to build and manage workflows, and how to troubleshoot issues.

This section comprises the following chapters:

- *Chapter 1, Introduction to Business Process Automation with Zapier*
- *Chapter 2, Preparing to Automate Your Processes*
- *Chapter 3, Building Your First Automated Workflow (Zap)*
- *Chapter 4, Managing Your Zaps*
- *Chapter 5, Troubleshooting and Handling Zap Errors*

1

Introduction to Business Process Automation with Zapier

Before you get started with building your first automated workflow, you should understand the basic principles of **business process automation** (**BPA**) and how it can make light work of manual and repetitive processes. We'll cover how applications connect with others to transfer data and how Zapier has impacted the no-code revolution to automate tasks without the need for developers. This background information will put you in a better position to grasp the terms and concepts used by Zapier and will help you to understand the features and functionality of Zapier, as well as how the platform works.

If you have only just started using Zapier, you may not know which pricing plan is most suitable for your business and when the right time to upgrade is. We cover the features available for each pricing plan in this chapter and explain the pros and cons of choosing one over another. Then, we describe how to set up a Zapier account, and we provide an overview of how the platform is structured to enable you to find your way around effectively. We conclude this chapter by working through how to customize your settings and preferences.

We will cover the following key topics in this chapter:

- How process automation helps businesses to increase productivity
- The "no-code revolution" and workflow automation with Zapier
- Understanding the key terms used by Zapier
- Choosing the right Zapier plan
- Creating a Zapier account
- Familiarizing yourself with navigation on the Zapier platform
- Changing your settings and preferences

Once you have worked through each of these topics, you will be ready to get stuck in with building your first workflow automation.

Technical requirements

To get started, we recommend that you sign up for a Zapier account, which will give you access to a 14-day free trial. We will discuss how to set up an account in the *Creating a Zapier account* section. The Zapier Free plan will be adequate to work through the content in this chapter.

How process automation helps businesses to increase productivity

Whether you are a solopreneur or your business has a team, every successful business strives to make the most of its resources and improve productivity so that there is more time for increasing revenue. Many companies have systems that may not communicate with each other, and as a result will have processes that are manual, time-consuming, and error-prone.

We live in a time where technology is continually evolving to help us make our work easier, and it is now more straightforward and cost-effective than ever to implement and run this technology ourselves. By introducing appropriate business technology tools, connecting those tools, and automating manual and repetitive tasks, businesses can significantly increase productivity.

Introducing business process automation

BPA is all about using technology to improve the way we work by automatically performing repetitive tasks that would typically require human intervention. It ultimately focuses on the human element in the process rather than the actual applications that are in use. Of course, the tools you use are fundamental and need to be the right ones for their jobs; however, the real goal is to help the people using those systems to be more productive and focus on the tasks that truly matter for the success and growth of an organization.

Here are a few examples of when BPA can help you get rid of manual tasks and increase productivity:

- Posting the same information on multiple social media channels
- Inputting new webform leads into your customer database
- Manually importing sales invoices and payment information from your e-commerce store into your accounting software
- Collating reporting information from numerous sources
- Processing feedback and testimonials from customers
- Adding meeting events to your calendar
- Sending documents for signing
- Following up with leads

It does take time to learn and adequately implement the principles of BPA; however, the resulting value far outweighs the time investment. These are just some of the benefits of using BPA:

- Reduced manual data entry and errors
- Reduced operational costs
- More time for growing sales

- Better customer service
- Increased employee engagement and job satisfaction

The most significant benefit of using BPA is the overall time savings. Automation platform users report time savings of a few hours a week by automating certain tasks such as social media posting, to more than 160 hours a month being saved by automating entire sales cycles or operation functions. The value of time savings is relative to the individual case. For example, a time saving of 2 or 3 hours a week may be of significant value to a solopreneur, whereas a 160-hours-per-month saving equates to having a full-time employee working for free. These savings in hours would translate to savings of thousands of dollars in resource time.

Zapier has several case studies and customer success stories published on their website, `https://zapier.com/customers`. Here are a few examples of successful use cases of automation that help businesses to become more efficient and grow:

- A real estate agent reduces lead management by 40%.
- A digital agency saves 30 hours a week with messenger funnel automation.
- A coffee shop powers online ordering with automation.
- A home entertainment company automates its entire sales cycle.
- A freelancer automates client onboarding and grows their business.

BPA essentially allows companies of all sizes and in any industry to innovate by using cloud-based technology to work better and more efficiently and stay ahead of the competition. The possible improvements you can make to your business with BPA are endless.

Although automation functions to make processes work better, it is essential to bear in mind that applying automation to an already inefficient operation will increase the inefficiency. As a whole, BPA requires you to take specific steps to look at your processes holistically, understand and simplify them, identify what systems can be connected, and only then decide on which tasks can benefit from automation. In *Chapter 2, Preparing to Automate Your Processes*, we will work through the steps required to map out our business processes and streamline them by identifying what can be simplified, digitized, and automated.

> **Important note**
> In this book, we will use the term **workflow automation** interchangeably with BPA.

Before we can focus on the practical aspects of improving and automating our operations, we need to understand how web applications communicate with each other and what options are available for businesses to connect their tools.

How your business applications communicate with each other

Allowing your business applications to communicate with one another and then automating tasks where possible is key to increasing productivity. Before we can explore how automation with Zapier comes into this picture, we need to understand how business applications can be connected using **API integrations**.

An **API** (short for **application programming interface**) is a means by which multiple software programs can communicate with each other. It essentially acts to allow data from different systems to pass between them. When two software programs are connected in this way by an API, they are said to be "integrated."

When an **integration** exists, this allows specific requests to be sent by one application, producing a response by another. The information requests are usually in the form of creating new (**create**), retrieving existing (**retrieve**), editing/updating existing (**update**), or deleting existing (**delete**) resources. Upon receipt of a request, the application will try to fulfill the request and send back a response in the form of a three-digit status code (success or error). If, for example, you type a website URL into your browser and the page is displayed, this would be a success response. If the page does not exist, an error message would be displayed, `The requested URL was not found on this server`, depicting a 404 error response. How API integration is created and customized defines what range of information can be requested.

As the goal of API integration is to share data efficiently between two connected apps, there must be a way to identify changes in these resources. For example, if you want a new row to be created in your spreadsheet app when a new subscriber is added to your email marketing app, you need to know that the new contact has been created in the first place. The two most popular methods for identifying changes are currently **polling** and **webhooks**.

With the polling method, requests for new events (for example, creating, retrieving, and deleting resources) are repeatedly sent at pre-defined intervals, waiting for a response. If there is no response, this signifies that there are no new events. So, in the example, the polling method would periodically search for new occurrences of contact records being created, say every 15 minutes.

With webhooks, however, instead of sending requests, you provide the app with a URL that your originating app monitors for new events, thus receiving information in real time. So, in the example, when a new contact record is created, the information would be provided instantly. Webhooks are an instant and much more efficient way of communicating event information. We will discuss webhooks in more detail in *Chapter 11, Advanced Built-In Apps by Zapier – Part 2.*

The options available for businesses to connect their tools

Building API integrations requires software programming and development skills and can be a lengthy and costly process. Most applications that you are currently using for your business processes are likely to have a section on their website containing a list of the other applications with which they integrate. These applications listed in these app marketplaces, or **app ecosystems**, have integrations created using APIs to enable the two apps to communicate with each other. Software providers invest time, money, and technical skills in building and maintaining these **native integrations**. Generally, these providers will create an integration that satisfies the highest-priority needs of most users to automate the most frequently used types of activities. They may also prioritize integration development resources on other more commonly used applications rather than smaller, less popular apps.

In some cases, a user of certain software might need to connect another tool that is not listed in the app ecosystem or may need to accomplish a specific task that is not available with the existing native integration. Under these circumstances, a business could employ a programmer to write **code** to create a **custom integration** with the API provided by the software provider. For most companies, the process of developing a custom integration is not a financially viable option. Therefore, there is often a reliance on what integrations are available in these app ecosystems and how flexible they are.

You now have a better understanding of what the basic principles of BPA are and how process automation helps to increase productivity. Next, we explore how this relates to Zapier.

The "no-code revolution" and workflow automation with Zapier

Thankfully, as technology has developed, it is now possible to create digital processes without the need to write any code. Therefore, anyone can learn how to build a website, create email templates, and connect their systems using, in many cases, visual drag-and-drop editors. These editors give you the ability to add and remove blocks in templates rather than writing code in a computer programming language. Instead of needing to use a developer to write this code, the average person with basic IT skills can create these processes themselves. These advances are described as a "**no-code** revolution," as software providers have pushed forward to develop solutions that will help the non-IT workforce to execute tasks that could previously only be done by software engineers.

Zapier is one of these technology solutions and allows you to automate and manage your business processes without writing code. Zapier essentially acts as a connector or translator between thousands of cloud-based applications that may not have direct native integrations with each other or for which the event requests are more limited, allowing them to communicate with each other. The platform enables users to build business-specific workflow automations with a visual editor using pre-built integrations to seamlessly perform manual and repetitive tasks without human intervention.

Zapier is the brainchild of forward-thinking founders Wade Foster, Bryan Helmig, and Mike Knoop. Wade, Bryan, and Mike recognized the productivity struggles that plague small and medium-sized businesses where many repetitive tasks are handled manually and with an ever-increasing chance of errors occurring. They developed a powerful solution to help businesses with their efficiency struggles, allowing them to connect their web applications together and automate their mundane and repetitive tasks using custom-built workflows. Most importantly, the solution allows the average business owner and their team to use the software without the need for writing code or having specialist help involved. The first release of the Zapier platform was in 2012, and since then, they have grown their integration marketplace to over 3,000 app connections. Zapier is based in California, USA, and as a company that actively supports an ethos of remote working, they have grown their global team to over 300 people located in the US and over 20 other countries around the world.

As well as allowing the less technical user to build custom workflows, the Zapier platform also has an open API, thereby allowing app developers to build integrations with Zapier to connect their apps to the platform. This, in turn, allows their customers to then create custom integrations with thousands of other apps, using Zapier as the connector. In essence, the Zapier user then becomes the developer without needing to use code. Using no-code technology, we no longer need advanced technical skills to harness the power of **integration automation**.

To help you understand a bit more about BPA and the "no-code" revolution, you can get access to a free masterclass here: `https://bit.ly/3e5BUkn`.

You now have a better understanding of how Zapier and BPA work hand in hand to help businesses increase productivity. In the next section, we cover the key terms that are used by Zapier and throughout this book.

Understanding the key terms used by Zapier

Zapier uses specific terminology throughout the platform. We will use these terms frequently throughout this book. It is useful to know and understand the most commonly used terms before we discuss the features available in each Zapier pricing plan.

What is an app?

An **app** (application) is a technology tool or cloud-based web service. Zapier integrates with thousands of apps to allow you to transfer data between them and automate your manual and repetitive tasks. Most apps are available for use regardless of which Zapier pricing plan you use, except for **premium apps**, such as **Salesforce**, **Facebook lead ads**, and **Xero**, which are only available on paid plans. Zapier has an **app ecosystem** of over 3,000 app integrations listed in a directory. We cover Zapier's app ecosystem directory in more detail in *Chapter 2, Preparing to Automate Your Processes*.

What is a Zap?

A **Zap** is a step-by-step automated workflow that allows a user to create a flow of data between two or more apps. When an event occurs in one app, this produces an activity such as an action or event in another app. Zaps allow you to connect your different apps and automate repetitive tasks between them. We cover how to create a Zap in *Chapter 3, Building Your First Automated Workflow (Zap)*.

What is a trigger?

A **trigger** is an originating event that starts an automated workflow. The trigger is always the first step in the workflow, and only one trigger step will ever exist in a Zap.

What is an action?

An **action** is the resulting activity that happens once a trigger starts an automated workflow. Zaps can have one or multiple actions. Actions can also include **searches**.

What is a task?

Once a Zap is built, tested, and turned on, a trigger in one app will cause an action to happen in another app. A **task** is an activity that the Zap successfully completes. Your Zapier pricing plan defines your monthly task limit. Successfully completed actions, searches, and passed filters count toward your monthly task limit.

> Tip
> Use BPA principles to strategize your workflows in advance of actually building your Zaps. Doing this will allow you to reduce the number of steps in your workflows and minimize task usage. Every task counts toward how much you spend on your Zapier pricing plan. Having simple processes from the start will enable you to use Zapier most cost-effectively. You can set up a workflow with the Zapier Manager built-in app to alert you on task usage related to your monthly allowance. We will discuss this is in more detail in *Chapter 12, Managing Your Zapier Account with Built-In Apps*.

What is the Zap editor?

The **Zap editor** is a visual editor that allows you to create and alter your Zaps using simple drop-down lists and a systematic process. The Zap editor enables you to add your trigger app and action app(s) and run conditions in your workflows. We will discuss the Zap editor in more detail in *Chapter 3, Building Your First Automated Workflow (Zap)*.

What is the update time/syncing interval?

The majority of app triggers use the polling method to retrieve new data on events. The **update time** (or **syncing interval**) refers to how quickly your automated workflow triggers and depends on how often the polling runs to check the triggering app for new information. Zapier checks for new activities to trigger an automated workflow every 1 to 15 minutes, and your Zapier pricing plan defines this time interval. Triggers using the polling method are denoted by the word **scheduled**.

> **Important note**
>
> Some app triggers use the webhooks (instant) method and allow an automated workflow to run as soon as new event information is available. These triggers are denoted by the word **instant**.

What is a filter?

A **filter** is a condition that you can add to a Zap to prevent the workflow from moving on to the next action step. Filters are only available on paid Zapier pricing plans. We cover using filters in detail in *Chapter 7, Getting Started with Built-In Apps*.

What is a formatter?

A **formatter** is a function that allows you to alter numbers, text, dates, and times, as well as performing tasks such as looking up data from a list. Formatters are only available on paid Zapier pricing plans. We comprehensively cover the various formatter apps built by Zapier in *Chapter 13, Formatting Date and Time, Chapter 14, Formatting Numbers, Chapter 15, Text Formatting Functions in Zapier – Part 1, Chapter 16, Text Formatting Functions in Zapier – Part 2*, and *Chapter 17, Zapier's Utilities Functions*.

What are paths?

Paths allow you to create complex Zaps that use "if this, then that" **conditional logic** to perform different actions based on multiple conditions. For instance, if X happens in the trigger app, then do Y in one or more action steps. Paths are only available on the Professional, Team, and Company plans. We comprehensively cover paths in *Chapter 7, Getting Started with Built-In Apps*.

What is a multi-step Zap?

A **multi-step Zap** is a workflow that involves one trigger and multiple actions, as opposed to a **single-step Zap**, which contains one trigger and only one action. With multi-step Zaps, you can also add filters, formatter steps, searches, and complex paths to your workflows, which allow you to create flexible automated workflows. Multi-step Zaps are only available on paid Zapier pricing plans. We cover how to build multi-step Zaps in detail in *Chapter 6, Creating Multi-Step Zaps and Using Built-In Apps*.

What is Zap history?

The Zap history shows a detailed log of activity for each of your Zaps. You can view data that has passed through each step of your workflow and use this to troubleshoot errors. We cover Zap history in more detail in *Chapter 5, Troubleshooting and Handling Zap Errors*.

What is Autoreplay?

Sometimes tasks will fail due to app downtime or temporary errors. If this happens, you can enable the **Autoreplay** feature, which allows Zapier to retry running these tasks immediately, and repeat this a few times if the error still exists. The Autoreplay feature is available on Professional, Team, and Company plans, and it can be found in your Task History. This feature is handy if you use a large number of tasks. We cover the Autoreplay functionality in more detail in *Chapter 5, Troubleshooting and Handling Zap Errors*.

You now have a better understanding of the key terminology used on the Zapier platform. Next, we discuss the different Zapier pricing plans, what is included in each, and how to choose the right plan for your needs.

Choosing the right Zapier plan

Zapier offers five pricing options to suit your business requirements, as follows:

- **Free plan**
- **Starter plan**
- **Professional plan**
- **Team plan**
- **Company plan**

The following figure gives a summary of the features available for each Zapier pricing plan:

	Free	Starter	Professional	Team	Company
Monthly price (starting at)	$0	$24.99	$61.25	$373.75	$748.75
Task quota (per month)	100	750	2,000	50,000	100,000
Extra task bolt-on?	No	Yes	Yes	Yes	Yes
Number of Zaps	5	20	Unlimited	Unlimited	Unlimited
Update time	15 minutes	15 minutes	2 minutes	1 minute	1 minute
Number of users	1	1	1	Unlimited	Unlimited
Number of Premium Apps	0	3	Unlimited	Unlimited	Unlimited
Multi-step Zaps		x	x	x	x
Filters		x	x	x	x
Formatters		x	x	x	x
Custom integrations (webhooks)		x	x	x	x
Custom logic (paths)			x	x	x
Autoreplay			x	x	x
Folder permissions				x	x
Shared app connections				x	x
Shared workspace				x	x
Unlimited workspaces					x
User provisioning (SCIM)					x
Apps access control					x
SAML Single Sign-On (SSO)					x
Account capture					x
Live training					x
Data retention	30 days	30 days	30 days	30 days	Custom
Support	Standard	Standard	Standard	Premier	Premier

Figure 1.1 – Summary of features available for each Zapier pricing plan

> **Important note**
>
> All prices and plan structures are correct at the time of publishing this book. You may also find that depending on your region, the pricing and plan structure may vary slightly.

Each pricing plan varies in features; however, primarily, the plans are categorized according to the number of tasks you have available monthly, the number of Zaps you can set up, and how short the syncing interval is. On most plans (except for the Free plan), you can retain features and add additional tasks for an extra fee. The availability of Zap history data and access to online customer service and technical support is included in all plans.

The Free plan is free forever, and all paid Zapier plans are available to be paid monthly or annually.

Zapier offers a 14-day trial plan, which gives you access to the majority of features on the Professional plan with 1,000 tasks, except for Autoreplay.

You can view a detailed list of the features and pricing for each plan and change your plan as needed by clicking on the links in the following navigation options:

- **Billing and Usage (Settings)**
- **Wallet** (expandable left sidebar)
- **Pricing** (top menu on information pages)
- **Pricing** (footer menu)

> **Important note**
> Your monthly task allocation does not carry over to the next month. Toward the end of each billing period, if you have unused tasks left over and you are using fewer tasks than you need to, you may be able to downgrade to a lower subscription and still retain your pricing plan features.

Next, let's take a look at different Zapier plans that will be suitable for your business.

Which is the right Zapier plan to use for your business?

Zapier is ideal for any size business that wants to automate their processes. It can be used by solopreneurs or companies with small or large teams. It can also be used by freelancers and consultants to manage their clients' processes.

The needs of your business will determine which price plan is best to use. How many processes you would like to automate and how complex these processes are will impact your decision.

Free plan

For businesses with one user that only have a few simple tasks to automate, this plan is the most appropriate. You will be able to build up to five single-step workflows using the majority of apps that Zapier integrates with (excluding premium apps). Zapier will search for new data in your trigger apps every 15 minutes and run your Zaps, allowing up to 100 tasks per month to be processed. The Free plan is the best plan to get started with while you get to grips with how Zapier works on a basic level.

Starter plan

If you still only have one user and a relatively small number of processes to automate, but you need to automate multiple activities in one or more apps (including up to three premium apps), try the Starter plan. You can take advantage of additional features, such as using conditions in filters, formatting text, numbers, and dates, as well as creating custom integrations with webhooks. You can build up to 20 Zaps and will have access to 750 tasks per month (1,500 for a higher subscription payment). The update time remains at 15 minutes.

Professional plan

The Professional plan is for single users that want to level up and use Zapier optimally. This plan is best for you if you have a large number of complex, multi-step processes that require conditional logic and you use more than three premium apps in your business. All Starter plan features are included, as well as paths and task Autoreplay. You can take advantage of unlimited premium apps, unlimited Zaps, a quicker update time of 2 minutes, and access to between 2,000 and 2,000,000 tasks per month (depending on subscription payment).

Team plan

Businesses with two or more team members that are responsible for automating and managing processes should take advantage of the features available on the Team plan. All elements of the Professional plan are included, with the added benefits of a faster update time of 1 minute and a much higher task allocation compared to the Professional plan (50,000 to 2,000,000 based on subscription payment). The Professional plan allows teams to collaborate and automate their processes securely and in an organized way. Team members can securely access multiple apps without the need to share passwords and **API keys** between them, share workspaces, and select who has access to specific folders. An additional bonus of this plan is access to a dedicated premier support team with faster, prioritized responses.

Company plan

The Company plan is for organizations that require enterprise-grade security considerations and want to separate their users into teams. You still have access to all the features of the Professional plan, between 100,000 and 2,000,000 tasks per month (depending on subscription payment), plus access to multiple workspaces. Security features include user management, app access control, secure **Single Sign-On (SSO)**, and top-level account management.

An additional bonus of this plan is the ability to customize Zap history data retention for shorter periods than the standard 30 days to fit with your company's regulatory requirements.

You now have a better understanding of what features and functionality are included in each Zapier plan and which plan would suit your business most. Next, we cover how to set up your Zapier account.

Creating a Zapier account

For you to get started with Zapier, the first thing you will need to do is create a Zapier account.

Important note

The Zapier team are very proactive with trying to create the best experience for the user and often test different **User Interface (UI)** changes on user groups. UI updates, new features, and changes to navigation are released regularly, so don't be surprised if as you work through this book, the screenshots we have used differ slightly from the current, live state.

Work through the following steps to create your new Zapier account:

1. Open your web browser and navigate to the Zapier website home page: `https://zapier.com/`.

2. Create a Zapier account by entering your business email address and your first and last name, and then click on **Get Started Free**, as shown in the following screenshot. Alternatively, you can sign up using your Google or Facebook credentials:

Figure 1.2 – The sign-up area on the Zapier home page

3. Add a password and click on **Sign Up**, as shown in the following screenshot:

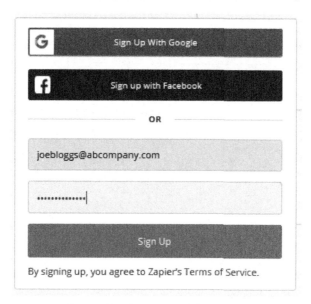

Figure 1.3 – Filling in details on Zapier's home page sign-up area

4. Complete the first step in the onboarding process by identifying your role and clicking **Continue**, as shown in the following screenshot:

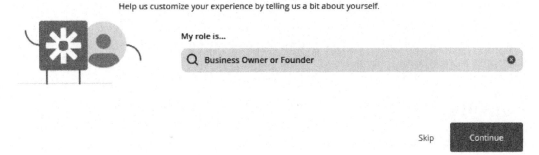

Figure 1.4 – The first step of the Zapier sign-up onboarding process

5. Complete the second step in the onboarding process by selecting the apps that you use in your business, then choose whether you want to receive marketing emails from Zapier and click **Finish Setup**, as shown in the following screenshot:

Figure 1.5 – The second step of the Zapier sign-up onboarding process

> **Important note**
> By completing this two-step onboarding process accurately, Zapier will be able to customize your user experience and provide you with tailored workflow suggestions. These recommendations will give you ideas of what types of tasks you can automate using your business apps as examples. You can choose to fill this information in as appropriate or skip these steps.

Now that you have set up your Zapier account, you're one step closer to building your first workflow automation. In the next section, we cover navigation on the Zapier platform.

Familiarizing yourself with navigation on the Zapier platform

Zapier has made its UI helpful for navigating easily around the platform. When you sign in to Zapier, the first thing you will see is the main **dashboard**. The central dashboard area provides you with useful information to help you get started with tutorials, creating your own workflows, and using some pre-built workflow examples.

The dashboard layout is as shown in the following screenshot:

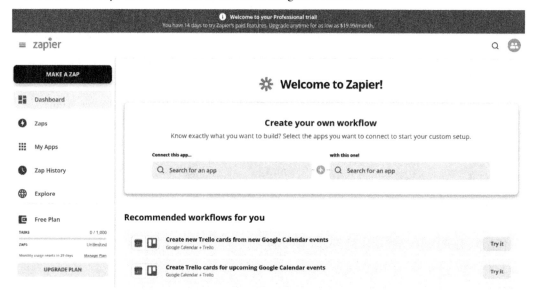

Figure 1.6 – The Zapier main dashboard layout

From the majority of pages within the platform, you have multiple navigation options:

- Icons in the left sidebar
- Icons on the top right
- Footer menu

> **Important note**
> These navigation options are available on most Zapier pages except within the **Settings** and Zap editor modules.

Icons in the left sidebar

The left sidebar is the most commonly used navigational bar in Zapier. It is found on every page within the platform (except on information pages and within the **Settings** and Zap editor modules). The sidebar can be expanded and reduced using the hamburger menu next to the Zapier logo. The following screenshot shows the navigation options in this bar:

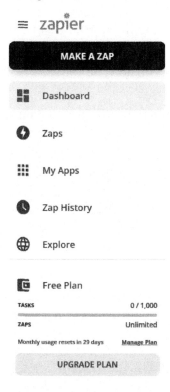

Figure 1.7 – Navigation options in the left sidebar

These navigation options are as follows:

- **MAKE A ZAP**: This button takes you straight into the Zap editor, where you can start building a Zap. We cover the Zap editor in more detail in *Chapter 3, Building Your First Automated Workflow (Zap)*.

- **Dashboard**: This icon link will take you back to the main dashboard at any time.

- **Zaps**: This icon link will take you into your Zap management area. This area gives you a list of all of your Zaps, where you can organize them into different folders and change team sharing preferences. We cover the Zap management area in more detail in *Chapter 4, Managing Your Zaps*.

- **My Apps**: The **My Apps** icon link will take you into your list of connected apps. From there, you can connect and authenticate all your relevant business apps. We cover the My Apps module and how to connect your apps in more detail in *Chapter 3, Building Your First Automated Workflow (Zap)*, and *Chapter 4, Managing Your Zaps*.

- **Zap History**: This icon link will take you into your Zap history, where you can review data that has run in your triggered Zaps. We cover Zap history in more detail in *Chapter 5, Troubleshooting and Handling Zap Errors*.

- **Explore**: This icon link will take you into the **Explore** area, where you will find a wide range of information on different ways to use Zapier to automate your business processes.

- **Get Help**: The **Get Help** icon link will take you into the help center, with comprehensive how-to articles, FAQs, and support options. We cover this in more detail in *Chapter 5, Troubleshooting and Handling Zap Errors*.

- **Wallet**: This gives you a handy snapshot view of your current plan, task usage relative to your monthly limit, and the number of Zaps relative to your plan limit. From here, you can also manage or upgrade your plan using the links provided.

Icons on the top right

In the top-right corner, you will find the following icons:

- **Magnifying glass**: This icon gives you the ability to search for apps to find out whether Zapier integrates with them. The app ecosystem directory contains a comprehensive list of app integrations and details about them.

- **People icon**: This icon displays a drop-down menu with your account settings and an option to log out of Zapier.

Footer menu

In the footer menu, you will find additional navigation options that are available on all pages. The two most useful ones are as follows:

- **Pricing**: This link will take you to the **Plans** page, which will show you the different Zapier plans, features, and associated prices. You can choose to trial, upgrade, or downgrade your plan, while reviewing the features and pricing of different plans.

- **Help**: This link will take you into the **Help** area, which we described earlier.

You now have a better understanding of and have become familiarized with navigation in the Zapier platform. Next, we discuss how to change our settings and preferences.

Changing your settings and preferences

Ensuring that your settings are correct and understanding how specific settings impact other areas of your account is essential for successful account management.

You can access your settings by clicking on the circle icon with your initials in the top right of your dashboard and selecting the cogwheel icon/settings option. The settings menu will be shown in a left sidebar, as shown in the following screenshot:

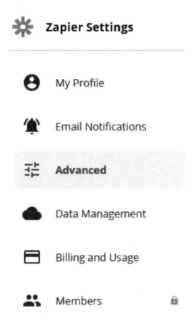

Figure 1.8 – The left sidebar menu in the settings area

> **Important note**
> Team and Company plans have an extra **Organization** menu item, and the Company plan has an **Advanced Security** option. We cover these settings in *Chapter 5, Troubleshooting and Handling Zap Errors*.

My Profile

This area contains basic data about you and allows you to do the following:

- Authenticate your email address.
- Add/change a profile image using Gravatar (an online service that links a picture of you with your email address).
- Change your email address, first and last name, password, and company.
- Change your role.
- Adjust your timezone.

The following screenshot shows the layout of the **My Profile** area:

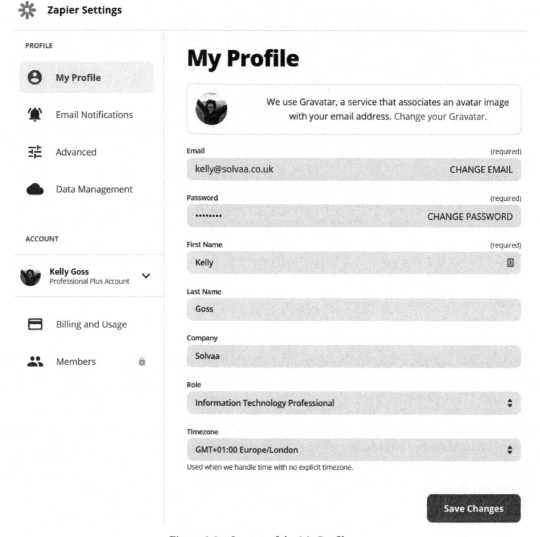

Figure 1.9 – Layout of the My Profile area

Important settings to customize in My Profile

There are a few things that you should do once you have set up your Zapier account:

- Validate your email address.
- Add your role.
- Add your timezone.

Let's go through how to do each of these in Zapier.

Validating your email address

Work through the following steps to adjust these settings:

1. Click on the highlighted text (marked as important) to confirm your email address.

2. Follow the instructions in the email you are sent from Zapier.

This is the first step to protecting your account and allowing Zapier to ensure that it has the right email address to send notifications.

Adding your role

If you did not add your role in the two-step onboarding process when you set up your Zapier account, you can do it here. To do this, scroll to **Role** and choose the closest match to your role from the drop-down list. Completing this step will enable Zapier to make workflow suggestions based on what other users with the same role might be using.

Adding your timezone

To adjust these settings, scroll to **Timezone** and choose your **timezone** from the drop-down list.

Completing this step will enable Zapier to use your timezone when displaying and handling time in your account. The default is **UTC (Coordinated Universal Time)**.

An example of this would be in your Zap history. Times would be displayed in your timezone rather than in UTC. It is much easier to keep track of times when investigating errors if they are in your timezone.

Email Notifications

This area will enable you to alter your preferences for how and when you want to receive email communications. The following screenshot shows the layout of the **Email Notifications** area:

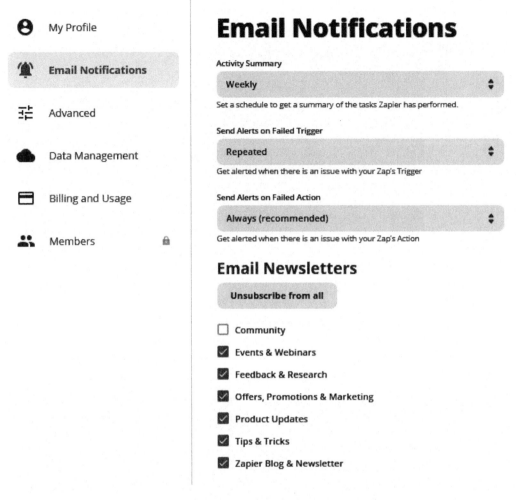

Figure 1.10 – Layout of the Email Notifications area

You can change your preferences for the following:

- **Activity Summary**: Zapier regularly sends you summaries of all the tasks that have been performed over a period of time (within the set frequency). You can choose to receive activity summaries daily or weekly, or if you prefer, never.

- **Send Alerts on Failed Trigger**: You can choose to receive alerts if any of your triggers have issues. It is useful to have this information so that you can sort out a problem soon after it happens. You can choose to receive failed trigger alerts repeatedly, always (this is the recommended setting), or if you prefer, never. Another option available is **Only Zapier Manager Trigger**, which we will discuss in more detail in *Chapter 5, Troubleshooting and Handling Zap Errors*.

- **Send Alerts on Failed Action**: As with failed trigger alerts, you can choose to receive alerts if any of your actions have issues.

- **Email Newsletters**: You can choose what kind of content you want Zapier to send you. You can also unsubscribe from receiving any newsletter content.

Advanced

In the **Advanced** area, you can change your preferences for the following:

- **Two-Factor Authentication**: **Two-Factor Authentication** (**2FA**) gives you more security by requiring you to enter your standard login details (email address and password) as well as an authentication code generated and sent to a nominated email address or mobile phone number. It is recommended that you set up 2FA on your account.

- **Authorized Applications**: This shows a list of apps that you have granted access to your Zapier account. You can remove apps from this area as needed. This area differs from your connected apps in **My Apps**.

- **SSL Checks**: SSL certificates allow scrambled information to be sent between Zapier and its partners. These settings are turned "on" by default and should only be altered if you have experience with changing them and know the consequences or if you have been advised to do so by the Zapier support team.

- **Sign-in With**: This allows you to change your sign-in settings to use your Google account instead of the standard email and password.

- **Delete My Account**: If you want to close your Zapier account and delete all your account data, you can use this area to proceed. If you wish to delete some data periodically, you can do so through the **Data Management** area.

Data Management

Zapier gives account owners the ability to control their data. In this area, you can export and delete your data periodically and read more about data regulation and GDPR compliance.

Team and Company plans have additional **Data Management** settings that allow you to import and export Zaps in bulk (in a **JSON** file) so that you can make backups or share them with others.

Account

If you have access to your personal account as well as one or more Team or Company accounts, a drop-down option will be displayed allowing you to navigate between your different accounts to view the settings for each account.

Billing and Usage

This area is essential for anything related to billing, task, and Zap usage. You will have access to more detailed information about your usage than in the snapshot wallet in the expandable left navigation bar. You can see how many tasks have been used and how many Zaps have been built in relation to your limit and what date your usage resets on. You will also be able to adjust your price plan, payment method, and billing information and view your invoices.

Members

Unless you are on a Team or Company plan, this area will be locked, denoted with a padlock icon.

The **Members** area gives you an overview of tasks related to Zaps built and owned by this member. You can adjust team member settings as follows:

- Add or remove members.
- Change member roles (**Admin** or **Member**).

You now have a better understanding of how to change your settings and preferences.

Summary

In this chapter, we started with an overview of the principles of BPA and how we can use it to increase productivity. We discussed how applications integrate using APIs and transfer data between them. We then introduced Zapier, a no-code tool that integrates with thousands of business apps to help you automate tasks without the need for developers. We presented the key terms used on the Zapier platform and covered how to choose the right pricing plan for your business needs. Then, we discussed how to set up a Zapier account and familiarize yourself with navigation around the platform. Lastly, we covered how to customize the settings.

You now know how to choose the right Zapier pricing plan for your business, set up your Zapier account, navigate the Zapier platform with ease, and customize your settings.

In the next chapter, we will cover how to use the principles of BPA to improve our processes before we jump into automating them. We'll then discuss how to strategize and plan a workflow in preparation for building a Zap and how to explore Zapier's ecosystem of app integrations and use its features.

2
Preparing to Automate Your Processes

In this chapter, we will use the principles of business process automation to prepare to automate your processes. As we discussed in the previous chapter, it is vital to simplify your processes before attempting to automate them. We will, therefore, start by describing how to improve your business processes and then identify what can be automated. We will then explore how to find information about your business apps and how your apps integrate with Zapier. We will expand on this in the *Getting the most out of the app ecosystem directory* section of the chapter, where we will cover navigation in the directory of app integrations and how to find new apps to use.

We will cover the following key topics in this chapter:

- Simplifying your processes and assessing what can be automated
- Establishing how your business apps integrate with Zapier
- Getting the most out of the Zapier app ecosystem directory

Once you have worked through each of these topics, you will have successfully improved and simplified your processes and understood how your business apps connect and how to navigate Zapier's directory of app integrations.

Technical requirements

To work through the content and exercises in this chapter, you will need access to a Zapier account. The Zapier Free plan will be adequate to work through the content in this chapter. You can get access to the systems and process audit template used in this chapter at `https://bit.ly/3e5BUkn`.

Simplifying your processes and assessing what can be automated

Before looking to gain from the benefits of automating your processes, it is essential to analyze, understand, and simplify your existing manual processes. Following this method will ensure that you have more robust processes as well as helping to reduce the number of steps you have in your Zaps. This will, therefore, help to lower the number of tasks that will contribute to your monthly Zapier task limit when your workflows run.

When you hear the term **process mapping**, you might immediately think you will need to employ someone with analytical skills to help you detail your processes in flowcharts and documents. You may also believe that it does not apply to you or your business. The fact is that you most likely already map out your processes in one way or another, such as when you create training documents and checklists for new staff. Having documented procedures allows you, the business owner, the manager, and the team members that use the process to have a clear view of how specific tasks are meant to be done consistently. All businesses, small or large, can benefit from documenting the way they do things, and we will break this down into an easy-to-follow exercise to help you accomplish this.

To establish how business process automation can best work for your business, we recommend that you take a holistic view of all of your processes and systems, alongside assessing your business goals, then look at each process individually. This exercise involves the following key areas:

- Assessing your top-level management goals
- Involving your team
- Brainstorming your processes and prioritizing them
- Analyzing and simplifying your processes
- Identifying what can be automated
- Documenting the new process

As you're working through each stage, using an adapted version of a well-known problem-solving technique called the **5W1H method**, you should bear in mind the following questions:

- *Where?*: Where does this task occur? What app(s) is involved in the process? If there is no app, is human intervention required for it to work accurately?

- *How?*: How is the task accomplished? What steps will you need?

- *When?*: When does this step occur in the process?

- *What?*: What do you need to accomplish the task? What data is required?

- *Who?*: Who is involved in the process? This could be members of the team, or your leads or customers.

- *Why?*: Why is this step important and why could it benefit from being automated?

You can read more about the 5W1H method here: `https://en.wikipedia.org/wiki/Five_Ws`.

Let's dive into the details of each of these steps to improve and streamline your business processes.

Assessing your top-level management goals

Firstly, reviewing your top-level business objectives will make the overall intentions clearer and easier to communicate to your team. Document the answers to the following questions:

1. What are your business goals for the next 6 to 12 months?

2. What are the top five most time-consuming manual process problems that you want to solve?

3. What benefit would simplification and automation bring to these processes and the team members involved?

4. How do these benefits align with your business goals?

5. How much time are you willing to allow you and your team to spend on improving and automating your processes?

As you work through the next sections, keep these answers in mind.

Now that you have a clearer picture of your top-level goals, we will have a look at the importance of involving your team in the exercise.

Involving your team

It is vital to involve the people who use the processes regularly. It is especially important if you have a team (small or large) and tasks that span different departments or roles. Including all relevant team members will ensure engagement and empowerment in the change process and allow teams to take ownership of and manage the processes collaboratively on an ongoing basis. It is also essential to explain the purpose of the exercise (remember your top-level goals) and remind your team that automation will help them to do their jobs better and more efficiently. Encouraging your team to learn how to use business process automation in their daily roles will boost productivity and job satisfaction.

Next, we need to produce a list of all your processes and prioritize them so that we know what to start working on first.

Brainstorming your processes and prioritizing them

This exercise is best conducted visually. You can use sticky notes added to a board or wall and then formalize them in a spreadsheet format to record the various datasets. Take photographs of your brainstorming exercise; this will help you to visualize and structure other parts of your process improvement exercise. You can also use digital whiteboard tools such as **Miro** (https://miro.com/) or **Mural** (https://www.mural.co/) to collaborate with your team online.

To get started with this exercise, nominate a team member to facilitate and own the overall project. Then, work through the following steps with your core team members:

1. Brainstorm a list of all of your processes and what the purpose of each is. Categorize these processes into marketing, sales, operations, and finance, or whatever business functions make the most sense to you. You may find that some processes cross over between departments; therefore, make a note of this. An example of this using the Miro app is shown in the following figure:

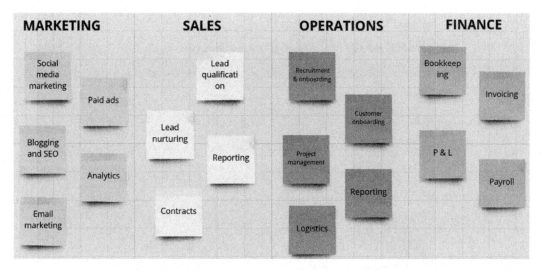

Figure 2.1 – A digital whiteboard brainstorming exercise using Miro

2. Brainstorm a list of all the apps and tools you use in your business, make a note of their specific function, and other apps that you have been considering potentially replacing them with. Again, you can use a whiteboard or add them to a spreadsheet. An example of this using a spreadsheet is shown in the following screenshot:

TYPE	CURRENT SYSTEM (S) e.g. Excel spreadsheet	ANY SYSTEMS YOU ARE CONSIDERING
LEAD GENERATION/ MARKETING		
EMAIL MARKETING	Klaviyo	Mailigen
MARKETING AUTOMATION		
DIRECT MAIL MARKETING		
SOCIAL MEDIA POSTING	Publer	
WEBSITE PLATFORM	Wordpress	
WEBSITE CHAT	Intercom	ManyChat
SALES		
CRM (CUSTOMER DATABASE)	Salesforce	
CONTRACTS/ PROPOSALS/ DIGITAL SIGNATURES	Adobe	
E-COMMERCE PLATFORM	Shopify	Woocommerce
OPERATIONS		
PURCHASING		
STOCK MANAGEMENT	Xero inventory	

Figure 2.2 – A systems audit document

If you would like a copy of a systems and process audit template, you can get access here: https://bit.ly/3e5BUkn.

3.   Identify and list all the process users.

4.   Nominate one process user to own each ongoing process.

5.   Give each process a score between 1 and 5 (where *1* is low and *5* is high) for each of the following:

  •   How time-consuming it is when performing it currently

  •   How error-prone it is when performing it currently

6.   Add these scores together to calculate the total, which will give the overall pain-point score for each process.

7.   Add an explanation for each score to elaborate on the pain point and why the problems are necessary to address.

An example showing *steps 3* to *7* is shown in the following figure:

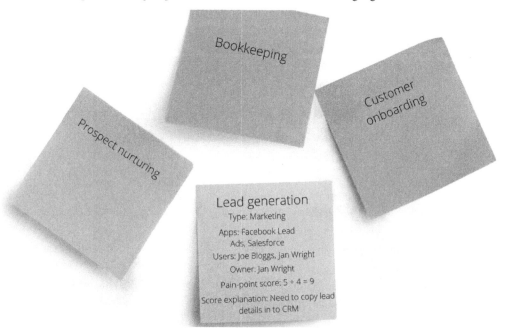

Figure 2.3 – A business process brainstorming exercise with more granular detail

8.   Number each process in order of priority of what to work on first.

9.   From the priority list, choose the top five processes with the highest pain-point score. Review your top-levels goals and ask yourself whether this list aligns with what you noted as your top-level management goals.

Now that you have a list of priority processes to work on, let's take a look at the best way to analyze and simplify each of them.

Analyzing and simplifying your processes

For the top five priority processes that you identified, work through the following steps for each, one by one. Be sure to involve your team of users specific to each process. Once again, this exercise is best done visually by using a traditional whiteboard or digital whiteboard for remote collaboration. Let's explore how to do this:

1. Describe the importance of the process and what it achieves.

2. Break the process down into manageable and systematic steps.

3. If the process spans business functions, then categorize each step into marketing, sales, operations, or finance functions, or use other categories that suit your business better.

4. From your list of apps (that you created earlier), identify what business tools you currently use for each step.

5. Review, understand, and describe the importance of each step.

6. Identify steps that can be modified and improved, potentially by introducing other apps.

7. Eliminate irrelevant, ineffective, unnecessary, or wasteful steps.

8. Review the new process for accuracy and assess any change risks.

Repeat this method for each of the remaining top-priority processes.

To help you visualize this process, let's take a look at an example.

The reception team of a small chiropractor practice currently logs all inquiries in **Smartsheet**. The inquiries come from multiple sources, such as a web form on their website, and by email. Any inquiries that are not booked in for an appointment at first contact need to be followed up with a second call. These tasks are created in **Trello** and once the appointment is booked, a patient record and booking are created in the practice management system. All updates to follow-ups and appointment bookings are recorded on the sheet so that there is traceability. The process is very manual and prone to error as tasks are often forgotten. The following figure shows *steps 1 to 4*:

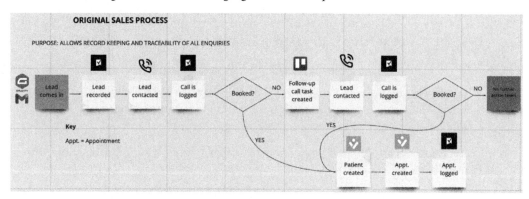

Figure 2.4 – Analyzing the existing process

The team then discusses and records the elements of *step 5* separately.

In this example, the practice staff has established that their practice management system has new functionality that allows them to extract reports and use tasks, so they no longer need to use Smartsheet for reporting or Trello for task management. They can now simplify the process and eliminate unnecessary steps. *Steps 6* and *7* are shown in the following figure:

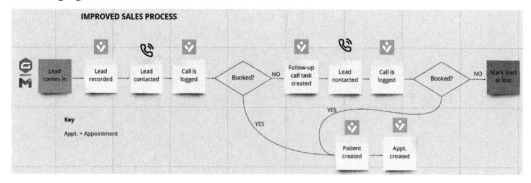

Figure 2.5 – Simplifying the process

The team agrees that there are no significant risks involved with using this new process, as per *step 8*.

Now that we have streamlined our top-priority processes and broken them down into manageable steps, we can establish whether each one of them can be partially or fully automated. Let's look at this next.

Identifying what can be automated

Work through your priority list and steps from the previous section to identify what can be automated as follows:

1. Ask the following questions:

    a) Is it repeatable?

    b) Can it be done with minimal logical thinking and human intervention?

    c) Is it prone to error when done manually?

    d) Is it consistent across all our business operations?

    If the answer to each of the above is "yes," then this process is a prime candidate for automation. If you answered "no" to any of those, discuss the options to part-automate the process, where possible. If the process is not consistent across all business operations, as long as you answered "yes" to the first three questions, it may be possible to duplicate workflows across business operations to encompass various nuances.

2. If your process can be partially or fully automated, make a note of two or three quick-win solutions and the longer-term solution, with expected timeframes to accomplish each.

Using our example from the last section, the practice team discusses and records the answers, as shown in the following figure:

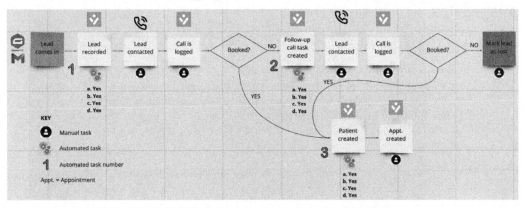

Figure 2.6 – Establishing what steps can be automated

Tasks 1, 2, and 3 can be fully automated as follows:

- Task 1, the recording of the lead in the practice management system, can be automated as the practice management system integrates with Zapier and so does the existing web form app. Emails can be forwarded and parsed to extract information then added via Zapier.

- The follow-up task creation, task 2, can be fully automated as workflow automation is available in the software.

- The practice management system allows for the automation of lead conversion to new patients applicable to task 3.

All of the automated tasks can be implemented within a week of the decision being made to change the process.

You can now repeat this method for each of the remaining processes. You do not need to do this all at one time; however, this will give you a better picture of how your apps are linked and can work together.

Next, let's discuss how to adequately document your new processes.

Documenting your processes

So far, we've been using a whiteboard tool to illustrate our examples. This method might not work for you; however, whichever method you have used for simplifying your processes and establishing what can be automated, we suggest that you formally document them once you have completed the exercise. You can document your new process in a spreadsheet, using a digital whiteboard tool such as Miro or Mural, or a flowchart tool such as **Microsoft Visio** or **Draw.io**. You can also use checklist-style, workflow management tools such as **Process Street** or **Process Bliss** that allow you to create digital **Standard Operating Procedures** or **SOPs**.

> **Important note**
> When documenting the new process, keep the critical information to a minimum. A simple but effective way of documenting the process involves stating the app it involves, what happens in the task, and whether it requires manual intervention or is automated.

Another example of a visually documented process is shown in the following figure:

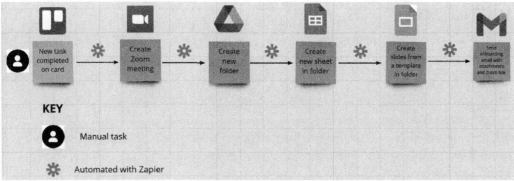

Figure 2.7 – A digitally documented process using Miro

> **Tip**
> If using whiteboard tools or flowcharts, you can represent your process map
> vertically or horizontally.

If you want to have a bit more detail in your process maps, you can incorporate the information you have pulled together during your problem-solving process using the 5W1H method. This method serves as a reminder to ensure that you should capture all the relevant information as a summary in your process maps:

- *Where?*: What app(s) is involved in the process?

- *How?*: How is the task accomplished? What steps will you need? Identify whether the step is automated or requires human intervention.

- *When?*: When does this step occur in the process?

- *What?*: What do you need to accomplish the task? What data is required? Make a list of key data values, such as names or email addresses.

- *Who?*: Who is involved in the process? This could be members of the team, or your leads or customers.

- *Why?*: Why is this step important and why it will benefit from being automated? Make a note of some critical pain points.

We'll show you a visual example of this is in *Chapter 3, Building Your First Automated Workflow (Zap)*.

Now that you have simplified your processes and assessed what parts could be automated, let's discuss the best way to establish how Zapier integrates with your apps so that you can begin to automate those processes.

Establishing how your business apps integrate with Zapier

Before we can start automating any tasks, we need to determine which of your business tools integrate with Zapier, as well as what trigger, action, and search functions have been developed into the integration if one is available.

When working through the exercises in the last section, you created a list of all of your business apps. You also noted which apps were associated with each step in your mapped-out processes. Starting with your five top-priority processes, we can now go through the list of apps related to those processes one by one to establish which of your apps integrate with Zapier.

The steps you should take to establish how your business apps integrate with Zapier are as follows:

1. Search for information about your app.

2. Review information on the **app profile** page.

3. Assess how to use your app with Zapier.

Let's review each of these.

Searching for your app

The easiest way to find out if your app integrates with Zapier is by clicking on the magnifying glass icon in the top menu bar to search by app, as shown in the following screenshot:

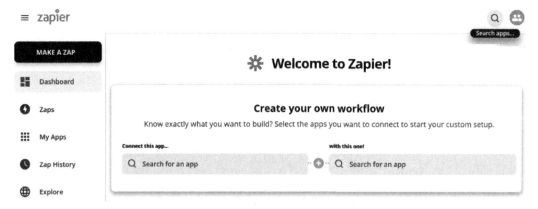

Figure 2.8 – Using the magnifying glass icon to search by app in Zapier

A search bar will appear, and you can type in the name of your app. As you type, any matching name suggestions will be highlighted in a drop-down list, as shown in the following screenshot:

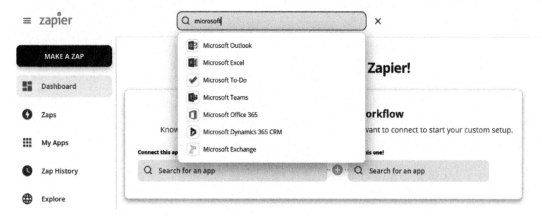

Figure 2.9 – The drop-down list of apps when searching by app in Zapier

From there, you can select your app and will be taken to the **app profile** page.

> **Important note**
>
> If you are using a less popular app, you may find that your app does not come up in a search. First, check that the spelling you are using matches with the official naming convention of the app. If it still does not appear, this most likely means that an integration does not currently exist with Zapier or has not been published in the directory. We will discuss what to do in this scenario in the *Getting the most out of the Zapier app ecosystem directory* section.

Next, let's explore how to review the information about the app.

Reviewing information on the app profile page

App profile pages show a wealth of information about a specific app and how to use that app with Zapier. We recommend that you review the information on the app profile page thoroughly, as it will help you to understand the automation capabilities of using Zapier with your app.

Each page is structured with navigation tabs as follows:

- **Integrations**
- **Help**

We will use **Calendly** to illustrate this, as shown in the following screenshot:

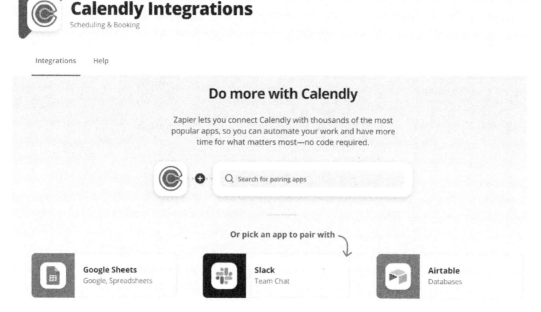

Figure 2.10 – The Calendly app profile page

At the bottom of the page of both the **Integrations** and **Help** tab, you will find some details about the app. This shows a logo image of the app, a short descriptive summary, and a link to the app website.

> **Tip**
> As you navigate through the information available for your app on the app profile page, keep in mind all your processes that involve this specific app. Refer back to the visuals of your brainstorming exercise, so that you can see how all your apps fit together. Creating diagrams specific to apps will help. Make notes of any key points that will help you to visualize and strategize your workflows.

Let's cover the information shown in each of the different tabs.

Integrations

The **Integrations** tab presents you with detailed information about the app, structured in the following sections:

- **Do more with…**: This section provides a **Search for pairing apps** search bar, allowing you to search for other apps to connect with.

  Or pick an app to pair with: This section shows a visual representation of several **pairing apps**. Clicking on the logo icon and text of each will take you to an **Integrations** page specifically for that app pairing. Scrolling on the arrows under the list will show you additional apps. We will use the **Calendly** and **Slack** integration to highlight this as in the following screenshot:

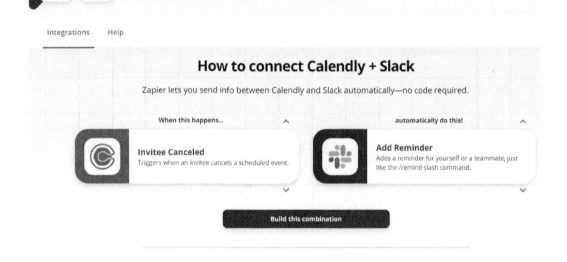

Figure 2.11 – The Calendly and Slack Integrations app pairing page

On that page you can use the **Build this combination** button to start using the pre-built workflow.

- **Popular ways to use…workflows**: This section lists popular pre-built workflows with your app. You can enter the name of another app from your list of business tools into the search bar and bring up the list of guided workflows to use. We will use **Twitter** to highlight this in the following screenshot:

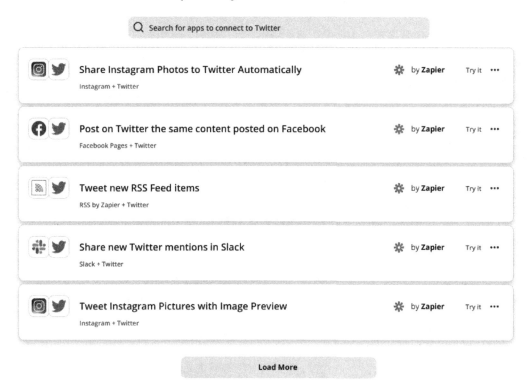

Figure 2.12 – Twitter integrations – connect to over 3,000 apps

Clicking on the **Load more** button will expand the list. Click on any of the guided workflows, then either the **Try it** button to use the workflow, or the **See Zap details** button for more information.

- **Supported triggers and actions**: This section provides information about the available trigger, action, and search functions supported by Zapier, which can be selected from the drop-down menu. Each function has a short descriptive title and a summary of what it does. We will use **Intercom** to highlight this in the following screenshot:

Figure 2.13 – Intercom triggers, actions, and searches shown in the Integrations tab

We will discuss using triggers, actions, and searches in more detail in *Chapter 3, Building Your First Automated Workflow (Zap)*, and *Chapter 6, Creating Multi-Step Zaps with Built-In Apps*.

> **Tip**
> Use the **Supported triggers and actions** section as a quick reference to find out how your app integrates with Zapier and what triggers, actions, and searches are available to use.

Next, let's take a look at the **Help** tab.

Help

The **Help** tab is structured as follows:

- **Help & Support**: This section presents you with helpful articles on how to get started and tips on using the app with Zapier, as well as common errors and problems seen with app integrations and how to solve them.

- **Tutorials**: This section displays content created by Zapier to help you get started with using your app in question with Zapier. This includes how to solve common problems, presents examples of popular pre-built Zaps that use your app, and provides other useful content.

- **Alternatives**: This section provides you with a snapshot of a few alternative apps (with app name and type) to your app. The other options represent apps that are similar in functionality and use to the app you have searched for. This information is handy if you are looking to change from your current app and want to review other apps with similar functionality that may have more or slightly different integrations with Zapier. Clicking on the logo icon will take you to the app profile page for that app.

Let's explore how to use your chosen apps with Zapier.

Assessing how to use your app with Zapier

Now that we have reviewed the information about your app in the app profile page, we should pay particular attention to the **Supported triggers and actions** section found in the **Integrations** tab.

For each of your apps, make a list of all the function titles and types. For triggers, record whether it is scheduled or instant. For example, for **Google Sheets**, one available trigger is **New Spreadsheet Row**, which is instant. Also note whether your app is labeled as Premium, as you will need to ensure you are subscribed to a price plan that supports premium apps, as discussed in *Chapter 1, Introduction to Business Process Automation with Zapier*.

An example is shown in the following figure:

	A	B	C	D	E
1	APP	APP TYPE	FUNCTION	TRIGGER TYPE	WHAT
2	Salesforce	Premium	Trigger	Polling	New Record
3			Trigger	Polling	Updated Record
4			Trigger	Polling	Updated Field on Record
5			Trigger	Instant	New Outbound Message
6					

Figure 2.14 – Recording the Zapier integration options for Salesforce trigger types

You can now repeat this method for each of your associated business apps in the top five priority processes. Once that is done, you can work through your other business apps. You do not need to do this all at once; however, taking a holistic view of your apps and business processes will position your thoughts better for when you create your workflows in Zapier.

> **Important note**
>
> As a bare minimum, it is crucial to work through what we have described for the apps in your first top-priority process. This will give you a clearer picture of how your apps can be connected so that you can start automating your processes.

Now that you understand how to assess how Zapier integrates with each of your apps, we can take a look at the benefits of using the app ecosystem directory.

Getting the most out of the Zapier app ecosystem directory

In the previous part of this chapter, we discussed how to use the magnifying glass icon in the top menu bar to search for your app. Another place to do this is from within the app ecosystem directory. The app ecosystem directory is not only useful for searching for your existing apps, but it also serves to direct you if your app does not have an integration with Zapier. Most importantly, the app directory is a comprehensive resource to help you find apps that you may want to start using in your business.

The app directory can be found via the top menu navigation on information pages, as described in *Chapter 1, Introduction to Business Process Automation with Zapier.* It can also be found using the following URL: `https://zapier.com/apps`.

Let's start by familiarizing ourselves with the app directory.

Navigating the app ecosystem directory

The app directory consists of a left navigation sidebar and a central navigation pane, as shown in the following screenshot:

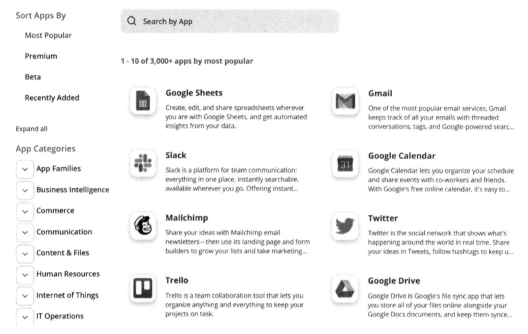

Figure 2.15 – The Zapier app ecosystem directory

We will now look at each of these navigation options.

The app ecosystem directory central navigation pane

The central navigation area displays information that we had become familiar with when we discussed app profile pages in the previous part of this chapter and is structured as follows:

- **Search bar**: The search bar allows you to search the directory by app. It functions similarly to the magnifying glass icon-search bar we discussed in the previous part of this chapter.

- **1-10 of 3,000+ app by most popular**: This section provides a list of the 10 most popular apps out of all the apps listed in the directory with snapshot details.

- **Featured, New Actions Added, Coming Soon, Recently Added**: This section shows four different apps that are either being featured by Zapier; have had new triggers, actions or searches added; are soon to integrate with Zapier; or have integrated recently with Zapier.

- **3,000+ apps by most popular**: This section provides a more extensive list of the most popular apps without the snapshot details. If you scroll down to the bottom of the list, by clicking on the **Load more** button, the list will expand.

The left navigation sidebar

The left navigation sidebar is useful for displaying apps by group and is shown in the following blocks:

- **Sort Apps By**: You can sort apps by popularity, their Premium or **Beta** (an integration undergoing testing that has not officially been released) status, or if they have recently been added. Clicking on each link will change the app lists in the central navigation pane.

- **App Categories**: You can sort apps by their category and sub-category; for example, category **Commerce**, sub-category **Accounting**. The central navigation pane view changes slightly to display a useful blog article related to the category/sub-category and lists the top apps, as shown in the following screenshot:

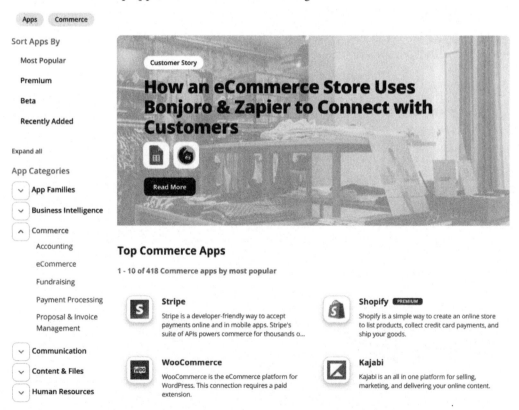

Figure 2.16 – The central navigation pane of the app directory showing accounting apps

- **Request an App**: If your app does not exist in the app directory, it might mean that an integration has not yet been built with Zapier or it is not yet listed in the directory. You can reach out to the customer service team of the app provider to inquire about whether the app integrates with Zapier. Alternatively, the app provider might list details of a Zapier integration on their website, or you might find the information by doing a Google search. From the **Request an App** block, you can click on the **Email us the apps you'd like added today!** link and submit a request to have the app added to Zapier.

- **Add an App**: If you are a software provider or developer, you can access the developer portal to integrate your app and create triggers, actions, and searches by clicking on the **Go to the Developer Platform** link.

- **Get Updates**: Clicking on the **Go to the Updates Blog** link takes you to the updates blog page, where you can sign up for blog updates on new apps and feature releases.

Clicking on any app logo brings up an app profile summary popup, which we discuss next.

The app profile summary popup

When you click on any of the app logos in the app directory, you will see a popup as shown in the following screenshot for **Pandadoc**:

Figure 2.17 – The Pandadoc app profile summary popup

This is a quick-reference summary of the app profile page and is also structured with a left sidebar and a central navigation pane.

Left sidebar

The left sidebar contains the following:

- **App logo**: This shows the logo of the app.
- **Guided workflows**: This shows the number of pre-built workflows that have been created by Zapier using this app.
- **Paired apps**: This shows the number of other apps that this app is commonly paired with in workflows.
- **View app profile**: Clicking on this button takes you to the app profile page.
- **Get started with**: Clicking on this button takes you directly into the Zap editor to start building a Zap with this app as a trigger.

Central navigation pane

The central navigation pane contains the following:

- **App name**: The name of the app.
- **Summary**: A few sentences describing what the app is and how it can be used.
- **Great pairing apps**: This tab shows logos of 10 apps that work well together with this app. Clicking on **See more apps** will take you to the **Integrations** tab of the app profile page.
- **Guided workflows**: This tab shows two popular pre-built workflows. Clicking on **See more workflows** will take you to the **Integrations** tab of the app profile page.

Next, let's discuss how to choose new apps for your business.

A brief guide to choosing new apps for your business

The intricate considerations of **digital transformation** could be an entire book on its own. However, it is essential to mention a few points that will help you in your search for new apps to add to your business or alternatives to the ones you are currently using. These are listed here:

- Explore your options.
- List your key features and requirements.
- Define your core app.
- Search app ecosystems.
- Search the Zapier app ecosystem directory.
- Search app comparison directories.
- Review feedback.
- Arrange product demonstrations and test support resources.
- Trial your app shortlist adequately.
- Plan to transition to the new app.

> **Important note**
>
> If any of your processes are interconnected, and you would benefit from having multiple apps connected to automate tasks, always establish whether your current apps and the apps you are considering integrate with Zapier and in what way. Keep this in mind when you are creating your shortlist.

We will now look at each point in turn.

Exploring your options

Although it may seem logical to settle on an app because it is well known, it is always wise to explore your options. With **Software as a Service (SaaS)** becoming a more popular industry, the release of thousands of new applications to the market has become commonplace over the last few years. There is plenty of competition and there are many different apps available to fit every use case. Therefore, spend more time investigating your options.

Listing your key features and requirements

If you are looking for an alternative to an app you currently use, make a list of all the features from your existing app that are essential to the way you do business. Also, review what you defined earlier in the chapter in the *Simplifying your processes and assessing what can be automated* section. This information will help you to assess what additional functionality you will require. Equally, if you are looking for a new app to digitize your existing processes, this information is vital. Make a note of what features are critical and what are only "nice-to-have" features.

Defining your core app

We have previously mentioned that it is important to take a holistic view of your apps and processes so that you know how apps and processes link together. It is also essential to identify the most key application in your business – the app that you consider to be the one source of truth. For example, this might be your **Customer Relationship Management** (**CRM**) tool or your project management tool. If this app is key to your business, knowing what apps it integrates with natively and in what way will allow you to make better decisions about the new apps you intend to introduce. As we discussed in *Chapter 1, Introduction to Business Process Automation with Zapier,* your cloud-based apps are most likely to have a list of other apps that they integrate with and can be found in the app marketplace or ecosystem.

Searching app ecosystems

App ecosystems usually contain a wealth of information about how apps integrate with your core app. You are likely to find user feedback, comprehensive help documents, and videos as well as pricing and functionality information. These ecosystems are excellent places to start if you are looking for new apps to use with your existing core app and subsidiary apps.

You can now start to create a shortlist with feature comparisons, pricing, and how they integrate with your core app.

Searching the Zapier app ecosystem directory

The Zapier app ecosystem directory is a good starting point to find information about alternative apps that are the closest matches for you in terms of functionality. You can also look for new apps to use by using the left sidebar to sort apps by categories and sub-categories. You can also navigate to the **Alternatives** section of the **Help** tab on your current app's profile page to look for apps with similar functionality.

You can now build on your shortlist with how the potential apps integrate with Zapier (triggers, actions, and searches).

Searching app directories

Free directories such as **Get App** (`https://www.getapp.com/`) allow you to search for apps in specific categories, by industry and use case. You will have access to verified user reviews, comparison tables, and articles. You can also use their app finder tool to create a list of recommended apps based on your company size, industry, and the apps you currently use.

Product Hunt (`https://www.producthunt.com/`) is another directory that shows information and up/down votes for products and new features.

You can now compare your apps and add information to your shortlist.

Reviewing feedback

Get App is not the only place to find feedback on apps. You can search social media, forums such as **Reddit** `https://www.reddit.com/`, and trust sites such as **Trustpilot** (`https://www.trustpilot.com/`). Considering reaching out to users that have posted comments or asking for feedback on online business groups and communities, such as Facebook or LinkedIn, can be beneficial too. Review feedback carefully and evaluate the pros and cons.

Arranging product demonstrations and testing support resources

Product demonstrations (demos) offer a much better way of initially assessing a tool, more than a free trial will. You might initially think that only larger software providers provide demonstrations of their products. As mentioned earlier, the SaaS industry is becoming more competitive, and even smaller providers offer one-on-one walk-through demos, which then allow you, the potential buyer, to ask questions tailored to your use case. Simply enquire with their customer service team to assess the possibility of a product demo if not explicitly offered on the website of the software provider. Providing some flexibility with providing a demo will also give you an indication of what customer support and service levels are likely to be once you have committed to purchasing the product.

> **Tip**
> Customer service availability and levels of service are often crucial when you are just starting out with a new app. Establishing customer service availability in relation to your timezone and query response time will help you to make a judgment on whether this fits your needs.

Trialing your shortlist of apps adequately

Once you have made your comparisons, choose two apps to trial alongside each other and the existing app, if appropriate. Using representative data from your existing app or process (if you do not have an app in place currently), run a trial for a few weeks to adequately assess functionality side by side. Free trial periods are often not long enough to properly evaluate the suitability of an app, so enquire prior to starting your trial about whether trial extensions are available.

> **Tip**
> Choosing more than two apps to trial may be time-consuming and overwhelming for your team. It is time well spent to invest in your comparison groundwork to reduce your list to two apps.

Ensure that you have set up the app following the guidance and best practice provided by the software provider, and make sure that a selection of the key users of the process are involved in the testing. Software providers generally supply comprehensive how-to and training videos and will likely be on hand to address certain issues. You may also find that some providers provide free setup and onboarding services.

Planning for transition to the new app

Once you have decided on the app that you want to implement permanently, ensure that you have created a detailed project plan to manage the transition to using the new app and phase out the old app and process. This plan should include system setup review and customization, data backup, data import, process documentation, and staff training.

You now have a better understanding of how to use Zapier's ecosystem directory of app integrations effectively, can find information about how Zapier integrates with your apps, and can find and assess new apps to use in your business.

Summary

In this chapter, we started by working through how to improve your business processes and then identify what can be automated. We explored how to find information about your business apps and how your apps integrate with Zapier. We discussed navigation in the app ecosystem directory and how to use it effectively to explore new apps to use in your business. We concluded by briefly describing how to find and assess apps to use in your company.

You now know how to simplify your processes, identify what can be automated, navigate the app directory, and find apps to use in your business.

In the next chapter, we will discuss how to strategize and plan individual workflows before automating them. We will cover the steps required to connect your apps to Zapier, discuss navigation in the Zap editor, and work through an example to create your first Zap. We will show you how to find and use pre-built workflows, explain field types and data handling, and, lastly, cover continuous improvement.

3
Building Your First Automated Workflow (Zap)

In this chapter, we cover all the need-to-know information to enable you to start automating manual and repetitive tasks in your business. We start by covering how to strategize and plan individual workflows before automating them. We then dive into working through a step-by-step process of connecting your apps to Zapier, introduce the Zap editor, and work through an example to create your first Zap from scratch. We show you how you can access a wide range of pre-built or guided workflows created by Zapier, to speed up your Zap building process. We explain the different field types you may see in your action steps, and how to use the correct data formats for their fields. We conclude the chapter by delving into best practices for ensuring the continuous improvement of your processes.

We will cover the following key topics in this chapter:

- Strategizing your first workflow

- Connecting your apps to Zapier

- How to create your first Zap in the Zap editor

- Understanding field data types

- Ensuring your processes and automations stay current

Once you have worked through each of these topics, you will have successfully built your first workflow automation using Zapier.

Technical requirements

To work through the content in this chapter, you will need access to a Zapier account. The Zapier Free plan will be adequate to work through the content in this chapter. You can get access to the **Zap templates** used in this chapter here: `https://bit.ly/3e5BUkn`. Using the templates will help you visualize how the process works.

Strategizing your first workflow

So far, in this book, we have worked through how to simplify your processes, establish what can be automated, and assess how your business apps integrate with Zapier. We are now suitably prepared to get started with planning your first workflow.

The following steps are required to strategize your workflows:

1. Reviewing your process and app information
2. Creating a step-by-step workflow plan

Let's take a look at each of these.

Reviewing your process and app information

From your list of processes, choose one of your five top-priority processes that satisfy the following criteria:

- The process can be automated partly or fully.

- One or more apps associated with the process integrate with Zapier.

- You have made a list of triggers, actions, and searches for each of your apps.

Let's now explore how to create a workflow plan.

Creating a step-by-step workflow plan

From your chosen process, select one of the most straightforward quick-win solutions that you identified earlier that could be automated. Use this part of your process to work through the following steps to strategize the workflow. We will then create this workflow automation in Zapier in the next part of the chapter.

We will use the following example in a sales process to illustrate the steps we need to take to strategize the workflow.

Your company does not have a complex sales process. You have two salespeople that are using **ActiveCampaign** to manage your sales pipeline. New deals are created in the pipeline when marketing leads hit a certain lead score from automated marketing campaign opens and link clicks. There are also members of your admin team that do not need access to ActiveCampaign but need to know a summary of specific details associated with these new deals. This information is manually added to a Google Sheets spreadsheet by the sales team after they have created the deal in ActiveCampaign. The admin team has identified that, on occasion, deals have not been added to the spreadsheet, and there are often transcription errors in the data. The sales team has mentioned that the process is time-consuming and prone to error, which increases with volume. You have already worked through all the steps in the previous sections to simplify the process, establish whether it can be automated, and assess whether ActiveCampaign and Google Sheets integrate with Zapier and in what way.

The following figure shows the preceding example as a mapped-out process with the 5W1H method that we covered in *Chapter 2, Preparing to Automate Your Processes*:

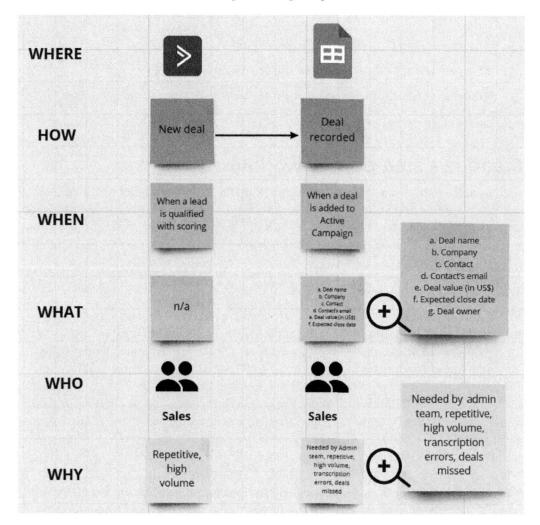

Figure 3.1 – A process map to visualize the example (courtesy of Miro)

Let's use this example to work through a step-by-step process to strategize a workflow:

1. *Identify your trigger app*: In our example, the trigger app is **ActiveCampaign**.

2. *Identify your trigger step event*: In our example, the Zapier trigger step is **New Deal Added or Updated**. This event triggers the start of the workflow in Zapier when a new deal is created in ActiveCampaign. This is shown in the following screenshot:

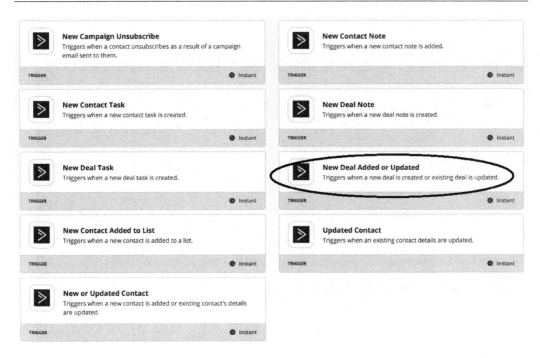

Figure 3.2 – ActiveCampaign app profile showing the "New Deal Added or Updated" trigger event

3. *Identify whether the trigger is scheduled or instant*: In our example, this trigger is instant, which means that immediately after a deal is created in ActiveCampaign, the workflow in Zapier will be triggered.

> **Tip**
> It is handy to know how often your workflows will update. If you have noted that your trigger is scheduled rather than instant, review your Zapier pricing plan to establish how often your workflow is likely to start. For example, if you are using the Free plan, the update time is every 15 minutes, which means that Zapier will look for new data in that trigger app every 15 minutes, to start your workflow. This is discussed in *Chapter 1, Introduction to Business Process Automation with Zapier*.

4. *Identify your action app*: In our example, the action app is **Google Sheets**.

5. *Review the data you require for your action step*: In our example, we want to capture the following information from the deal in ActiveCampaign and add it to our Google Sheets spreadsheet:

a) Deal name

b) Company

c) Contact

d) Contact's email

e) Deal value (in US$)

f) Expected close date

g) Deal owner

Our ActiveCampaign deal is shown in the following screenshot:

Figure 3.3 – An ActiveCampaign deal to be used as a working example (courtesy of ActiveCampaign)

6. *Identify your action step event*: In our example, the Zapier action step is **Create Spreadsheet Row**. This action will create a new row in a spreadsheet that you will specify. This is shown in the following screenshot:

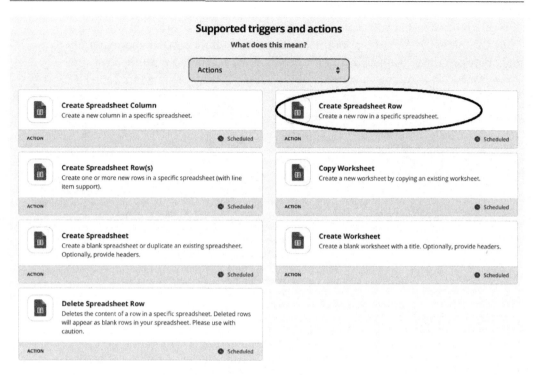

Figure 3.4 – Google Sheets app profile showing the "Create Spreadsheet Row" action event

Next, we need to understand what data we need to capture in our action app. In this case, it is a Google Sheets spreadsheet, and the structure is shown in the following screenshot:

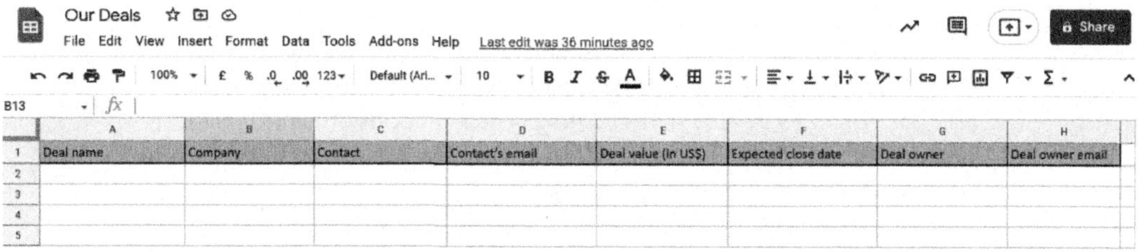

Figure 3.5 – A Google Sheets spreadsheet to be used in our example (courtesy of Google)

It is often the case that your data headings may have slightly different wording in your various apps; thus, it is good practice to make a note of what you may want to map between the two apps. This exercise will make our **data mapping** steps more straightforward to follow when we start building out the workflows in Zapier. Our example is shown in the following figure:

ActiveCampaign	Google Sheets
Deal Title	Deal name
Account	Company
Deal Contact First Name + Deal Contact Last Name	Contact
Deal Contact Email	Contact's email
Deal Value	Deal value (in US$)
Forecasted Close Date	Expected close date
Deal Owner First Name + Deal Owner Last Name	Deal owner

Figure 3.6 – Data mapping between the trigger and action steps

Now that you have strategized your workflow, we can get stuck into connecting our apps to Zapier and then creating your first workflow automation on the Zapier platform.

Connecting your apps to Zapier

Before we can start building our automations, we need to connect our apps to Zapier to allow Zapier to retrieve and post data in them.

> **Important note**
>
> Knowing how your data and security are handled by Zapier is an important topic. Allowing Zapier access to your apps using authentication protocols is essential for Zapier to be able to perform task automations on your behalf. The credentials that you use to authenticate your apps so that Zapier can connect with them are stored with bank-level encryption. Zapier has created a comprehensive resource on data privacy and security, which you can read here: `https://zapier.com/help/account/data-management/security-at-zapier`.

App connection can be performed from two places:

- The **My Apps** link in the left sidebar
- The Zap editor in our trigger, action, or search steps

Let's look at the **My Apps** method first.

Connecting your apps in My Apps

Follow these steps to connect each of your apps:

1. Start typing in the name of your app in the search bar to reveal a drop-down list, then select your app, and click on the **Connect** button. You can also just click on the **Add connection** button to reveal a popup where you can use the search bar to search for an app. This is shown in the following screenshot:

Figure 3.7 – Connecting a new account in My Apps

2. Once you have chosen your app, a new window will open, giving you instructions on how to authorize the app. You could be asked to enter some of the following details:

    a) Google account details (to use **Sign in with Google**)

    b) Username and password

    c) App domain or subdomain URL

    d) API key or token

    > **Tip**
    > Zapier provides instructions to explain which are required fields that you need to fill in and how you can find this information if it is not immediately apparent.

The following screenshot shows an example of a subdomain and API key request for **Freshdesk**:

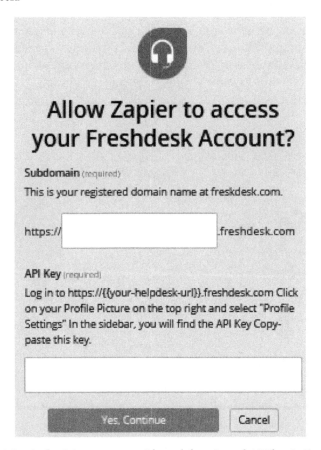

Figure 3.8 – Authorizing your app with a subdomain and API key in Freshdesk

> **Important note**
> If a new browser tab or window does not appear when you select the app that you want to connect, try to disable your browser's pop-up blocker.

3. You will then be taken to an approval page, advising you that Zapier wants to access your account and what Zapier will be allowed to do if you approve access. You can read further about privacy and risks, and if you are happy to continue, click **Allow**. This text may differ between apps. An example using a Google account is shown in the following screenshot:

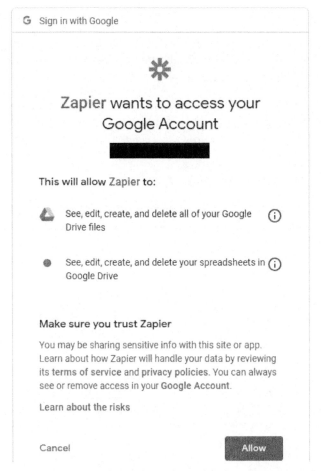

Figure 3.9 – Google approval page to confirm allowing Zapier to access the app

---

Important note

You might need to reconnect your app if you have connected the app to Zapier using a username and password and you have changed your password in the app. Here are more details on app authentication and reconnection requirements: `https://zapier.com/help/manage/app-connections/what-should-i-do-in-zapier-if-i-change-an-app-account-password`.

Follow *steps 1* to *3* for all apps involving a trigger and an action step.

You will now be able to use your connected apps in your workflows, and you can now focus on creating your first Zap. We will discuss how to connect apps from within the Zap editor in the next part of this chapter.

How to create your first Zap in the Zap editor

There are two ways that you can create a Zap. You can use workflow templates that Zapier has created, which we will cover later in this chapter; however, the best way to learn how to use Zapier to automate your processes is to build your Zaps from scratch.

All workflows are created, edited, and maintained in the Zap editor. The Zap editor is accessible at any time from the expandable left sidebar menu, by clicking on the **Make a Zap** button. Let's first have a look at how to navigate through the Zap editor.

Navigating in the Zap editor

The Zap editor is structured with text fields, icons, and buttons along the top bar and right-side panel, as well as a central section that serves as the visual editor. This is shown in the following screenshot:

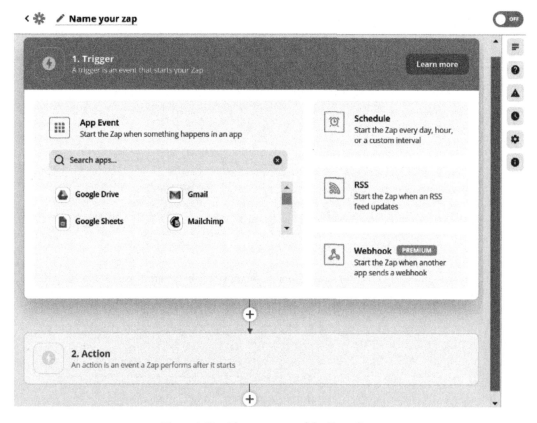

Figure 3.10 – The structure of the Zap editor

Let's take a look at this structure in more detail to understand what each section offers us.

The top bar

The top bar contains the following text fields, icons, and buttons, from left to right:

- **Zapier logo icon with back arrow**: Clicking on this icon takes you to the Zap management area. We discuss this area in more detail in *Chapter 4, Managing Your Zaps*.

- **Name your zap**: This is an editable text field that allows you to give a custom name to your Zap. Adequately naming your Zap is an important part of managing your workflows. We discuss this in more detail in *Chapter 4, Managing Your Zaps*.

- **The "Share" button**: This button allows you to share the Zap you have created with anyone who has a Zapier account. It will only be visible once you have turned your Zap **On**. We discuss Zap sharing in more detail in *Chapter 4, Managing Your Zaps*.

- **The "On/Off" button**: This button becomes usable once you have created your Zap, tested it, and eliminated any errors. You must turn your Zap **On** to use it with live data.

The right-side panel

The right-side panel contains several icons that, once highlighted with your cursor, show the text that follows, from top to bottom:

- **Outline**: This section is represented by a list icon in the menu. It shows a summary of all of your steps in your Zap as built out in the visual editor. Selecting any of the steps in the **Outline** section highlights the step in the editor. Once you start to create complex multi-step Zaps, using the **Outline** section as a quick-reference tool is handy for identifying where certain steps are in the workflow. The search bar is just as important to use for searching for steps based on their title. We will discuss how to best name your Zaps in *Chapter 4, Managing Your Zaps*, and how to start creating multi-step Zaps from *Chapter 6, Creating Multi-Step Zaps and Using Built-In Apps*, onward.

- **Guide**: This section is represented by a question mark icon in the menu. It is a useful built-in helpdesk that shows "how-to" help articles and videos that can be viewed from within the Zap editor. If you are having a problem with your Zap, at the bottom of the page, you will find a **Get Help** link, which will take you to the Zapier support page where you can submit a support query.

- **Errors**: This section is represented by an exclamation mark icon in the menu. Any errors related to specific steps in your Zap will be highlighted here. You can get more information on the specifics of the error by clicking on the notification. It is important to address any errors highlighted before you attempt to turn your Zap on.

- **Zap history**: This section is represented by a clock icon in the menu, and links to the **Zap History** module. We will cover Zap History in detail in *Chapter 5, Troubleshooting and Handling Zap Errors*.

- **Settings**: This section is represented by a cog icon in the menu, and allows you to manage your Zap from within the Zap editor. You can edit the Zap name, change the folder it is stored in, add or alter a description (this is useful for making notes), and change the timezone settings of the Zap. We will discuss this in detail in *Chapter 4, Managing Your Zaps*.

- **Zap Details**: This section is represented by an i (information) icon. Clicking on this icon will take you to the **Zap Details** page for the Zap. We will discuss this in detail in Chapter 4, Managing Your Zaps.

Visual editor

The visual editor is where the real magic of Zapier happens. This is where you create workflow automations step by step. The visual editor is structured as follows:

- **Trigger step box**: This is your trigger step. You can start building your Zap by searching for or selecting an app to add to your trigger step.

- **Plus sign (+) icon**: These icons appear between all steps and after the last step. Clicking on this icon allows you to add action, search, filter, delay, and formatter steps between existing steps, as well as paths after the last step. We will discuss this in more detail from *Chapter 6, Creating Multi-Step Zaps and Using Built-In Apps*, onward.

- **Action step box**: This is your action step. Click on the step to begin setting up your action step.

- **The Share feedback button**: Clicking on this button will bring up a pop-up box for you to share your experience of using the Zap editor with the Zapier team or create a support request. This button is normally only visible in new accounts.

Once you have added an app to your trigger or action step, two icons will be revealed in the top-right corner.

The two icons are represented as follows:

- **Question mark icon**: Clicking on this icon will open up or close the **Guide** section of the left-side panel.
- **Three dots icon**: Clicking on this icon will allow you to rename your step for either trigger or action steps. For action steps, you also have the option to delete this step. You cannot delete a trigger step but you can edit it. We will discuss this in more detail later in this chapter.

Now that we have a better understanding of how to navigate through the Zap editor, we can start creating our Zap. We previously identified our trigger and action apps, our related steps, and the data we will map between our apps. We will now use our working example from earlier in the chapter to illustrate how to create a Zap. You can work through the steps using the workflow you strategized earlier.

Setting up your trigger step

Firstly, we will start with the trigger step. Let's work through a step-by-step guide to set up our trigger step using our example:

1. *Start editing the trigger step*: When you open up the Zap editor, the trigger step will already be open.

2. *Choose your trigger app*: From the list of apps presented in the trigger step, choose one to connect as the trigger app. If you don't see it in the list, search for it in the search bar just above. The search bar allows you to search for your chosen app if it is not shown in the list of apps. Selecting any of the apps will allow you to start customizing your trigger and action steps. In our example, we will select **ActiveCampaign**.

3. *Choose your trigger event*: Now select your trigger event. In our example, we will select **New Deal Added or Updated** as our trigger event, as shown in the following screenshot:

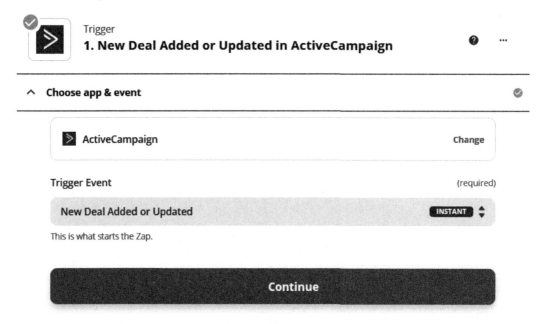

Figure 3.11 – Using the ActiveCampaign app New Deal Added or Updated trigger event in the Zap editor

Click on the **Continue** button.

4. *Choose your trigger app account*: Select your app account from the drop-down list. The list will only show accounts specific to the app you selected in *step 2*, and those you have previously connected to Zapier. You can also click on the **Connect a New Account** link to connect and authenticate a new app account. This will take you through the same procedure that we discussed in the *Connecting your apps to Zapier* section of this chapter. Another option is to click on the **Edit Accounts** link, which will enable you to edit your connections in the **My Apps** module. This is shown in the following screenshot:

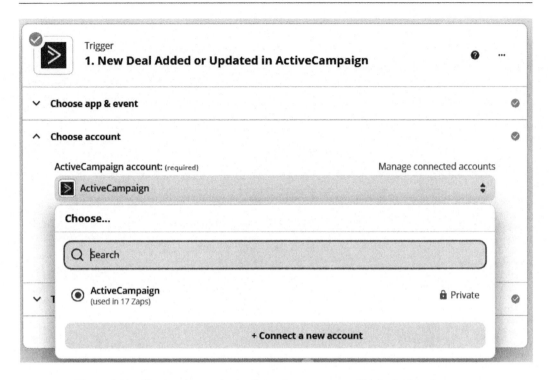

Figure 3.12 – Connecting an ActiveCampaign account to Zapier in the trigger step

Click on the **Continue** button.

5. *Choose your sample data and test your trigger*: Next, we need to find sample data from our app (ActiveCampaign, in our example) to test our trigger. This will confirm that we are using the right app account and that the trigger step is working correctly. Click on the **Test trigger** button. Zapier will search for data in your app, which, after a few seconds, will be pulled through into the Zap editor.

> **Tip**
> We recommend creating test data sample sets of data or dummy data wherever possible when you are testing your Zaps. This can help avoid live data corruption in your app accounts.

6. *Review your sample data*: You should review your data to ensure it is what you are expecting. Note that data labels will be highlighted in bold and the data value will be in normal text. In our example, we created a deal called `Test Company deal`, associated with the `deal_title data label`. We use the name of this deal as the **unique identifier** to check that we have the correct sample data to use in the test, as shown in the following screenshot:

Figure 3.13 – Using a unique identifier to search for data in the sample

You can scroll through the data or use the search bar to find your data.

7. *Change your sample data*: You can change your sample data by selecting the sample header with the up and down arrows (for our example, the preceding screenshot shows this labeled as **Deal G**) and select another option if available. To retrieve more sample data, select **Load more**.

8. Select **Continue** to move on to your action step. If your trigger has been set up correctly, you will see a green check mark next to the app logo, as shown in the following screenshot:

Figure 3.14 – A completed trigger step in the Zap editor

> **Important note**
>
> Some app integrations only allow a limited number of sample datasets to be brought through. In some cases, only recently created data will be pulled through. You may have to create additional sample sets as you are testing your trigger.
>
> Also, some app integrations have issues pulling through any existing sample data from the app and will provide you with dummy sample data to use instead. In these situations, use the dummy sample data to test your trigger step. Your Zap will work correctly with "live" data when the Zap is turned on. Contact Zapier support if this does not work.

Next, we'll set up our action step.

Setting up your action step

In action steps, you will find two main field types:

- **"Choose value…"** from which you can choose set values from a drop-down list brought in from our action app or add **custom values**. We will discuss using custom values in more detail when we explore multi-step Zaps in *Chapter 6, Creating Multi-Step Zaps and Using Built-in Apps*.

- **Type or insert…** from which you can either manually type in static text, if you want that value to always be displayed, or insert **dynamic data** that updates every time the Zap runs. You can also add a combination of static and dynamic data. In our example, if we wanted the `Deal name` cell in the Google Sheets spreadsheet to always display the text `Test Deal` when a new row is created, we would enter the text `Test Deal` into the field in that step. Using dynamic data, on the other hand, means that the value will represent live data when the Zap runs. This data is retrieved from your trigger app (or previous action steps if using multi-step Zaps).

> **Tip**
>
> Mapping out your data in a table helps to identify the dynamic data names in the different apps. Often, the title of the data may be named differently from what you expect. These naming conventions are based on what title the API field is given in the app. With reference to the data table in *Figure 3.6* and trigger data in *Figure 3.13*, in our example, we may expect to see a value for "Deal name" but we see `deal_title` instead, and for "Account" we see `contact_orgname` or `deal_orgname` instead. As you become more familiar with how field data is named and presented from your trigger and action steps, you can add an additional column to your data mapping table that shows the API field name.

An example is shown in the following screenshot where static text and dynamic text are used in the Deal Name field in two separate action steps:

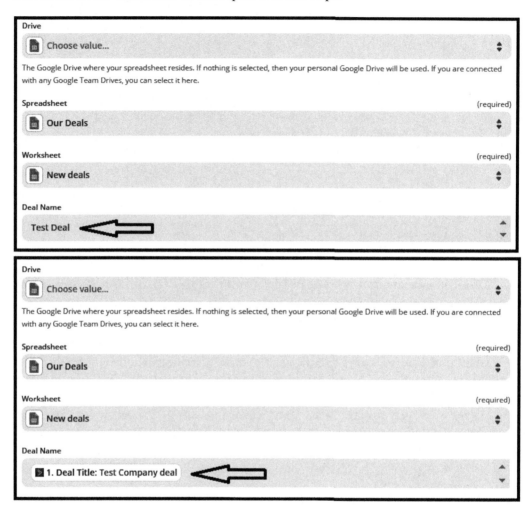

Figure 3.15 – Using text (at the top) or dynamic data (at the bottom) to map a Google Sheets action step field

Let's now work through a step-by-step guide to set up our action step, as follows:

1. Click on the second step marked as **2. Action** to reveal the app list.

2. *Choose your action app*: From the **My Apps** list, select your action app. If you don't see it in the list, search for it in the search bar just above. In our example, we will select **Google Sheets**.

3. *Choose your action event*: Now select your action event. In our example, we will select **Create Spreadsheet Row** as our action event. Click on the **Continue** button.

4. *Choose your action app account*: Select your app account from the drop-down list. This step functions in the same way as in the trigger app account step. Click on the **Continue** button.

5. *Customize your action step*: Next, we need to customize our action step. In our example, the first thing we need to do is choose which spreadsheet we want Zapier to add data to. Using **Choose value…** fields, Zapier will bring in a list of fixed values from our action app. In the case of our example, Zapier will bring in a list of spreadsheets, and once a spreadsheet has been selected, a list of worksheets within that sheet. This is shown in the following screenshot:

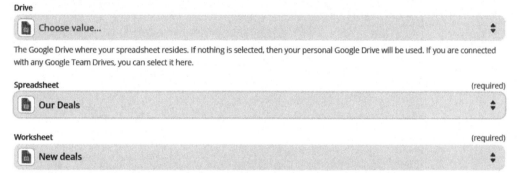

Drive

| 📄 | Choose value... | ↕ |

The Google Drive where your spreadsheet resides. If nothing is selected, then your personal Google Drive will be used. If you are connected with any Google Team Drives, you can select it here.

Spreadsheet   (required)

| 📄 | **Our Deals** | ↕ |

Worksheet   (required)

| 📄 | **New deals** | ↕ |

Figure 3.16 – Choosing a Google Sheets spreadsheet and worksheet to use in a Zapier action step

In our example, the rest of the field types are **Type or insert…**, and we will use this to describe how to map your fields.

Once you have selected the field you want to map (using a **Type or insert…** field in this case), a drop-down list of dynamic data will be shown. This dynamic data will be presented in the following format:

- *An icon*, which represents the originating app (in our example, ActiveCampaign). It will look similar to the app's logo.

- *A number*, which denotes which step the data has originated from. In single-step Zaps, this will always be 1 .. In multi-step Zaps, this numbering will help you identify which step to map data from.

- *Text styled in bold with a colon*, which represents the name of the field as coded within the app, that is, the **API field name**.

- *Text normally styled*, which represents the dynamic data from the app.

This is shown in the following screenshot:

▶ 1. Deal Title: Test Company deal

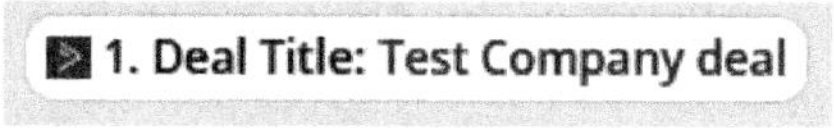

Figure 3.17 – The structure of dynamic data

You can select **Show all options** to show all data, which you can scroll through or use the search bar to search for specific text.

We can now use the information from *Figure 3.6* to assist us with mapping our field data. Using our example, we can search for the deal title Test Company deal by typing this in the search bar, as shown in the following screenshot:

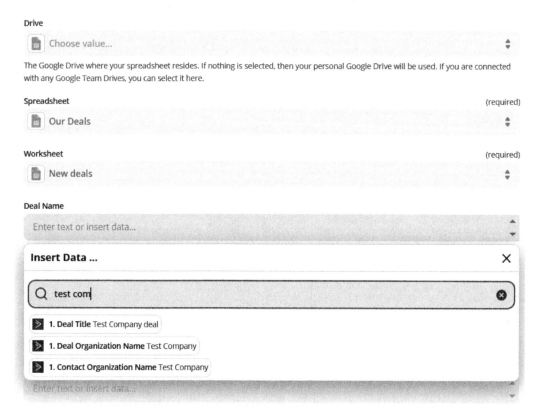

Figure 3.18 – Searching for dynamic data in an action step

Identify the correct dataset to map to that field and select the relevant one. Repeat this for each field.

> **Important note**
> Fill in any fields that are marked as **required**. You will not be able to test your action step without these fields.

Once you have mapped all the fields, the resulting action step form will look similar to what is shown in the following screenshot (using our example):

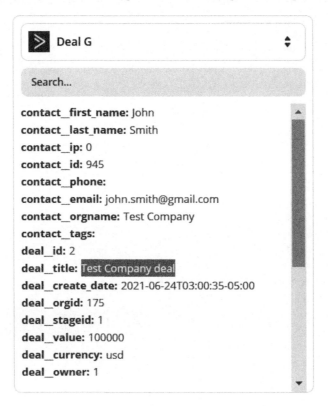

Figure 3.19 – A completed action step form with mapped fields

As you can see from *Figure 3.19*, you can map into the field two or more values dynamically to form a new word. For example, in the `Deal Owner` field, we have added the `Deal Owner First Name` data value and the `Deal Owner Last Name` data value to show the full name.

6. *Test your data*: Once you are satisfied that your **field mappings** are correct, select **Continue**. Next, we need to test our data by sending it to our action app, Google Sheets. You can review the data that we will send and select **Test & Review** to stay in the **Test action** block to see the result or **Test & Continue** to move on to another step if you have one set up. This is shown in the following screenshot:

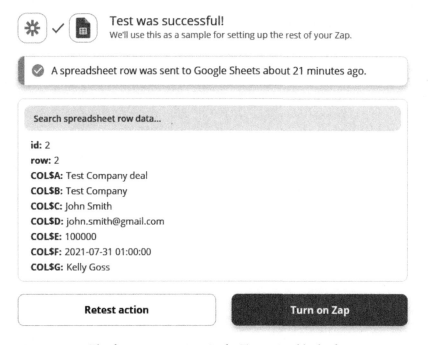

Figure 3.20 – The data testing options in the Test action block of an action step

You can also select **Skip test** if you do not want test data to be sent.

If your request is successful, you will be shown a highlighted success message. You can choose to select **Retest action** to stay in the **Test action** block to see another result or **Turn on Zap** to turn your Zap **On**.

7. *Check your data in your action app*: Always check your data has been sent correctly to your action. This is shown in the following screenshot:

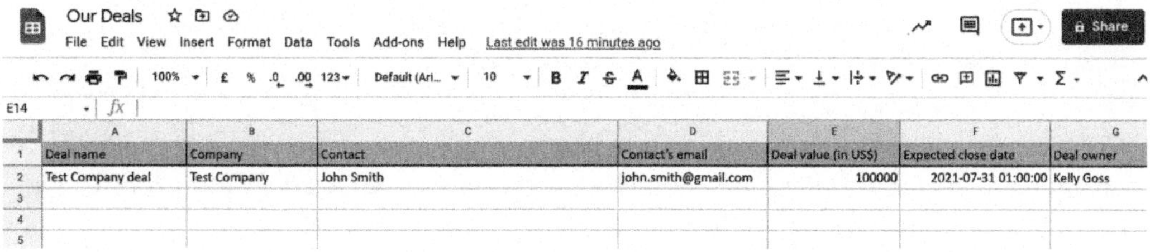

Figure 3.21 – Successfully sent test data from the action step shown in Google Sheets (courtesy of Google)

> **Tip**
>
> Zapier assigns a standard name to trigger and action steps based on what the step does. Get into the habit of changing these standard names and renaming your action steps with keywords applicable to your workflow. You can then search for steps using the **Outline** icon in the expandable right-side menu. This is handy when you have complex multi-step Zaps and you're working with a team.

You can get a template of this Zap here and add it to your Zapier account: `https://bit.ly/3e5BUkn`. Using the Zap template will help you to visualize how the process works.

> **Tip**
>
> With our example, you need to bear in mind that the trigger will run every time a new deal is added or updated in ActiveCampaign. This means that we will also be adding updated deals to the Google Sheets spreadsheet as new rows. You can use a search action step to check the Google Sheets spreadsheet to see whether the deal already exists on the sheet, then a Filter by Zapier step straight after to only allow the Zap to continue if the deal is not on the sheet. We will discuss using search action steps in *Chapter 6, Creating Multi-Step Zaps and Using Built-In Apps*, and using Filter by Zapier in *Chapter 7, Getting Started with Built-In Apps*.

Now that you have created your trigger and action steps, and tested your Zap, you will need to name it and turn it on so that it can trigger on your selected event in your trigger app and run with live data.

Naming your Zap and turning it "On"

Let's name the Zap so that it is easily identifiable. We can do this in the top-panel **Name your Zap** editable text field or in the expandable right-side panel **Settings**. Choose a name that represents it well. In our example, we will use `Create new Google Sheets row when new deal is added in ActiveCampaign`. We discuss the best way to name your Zaps in more detail in *Chapter 4, Managing Your Zaps*.

The last thing to do is turn your Zap **On**. This can be done using the **On/Off** toggle in the top menu. Well done, you have just created your first workflow automation from scratch!

Now let's discuss using pre-built workflows.

Using Zapier's guided workflows (Zap templates)

Using the Zap editor to start building out your Zaps is the best way to learn how to use Zapier. You can save time, however, by exploring and using pre-built templates or guided workflows called Zap templates. Zapier has created thousands of single-step Zaps using popular combinations of apps and corresponding trigger or action events. These Zap templates can be accessed from various locations, as we have mentioned throughout this chapter; however, the most practical place to start using guided workflows is from the main dashboard, using the **Create your own workflow** interactive tool.

All you need to do is enter the two apps you want to connect, as well as your trigger and action events. Zapier will then present you with a pre-built Zap to use. Select **Use Zap** to continue, which will take you directly to the Zap editor, or **Cancel** to start again. This is shown in the following screenshot using our working example:

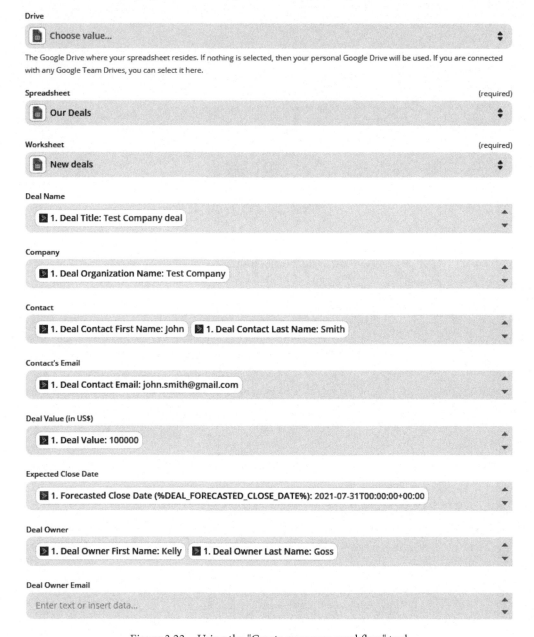

Figure 3.22 – Using the "Create your own workflow" tool

Zapier provides variations of the interactive tool, such as with the **Get started with our most popular workflows** option on the main dashboard. This offers a more specific approach by naming the objective. For example, you could choose a template to notify your team about new leads, then follow the steps to add in your lead generation trigger app, your messaging action app, review the guided workflow, and start using it in a Zap. An example is shown in the following screenshot:

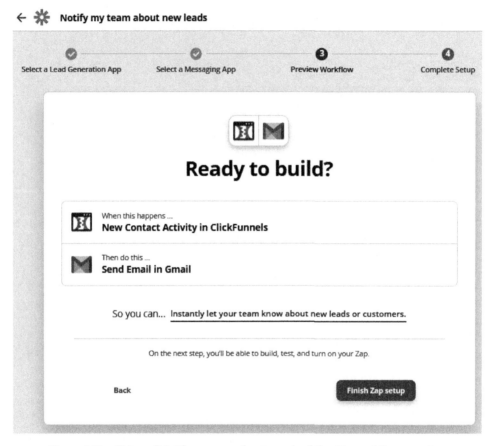

Figure 3.23 – Using a "Notify my team about new leads" guide workflow template

You should now have a better understanding of how to create a Zap from scratch, and how to use pre-built workflows created by Zapier. Now, let's take a look at the different field types that may be shown in action steps.

Understanding field data types

Now that we've created our first Zap, it's important that we elaborate on the different types of fields that you may see in Zapier action steps.

In the last section, we covered the two general types of fields, **Choose value...** and **Type or insert...**, and how to use them to map fields in your Zaps. In addition to these two general field types, there are five different field data types that only allow you to add data in specific formats. Each field data type is represented by an icon, as shown in the following table:

Icon	Field Data Type
 🗓️🕐	Date/time
1 2 3	Number (integer)
 ●○	Boolean (true/false)
 🗋	File
1.0	Decimal

Figure 3.24 – Action step field data types

These field data types are dictated by the data posting format requirements of your action app. For example, if your action app is Xero (an accounting app), and you want to create a new invoice, your invoice date field will only allow you to add date/time data values for the request to be successful.

We will discuss each of these field data types in turn.

Date/time

The **Date/time field** type is represented by a calendar and clock icon side by side. This field requires data in the form of a date with or without a time.

An example of a date/time field from an accounting app action step is shown in the following screenshot:

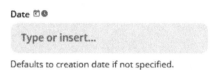

Figure 3.25 – A date/time field from an accounting app action step

Supported formats

Zapier recognizes and supports various time/date formats as follows:

- Standard international date format (ISO), for example, 2020-07-15T13:05
- Unix timestamps (the number of seconds since January 1, 1970), for example, 1591537509
- Today at noon
- Next Monday at 5pm
- 5/15/2020 9pm EST

Timezone settings

In *Chapter 1, Introduction to Business Process Automation with Zapier*, and earlier in this chapter, we discussed altering your account timezone settings and your Zap timezone settings. If you do not specify a timezone in the time/date data, for example, today at noon, Zapier will use your account or Zap timezone settings.

The format you should use in the field is that needed for the action app. Every app has a different required date/time format and timezone setting. Each app will recognize certain time formats/timezone settings and not others. If you're unsure of the exact format needed for your action app or if the data is not posted as expected, you should contact Zapier support.

We will cover how to format date and time values in *Chapter 13, Formatting Date and Time*.

Number (integer)

The **Number (integer)** field type is represented by the numbers **1 2 3**. This field requires data in the form of an integer, which is a positive or negative whole number (which can also be zero). This field is quite often used for selecting unique identifier records such as ID numbers for users, companies, and projects, as well as posting strings of numbers in number-specific fields in the action app.

An example of a number (integer) field from an SMS messaging app action step is shown in the following screenshot:

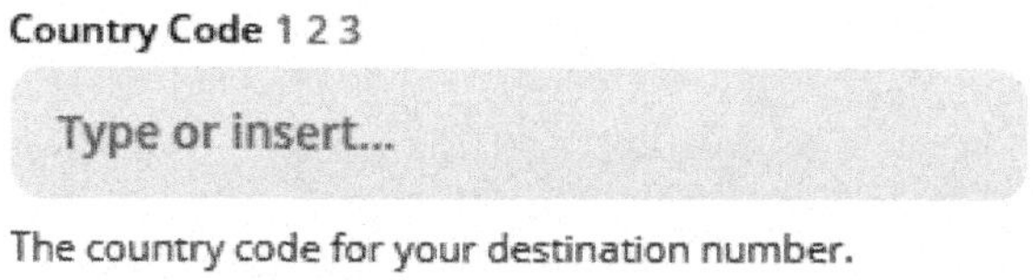

Country Code 1 2 3

Type or insert...

The country code for your destination number.

Figure 3.26 – A number (integer) field from an SMS messaging app action step

Boolean (true/false)

The **Boolean (true/false)** field type is represented by **two dots side by side**, one filled and the other not. This field requires data in the form of a true or false value and denotes how the field is represented in the action app. These values may be converted as follows:

- true, yes, t, or 1
- false, no, f, or 0

In the example shown in the following screenshot, when creating an invoice in the Xero accounting software, you can select to mark the invoice as **Sent To Contact**. A value of **True** would signify yes and a value of **False** would signify no:

Figure 3.27 – A Boolean (true/false) field from a Xero accounting app action step

File

The **File** field type is represented by a **document icon**. These fields require data in the form of an actual document file and not the name of a document. Often these document files are represented by the text in the dynamic data labeled **(Exists but not shown)** and can be in various file formats.

An example of a file field from an email app action step is shown in the following screenshot:

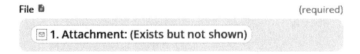

Figure 3.28 – A file field from an email app action step

You can type text into the field and this will be converted by Zapier into a .txt file containing the filled contents, and uploaded to the action app. You can also add a URL and Zapier will inspect the content, attempt to transcribe it, name it accordingly, and upload it to the action app. For example, if you added the URL to an image, rather than the image file itself.

Decimal

A **Decimal** field type is represented by the icon **1.0**. These fields require data in the form of a number with a decimal and can be of variable decimal places. The theory is similar to the number (integer) field; however, if the decimal is missing, Zapier will add it before posting the data in the action app.

An example of a decimal field from an accounting app action step is shown in the following screenshot:

Figure 3.29 – A decimal field from an accounting app action step

---
Note
It is only possible to add a single file to one field.

You should now have a better understanding of the different types of field data used in action steps. Let's now explore how to keep your workflow automations current.

Ensuring your processes and automations stay current

In *Chapter 1*, *Introduction to Business Process Automation with Zapier*, and *Chapter 2*, *Preparing to Automate Your Processes*, we covered using business process automation principles to improve the way you manage your processes and make them more efficient with automation. We now need to discuss the importance of building your workflows with continuous improvement in mind.

Businesses continually change with economic influences, staff turnover, priorities and goals, and growth. Thus, the way companies work and how tasks are performed is bound to change often. In addition, app integrations are frequently updated and improved. Regularly reviewing your processes will ensure you benefit from these upgrades and align with the way your business functions currently. Business process automation principles take into consideration that businesses and technology evolve constantly, and promote having a plan for continuous improvement.

These are the five key steps to implement effective workflow automation in your business successfully:

1. *Discover*: Analyze and simplify your processes and plan your workflows step by step.

2. *Create*: Build your workflows and test them. Adjust your workflows as required.

3. *Implement*: Document your workflows, train all users, and make other relevant team members aware of the new process. Set your workflows to live.

4. *Review*: Continually monitor workflow performance. Regularly review your processes to assess whether they can be improved. You can do this by repeating the exercise described in the *Analyzing and simplifying your processes* section of *Chapter 2, Preparing to Automate Your Processes*, and check whether they are still relevant, useful, and not redundant or wasteful.

5. *Improve*: Evaluate what steps can be changed and improved.

Once all five steps are completed, repeat them from *step 1* at planned, regular intervals.

By reassessing your Zapier workflows regularly, you will be able to remove unnecessary steps, which will ultimately reduce your task usage. Following these principles will ensure that your processes and subsequent automations align with the current situation, and remain lean and error-free.

Summary

In this chapter, we started off by discussing how to strategize individual workflows before diving into working through the step-by-step process of connecting your apps to Zapier, and creating your first workflow automation (Zap) in Zapier. We covered how you can access and use a wide range of pre-built workflows. We also explored the different types of fields found in action steps and how to use these fields correctly. We concluded the chapter by delving into best practices for ensuring the continuous improvement of your processes.

You now know how to plan your workflows and create them in Zapier from scratch or using Zap templates. You also know how to use different types of field data and perform continuous improvement in your processes. You have also created your first automated workflow.

In the next chapter, we cover the best ways to organize your Zaps by naming them and using folders. We discuss how to manage individual Zaps and help you to understand Zap statuses. We cover how to manage the apps you have connected to your Zapier account, and finally, we describe how to share copies of individual Zaps with other Zapier users and how to share Zaps and folders with your team.

4
Managing Your Zaps

In this chapter, we discuss the best ways to manage and maintain data in your Zapier account. As you build more Zaps, keeping them all organized will become more of a priority for preserving structure. We therefore start this chapter by explaining how to keep your workflows organized in the Zap management area by using the best naming conventions and by using folders. We then discuss how to manage individual Zaps and utilize the Zap **Settings** area. Next, we help you to understand Zap statuses and then cover how best to manage your connected apps. Finally, we discuss sharing your workflows with other Zapier users.

We will cover the following key topics in this chapter:

- Keeping your Zaps organized
- Managing your Zaps
- Understanding Zap statuses
- Managing your connected apps
- Sharing your Zaps and folders

Once you have worked through each of these topics, you will know how to keep your workflows organized, how to maintain and share them, and how to manage your connected apps.

Technical requirements

To work through the content and exercises in this chapter, you will need access to a Zapier account. The Zapier Free plan will be adequate to work through most of the content in this chapter. For some of the *Sharing your Zaps and folders* section, you will need access to a Zapier account on a Team or Company plan.

Keeping your Zaps organized

In *Chapter 3, Building Your First Automated Workflow (Zap)*, we worked through the steps required to create your first workflow automation. As you repeat that process, you will build more Zaps to automate your other business processes. It will eventually become more of a priority to ensure that you have created a system for organizing your workflows. It is, therefore, good practice to understand how best to keep your Zaps organized and start this process when you only have a few workflows built.

These are a couple of steps you can take to help you to keep your Zaps organized:

- Labeling your zaps adequately
- Using folders in the **Zap management** area

Let's discuss each of them.

Labeling your Zaps adequately

From an organizational perspective, you should name your Zaps with sufficient information to ensure a title is descriptive enough to understand what the Zap does. Labeling your Zaps in the right way will allow you to sort them into groups, search for them, and quickly identify them in the **Zap history** and when troubleshooting errors.

There are several ways that you can name your Zaps, and how you choose to do this will come down to what seems most logical for your business and also personal preference. The following are some commonly used methods for Zap naming:

- Using trigger and action descriptions
- Using unique identifiers
- Adding numbers, letters, or roman numerals

As we review each of these, think of keywords that could help you to identify your Zaps.

Using trigger and action descriptions

The most obvious method is to use a brief description of what happens in action steps when an event is triggered in the trigger app. In *Chapter 3, Building Your First Automated Workflow (Zap)*, we used a working example to illustrate the Zap building process. In our example, we built a workflow that triggers when a new deal is created in ActiveCampaign, which then results in a row being added to a Google Sheets spreadsheet. We chose to name that Zap `Create new Google Sheets row when new deal is created in ActiveCampaign`. If your Zap triggered on a new contact being added to **SendinBlue**, which then created an item in **monday.com**, we could name the Zap `Create new item in monday.com when new contact is added to SendinBlue`.

This is the typical arrangement that you will see used in most Zapier pre-built/guided workflows.

Using unique identifiers

You may also choose to specify a unique identifier, such as a user, file, or app account that is involved in either your trigger or action step(s), if highlighting this is of particular importance. For example, if you have multiple Zaps that accomplish a similar outcome but trigger based on different conditions, such as something user-specific, you could add the user's name to the title to help you identify the difference between those workflows. In our example, we may choose to highlight the Google Sheets spreadsheet we are using and name the Zap `Create new Google Sheets (Our Deals) row when new deal is created in ActiveCampaign`.

> **Tip**
> As you start to build multi-step Zaps, naming your Zaps using this method could get complex. Don't overcomplicate the naming process. Abbreviate where possible, use keywords, and keep your Zap titles short yet descriptive.

Using unique identifiers is especially useful for filtering and searching for Zaps based on keywords.

Adding numbers, letters, or roman numerals

Another frequently used Zap naming method is to add numbers, letters, roman numerals, or a suitable combination preceding the short trigger/action description. In our example, we may choose to number and name the Zap `1a. Create new Google Sheets (Our Deals) row when new deal is created in ActiveCampaign`. This method is especially useful if you have split your workflows so that they mirror steps in the actual processes you are automating. As Zaps are listed alphanumerically in the Zap management area, naming your Zaps in this way is also helpful if you want to see your Zaps in a particular order. Numbering your Zaps will also help for quick reference purposes when looking at Zap history information.

Starting to use a suitable naming system soon after you begin using Zapier to automate your processes will save you time and headaches in the future when organizing your Zaps.

> **Tip**
> Zapier also does not show a detailed changelog or revision history of a Zap. If you work with a team, you may find it useful to add version numbers and revision dates to the end of your Zap name. These details can also be added to the Zap **Settings Description** box, which we will discuss later in this chapter, in the *Utilizing the Zap Settings tab in the Zap editor section*.

Now let's review how to use folders to bring further organization to your Zapier account.

Using folders in the Zap management area

Adequately naming your Zaps is most certainly a good practice. If we combine that with sorting Zaps into folders, your Zaps will be easy to find and maintain. Folders can be created and managed in the Zap management area, which can be found by clicking on the **Zaps** icon in the left sidebar or by navigating to `https://zapier.com/app/zaps`.

The Zap management area is split into a left-side panel and a central panel, as shown in the following screenshot:

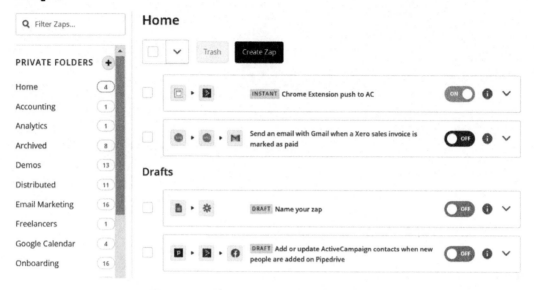

Figure 4.1 – The Zap management area of Zapier

We will discuss the central panel in the *Managing your Zaps section*, so let's dive into reviewing how we can use the left-side panel for managing folders.

The left-side panel is used for managing folders and is structured as follows:

- **Search bar**: You can use the search bar to filter your Zaps using keywords. These filtered Zaps will be displayed in the central panel with a header showing the number of results for that keyword search. This is shown in the following screenshot:

Figure 4.2 – Filtering your Zaps using a keyword search

- **PRIVATE FOLDERS**: This section shows all the folders that you have created with Zaps that are owned by you. If you are using a Team or Company plan, these folders and Zaps within them will only be visible to you.

- **SHARED FOLDERS**: This section will only be available for use if you subscribe to a Team or Company plan. Folders created here can be shared with individual users or if you are using a Company plan, specific groups of users that you have set up in teams. We will discuss using shared folders in more detail in the *Sharing your Zaps and folders section*.

- **Trash**: This folder holds Zaps that have been deleted. Deleted Zaps are held in this folder for 30 days before being permanently deleted.

> **Tip**
> You can archive your Zaps rather than permanently delete them. Create a folder called Archived to store Zaps that you may need to refer to in the future so that they are not permanently deleted if you add them to **Trash**.

From the left-side panel, you can do the following:

- Create and name a folder
- Select a folder to view its contents
- Manage your folders

Let's take a look at each of these.

Creating and naming folders

You can create a new folder by clicking on the + icon next to the section names **PRIVATE FOLDERS** and **SHARED FOLDERS** (if using a Team or Company account). To the right of the pen icon, add text that will help you to identify the folder. Then, press *Enter* on your keyboard to continue.

Naming your folders

As we discussed earlier in this chapter, suitably naming your Zaps is essential for organizing them. The way you choose to group your Zaps into folders is just as important. Once again, this will come down to personal preference and what fits your business needs. However, these are a few examples of ways to sort your folders:

- *By focus app or app category*: You could group your Zaps according to the main app used in trigger and action steps, for example, "Salesforce". Alternatively, you could group them by the app category, for example, "Surveys."

- *By department or business function*: You could separate your Zaps into groups such as "Marketing," "Sales," and "Operations."

- *By client*: If you are a freelancer or contractor and you manage several of your client's workflows within your own account, you could separate your Zaps accordingly.

As with Zaps, folders are listed in numerical and alphabetical order. Each folder is displayed with the name and number of Zaps stored within it.

Selecting a folder to view its contents

You can select a folder to display and manage the Zaps in the folder in the central panel.

Managing your folders

Hovering over a folder (except for the **Home** folder) will show a clickable **cogwheel icon**, which, once selected, will display a drop-down list allowing you to do the following:

- **Rename**: Selecting this option will allow you to edit a folder name.

- **Delete**: Selecting this option will allow you to delete the folder. All Zaps held in this folder will be automatically moved back into the **Home** folder, and will not be deleted. This option will only be available to folder owners.

- **Share or Share with…**: You can share a folder along with all the Zaps in that folder. The **Share** option will be available in **PRIVATE FOLDERS** to the owner of the folder. Once shared, the **Share with…** option is displayed in **SHARED FOLDERS** and will be available to admin users only. This option will be displayed if you are using a Team or Company account. We will discuss this in more detail in the *Sharing your Zaps and folders section*.

- **Export**: You can export the Zaps in a folder as a JSON file. This option is displayed if you are using a Team or Company account, and is only available to admin users.

> **Important note**
>
> The Home folder is the default folder, and cannot be renamed, deleted, or shared. Zaps can, however, be added to and removed from this folder.

Now that we have explored how to keep your Zaps organized by using naming techniques and sorting them with folders, let's dive into how to manage your individual Zaps.

Managing your Zaps

The central panel shows a list of your Zaps, from either a folder you have selected or the results of using the search bar. The view defaults to the **Home** folder when you first navigate to the Zap management area. You can manage your Zaps from the central panel, and this displays the folder title as a header, a top navigation bar, and a list of your Zaps.

Each Zap is presented in a clearly defined box, and clicking on this box will take you directly into the Zap editor where you can edit that specific Zap. You will also find a checkbox on the left-hand side of each Zap box. You can use the checkbox to select one or more Zaps to manage using the options in the top navigation bar. Individual Zaps can be managed by doing the following:

- Using the top navigation bar
- Using the options within specific Zap boxes
- Utilizing the Zap **Settings** tab from within the Zap editor

We will review each of these in turn.

Managing your Zaps using the top navigation bar

The top navigation sits just below the folder header and can be used to manage your Zaps using the following options:

- **The down arrow icon**: You can use the down arrow icon to select multiple Zaps depending on whether they are paused (**Off**), to select drafts, or to select all Zaps. You can also use this dropdown to deselect the Zaps that have been previously selected. This is shown in the following screenshot:

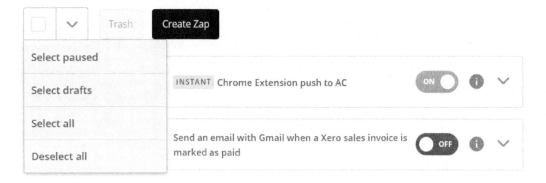

Figure 4.3 – Zap multi-select drop-down arrow in the Zap management area

- The **Trash** button: Once you have selected any Zap, clicking on this button will add that Zap to the **Trash** folder. You can choose and send multiple Zaps to the **Trash** folder at one time.

- The **Export** button: If you are using a Team or Company account, you can export Zaps in a folder as a JSON file. This option is only available to admin users.

- The **Create Zap** button: Although this button does not help to manage the Zaps within the Zap management area, it is a conveniently placed navigational tool to allow you to create a new Zap from this view. By clicking on this button, you will be taken straight into the Zap editor to build a new Zap.

Now let's discuss managing Zaps from within their Zap box.

Managing your Zaps from within their specific Zap boxes

Each Zap is displayed within a box that shows the following:

- **App icons**: Single-step Zaps are displayed as a trigger and action app separated by an arrow. Zaps with two action steps are displayed with the trigger and the two action steps in sequence, separated by arrows. Zaps with multiple action steps are displayed as the trigger and the action app separated by an icon with the number of action steps, separated by arrows. This is shown in the following screenshot:

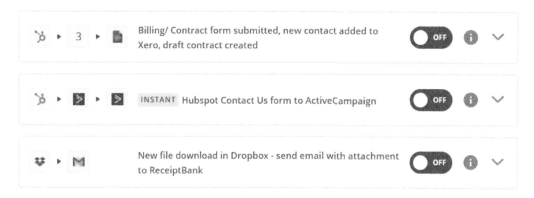

Figure 4.4 – Distinguishing between single - and multi-step Zaps

- **Zap title**: The full Zap title is displayed here.

- **On/Off toggle button**: You can turn your Zap **On** or **Off** using this toggle button.

- **Information icon**: Clicking on this icon will take you to the **Zap Details** screen for a specific Zap. This is a handy management area for your Zap, allowing you to perform specific functions all from one location, such as adding or changing Zap details such as the Zap title, **Description**, and **Timezone**, viewing and testing the connection for the connected apps, and toggling the Zap **On** or **Off**. You also have buttons available to **Open in editor**, **Move to folder**, **Run Zap** (if the trigger uses the polling method), **Share with others**, or **Move to Trash** (if it is turned **Off** or a draft). This is shown in the following screenshot:

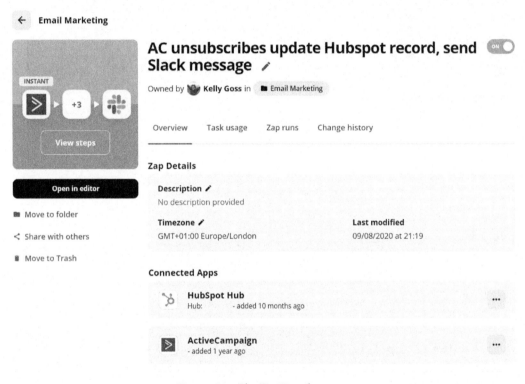

Figure 4.5 – The Zap Details screen

You will also be able to see a bar chart representation of your task usage in the **Task usage** tab, information on Zap runs in the **Zap runs** tab, and some basic Zap change log history in the **Change history** tab. All of these are very useful for getting insights into how your Zaps are running. An example of data in the **Task usage** tab is shown in the following screenshot:

Figure 4.6 – Task usage information for a Zap

- **The down arrow icon**: When this icon is clicked, a drop-down list will be displayed, giving you several options to manage your Zap. This is shown in the following screenshot:

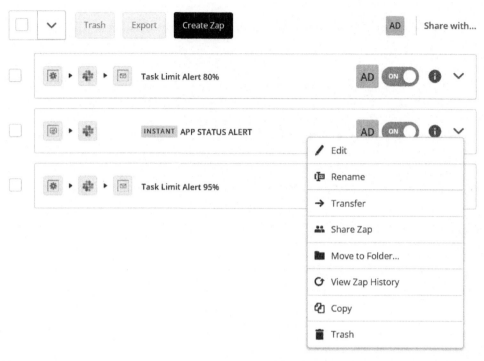

Figure 4.7 – Managing your Zaps using the drop-down options within the Zap box

The drop-down menu gives you the following options:

- **Edit**: Clicking on this option takes you directly into the Zap editor, where you can edit your Zap.

- **Rename**: You can conveniently rename your Zap directly from the Zap management area without having to navigate to the Zap editor.

- **Transfer**: You can transfer ownership to another user, which will grant the new user access to all associated folders and connections. This option is only displayed if you are using a Team or Company account and is only available to the owner of the Zap.

- **Share Zap**: You can share a copy of your Zap with a link. We will discuss this in more detail in the next section.

- **Move to Folder**: Clicking on this option will allow you to move your Zap to another folder.

- **View Zap History**: Clicking on this option will take you straight to the Zap history of this specific Zap. We will discuss the **Zap history** module in detail in *Chapter 5, Troubleshooting and Handling Zap Errors.*

- **Copy**: You can make a copy of any Zap, which can then be used as a template for creating another Zap.

- **Trash**: You can send your Zap to the `Trash` folder by clicking on this option.

> Tip
> The **Copy** option is handy if you intend to build multiple workflows that have similar steps but may differ with some variations. Using this option allows you to duplicate a Zap and essentially use it as a template. This function is especially useful as a time-saver if you have complex multi-step workflows that you want to use with different conditions.

Let's review how to restore Zaps that have been moved to the `Trash` folder.

Restoring Zaps from the Trash folder

Zaps that have been sent to the **Trash** folder are held there temporarily for 30 days before being deleted permanently. Once a Zap is in the **Trash** folder, you will not be able to make edits to it until it is restored; however, it can be restored within this time period.

While a Zap is in the **Trash** folder, clicking on the **down arrow** icon will allow you to share the Zap, move it to another folder, or review the task history, as shown in the following screenshot:

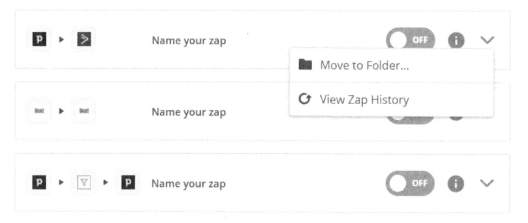

Figure 4.8 – Restoring Zaps from the Trash folder

Select the **Move to Folder** option and choose a specific folder to restore the Zap in.

> **Important note**
> Zapier does not show a detailed history of changes to the Zap, so it will not
> be possible to know how long the Zap has been in the **Trash** folder and when
> it will be permanently deleted. Remember, you can create another folder to
> archive Zaps in so that they are not permanently deleted.

Now let's cover how to best use the Zap **Settings** tab in the Zap editor to manage
your Zaps.

Utilizing the Zap Settings tab in the Zap editor

As we discussed in *Chapter 3, Building Your First Automated Workflow (Zap)*, you can
manage your Zap using the **Settings** section from within the Zap editor. The **Settings**
section can be found by clicking on the **Settings** icon in the expandable right-side menu.
The options are presented as follows:

- **Name**: The name of your Zap will be displayed here. You can quickly alter it without
  having to change it in the Zap editor.

- **Add to Folder…**: You can change the folder your Zap is stored in by using this
  option.

- **Description**: You can add new text or alter any existing notes here. This is useful
  when you need to add extra details to your Zap where the name might be too long.
  For example, adding the date it was last edited, the user initials if appropriate, and
  additional details about what the Zap does and the logic behind it to help other
  users understand it better.

- **Timezone**: You can alter the timezone settings of the Zap if you want your Zap to
  run in a different timezone than that specified in your account settings.

This is shown in the following screenshot:

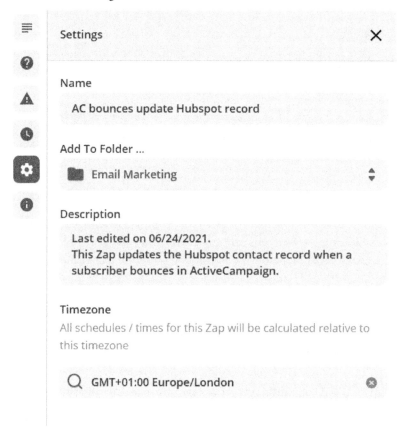

Figure 4.9 – The Zap Settings section in the Zap editor

Tip

With the exception of customizing a step title, Zapier does not allow you to
make notes within individual steps in a Zap. In addition, Zapier also does not
show a detailed changelog or revision history of the Zap. The **Description** box
is, therefore, handy for adding notes to describe steps in detail and specify
changes to the Zap with dates. If you work in a team, you could record the
initials of the user who made the revision and record other notes for the benefit
of other team members.

You should now have a better understanding of how to manage your Zaps. Let's now take
a look at the different statuses that might be assigned to your Zaps. This will help you to
manage your individual Zaps better.

Understanding Zap statuses

Now that you know how to manage your individual Zaps, it's useful to know what the different statuses are, and when you are likely to see your Zaps in those statuses. When you view your Zaps in the Zap management area, they will be displayed with one of the following states:

- **ON**: As we discussed in *Chapter 3*, *Building Your First Automated Workflow (Zap)*, once you have built and tested your Zap, you must turn it **ON** for it to work with live data from your trigger app. Once a Zap is turned **ON**, Zapier will look for new data in the trigger app to then kick off the workflow and perform the action steps.

- **OFF**: If your Zap is turned **OFF**, Zapier will not actively look for new data in the trigger app. Zapier may automatically turn a Zap that you have **ON** to the **OFF** status for the following reasons:

  a) Your Zapier pricing plan is downgraded to the Free plan from a paid plan, and you therefore lose access to paid plan features such as multi-step Zaps or Premium apps.

  b) Your Zap experiences multiple errors when it runs. Zapier will send an email to the account owner to notify you of the Zap being turned **OFF**.

- **DRAFT**: Draft Zaps generally do not have adequate information. They will either be missing a trigger or action step or both. Draft Zaps are shown in a separate section below Zaps with a status of **ON** or **OFF**, and labeled accordingly, as shown in the following screenshot:

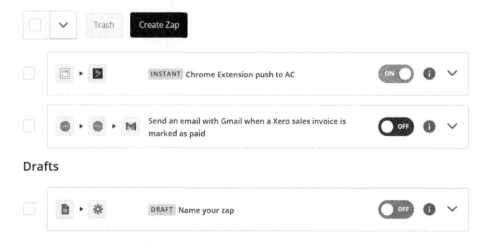

Figure 4.10 – The Zap management area showing ON, OFF, and DRAFT Zaps

On occasion, your Zaps may be displayed with the following statuses in addition to being **ON** or **OFF**:

- **HELD**: You may see your Zaps highlighted with the label **ZAP RUNS HELD**, as shown in the following screenshot:

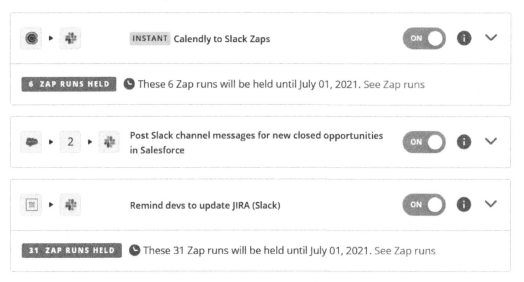

Figure 4.11 – Zaps displaying a HELD status

One reason this might happen is when your Zaps are triggered too many times during a short interval. Zapier will then notify you that tasks are being held, and you will not be able to run the Zap until you have replayed or deleted the tasks. We will discuss this in more detail in *Chapter 5, Troubleshooting and Handling Zap Errors.*

- **EXPIRED AUTH**: Sometimes, your connected apps may disconnect. If this happens, your Zap will show an **EXPIRED AUTH** status, indicating which app has disconnected. You can reconnect your app by clicking on the **Please reconnect here** link. This is shown in the following screenshot:

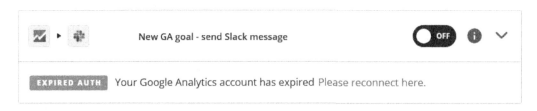

Figure 4.12 – A Zap displaying an EXPIRED AUTH status

Now that you understand Zap statuses, let's look at how to manage your connected apps.

Managing your connected apps

Once you have connected your apps to Zapier, it's useful to know how to manage the connections. This can all be done from the **Apps** module. You can navigate to this module by clicking on the **My Apps** icon link in the left sidebar or navigating to `https://zapier.com/app/connections`.

From within your personal account in the **Apps** module, you will be able to see a list of your connected apps under the **All apps tab**, how many connections have been added and how many Zaps they are involved in. You will also see a tab called **Custom Integrations**, which will list any custom integrations with non-public apps involved in your account.

If you are using a Team or Company plan, your connections will be separated into two sections as follows:

- **My apps**: Only you can use these accounts. You can, however, choose to share your app connections with your team.

- **Shared with me**: These are accounts that are owned by others in the team, but have been made available by other team members for you to use.

We will discuss sharing connections later in this section.

This is shown in the following screenshot:

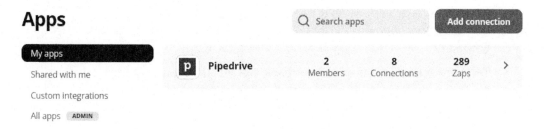

Figure 4.13 – Connected apps in the Apps module

You can manage your connected apps by clicking on the **arrow** button and then selecting the **three-dot** drop-down menu, as shown in the following screenshot:

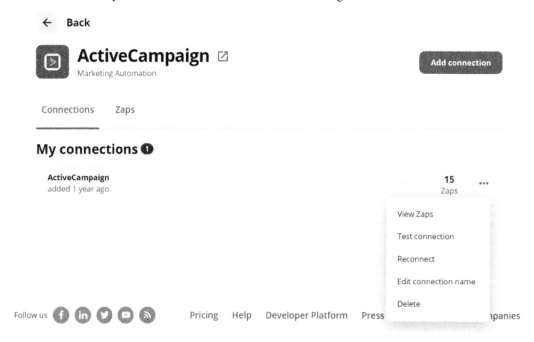

Figure 4.14 – An app connection in My Apps

You can then select one of the following options:

- **View Zaps**: You can view all the Zaps associated with the connection by clicking on the **View Zaps** option in the three-dot drop-down menu. Alternatively, click on the **Zaps** tab.

- **Test connection**: It is useful to be able to test whether your app has connection issues. You can do this by clicking on the **Test connection** option in the drop-down menu. A successful connection will be highlighted in green with the words **Success** and therefore, no further action is required.

- **Reconnect**: When Zapier identifies an app as requiring reconnection, these apps are highlighted with a warning triangle. You can reconnect your app by clicking on the **arrow** icon button and following the prompts. This is shown in the following screenshot:

Figure 4.15 – Apps requiring reconnection

- **Edit connection name**: You can edit the name of your connection by clicking on the text next to the pencil icon. Being able to alter the connection name is handy if you want to differentiate between different accounts for the same app; for example, if you are connecting multiple email accounts.

- **Delete**: You may wish to disconnect an app connection entirely from your Zapier account. You can do this by clicking on the **Delete** option. You will be prompted to confirm. Once confirmed, the app connection will no longer be listed in your **My Apps** list.

- **Transfer connection**: You will be shown this option in Team and Company accounts, which allows you to transfer your connections to other users. This is especially useful if you will no longer have access to the Zapier account, for example, if your employment has been terminated and you need to transfer ownership of the app connection to an admin user.

Lastly, clicking on the **Zaps** tab allows you to see details of the Zaps your app is associated with, including their status, when they were last changed, and how many tasks have run. This is shown in the following screenshot:

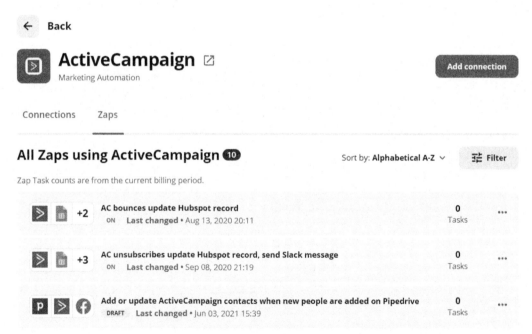

Figure 4.16 – A list of Zaps using ActiveCampaign as a connected app

Let's discuss how to share your connected apps next.

Sharing your connected apps

When you work with a team, you might want the flexibility for other members of your team to use particular app connections that are owned by you. For example, if your team all have access to a specific app, you could connect that app to Zapier and allow them to use that app connection by sharing it with them.

Sharing connected app accounts

You can share your app connection with others in your team as follows. By clicking on the **Only you** sharing status button, a popup will appear as shown in the following screenshot:

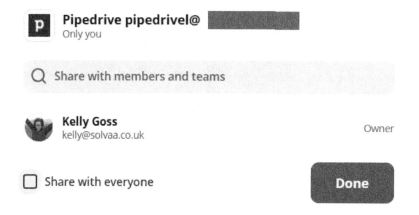

Figure 4.17 – Sharing options for private app connections

Add a specific member or team or check the **Share with everyone** box, and then click on the **Done** button to confirm. Click on **Share Account**. Some apps will ask you for authorization to give access and another popup will appear asking you to authorize granting your team access to the app connection. This is shown in the following screenshot using Cognito forms as an example:

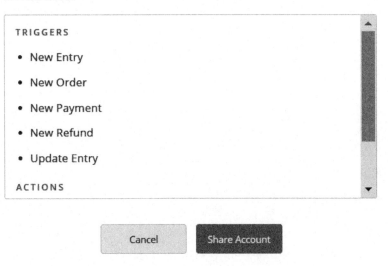

Figure 4.18 – Authorizing a connected app to be shared with your team

Just click on the **Share Account** button to continue. The sharing status button will change to **Everyone**.

> **Important note**
> If you are using a Company plan, you will be able to specify which user or team you want to share the connected app with. You can also share the app connection with everyone.

Once an app connection has been shared with your team, all users will be able to do the following:

- View sample data from the app when used as a shared app connection in a trigger step.
- View Zap history information from this shared app connection.
- Use the shared app connection in private and shared Zaps in triggers and actions to retrieve data from and update the app.
- Edit steps in Zaps that use this shared connection.

> **Important note**
> Only share access to an app connection if you are sure you want other team members to access data in that account. For example, if you share your private email app connection, other team members will be able to access all emails received and will be able to send emails from that account. You could instead create a shared email account for a specific purpose, such as for sending invoices and receiving bills, for example, accounts@yourcompany.com.

Stopping sharing a connected app account

You can remove access to a shared connected app as follows:

1. Click on the **sharing status** button.
2. Untick the **Share with everyone** box.
3. Click on **Done** to continue.

> **Important note**
> Once you make a shared app connection private again, any Zaps that have been built using that connected app will continue to run and use that account data. Your team members will still be able to see data in any steps using that connected app, although only you will be able to edit these steps. To stop data from being accessed in these steps, you will need to remove the app connection from each step and replace it with another app connection.

You should now have a better understanding of how to manage and share your connected apps on the Zapier platform. Let's now discuss how to share individual Zaps and folders.

Sharing your Zaps and folders

Working through your processes and then creating your Zaps will require some initial time investment. However, once you harness the power of using workflow automation tools such as Zapier, you'll begin to benefit from the time-saving and productivity gains of automating your workflows. You may want others to benefit from the time you have invested in building your workflows and, therefore, Zapier offers you some options to be able to share your workflows with others. This is especially useful if you work with a team of people with whom you can collaborate to automate company processes by building and maintaining your Zaps together.

You can share your Zapier workflows in two ways:

- Sharing copies of your Zaps with other Zapier users outside your company
- Sharing your Zaps and folders with other team members, if you subscribe to a Team or Company plan.

First, we will have a look at sharing copies of your Zaps with other Zapier users.

Sharing a copy of your Zap

If you want to share a copy of your Zap, you can do this without the risk of your connected accounts, data, and Zap history being shared with the recipient. A copy of the Zap will be shared by generating a link that can be disabled if required. You can only share a copy of a Zap that has been completely set up and turned **ON**.

> **Important note**
> Zaps with Paths by Zapier steps cannot be shared with other users outside of your Zapier account.

Enabling a copy of your Zap to be shared

You can share a copy of your Zap from two locations:

- *Zap management area*: Click on the **down arrow** icon and select **Share Zap**.
- *Zap editor*: Click on the blue **Share** button in the top bar.

Once you have selected the share option, a popup will appear, as shown in the following screenshot:

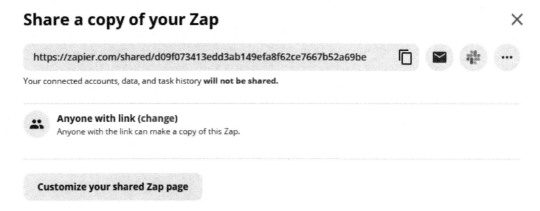

Figure 4.19 – Sharing a copy of your Zap

You can then work through the following options:

- **Copy or share**: Copy the link by clicking on the **copy icon** button or share the link by email, Slack, Facebook, Twitter, or LinkedIn using the relevant icons.

- **Choose who can copy this Zap**: Click on the **change** link to choose whether you would like the copy of the Zap to be shared with anyone with a link or you can disable the sharing of the link. This is shown in the following screenshot:

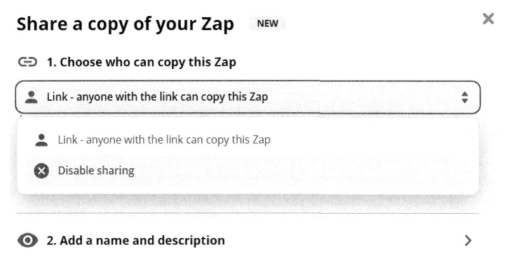

Figure 4.20 – Zap sharing options

- **Customize your shared Zap page**: Click on this button to add a name and description to help the recipient identify the Zap and understand what its purpose is. It is also useful if you intend to share the link on social media. The name of the Zap and description must be specified before you can share your Zap copy. You can edit either by clicking on the **Edit** link. In the description field, you can enter additional information, such as instructions on what to customize in the Zap; for example, changing the email signature in an email-related action or changing field data mapping that will differ between account connections. This will be very useful for the people you are sharing the Zap with. This is shown in the following screenshot:

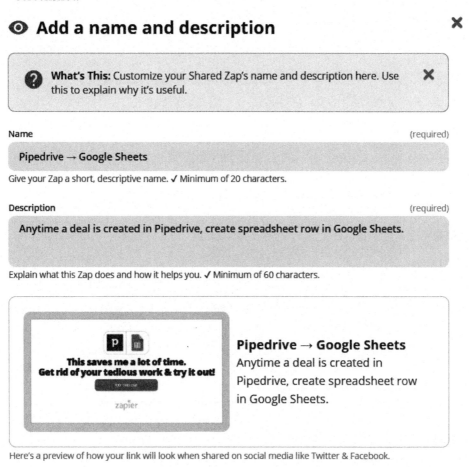

Figure 4.21 – Adding a name and description when sharing a copy of a Zap

Once you have worked through the options, click on the **tick icon** to save your changes or **x icon** to cancel.

> **Important note**
> Updates to a Zap will not be reflected in the copy shared with a link. To share the updates, you must update the link. You can do this by navigating to the **Sharing Preferences** option in the Zap editor and follow the prompts.

Now let's take a look at how to disable link sharing.

Disabling Zap link sharing

You can disable the Zap link at any time from the Zap management area as follows:

1. Click on the **down arrow** icon and select the **Sharing Permissions** option.

2. Click on the **change link** and choose the **Turn off** option.

3. Save your new preferences by clicking on **x icon**.

You can share copies of Zaps with a link regardless of which pricing plan you subscribe to. If you have a Team or Company plan, however, you have the additional benefit of sharing Zaps and folders with team members in your Zapier account.

Sharing Zaps and folders in your Team or Company account

If you have a Team or Company plan account, you can share individual Zaps and folders that you own with members of your team. You can also transfer ownership of a Zap to another member of your team.

Sharing folders with your team

As we discussed earlier in this chapter, folders are managed from the left-side panel. To share a private folder, hover over a folder to show a clickable **cogwheel icon**. Once this icon is clicked on, select **Share**. This will move the folder into the **SHARED FOLDER** section and the folder will, by default, be shared with team admin and team owner users. All team members will be able to view and edit any Zaps in shared folders.

> **Important note**
> You cannot unshare a folder. Once you have shared a private folder, if you want to remove sharing access, you need to move individual Zaps back into a private folder.

Next, let's review how to manage shared folders.

Managing shared folders

Once you have shared a folder, you can change sharing preferences in two places:

- **Left-side panel**: You can do this by clicking on the **cogwheel icon** of any folder and selecting the **Share with...** option.

- **Central panel**: Select the **Share with...** option, on the far right of the top bar, next to the set of Gravatars or initials.

This is shown in the following screenshot:

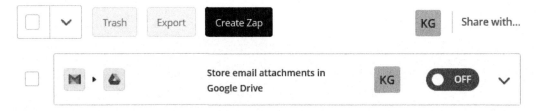

Figure 4.22 – The "Share with…" option in the central panel

Once selected, you can then choose to share the folder with every user by choosing **Share with everyone** or select users by entering their names or email addresses in the search bar. If you have a Company account, you can also select groups of users in teams.

You can identify who has access to a folder by hovering over the Gravatars or initials of users displayed in the top bar to the left of the **Share with...** button.

Transferring ownership of a Zap

You can identify the owner of a Zap as their Gravatar or initials will be displayed to the left of the **On/Off** toggle button in the individual Zap boxes. If you are the owner of the Zap, a team admin, or team owner, you can transfer ownership of a Zap to another team member. You can do this by selecting a Zap, clicking on the **down arrow icon**, and then selecting the **Transfer** option. You can then enter the name or email address of another member on the account to transfer Zap ownership to. This is shown in the following screenshot:

Figure 4.23 – Transferring ownership to another team member

Now let's cover how to move your Zaps between personal and team accounts.

Moving Zaps between personal and team accounts

If you have a personal account and you are a member of a team account, you can move individual Zaps and folders between accounts. You can do this by navigating to your Gravatar or initials in the top-right menu bar and selecting the **Move Zaps** option in the drop-down menu or by navigating to https://zapier.com/app/move-zaps/.

You can then select the personal account you want to transfer the Zap from and the team account you wish to move it to, as shown in the following screenshot:

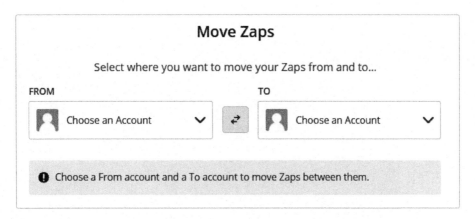

Figure 4.24 – Moving your Zaps from one account to another

You will be shown a list of folders and Zaps. You can then choose which individual Zaps or entire folders you might want to share, and select **Move these Zaps**.

> **Important note**
> Data transfer can take some time, depending on how many Zaps you are transferring. Ensure that you do not navigate away from the page while the transfer is in progress.

You should now have a better understanding of how to share copies of Zaps. In addition, you should know how to share individual Zaps and folders with your team.

Summary

In this chapter, we began by describing how to keep your workflows organized in the Zap management area by adequately naming them and using folders to sort them. We then discussed how to manage individual Zaps and covered the different Zap statuses. We explored managing your connected apps, and lastly, we discussed how to share your Zaps with your team and other Zapier users.

You now know about the best ways to manage and maintain your Zaps and app connections in your Zapier account, how to keep your workflows organized, as well as how to share them with your team or other Zapier users outside of your company.

In the next chapter, we will discuss how to best use Zap history information, and we will cover typical Zap behavior and the best ways to handle and troubleshoot errors. We will help you to manage Zap alerts by adjusting your account settings, and by setting up a Zap with the Zapier Manager built-in app. We will also discuss the various channels of support available to users.

5
Troubleshooting and Handling Zap Errors

As you get more familiar with Zapier and start to build complex workflows, you are likely to run into problems occasionally with your workflows. In general, when errors occur, they might originate from the way the Zap was set up, from issues with one of the apps in the workflow, or from general performance problems of the Zapier app itself. The best way to learn how to address these problems is to do some initial investigation work yourself before reaching out for additional help.

In this chapter, we discuss the critical information that you will need to deal with unexpected errors when using Zapier. We begin by discussing how to manage Zap error notifications by adjusting your account settings, and by setting up a Zap with the **Zapier Manager** built-in app. Then, we cover how to manage app status alerts by monitoring the Zapier status page, and by setting up a Zap with the **App Status by Zapier** built-in app. After, we show you how to best use Zap history information to assess how your Zaps have run and to gather information to help with troubleshooting. Lastly, we cover the channels available to seek additional support on the Zapier platform.

We will cover the following key topics in this chapter:

- Managing Zap error alerts
- Managing app status alerts

- Utilizing Zap history information for troubleshooting

- Finding help: help center, customer support, community, and experts

Once you have worked through each of these topics, you will understand how Zapier processes data, know how to use Zap history for troubleshooting, and adjust your alert notification preferences.

Technical requirements

To work through the content in this chapter, you will need access to a Zapier account. The Zapier Free plan will be adequate for most of the content in this chapter. To work through the *Managing Zap history data* section, you will need access to a Starter plan or higher for some parts and access to a Professional plan or higher for the content on the Autoreplay function. You can get access to the Zap templates used in this chapter here: https://bit.ly/3e5BUkn.

Managing Zap error alerts

One of the benefits of using a workflow automation tool such as Zapier is that your processes can run on autopilot while you focus on other things. You will, however, want to know when your workflows run into errors so that you can address any problems promptly, to ensure continuity. Zapier monitors all Zaps for performance when they are running. Whenever a fault is detected with the way any of your Zaps are expected to work, Zapier generates an error code. The best way to monitor any problems with your workflows and deal with them quickly is to ensure you receive notifications when any issues arise.

You can manage the way you receive your alerts by doing the following:

- Adjusting your email notification settings

- Setting up an error alert workflow with the Zapier Manager built-in app

You will then be able to manage your alerts and take action in a more timely manner.

> **Tip**
> Using alerts with the Zapier Manager built-in app is particularly useful if you are the system administrator for the Zapier account and need to receive alerts because perhaps you don't have access to the Zapier account owner's emails to receive email notifications. It is also handy for Team or Company account users for the same reason.

Now let's take a look at each method to manage alerts.

Adjusting your email notification settings

As standard, Zapier sends out email notifications for trigger and action error alerts, as well as for issues with connected apps in your Zaps. As discussed in *Chapter 1, Introduction to Business Process Automation with Zapier*, you can adjust the frequency of these alerts in the **Email Notification** area of your **Account Settings**. The settings available for both **trigger** and **action** alerts are as follows:

- **Never**: Choose this option if you do not want to receive error alerts at all.

- **Repeated**: Choose this option to receive repeated alerts until the issue is sorted out. This will remind you to address the issue.

- **Always**: This is the recommended option to use. Zapier will alert you any time your trigger or action steps run into problems.

- **Only Zapier Manager Trigger**: Choose this option if you want to customize what alerts you see. We will discuss this next.

> **Tip**
> Although Zapier will include alerts relating to the connected apps in your workflows in email notifications, you may want to set up app-specific status alerts. This will give you timely information on incidents occurring with your connected apps. We will discuss this in more detail in the section called *Managing app status alerts*.

Now let's review how to use the Zapier Manager built-in app to trigger an alert workflow.

Setting up an error alert workflow with the Zapier Manager built-in app

You can customize the alerts that you want to receive notifications for by setting up a Zap with the Zapier Manager built-in app as a trigger. I will now explain how to set up a Zap error alert workflow using Zapier Manager as the trigger app and give you a few examples of apps and events that you could use for your action step. You can use the detailed steps we described in *Chapter 3, Building Your First Automated Workflow (Zap)*, to set up your Zap effectively.

Selecting your trigger event

Once you have navigated to **Zap editor**, select the Zapier Manager built-in app to use in your trigger step. Next, select your chosen trigger event to use. The Zapier Manager built-in app has several trigger events to choose from; however, there are three trigger event options specific to managing errors. These are as follows:

- **New Zap Error**: You can select this trigger event if you want this alert workflow to trigger when one of your Zaps encounters an error.

- **Zap Turned Off**: You can select this trigger event if you want this alert workflow to trigger when one of your Zaps is turned off or paused by Zapier. This usually happens when a Zap is experiencing several errors repeatedly.

- **New Halted Task**: You can select this trigger event if you want this Zap alert to trigger when one of your tasks in a workflow has the status **Stopped Halted**. We will discuss task statuses in the *Understanding task statuses section*.

These are shown in the following screenshot:

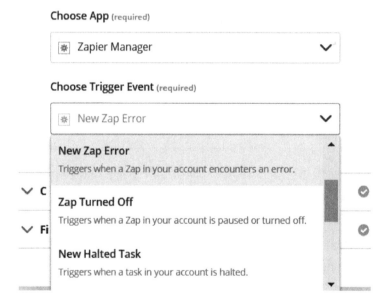

Figure 5.1 – Setting up a Zapier Manager trigger

We will cover the other Zapier Manager trigger events in *Chapter 12, Managing Your Zapier Account with Built-in Apps*.

Customizing your trigger event

Next, customize the trigger event to specify the following:

- **Account**: If you are a member of multiple Team accounts, you can stipulate which account you want to receive alerts for.

- **Folder**: You can stipulate which specific folder you want to receive alerts for. If you specify a folder, this error alert workflow will trigger for all Zaps in that folder, unless you specify a Zap in the next field.

- **Zap**: You can stipulate which specific Zap you want to receive alerts for.

None of these fields are required for the trigger to work, so if you want to receive alerts for all Zaps in all accounts, you can leave each of them blank.

Once you've customized your trigger event, you can confirm the sample data you want to use to test the trigger, test it, and move on to setting up your action step.

Now let's discuss some examples of apps and events that you could use in your action step.

Setting up your error alert action step

After you have set up your trigger step, you can proceed to add one or more action steps and map the sample data to the relevant fields. To complete the workflow, we need to add an action step that will allow Zapier to send a notification to one or more people. Here are a few examples of communication apps and events we could use:

- Send a direct, private, or channel message to your team in **Slack**.

- Send an email to you and your team using **Gmail**, **Microsoft Outlook**, or **Email by Zapier**.

- Send an SMS to yourself using **SMS by Zapier**.

If you're using a Starter plan or higher, you will be able to create multi-step Zaps and add additional steps to your workflow. You could then add further steps to add a log of all your Zap error alerts to a Google Sheets spreadsheet and create a task to review the alert in a task management app, such as Trello.

We've created a template of a Zap error alert with Slack as the notification app, a Google Sheets spreadsheet to record the history of alerts, and a Trello task to check the alert. You can get access to a copy of this Zap template here: `https://bit.ly/3e5BUkn`.

> **Tip**
>
> If you only want to receive notifications for error alerts that trigger using the Zapier Manager workflows you have built, remember to change your email notification settings to **Only Zapier Manager Trigger**.

You should now have a better understanding of how to adjust your notification settings and manage Zap error alerts using the Zapier Manager built-in app.

Now let's take a look at how to manage app status alerts.

Managing app status alerts

In the previous section, we described how to manage Zap status alerts for issues arising with your Zap triggers, actions, and connected apps. When troubleshooting, you will also find it useful to understand how to find information on the overall performance of the Zapier app itself and see updates on any known issues with the connected apps in your workflow. This will help you to exclude these external issues when you begin to investigate problems with specific Zaps.

You can find information on the Zapier app performance and manage app status alerts by doing the following:

- Monitoring the Zapier **Status** page
- Setting up an app status alert workflow with the App Status by Zapier built-in app

Let's take a look at each one.

Monitoring the Zapier Status page

When trying to investigate unexpected issues with your workflows, you will find it useful to check for incidents relating to how the Zapier app itself is functioning or any known problems with other connected apps in your workflow. The best place to check for known incidents is the Zapier **Status** page. You can navigate to the **Status** page using the URL `https://status.zapier.com/`.

The **Status** page is split into two sections focusing on summary information and then more detailed metrics and statuses.

In the **Summary** section, Zapier reports on known incidents that affect the following:

- **Website**: This relates to the `zapier.com` website where you manage your Zaps and associated tasks resulting from your running workflows.

- **Zaps**: This relates to the general working of Zaps, including **Instant Triggers** (powered by webhooks or other instant methods), **Polling Triggers** (powered by periodic polling), and **Searches & Writes** (actions such as searches, filters, and data writing).

- **Apps**: This relates to all apps that Zapier integrates with and provides general reporting on significant issues.

- **Developer platform**: This relates to the Zapier developer platform.

If any of those systems are not operational, Zapier will highlight this and specify the issue.

In the next section, Zapier reports in more detail on the following in separate tabs:

- **System Metrics**
- **App Status**
- **Incident History**

Let's look at each of these.

System Metrics

The **System Metrics** tab shows details of polling and instant trigger reliability and response times, as follows:

- **Trigger Reliability**: This signifies the success rate of an average Zap shown as a percentage.

- **Trigger Response Time**: This signifies the average speed of an average Zap powered by either polling or an instant trigger, and is shown in milliseconds.

> **Important note**
> The **Polling Trigger Response Time** displayed does not include the polling time based on your pricing plan of either 1, 2, or 15 minutes. It purely reflects the response time once a new event is found by Zapier.

The metrics are displayed graphically, and you can select to show them by day, week, or month. You can also move your cursor along the graph to show an exact date and time with the metric, as shown in the following screenshot:

Figure 5.2 – Graph of Polling Triggers Response Time metrics

System metrics are particularly useful when trying to understand whether a Zap error event is associated with the downtime and performance of Zapier and can help to exclude problems with a particular app. This is important to review alongside the information in the **Incident History** tab, as this will give more context to the problem.

App Status

The **App Status** tab shows a list of apps demarcated in boxes displaying the following details for each:

- **App icon**: This shows the image that represents the app.
- **App name**: This shows the name of the app, displayed as a clickable link that will take you to the app profile page.
- **Response time**: This shows the app response time to Zapier queries in milliseconds.
- **Past hour**: This shows a graph of the app response time over the last hour.
- **More Options menu**: This is represented by an icon of three horizontal dots. If you click on this icon, you will be presented with the options to use pre-built workflows to create alerts using the App Status by Zapier built-in app. We will discuss this in more detail in the section named *Setting up an app status alert workflow with the App Status by Zapier built-in app*.

You can search for an app using the search bar just above the list of apps.

It is important to review **App Status** data alongside the information in the **Incident History** tab as this will give more context to the problem.

Incident History

The **Incident History** tab shows a log of recent incidents by day and noted with the time of the last update. This log is especially useful if you are trying to trace back to the source of an issue or if you were experiencing problems with your Zaps on a specific day or period. You can click on the **Incident history** link at the bottom of the page or navigate to https://status.zapier.com/history to view historical incident history. You can use the back and forward arrows to scroll by month.

> Tip
> You can also subscribe to updates so that you are notified when Zapier creates a new incident, and updates or resolves an existing incident. This is handy if you have access to multiple Zapier accounts and need to monitor issues. You can do this by clicking on the **Subscribe to Updates** button at the top of the **Status** page.

Now let's review how to use the App Status by Zapier built-in app to trigger an app status alert workflow.

Setting up an app status alert workflow with the App Status by Zapier built-in app

You can set up custom workflows to alert you about issues with app statuses by using the App Status by Zapier built-in app as a trigger. You can build a Zap from scratch from within the Zap editor, or you can choose from three pre-built workflows directly from app boxes within the **App Status** tab on the Zapier **Status** page. We will now explain how to set up an app status alert workflow using App Status by Zapier from pre-built workflows. You can use the detailed steps we described in *Chapter 3, Building Your First Automated Workflow (Zap)*, to set up your Zap effectively.

Choosing which pre-built workflow to use

From the Zapier **Status** page, navigate to the **App Status** tab and search for the app you want to monitor using the search bar. Then, use the **More Options** icon to show the following drop-down menu of pre-built Zaps:

- **Slack Alert**: Choose this option to use a template that sends a Slack message as an action step. You can customize this step to send a direct, private, or channel message to your team in Slack.

- **SMS Alert**: Choose this option to use a template that sends an SMS as an action step. You can customize this step to send an SMS to yourself using SMS by Zapier.

- **Email Alert**: Choose this option to use a template that sends an outbound email as an action step. You can customize this step to send an email to you and your team using the Email by Zapier built-in app.

These options are shown in the following screenshot:

Figure 5.3 – App status for ActiveCampaign displaying options for pre-built Zaps

Select an option, and you will be taken to the Zap editor where you can customize the template.

Next, let's review how to set up the App Status by Zapier built-in app to use in your trigger step.

Customizing your trigger event

App Status by Zapier has only one trigger event option, **New or Updated App Incident**. This event will trigger on new, updated, and resolved app status incidents. We can therefore move on to customizing your trigger event to specify the following:

- **App(s) to Monitor**: If you are using a template and have been directed from the **Status** page, the app you selected will show here. You can add multiple apps to the list by searching in consecutive fields. You can also reorder the apps by selecting, dragging, and dropping. You can leave this section blank if you want to receive alerts for all apps.

- **Status**: From the drop-down menu, select which statuses you want to receive alerts for. You can choose from **Scheduled**, **Investigating / In-Progress**, **Resolved / Completed, Monitoring / Verifying**, and **Identified / In-Progress**. You can add multiple statuses to the list by searching in consecutive fields. You can also reorder the statuses by selecting, dragging, or dropping. You can leave this section blank if you want the Zap to trigger alerts for all statuses.

This is shown in the following screenshot:

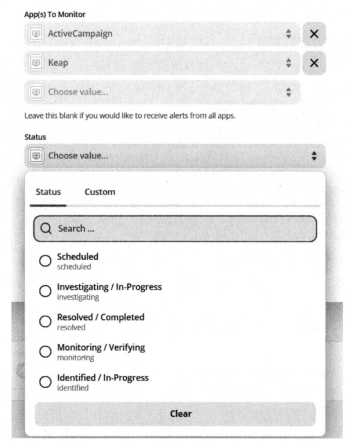

Figure 5.4 – Customizing the App Status by Zapier trigger

Once you've customized your trigger event, you can confirm the sample data you want to use to test the trigger, then test it, and move on to setting up your action step.

Setting up your error alert action step

After you have set up your trigger step, you can proceed to customize your templated action step to your requirements. You can also add additional action steps if required.

We will discuss using SMS by Zapier and Email by Zapier in more detail in *Chapter 8, Built-In Communication Apps*.

You should now have a better understanding of how to review information on the Zapier **Status** page as well as how to manage your app status alerts using the **App Status** by Zapier built-in app.

Now let's discuss how to troubleshoot errors by using Zap history information.

Utilizing Zap history information for troubleshooting

So far in this chapter, we have helped you to understand how to manage Zap error and app status alerts so that you can act promptly on any issues that arise. In addition, we've discussed how to assess the information that Zapier provides on the **Status** page, as having this information to hand will help you to exclude the impact of external issues when investigating problems with individual Zaps. Next, we will discuss how to troubleshoot errors with your individual Zaps by using the information available in the **Zap history** page.

Let's get started with understanding what Zap history is and how you can use it when troubleshooting problems with your workflows.

Understanding the Zap history page

The **Zap history** page provides you with a detailed log of activity of all of your Zaps. This log shows a list of all Zaps that have triggered successfully when new data has been found in the trigger app. It also shows action steps in a Zap that have been successfully completed and those that have not. The **Zap history** page captures all the data that passes in and out of each of the steps in a Zap when triggered successfully. It also shows task usage. Being able to view this information is extremely useful when troubleshooting unexpected events that have happened with your workflows, as well as when assessing your task usage per Zap.

> **Important note**
>
> Zapier only guarantees to keep Zap history information for a maximum of 1 month. It is therefore important to review issues as promptly as possible or download history periodically. We will discuss downloading Zap history data in the *Managing Zap history data section*.

The **Zap history** page can be found by doing the following:

- Clicking on the **Zap History** link in the left navigation sidebar
- Clicking on the **Zap History** link in the drop-down menu of individual Zap boxes within the Zap management area
- Clicking on the **Zap History clock icon** link in the expandable right panel in the Zap editor
- Navigating to `https://zapier.com/app/history`

Navigating from the main dashboard or using the URL will take you to the **Zap history** log page showing a list view of workflow events. Navigating from a Zap (either from the Zap box in the Zap management area or from within the Zap editor) will take to you a log page showing a filtered list of task history for that specific Zap.

The **Zap history** page in the list view is shown in the following screenshot:

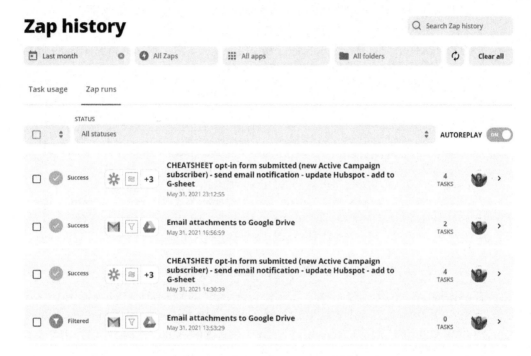

Figure 5.5 – The Zap history page list view

Let's now discuss the navigation options on the **Zap history** page.

Navigating the Zap history page

The **Zap history** page is split into two tabs as follows:

- **Task usage**
- **Zap runs**

Let's look at each of these.

The Task usage tab

The **Task usage** tab shows a list of your Zaps with task information related to each of them as follows:

- **App icons**: This shows you the icons of apps involved in each consecutive step of the workflow. Up to three app icons will be displayed, so if there are more than three steps involved in the Zap, the apps in the first two steps of the Zap will be shown plus a number depicting the additional app steps involved.

- **ZAP DETAILS**: This shows you the title of the Zap, whether the Zap is turned **On** or **Off**, and the time and date when it last ran.

- **TASKS USED**: This shows you how many tasks have been used in that billing period.

> **Tip**
>
> When performing a continuous improvement review of your Zaps, the information you see in the **Task usage** tab is really useful for gaining insight into which of your Zaps have high task usage. This information will help you to prioritize which Zaps to review first to assess whether you can remove steps to reduce task usage. You can gain further insight by navigating to the **View Zap details** screen from the **three-dot** dropdown menu on the Zap block.

- **Gravatar or initials**: This identifies the owner of the Zap.

- The **three-dots icon**: If you click on this icon, you will be presented with two options. If you click on **Open in Editor**, you will be taken to the Zap editor where you can edit that Zap. If you click on **View Zap runs**, you will be taken to the Zap history filtered specifically for that Zap. If you click on **View Zap Details**, you can see the detailed Zap information page.

An example of a Zap in the **Task usage** tab is shown in the following screenshot:

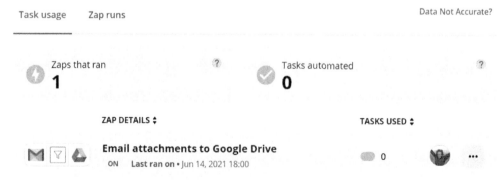

Figure 5.6 – The Task usage tab

You can sort the list of Zaps by clicking on the arrow icons in the respective headers, where **ZAP DETAILS** is sorted alphanumerically, and **TASKS USED** is sorted numerically.

> **Important note**
>
> The **Task usage** tab should only be used as a reference and may not accurately represent actual usage. For accurate information, you should refer to your monthly invoices.

Now let's have a look at the **Zap runs** tab.

The Zap runs tab

The **Zap runs** tab is the default view that you will see when you navigate to the **Zap history** page. This tab shows the history of the individual Zap workflow events that have run, with the most recent one at the top. You will only see Zaps that are turned **ON** in this history. Each workflow event is displayed with the following information in the list view:

- **Checkbox**: This allows you to select a specific workflow event and delete, download, or replay the event. We will discuss how to use the checkbox in the *Managing your Zap history data* section.

- **Task status icon**: This shows an icon of the status of the workflow event running. We will look at task statuses in more detail in the *Understanding task statuses* section.

- **App icons**: This shows you the icons of apps involved in each consecutive step of the workflow. This is similar to what is shown in the **Task usage** tab.

- **Zap details**: This shows you the title of the Zap and the time and date when the workflow event ran.

- **Tasks used**: This shows you how many tasks were used when the workflow event ran.

- **Gravatar or initials**: This identifies the owner of the Zap.

- **Forward arrow icon**: If you click on this icon, you will be taken to a detailed view of the workflow event. We will discuss this in the *Viewing detailed task information* section.

An example of a workflow event in the **Zap runs** tab is shown in the following screenshot:

Figure 5.7 – The Zap runs tab

10 workflow events are shown per page, and you can scroll through the pages by using the arrow buttons at the bottom of the **Zap runs** tab.

You will also find the following options just above the list of workflow events:

- **Checkbox icon**: You can use this dropdown to select or deselect workflow events in bulk. We will discuss using this checkbox for downloading, deleting, and replaying tasks in the *Managing Zap history data* section.

- **Task status**: You can use the drop-down list function to filter your Zap history log by task status. We will look at task statuses in more detail in the *Understanding task statuses* section.

- **Autoreplay ON/OFF toggle button**: You can turn the **Autoreplay** function **ON** or **OFF** using this toggle button. We will review using the **Autoreplay** feature in more detail in the next section, *Managing Zap history data*.

Now let's discuss how to view workflow events by filtering and searching.

Viewing workflow events as a list, searching, and filtering

The default view is to show all workflow events with the most recent event at the top of the list. You can use the search bar to search for workflow events by keyword. For example, you might want to find all workflow events that occurred that used the name Joe Bloggs, the email address joebloggs@abcompany.com, or file ID 12345. If you want to clear the search, hit the **x** icon in the search bar.

You can also filter workflow events using multiple filter options as follows:

- **Date range**: This filter allows you to select a date range relating to when workflow events ran. For example, you could filter to show workflow events for last week. Bear in mind that workflow events more than 1 month old will not be shown.

- **Folder**: This filter allows you to select a folder from a drop-down list to show only workflow events for Zaps housed in that folder. You can only select one folder to filter by.

- **App**: This filter allows you to search for an app and select it to filter workflow events for Zaps using that app. You can only select one app to filter by.

- **Zap**: This filter allows you to select a Zap from a drop-down list to show only workflow events that originate from that Zap. You can only select one Zap to filter by.

- **Status**: This filter allows you to select multiple options to show workflow events with those task statuses. For example, you could filter to show only workflow events that were successful or were filtered and stopped. We will look at task statuses in more detail in the next section, *Understanding task statuses*.

You can use the **Refresh** icon button to refresh the page with new results or the **Clear all filters** button to remove the filters and list all workflow events. You can also clear individual filter fields by hitting the **x** icon in any of the fields.

> **Tip**
> As we discussed in *Chapter 4*, *Managing Your Zaps*, if you have a large number of Zaps, ensuring that you label them adequately can help you to quickly identify them and associated workflow events in Zap history. Using numbers, letters, and roman numerals often helps to break the monotony of word descriptions in Zap names, which can help to easily identify them visually in the **Zap runs** tab and by sorting them in the **Task usage** tab.

Now let's discuss the different task statuses you are likely to see in Zap history.

Understanding task statuses

When you view your Zap history, you are likely to see workflow events listed with one or more of the following task statuses:

- **Success**: This indicates that the Zap ran, and all tasks in that workflow event were completed successfully.

- **Filtered**: This indicates that the Zap ran but had a filter at some point in the workflow that prevented it from continuing to process later steps in that workflow event.

- **Stopped**: This indicates that the Zap experienced an error while it was running that workflow event. Workflow events can have a task status of **Stopped Errored**, meaning that an issue occurred with the Zap running, or **Stopped Halted**, meaning that Zapier stopped a task from executing. **Errored** statuses one after another will cause Zapier to pause or turn **Off** the Zap, whereas **Halted** statuses do not cause this to happen.

- **Waiting**: This indicates that the workflow event is waiting to be completed because it has a **Delay** action step or is scheduled to replay using the **Autoreply** function. If the Zap has a **Delay** step, the status will be highlighted as **Waiting Delayed**. If the workflow event is scheduled to be run again using the **Autoreplay** function, the status will be highlighted as **Waiting Scheduled**.

- **Playing**: This indicates that the workflow event is still in process.

- **Holding**: This indicates that the workflow event is being held for several reasons.

Let's review the reasons for **Holding** task statuses.

Reasons for a task status of Holding

Workflow events may show a status of **Holding** for the following reasons:

- **High Task Use**: Multiple (100 or more) workflow events have triggered at the same time. Zapier uses this mechanism as a preventative measure to stop a high volume of tasks running until you have confirmed that you want to play the tasks. This prevents high task usage. It also prevents the possibility of you having to correct a large number of potentially incorrect records as a result.

- **Reconnect {app name}**: The named app has disconnected and must be reconnected before you can replay any held tasks. You can reconnect the app from the **My Apps** page.

- **Upgrade Needed**: Your account has surpassed its limit for Zaps, tasks, or Premium apps. If the upgrade is related to tasks, you will need to upgrade your plan before you can replay your tasks. Alternatively, you can delete held tasks or assess your number of Zaps and Premium apps instead of upgrading.

- **Payment Issue**: Your billing payment method has expired. You will need to update your payment method before you can replay your tasks.

We will discuss how to delete or replay tasks that have been held in the *Managing Zap history data* section.

Now let's discuss how to view detailed Zap run information related to individual workflow events.

Viewing detailed Zap run information

Being able to view detailed task information is the biggest benefit of the **Zap history** log. Having access to this information allows you to drill down to the specific causes of unexpected events. We'll cover the following key points in this section:

- Navigating detailed Zap runs pages
- Assessing step data
- Understanding **Data In** and **Data Out** information

Let's review each one.

Navigating detailed Zap runs pages

You can access the detailed task information by clicking on an individual workflow event in the **Zap runs** log. An example of a detailed task information page is shown in the following screenshot:

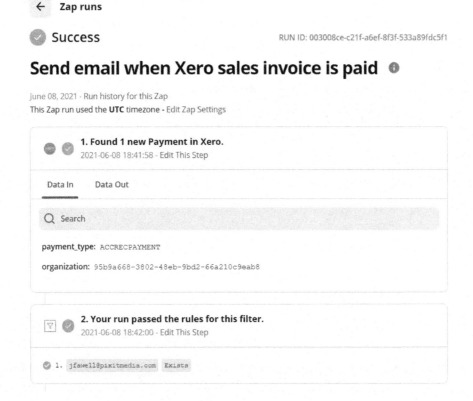

Figure 5.8 – An example of a detailed Zap information page

Detailed **Zap runs** pages show the following information:

- **Status icon**: The overall task status for that workflow event.

- **RUN ID**: This string signifies the ID for the workflow event and is displayed in the URL as well in the top right-hand corner where it can be copied to your clipboard if you click on it.

> **Important note**
> **RUN ID** is an important identifier that allows you to reference specific workflow events when communicating with Zapier customer support.

- **Zap name**: The name of the Zap.

- **Date**: The date the workflow event started to run. You can view the filtered task history log for the Zap by clicking on the link labeled **Run history for this Zap**.

- **Timezone**: The timezone associated with the Zap, for example, `America/Denver`. You can edit the timezone for the Zap by clicking on the link labeled **Edit Zap Settings**.

- **Step data**: History of all the data flowing in and out of each trigger and action step in the Zap is shown in separate tabs labeled **Data In** and **Data Out**.

From within **Stopped** tasks, you will be able to access app-specific help documentation by clicking on the **Documentation** button and can also raise a customer support query by clicking on the **Get Help** button. This is shown in the following screenshot:

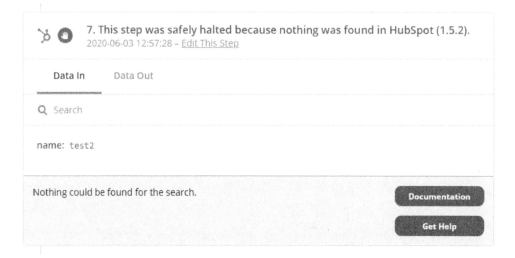

Figure 5.9 – Accessing documentation and help from Stopped tasks

By scrolling to the bottom of the page, you will see the total number of tasks used in the workflow event. You will also see a **Get Help** button that can be used to raise a customer support query, which prepopulates with the related Zap and specific task ID information.

You can navigate back to the **Zap runs** log by clicking on the **back arrow** icon at the top of the page.

Now let's review how to assess step data.

Assessing step data

Each step in a Zap will be shown in the detailed task information page and demarcated by a box showing the following information:

- **App icon**: This shows the app icon for the connected app for each step.

- **Task status**: This shows the status icon of each task. The status icon for individual tasks may be different from others in the workflow event.

- **Step number and result**: This shows the step number as configured in the Zap editor as well as the result of the trigger or action running in Zapier. For example, if your Zap triggers on receipt of a new email matching a search in Gmail, your trigger step number and result may show `1. Found 1 new Email Matching Search in Gmail`.

- **Date and time**: This shows the date and time that each step started in the workflow. This information is very useful for identifying when events occurred.

- **Edit this Zap link**: You can click this link to edit the Zap in the Zap editor.

- **Data In** tab: This displays all the data that was sent to the connected app for any given step.

- **Data Out** tab: This displays all the data received by a connected app for any given step.

The **Data In** and **Data Out** tabs hold crucial information about data that has passed through Zapier. Let's look at this next.

Understanding Data In and Data Out information

There are a few things that you may want to make a note of when reviewing **Data In** and **Data Out** information:

- Connected apps generally provide duplicate information of data that was added and received by the app, which is posted in the **Data Out** tab. However, there are some cases where a connected app does not post any information, and you may not see any data in this tab.

- You may find data posted to your action apps denoted by curly brackets, {{. This normally signifies that data for that field from the trigger step that you have mapped in the Zap editor is missing. You can find this string in the **Data In** tab of your action step. You can address this by finding the correct field to use in your **Data Out** tab of your trigger step and remapping the field in the Zap editor with new sample data from the trigger.

- You can enter keywords in the search bar to find specific information. This is useful when you want to find specific data that will identify what may have happened in a step when the Zap ran.

- Filter steps do not show **Data In** or **Data Out** information in tabs; they only display whether conditions of the filter have been met or not.

> **Tip**
>
> As we discussed in *Chapter 1, Introduction to Business Process Automation with Zapier*, ensure that your timezone is specified in your account settings so that dates and times are displayed according to that. This will help when you are trying to pinpoint when errors might have occurred on a timeline. You can also specify specific timezones applicable to that Zap within the Zap **Settings** in **Zap Editor**.

Now that you are able to assess **Zap history** data, let's review how best to manage your Zap history.

Managing Zap history data

Zapier allows you to delete, download, play, or replay tasks in the **Zap history** log individually or in bulk if you are using a paid Zapier pricing plan. If you want to select or deselect workflow events in bulk, you can use the **Checkbox** icon options as follows:

- **Select shown**: This allows you to select only the workflow events shown on that specific page (up to 10).

- **Select all (5000 at a time)**: This allows you to select all available workflow events displayed. You can use filters to display the events you want to manage.

- **Deselect all**: This allows you to deselect all selected checkboxes in bulk.

> **Important note**
> Use the filters to display the list of workflow events that you want to select ahead of using the **Checkbox** icon options. This is especially important if you are using the **Delete** function as using **Select all (5000 at a time)** will select the entire history if no filter is applied.

Selected workflow events will display a blue checkbox, and the workflow event box will be highlighted. When any workflow event(s) have been selected, the following options will be highlighted:

- **Play x**: The **Play** button will only be displayed if you are managing workflow events with the status **Holding** as these workflows have not run yet. Clicking this button will allow you to manually run these workflows.

- **Replay x**: Clicking this button will allow you to manually replay any tasks with the status **Stopped Errored** or **Stopped Halted**. The **Replay** button will not be displayed for held tasks. Using the **Replay** function will only replay any tasks in the Zap that have failed or have been unsuccessful and not the entire workflow event. For example, you may have two action steps in your Zap, the first to add a new deal to your **Customer Relationship Management** (**CRM**), and the second to send an email. If the first step is successful but the second has failed, the **Replay** function will only attempt to replay the second, so as to send an email.

- **Delete x**: Clicking this button will permanently delete any selected workflow events. Deleting successfully played tasks from the **Zap history** does not reduce your task usage in a billing period. This feature is, however, useful for deleting held tasks that you do not want to play.

- **Download x**: Clicking this button will allow you to generate a detailed .csv, which will be emailed to the email address associated with your profile, and accessible by a link that expires in 7 days. You can download up to 5,000 workflow events at one time; however, you can contact Zapier support if you want to download more. It is recommended that you download your **Zap history** regularly.

Each of the buttons will be shown with the number of workflow events selected in place of the **x**.

Now let's look at how to automatically replay your failed tasks using the **Autoreplay** feature.

Using the Autoreplay feature

We have already discussed how to replay tasks manually. If you are using a Professional plan or higher, you will have access to the **Autoreplay** feature, which allows you to automatically replay failed tasks due to temporary errors or downtime. You can switch on this feature by using the **Autoreplay ON/OFF** toggle button, as shown in the following screenshot:

Figure 5.10 – Locating the Autoreplay ON/OFF toggle button

Let's explore how the Autoreplay function works.

How the Autoreplay function works

Once you have turned the **Autoreplay** function **ON**, if a step in a workflow event fails, Zapier will attempt to retry it up to 5 times using the following schedule: after 5 minutes, after another 30 minutes, after another 1 hour, after another 3 hours, and finally after another 6 hours. Therefore, the last attempt to replay the task would be 10 hours and 35 minutes after the original error occurred. Zapier would not send error emails or trigger Zapier Manager until all replay attempts in the schedule have been completed, and only if the task failed to replay on the final attempt. During this time, you will not be able to manually replay a task, and all tasks that are being replayed or are scheduled to be replayed will display a status of **Waiting Scheduled**. The **Autoreplay** function will only start when the workflow event experiences errors; however, any tasks that have a status of **Halted**, **Errored**, and **Filtered** will be replayed. Triggers will never show as errored and do not replay because of the mechanism used for finding new data.

While the replay schedule is running, you can make small changes to your Zap to attempt to address any errors, and the **Autoreplay** function will incorporate these changes into the next scheduled replay. If, however, your Zap is switched off at the exact time the next replay is due or the **Autoreplay** function is turned off, all further scheduled attempts will be canceled.

Let's now take a look at how to interpret why tasks have not replayed.

Understanding why tasks have not replayed

You may find that after manually replaying tasks or when using the **Autoreplay** function that some of your tasks have still not replayed. This might happen if your Zap has been turned **Off** or is paused, if it has been deleted, or if significant changes have been made to it since the error occurred (as opposed to small adjustments). Zapier will send you notifications to remind you that tasks can be replayed before the replay time expires. Zap runs over 2 months old, those that have already successfully run, and those that are replaying or scheduled to be replayed, cannot be replayed.

In this section, we've reviewed how to use the **Zap history** page when troubleshooting problems. We discussed task statuses, detailed Zap information, and how to manage your Zap history data.

You should now have a better understanding of how to use Zap history information effectively to troubleshoot problems with your workflow events. Now let's take a look at how to find help on the Zapier platform.

Finding help: help center, customer support, community, and experts

Once you have done some initial investigations to troubleshoot errors in your Zaps and workflow events, you will find it useful to know where to look for additional help on the Zapier platform. Zapier provides you with several ways to get assistance, ranging from do-it-yourself information finding to hands-on support. There are a few ways in which you can get help on the Zapier platform:

- Finding app-specific help in app profiles
- Utilizing the Zapier help center
- Engaging with the Zapier community
- Reaching out to Zapier customer support
- Hiring a Zapier Certified Expert

These options are available to all users of Zapier regardless of which pricing plan subscription you use.

Let's explore each of these.

Finding app-specific help in app profiles

As we discussed in *Chapter 2*, *Preparing to Automate Your Processes*, each app that integrates with Zapier is listed in the Zapier ecosystem directory, and each app has an app profile. Under the **Help** tab of an app's app profile, you will find articles relating to common support issues raised by users. Many popular apps will have three popular articles listed in their app profiles, as follows:

- How to get started with (app name)
- Common problems with (app name)
- Tips and tricks with (app name)

If you're looking to solve a problem related to a specific app, this is an excellent place to start. It's also handy to know in advance what issues you may come across with your apps by researching this information when you first start using the app in your workflows.

Utilizing the Zapier help center

Another place to look when you have a problem with your workflows is to search for related solutions in the Zapier **help center**. The help center provides you with comprehensive articles on all aspects of troubleshooting. You can use the search bar on the main **Help** page to enter your search keywords and terms. Some articles also provide information in the form of videos and tutorials.

The help center is accessible as follows:

- The **Get Help** button in the lower right-hand corner (on some pages)
- The **Get Help** icon in the left sidebar
- The **Help** link in the footer menu
- The **Get Help** button in the **Zap history** area within stopped steps or at the bottom of individual detailed task histories
- By navigating to `https://zapier.com/help`

These are shown in the following screenshot:

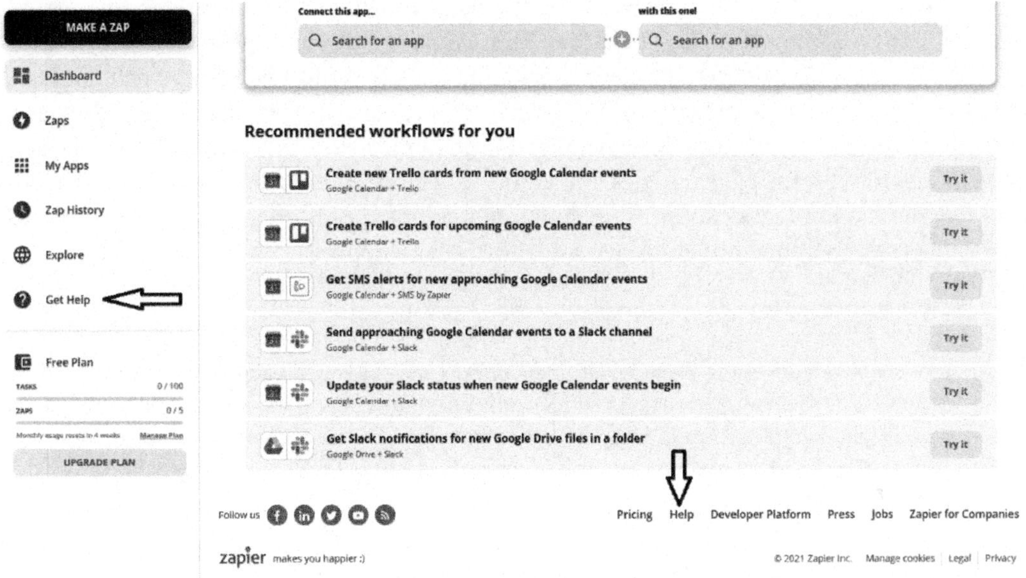

Figure 5.11 – Navigation to the help center

As discussed in *Chapter 3*, *Building Your First Automated Workflow (Zap)*, you can also access help articles from within the **Guide** section (in the expandable right-side panel) of the Zap editor. There is also a **Get Help** link at the bottom of the section that navigates to the **Zapier Customer Support** page.

For specific information on troubleshooting, you can navigate to `https://zapier.com/help/troubleshoot/`. You will find articles of particular interest that will help you address specific error notifications such as those involving status codes.

Engaging with the Zapier community

The **Zapier community** forum is a brilliant way to search for particular and niche solutions to problems. You can also post details of your issue and members of the community will respond with helpful suggestions and comments. It is even a great place to interact with other Zapier users, Zapier customer support staff, developers, and experts.

At the bottom of the main **Help Center** page and on each help article, you will find a link to the Zapier community. You can also navigate there using `https://community.zapier.com/`.

Reaching out to Zapier customer support

Sometimes you might need some additional, more personalized help to address issues you might be having with your workflows. The **Zapier customer support** team offers a free email support service to all Zapier users and typically responds within a few hours of you submitting the query, regardless of your timezone, ensuring problems are addressed promptly. They have access to more detailed backend information than what you will be able to see from **Status** page updates and alerts. If you use a Team and Company plan, you will have access to premier support, meaning that your support queries are likely to be responded to and sorted out quicker than with regular support.

> **Tip**
>
> When reaching out to Zapier customer support, give as much context as you can. Provide screenshots or video walk-throughs of the issue along with multiple examples from the **Zap history**, if possible. Detail what you have tried to rectify the issue, and be clear and specific. This will reduce the chances of miscommunication.

At the bottom of the main **Help Center** page and on each help article, you will find a link to the Zapier support page. You can also navigate there using `https://zapier.com/app/get-help`.

Hiring a Zapier Certified Expert

When you need help with troubleshooting really specific issues and have tried all other support avenues, you can hire a **Zapier Certified Expert**. Zapier Certified Experts are individuals or agencies that have gone through Zapier's certification program and are endorsed by Zapier to offer charged support to Zapier users. Zapier Certified Experts are listed on the **Zapier Expert Directory** and are given a badge to display on their websites and social media channels. As they are all independent consultants, there will be nuances in their backgrounds, experience, and service offerings; however, they generally offer training, technical support, and advanced workflow building services. Most Zapier Certified Experts are likely to offer a one-on-one experience such as phone and video conferencing support.

At the bottom of the main **Help Center** page and on each help article, you will find a link to the **Zapier Experts Directory**. You can also navigate there using `https://zapier.com/experts/`.

You should now have a better understanding of the different support options available to you as a Zapier user.

Summary

In this chapter, we covered the essential information required to troubleshoot errors when using Zapier. We started by covering how to manage error alerts using email notifications and by using the Zapier Manager built-in app. Next, we covered how to manage app status alerts by monitoring the Zapier **Status** page and by using the App Status by Zapier built-in app. We then looked at using Zap history information in detail to help you to troubleshoot problems with Zaps, apps, and individual data issues. Lastly, we reviewed the channels available to get extra support on the Zapier platform.

You now know how to manage your alerts by updating your email notification preferences and how to understand information on the Zapier **Status** page. You also now know how to create alert workflows using the Zapier Manager and App Status by Zapier built-in apps, and how to understand Zap history information to help with troubleshooting errors. Lastly, you now know how to find help on the Zapier platform.

In the next chapter, you will learn how to set up and customize multi-step Zaps, and use the all-important search functionality of Zapier. You will also be introduced to the most commonly used built-in Zapier apps and you will be able to test your knowledge by building your first multi-step Zap.

Section 2:
Customizing Your Zaps with Built-in Apps by Zapier – Functionality and Practical Uses

When this section is complete, you will understand the functionality of the Zapier platform, how to customize your Zaps using Zapier's built-in apps, and how to create your first multi-step Zap. We will discuss the functionality of built-in apps, teach you practical tips on how to use them, with examples, and you will be able to test your knowledge with a few exercises.

This section comprises the following chapters:

- *Chapter 6, Creating Multi-Step Zaps with Built-In Apps*
- *Chapter 7, Getting Started with Built-In Apps*
- *Chapter 8, Built-In Communication Apps*
- *Chapter 9, Exploring Built-In Apps for Extracting and Compiling Data*
- *Chapter 10, Other Useful Built-In Apps by Zapier*
- *Chapter 11, Advanced Built-In Apps by Zapier*
- *Chapter 12, Managing Your Zapier Account with Built-In Apps*

6
Creating Multi-Step Zaps and Using Built-In Apps

As you become more comfortable with using Zapier to automate your business workflows, you will find that in many situations, you may need more flexibility than what single-step workflows can offer. You will start to build more complex workflows, which will allow you to automate multiple action steps in your processes involving tasks in various apps. You may find that often the data you need to use in subsequent actions is not available in the trigger and existing action steps. In these cases, you will need to know how to use search action events to retrieve data. To complement using triggers and actions, you may also want to customize your Zaps further by using the myriad of build-in tools that Zapier has created to allow you to transform and manipulate data, all from within the Zapier platform.

In *Chapter 3, Building Your First Automated Workflow (Zap)*, we covered the basics of how to create a single-step Zap. In this chapter, we will build on the knowledge you have gained and discuss how to develop multi-step Zaps using multiple actions and searches, and introduce you to the various built-in apps created by Zapier. We begin by covering how to create multi-step Zaps by recapping using action steps and adding search steps. You will also be able to test your knowledge with an exercise involving a multi-step Zap. Then, we will briefly introduce the functionality of all the built-in apps by Zapier, all of which will be covered in detail in subsequent chapters.

We will cover the following key topics in this chapter:

- Creating multi-step Zaps with multiple action and search steps
- Introducing apps by Zapier

Once you have worked through each of these topics, you will know how to create a multi-step Zap and use search functionality in your action steps. You will also have a better understanding of the basic functionality of all Zapier's built-in apps.

Technical requirements

To work through the content in this chapter, you will need access to a Zapier account. To build multi-step Zaps, you will need to subscribe to the Zapier Starter plan as a minimum. You can get access to the Zap templates used in this chapter here: `https://bit.ly/3e5BUkn`. Using the templates will help you to visualize how the process works.

Creating Zaps with multiple action and search steps

In *Chapter 3, Building your First Automated Workflow (Zap)*, we walked through a step-by-step process to create your first single-step Zap. In *Chapter 5, Troubleshooting and Handling Zap Errors*, we used this knowledge to create alert Zaps using Zapier Manager and App Status by Zapier. Now that you've experienced first-hand what Zapier can offer in just a single-step workflow, it's time to explore the infinite automation possibilities of multi-step workflows to power your productivity.

As we discussed in *Chapter 3, Building Your First Automated Workflow (Zap)*, once you have set up your trigger step, you can add actions, searches, filters, and delays after the trigger and between any action step, and add paths at the end, using the + icon.

> **Important note**
> You can add up to 99 action steps to a Zap.

We will discuss how to add filters, delays, and paths to your workflows later in *Chapter 7, Getting Started with Built-In Apps*, when we will explore some of Zapier's built-in apps. Before we do that, we need to understand how to use search functionality in your action steps. Search functionality allows you to dynamically look up data that may not be present in your trigger and existing action steps. This is possible if the app you intend to search for data has search action events available through the integration.

> **Important note**
> Many apps offer you the option of searching for data. It's difficult to express in words the usefulness of search action functionality. It really gives the user the ability to extract information that you might not have available from the trigger steps or previous action steps. A common example would be when you make a sale in **Shopify** and you're given the product ID of the product associated with the sale. You might then want to search for other information associated with the product to then use in other steps.

There are two ways to add **search** actions steps to your Zaps:

- Using the + icon
- From a **Choose value…** field using the **Custom** header option

Let's look at each in turn. As we progress through this section, you will see that many of the examples and screenshots refer to **Pipedrive CRM**. We've used this example as it illustrates the search action functionality well. Bear in mind that many apps have search action functionality, which you can utilize as required.

Adding a search step using the + icon

If the app you are using has search action events available through the integration, they will be denoted by **Find...** plus the item. For example, in Pipedrive the following search action events are available:

- **Find Person**
- **Find User**
- **Find Organization**
- **Find Deal**
- **Find Activity**
- **Find Product**
- **Find Product(s)**

Searches are most commonly performed using unique identifiers for items, such as names, email addresses, subjects, codes, and record IDs. Most apps with search action event integrations will allow multiple ways to search for items.

> **Important note**
>
> A common mistake that many users make is to search by the "name" associated with a record ID. Record IDs are generally the best way to search for an item as in most cases record IDs are completely unique between items in an app. For example, in a CRM, duplicates may exist for a contact that may have variations in data; however, only one record ID will exist to differentiate between those duplicates.

Let's use an example to illustrate implementing a search action event. We will use an altered version of the working example from *Chapter 3, Building Your First Automated Workflow (Zap)*, where we will change the trigger app to Pipedrive and the trigger event will be **New Deal**. In this case, we may want to add the contact's full name as well as their first and last name to columns in our Google Sheets spreadsheet. When we try to search for the person's first name we see that the data that pulls through from the trigger step only presents the contact's full name. This is shown in the following screenshot:

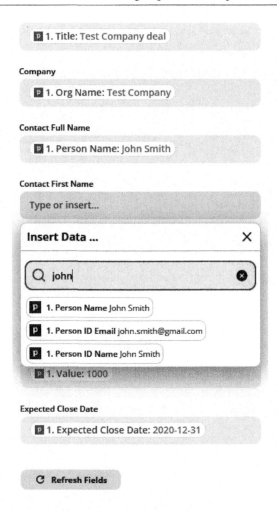

Figure 6.1 – Search for first name yielding no results

In this case, as the Pipedrive integration has a **Find Person** search action event, we can add a search action step between our trigger and the existing action step to retrieve these details. We would do this by clicking on the + icon.

> **Tip**
>
> Another option would be to add a step using the Zapier built-in app Formatter by Zapier **Text** action event with a **Split Text** transform option to split the text in Person Name data so that we can extract the first and last name. We will cover the Formatter by Zapier text splitting function in *Chapter 16, Text Formatting Functions in Zapier – Part 2*.

Next, we can add Pipedrive as our app and **Find Person** as our action event, as shown in the following screenshot:

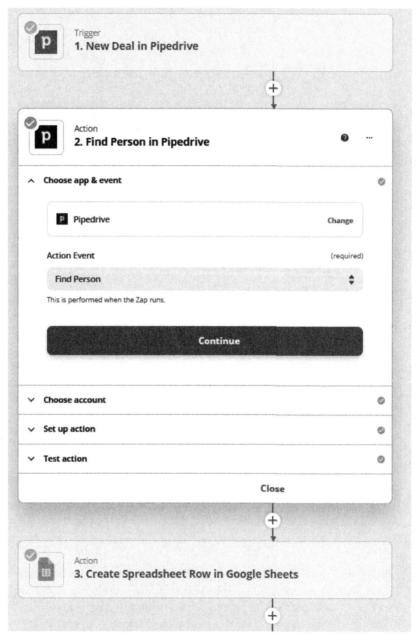

Figure 6.2 – Find Person action event

After adding in our Pipedrive account, we can customize our search, in this example, by adding in the following:

- **Field To Search By**: In this case, we are able to use the person's record ID to search with, so we will choose the **ID** value for the dropdown.

- **ID (Term)**: In this case, we would map the **Person ID** dynamic data value from our trigger step to this field. The ID field is a number (integer) field and the value we enter (whether static or dynamic) should be as such.

- **Search For Exact Match?**: In this case, we choose **Yes** option as we want to search for an exact match.

- **Should This Step Be Considered A "success" When Nothing Is Found**: Use this Boolean field to select **True** or **False** from the drop-down menu, enter text, or insert data from previous steps for this step to be considered a "success" if nothing is found in the search. The default for this field is **False**, which you should choose if you want the step to "halt" if nothing is found, as this is the most common use case. This means that Zapier will produce a soft error that you will not be notified of; the Zap will not pause. However, all subsequent steps that depend on the data in this step will be skipped. Use the **True** option when you want to allow the Zap to continue and subsequent steps to run. If you choose this option, it is best practice to have more control in your workflows by adding **Filter by Zapier** or **Paths by Zapier** conditional logic and allowing those steps to pass or stop based on whether the search returned a result or not. Refer to *Chapter 7, Getting Started with Built-In Apps*, for more information on how to use conditional workflows with this field option.

- **Create Pipedrive Person if it doesn't exist yet?**: Tick this checkbox if you want a new record to be created if the search does not return an existing record. Once ticked, the step will refresh and display fields as with the **Create Person** action event. The entity you want to search for in your specified app, for example, **Pipedrive Person**, will differ between apps, and so will the **Create** entity.

This is shown in the following screenshot:

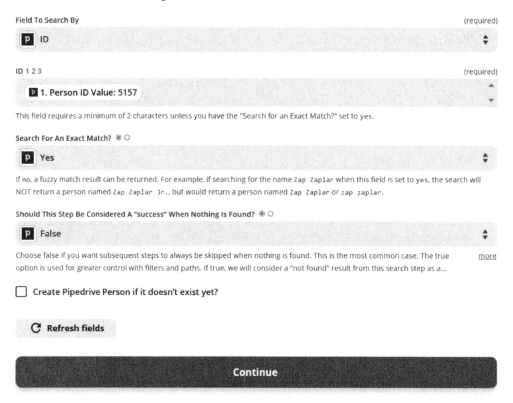

Figure 6.3 – Customizing the Find Person in Pipedrive search action step

We could, however, choose to use any other existing data value, either static or dynamic, to search by. For example, we could use the person's email address or name as the item to search by, if we are confident that they are likely to be unique enough to be able to find that specific record.

> **Important note**
> Search action event variables will differ between action events and apps, therefore what you see in the **Set up action** section is likely to be different from our example. The Zap Editor shows useful notes as to what you can include in each field.

Finally, if we have mapped our fields correctly, the **Test action** test will retrieve the correct contact with all the details we need to map the contact first name and last name in our **Create Spreadsheet Row in Google Sheets** action step. This is shown in the following screenshot:

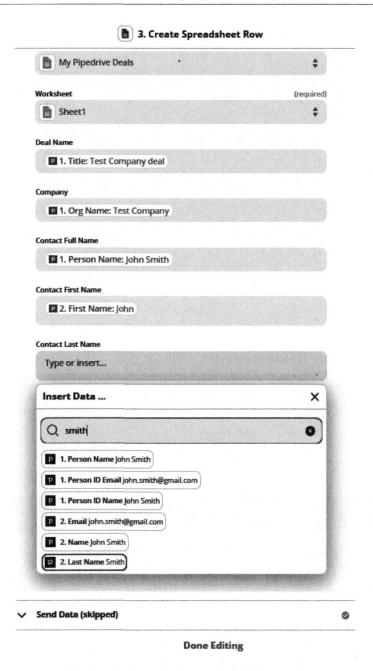

Figure 6.4 – Search for last name yielding a result

We can then go ahead and retest our action using the **Test action** test to see how our data pushes into our Google Sheets spreadsheet, or **Skip Test**.

As a comparison, the following screenshot shows a search action step using **Mailchimp** as the app:

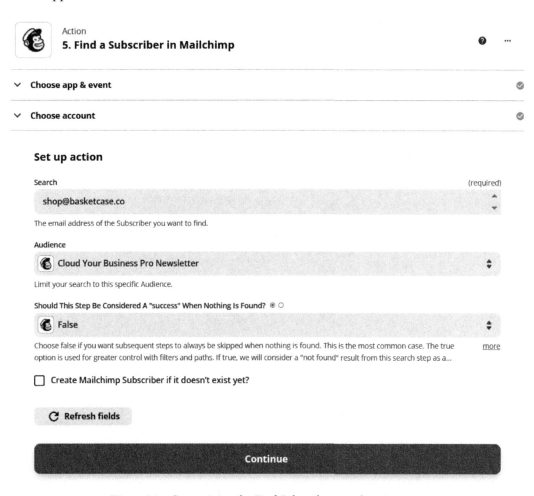

Figure 6.5 – Customizing the Find Subscriber search action step

You will see from the following screenshot that a large amount of data can be extracted from many search action steps that can be used in your other action steps:

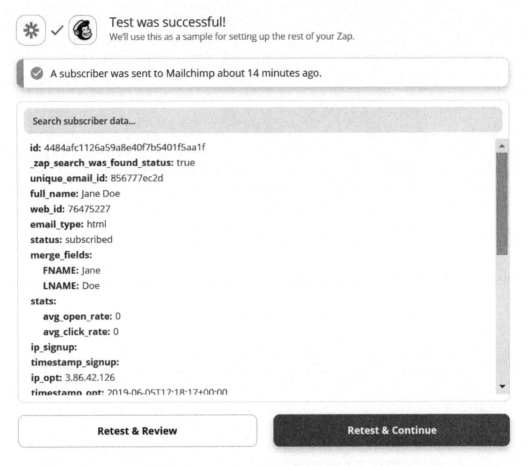

Figure 6.6 – The results of the Find Subscriber search

Now let's take a look at how to add a search action step from within a **Choose value...** field.

Adding a Search step in a Choose value... field

In *Chapter 3, Building Your First Automated Workflow (Zap)*, we introduced the two main field types that you will find in actions steps, **Choose value...** and **Type or insert...**. When using the **Choose value...** field type, you can map in either static or dynamic data. Dynamic data retrieved from trigger or previous action steps can be mapped in using the **Custom** header option. If the dynamic data that you specifically want to map does not exist in previous steps, you can add a search action if the app you are using allows this action through the integration.

Let's illustrate this by adding an extra requirement to the working example. Some CRMs such as Pipedrive have a product module that allows you to store set codes, descriptions, and pricing for products that you might charge your customers for. In our workflow, once we have created a new row in a Google Sheets spreadsheet, we may want to automatically add a product to our deal in Pipedrive. For our specific example, when the deal is created, a "product" is selected from a drop-down menu in Pipedrive, and we now want to use this to search for the actual product from our Pipedrive product module to add to the deal. This example may not be that relevant in real life, however, it serves to illustrate using the **Choose Value...** field type for searching.

First of all, we will need to add an action step after the **Create Spreadsheet Row in Google Sheets** action step using the + icon. We'll use **Pipedrive** for our app and **Add Product to Deal** for our action event. Under **Set up action**, in the **Product** field, we will select the **Add a search step** button under the **Custom** header option. This is shown in the following screenshot:

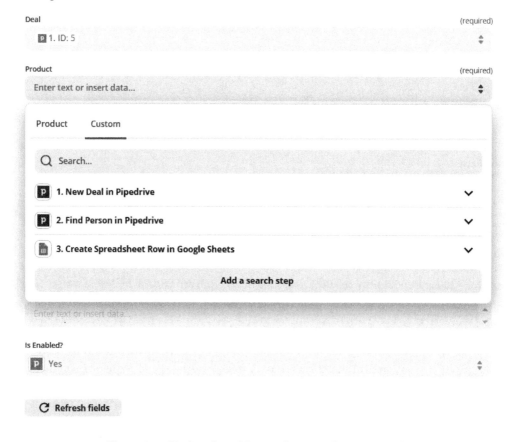

Figure 6.7 – Finding the Add a search step in the Custom tab

This will produce a popup with instructions as shown in the following screenshot:

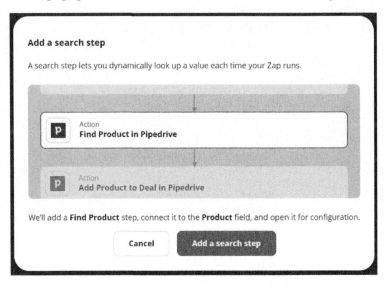

Figure 6.8 – The Add a search step popup

Once we have clicked on the **Add a search step** button, a Pipedrive **Find Product** search action step will be added automatically before the **Add Product** action step.

Next, after we have chosen the Pipedrive account we want to use, we need to map in a value to search with in the **Set up action** section. In our example, we would use the value entered from our Pipedrive product field from our trigger step. This is shown in the following screenshot:

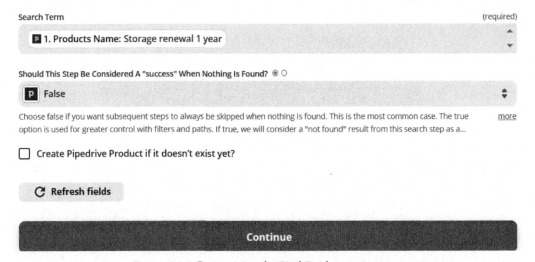

Figure 6.9 – Customizing the Find Product action step

Finally, the **Test action** test will retrieve the product information from the products module in Pipedrive and the ID will be automatically mapped to our **Add Product to Deal** action step. This is shown in the following screenshot:

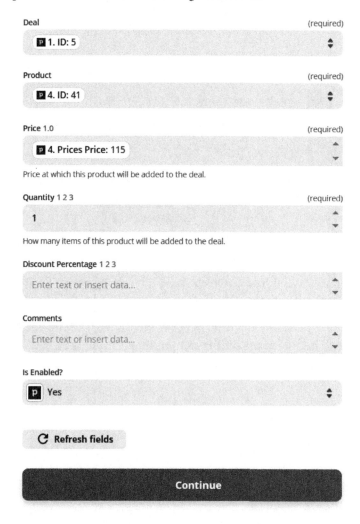

Figure 6.10 – The search step results automatically mapped to the originating action step

We can now fill in the other fields by adding static data or mapping dynamic data from previous steps, proceed to do a **Test action** test, and complete our workflow.

You can get a template of this Zap and add it to your Zapier account at `https://bit.ly/3e5BUkn`. Using the Zap template will help you visualize how the process works.

Now you can try this out yourself with the following exercise.

Exercise – Creating a multi-step Zap with a search action

Use one of the processes that you defined in *Chapter 2, Preparing to Automate Your Processes*, to work through the content in this section to create a multi-step Zap with a search action. Try to incorporate multiple apps in your workflow.

Here is an example that you could use:

1. *Trigger*: A webform is submitted.

2. *Action*: Add a new subscriber to your email marketing app.

3. *Action*: Add a new contact to your invoicing app.

4. *Action*: Search for a user ID on a Google Sheets spreadsheet lookup list.

5. *Action*: Add a new onboarding task to your task management app and assign it to the user from *step 4*.

6. *Action*: Send an email or a message in your messaging app to your team to notify them that new contact and subscriber records have been created.

You can repeat this exercise for any of your processes that you have documented and that would benefit from automation.

You should now have a better understanding of how to create and customize multi-step Zaps with custom values and search functionality. Let's now take multi-step Zap building even further and explore all the built-in apps Zapier has created to make workflow automation all-encompassing on the Zapier platform.

Introducing apps by Zapier

The basics of creating multi-step Zaps lie in knowing how to use triggers, actions, and searches adequately. Once you have got to grips with this, you may want to take advantage of the functionality of the many built-in apps that Zapier has created to allow you to perform common tasks without having to use another app and pay additional subscription fees. Zapier has created several built-in apps to help you supercharge your workflows.

We've categorized these apps as follows:

*   Apps that control run conditions and logic

*   Communication apps

*   Apps for extracting and compiling data

- Other useful apps

- Advanced apps

- Apps for managing your Zapier account

- The powerful Formatter by Zapier app

> **Important note**
>
> Zapier releases new features and built-in apps regularly. In this book, we will only cover the built-in apps that have been released from the beta phase with the triggers, actions, and search actions available at the time of publishing.

You can get access to a handy quick-reference cheatsheet to all of the Zapier built-in apps here: `https://bit.ly/3e5BUkn`.

Let's now briefly review the apps in each one of these categories.

Setting run conditions and using logic with apps by Zapier

You may want to customize your automations by controlling when your workflows will continue to run. You can do this by adding in logic to stop a Zap from running unless the data satisfies certain criteria or by adding timed delays and scheduling your Zaps to run at specific intervals. Zapier has created the following built-in apps that are commonly used for setting run conditions and using logic:

- **Filter by Zapier**: Filter by Zapier allows you to add conditional logic steps to your Zaps allowing the automation to continue only if certain criteria have been satisfied. For example, you may want to send an email when a new row has been added to your Google Sheets spreadsheet, but only if the data in a certain column exists.

- **Delay by Zapier**: By using Delay by Zapier, you can add time delays to subsequent action steps. You can set a delay to allow the rest of the Zap to run after a set period of time, such as 1 hour, at a certain time such as 2 P.M. or after a delay queue if there multiple delays in the workflow. For example, you may want to send a tweet on Twitter one week after an image or video has been added to Instagram.

- **Schedule by Zapier**: You can use Schedule by Zapier as a trigger step to run a workflow at set times, such as every hour, every day at a certain time, every week on a certain day, or every month on a certain day. For example, you may want to add a set of tasks to your task management app (such as Asana) at the start of every week.

- **Paths by Zapier**: Paths by Zapier allows you to add branching logic to your Zaps. This means that you can allow different paths with different actions to run based on set criteria. For example, you may want to either send an email or a text message to a customer that has filled out a contact form on your website based on the contact preferences they provide.

We will cover all of these Apps by Zapier in *Chapter 7, Getting Started with Built-In Apps*.

Now let's review the apps that Zapier has created that have communication functions.

Using apps by Zapier for communication

Zapier has created several communication-specific built-in apps that allow you to trigger workflow automations and perform actions. These are as follows:

- **SMS by Zapier**: Using SMS by Zapier, you can send a limited number of text messages to a specific number. This is useful for sending notifications or reminders.

- **Email by Zapier**: With Email by Zapier you can enable a unique `zapiermail.com` email address to use as a trigger or action step. You can then send outbound emails, and if you've enabled read receipts, you can trigger a workflow when someone opens your sent email. You can also trigger Zaps to run when you receive forwarded emails to your `zapiermail.com` address.

- **SMTP by Zapier: Simple Mail Transfer Protocol (SMTP)** allows email client apps to send emails. If you are using a mail server other than Gmail, Zoho Mail, or Microsoft Office 365, SMTP by Zapier allows you to send emails via these mail servers.

- **IMAP by Zapier: Internet Message Access Protocol (IMAP)** allows email client apps to retrieve emails from a server. If you are using a mail server other than Gmail, Zoho Mail, or Microsoft Office 365, you can use IMAP by Zapier to retrieve emails from these mail servers.

We will cover all of these apps by Zapier in *Chapter 8, Built-In Communication Apps*.

Now let's take a quick look at some of the other useful apps that Zapier has created and their associated functions.

Extracting and compiling data with apps by Zapier

Zapier has created a few built-in apps that allow you to extract data from emails, use RSS feeds in your automations, and create summaries of information. These are as follows:

- **Email Parser by Zapier**: Similar to Email by Zapier, you can enable a unique @ `robot.zapier.com` email address to which you can forward emails and enable data extraction from the email. For example, if you receive web form submission notifications by email you can use Email Parser by Zapier to extract data to be used in subsequent action steps.

- **RSS by Zapier**: **Really Simple Syndication** (**RSS**) feeds update whenever a site publishes new pages. The RSS by Zapier app allows you to use RSS feed updates as a trigger, which by then adding a notification action step such as an email, SMS, or Slack message will give you an update on new content. For example, you may want to receive updates on when your favorite business blog releases new articles. You can also create your own RSS feed with the app.

- **Digest by Zapier**: This built-in app allows you to capture data from multiple workflow trigger events and compile the data into single summaries that can be used in other action events. For example, send a weekly email with a summary of all sales invoices created over that week to your sales team. You can also search for existing digest data.

We will cover these apps by Zapier in more detail in *Chapter 9, Exploring Built-In Apps for Extracting and Compiling Data*. Now let's take a look at the apps that Zapier has created that have more advanced functionality.

Other useful apps by Zapier

There are several other built-in apps that Zapier has created that perform a variety of useful functions. These are as follows:

- **Zapier Chrome extension**: The Zapier Chrome extension, previously called Push by Zapier, uses a Google Chrome extension to trigger one-off automations from anywhere on the web manually. For example, you may want to create a new Trello card to review content in an article that you came across while browsing the internet.

- **URL Shortener by Zapier**: If you want to make long **Uniform Resource Locator** (**URL**) strings shorter and more easy on the eye, you can use URL Shortener by Zapier. This is especially useful if you have text length restrictions, for example, if you want to send an SMS or post a tweet to Twitter. This is similar to tools such as Bitly.

- **Translate by Zapier**: Translate by Zapier allows you to translate words, phrases, and web pages into over 100 languages, and it can be used to detect a language in text.

- **Lead Score by Zapier**: This app allows you to gather information from the web about a contact using their email address and can also be used to give them a qualification score. For example, if a new lead submits a webform, you may want to find out more details about the contact's company, company size, and location.

- **Weather by Zapier**: Weather by Zapier gives you access to weather conditions in your area. You can use it to get daily weather notifications and only to trigger if it will rain that day (for your local area based on your Zapier timezone settings). You can also search for current weather conditions and tomorrow's forecast for a specified location.

- **Retrograde by Zapier**: You can use Retrograde by Zapier to trigger your workflows based on Mercury retrograde astrological predictions. Choose from trigger events of Mercury entering or leaving retrograde or to trigger once a day when Mercury is in retrograde.

We will cover all of these apps by Zapier in more detail in *Chapter 10, Other Useful Built-In Apps by Zapier*.

Now let's take a look at the apps that Zapier has created that have more advanced functionality.

Advanced apps by Zapier

As you become more familiar with using apps by Zapier, you may want to experiment with a few more built-in apps that Zapier with slightly more advanced features. These are as follows:

- **Webhooks by Zapier**: We briefly introduced you to webhooks in *Chapter 1, Introduction to Business Process Automation with Zapier*. You can use webhooks as trigger or actions steps in your Zaps by using the Webhooks by Zapier app. As a trigger, you can use a Catch Hook or Catch Raw Hook event to wait for a new **GET** (retrieve), **POST** (create), or **PUT** (update) to a Zapier URL, or poll a URL for new entries. You then also use it as an action step for GET, POST, PUT, or custom requests.

- **Code by Zapier**: If you are familiar with **JavaScript** or **Python**, you can use Code by Zapier in your workflow automations. You can write code in JavaScript or Python to use in triggers or actions to manipulate data.

- **Storage by Zapier**: Storage by Zapier allows you to save and retrieve small data values. This allows you to store reference data each time a Zap runs and then share it with other Zaps by retrieving it. For example, you want to keep a running tally of how many new subscribers have been added to your email marketing app and then use this tally to be displayed in a dashboard reporting tool such as **Databox**.

We will cover all of these apps by Zapier in *Chapter 11, Advanced Built-In Apps by Zapier.*

Managing your Zapier account with apps by Zapier

If you're in charge of systems adminstration, then you will want to know how to use these apps. They allow you to build automations that help you to monitor issues with your Zapier account such as errors and task usage. These are as follows:

- **Zapier Manager**: We introduced the Zapier Manager app in *Chapter 5, Troubleshooting and Handling Zap Errors,* where we discussed how to use it to manage error alerts such as errors with Zaps, Zaps being turned off, or tasks being halted. You can also use Zapier Manager to notify you of new public apps being added to Zapier, changes to your account such as new folders or Zaps being created, task usage limits being reached, or new Zapier invoices being released. You can search for a Zap or public app, as well as turning Zaps on or off. If you are using a Team account, you can use Zapier Manager to invite a new user to your Zapier team or notify you of new team members being added.
- **App Status by Zapier**: We introduced the App Status by Zapier app in *Chapter 5, Troubleshooting and Handling Zap Errors,* where we discussed how to use it to get notifications of new, updated, and resolved incidents with public apps.

We will cover all of these apps by Zapier in *Chapter 12, Managing Your Zapier Account with Built-In Apps.*

Now let's discuss an overview of the versatile Formatter by Zapier app.

The powerful Formatter by Zapier app

The **Formatter by Zapier** app is by far the most versatile built-in app by Zapier. The functionality is so extensive that we will cover this app in four chapters. Using the Formatter by Zapier app allows you to format the following:

- **Dates and times**: You can convert date/time values to different formats (including timezones) and add/subtract time. We cover date and time formatting using the Formatter by Zapier app in *Chapter 13, Formatting Date and Time.*

- **Numbers**: You can manipulate numbers, phone numbers, currencies, and use spreadsheet-type formulas and math operations. We cover number formatting using the Formatter by Zapier app in *Chapter 14, Formatting Numbers*.

- **Text**: You can extensively format text using this function. There are so many things you can do that we will cover the functionality in two chapters. In *Chapter 15, Text Formatting Functions in Zapier – Part 1*, we explore adjusting titlecase, uppercase and lowercase, finding and replacing text, trimming whitespace, counting words and adjusting length, and pluralizing text. In *Chapter 16, Text Formatting Functions in Zapier – Part 2*, we discuss text splitting, truncating text, extracting patterns, URLs, phone numbers, numbers, and email addresses, and removing HTML tags and a fun one, creating a superhero name. We will also give an overview of advanced features such as how to convert Markdown to HTML, convert to ASCII, use Default Value, and URL Encode/Decode.

- **Utilities**: The Utilities function allows you to create and customize line items, convert text to line items and vice versa, use lookup tables and picklists, and import .csv files. We cover the Utilities functions in the Formatter by Zapier app in *Chapter 17, Zapier's Utilities Functions*.

You should now have a better understanding of what built-in apps are available on the Zapier platform.

Summary

In this chapter, we boosted your knowledge of how to use Zapier by introducing the benefits of building multi-step Zaps. We covered how to use search functionality in action steps and encouraged you to test your knowledge by creating a multi-step workflow for one of your own processes. Lastly, we introduced all of the built-in apps that Zapier has created to allow you to transform data all from within the Zapier platform.

You now know how to create workflow automations with multiple action and search steps. You also now have a better understanding of all the built-in apps created by Zapier.

In the next chapter, we will introduce you to some of Zapier's built-in apps. We will cover the specific functions of using conditional logic in your workflows with Filter by Zapier and see and how to add pathways with Paths by Zapier. We will also review how to use Delay by Zapier and Schedule by Zapier to apply time delays and schedule run times for your Zaps.

7
Getting Started with Built-In Apps

When you create your Zaps, you will specify what event you want your workflows to be triggered on, and the actions to take after that. You might find that there are occasions where you want to create conditions to stop your workflows from running unless they satisfy certain criteria or to run different actions depending on specific requirements. You might also want some of your actions to proceed to run only after a certain amount of time after the workflow is triggered or to trigger at a certain time. Using Zapier's built-in apps, we can apply conditional logic and run conditions on our workflows to achieve this.

In this chapter, we will introduce the four built-in Zapier apps that allow you to either control run conditions or use conditional logic in workflows by filtering, delaying, scheduling, or choosing pathways. We will give descriptions of their functionality and provide practical tips on how to use them.

First, we will cover how to use conditional logic in our workflows by using the Filter by Zapier app. Next, we take using conditional logic one step further and introduce how to use branching logic with the Paths by Zapier app. Next, we dive into how to use time delays in our Zaps using the Delay by Zapier app. Then we discuss how to schedule our workflows to run at specific times by using the Schedule by Zapier app. Lastly, we will work through an exercise to build a Zap with the features we will learn about in this chapter.

We will cover the following key topics in this chapter:

- Filter by Zapier – applying conditional logic to your Zaps

- Paths by Zapier – adding branching logic to your Zaps

- Delay by Zapier – adding delays to your Zaps

- Schedule by Zapier – scheduling your Zaps to run at intervals

- Exercise – creating a multi-step Zap with a scheduled trigger, search action, filter, path, and delay

Once you have worked through each of these topics, you will know how to apply conditional and branching logic and add delays or schedules to your workflows.

Technical requirements

To work through the content in this chapter, you will need access to a Zapier account. To build multi-step Zaps and use filters, you will need to subscribe to the Zapier Starter plan as a minimum. To work through the *Paths by Zapier – adding branching logic to your Zaps* section, you will need access to a Professional plan or higher to be able to use the Paths by Zapier app.

Filter by Zapier – applying conditional logic to your Zaps

Once your workflows have triggered, you may want to control whether they continue to run and follow through with subsequent action steps. This is useful for stopping your Zaps from running unless specific criteria from your trigger or previous action steps match the conditions you specify. We can use "if this, then that" conditional logic that has been built into the Filter by Zapier built-in app to achieve this.

Here are a couple of examples of when you can use conditional logic in your Zaps:

- You might record details of all bills and their payments on a **Smartsheet** spreadsheet. These are a combination of bills paid automatically by a credit card and those requiring a bank funds transfer to settle them. You mark a column called **Paid** with Yes or No accordingly. You may want to send an email to your accounts team when a new row has been added to your Smartsheet spreadsheet to notify them, but only if the bill requires payment (therefore if the data in the **Paid** column is No).

- You might want to add a copy of an email to **Evernote** only when you receive email updates from your favorite business blog. You have created an automation to mark these emails automatically with the label `My Favorite Blog`, and only want these emails to be added to Evernote.

In these scenarios, you can use the Filter by Zapier app to set conditional logic in your Zaps.

> **Tip**
> Filters only count toward your monthly task usage when the data passes successfully, allowing the workflow to move on to the next action step. This is very important as having this feature available allows you to have more control over your task usage and to be savvier with your allocated task quota.

Let's now take a look at how to use Filter by Zapier.

Setting up the Filter by Zapier app

Filter by Zapier can only be used as an action event that you can customize by setting up rules to specify when your workflow should continue to the next steps. You can add the app anywhere after the trigger step and have multiple filters within a Zap.

Adding a filter step and customizing your rules

Once you have added an action step, either by selecting the **Action** step or clicking on the + icon, and chosen **Filter by Zapier** as the app and **Only continue if…** as the action event, you can then edit the fields in the **Filter Setup & Testing** section as follows:

- **Choose field…**: Use the drop-down menu to choose a field from the previous steps to enter a dynamic data value. This is the value that you want the filter to check. As the value is dynamic, it will most likely change every time the Zap runs and will be used to decide whether the Zap should pass the filter step.

- **Choose condition…**: Use the drop-down menu to choose one condition (or logic) to cross-reference the dynamic value against a reference key. We will discuss filter conditions in detail in the next section.

- **Enter or select value…**: This field holds the data value that will be used as the reference value to check against the dynamic data value and condition.

For example, you might only want the workflow to continue if your dynamic value is the **Stage Name** deal from our trigger step, and the text exactly matches the Leads In reference value. This is shown in the following screenshot:

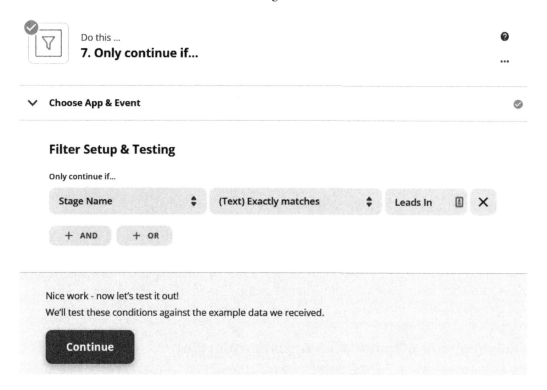

Figure 7.1 – Setting up a filter with the Filter by Zapier app

Next, you can customize your filter to have multiple criteria using the **+ AND** and **+ OR** buttons. Use **+ AND** logic if you want your filter to pass only when two or more conditions are satisfied. Alternatively, use **+ OR** logic if you want your filter to pass if either of the requirements is satisfied. Then, click **Continue**.

Testing your filter

Zapier will then test your conditions against sample data in the workflow. If the conditions pass, and the Zap would have continued, this will be indicated as shown in the following screenshot:

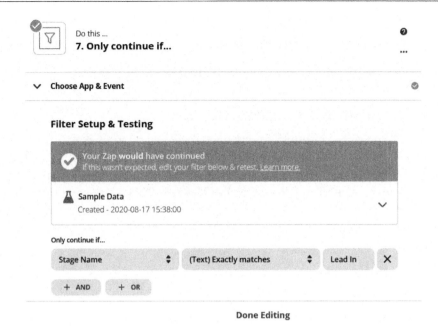

Figure 7.2 – A passed test filter in the Filter by Zapier app

If, however, the filter conditions do not pass, the Zap would be stopped. This will be indicated as shown in the following screenshot:

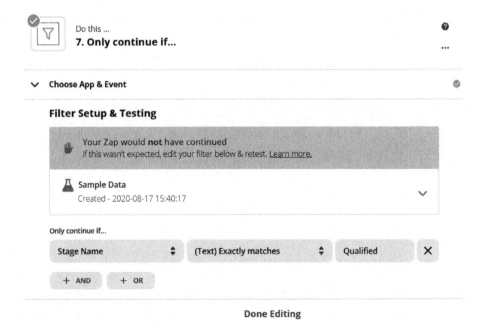

Figure 7.3 – A stopped test filter in the Filter by Zapier app

You can alter your conditions accordingly or click on the **Done Editing** button to continue, then proceed to add one or more action steps.

Now let's explore the different types of filter conditions and use cases.

Understanding filter conditions

Zapier has built multiple conditions into the app to allow you to work with various scenarios. When using the **Choose condition...** drop-down menu from the **Filter Setup & Testing** section, you will be presented with logic options involving five types of filter rules: **Text**, **Number**, **Date/time**, **Boolean, and Generic**. This is shown in the following screenshot:

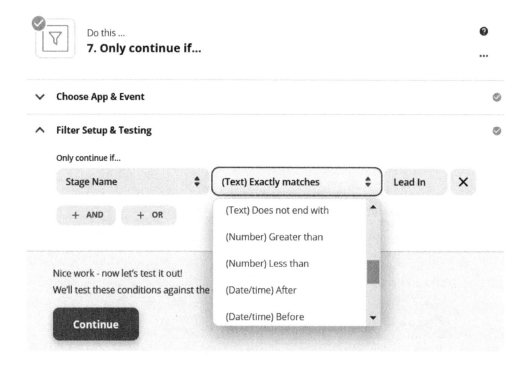

Figure 7.4 – The choice of logic options in the Filter by Zapier app

> **Important note**
> Each condition will only work with the type of filter rule specified in parentheses, unless it is generic.

Let's review each of these filter types in turn.

Text filters

There is a range of text filters to choose from, which can be case-sensitive depending on the type of rule that you use. The only case-sensitive rules are **(Text) Exactly matches** and **(Text) Does not match exactly**.

The following is a list of text filter options:

- **(Text) Contains**: This condition checks whether the dynamic data value contains the reference value.

- **(Text) Does not contain**: This condition is the opposite of **(Text) Contains**, and checks that the dynamic data value does not contain the reference value.

- **(Text) Exactly matches**: This condition checks that the dynamic data value matches the reference value exactly, letter for letter.

- **(Text) Does not exactly match**: This condition checks that the dynamic data value does not match the reference value exactly, letter for letter.

- **(Text) Is in**: This condition checks that the dynamic data value is in a specified list of reference values.

- **(Text) Is not in**: This condition checks that the dynamic data value is not in a specified list of reference values.

- **(Text) Starts with**: This condition checks that the dynamic data value starts with the reference value.

- **(Text) Does not start with**: This condition checks that the dynamic data value does not start with the reference value.

- **(Text) Ends with**: This condition checks that the dynamic data value ends with the reference value.

- **(Text) Does not end with**: This condition checks that the dynamic data value does not end with the reference value.

Next, let's take a look at number filters.

Number filters

In *Chapter 3, Building Your First Automated Workflow (Zap)*, we discussed using number (integer) field types. Number filters work in the same way, and in them, you can only use numeric values, such as 9.5 or 334.

The following is a list of number filter options:

- **(Number) Greater than**: This condition checks whether the dynamic data value is greater than the reference number value.

- **(Number) Less than**: This condition checks whether the dynamic data value is less than the reference number value.

Now, let's review date/time filters.

Date/time filters

In *Chapter 3, Building Your First Automated Workflow (Zap)*, we discussed using date/time field types. Date/time filters work in the same way, and you can use a variety of date/time formats but cannot use text such as today or tomorrow at 9 a.m..

The following is a list of date/time filter options:

- **(Date/time) After**: This condition checks whether the dynamic data value is after the reference date value.

- **(Date/time) Before**: This condition checks whether the dynamic data value is before the reference date value.

- **(Date/time) Equals**: This condition checks whether the dynamic data value is equal (identical) to the reference date value.

Next, let's take a look at Boolean filters.

Boolean filters

As we discussed in *Chapter 3, Building Your First Automated Workflow (Zap)*, Boolean values are either true or false.

The following is a list of Boolean filter options:

- **(Boolean) Is true**: This condition checks whether the dynamic data value is true.

- **(Boolean) Is false**: This condition checks whether the dynamic data value is false.

Finally, let's review generic filters.

Generic filters

Generic filters can be used with any type of field.

The following is a list of generic filter options:

- **Exists**: Checks whether a value exists (can be used with any type of field).

- **Does not exist**: Checks that a value doesn't exist (can be used with any type of field).

You should now have a better understanding of how and when to use the Filter by Zapier app to apply conditional logic to your Zaps. Next, let's dive into using branching logic in your Zaps with the Paths by Zapier built-in app.

Paths by Zapier – adding branching logic to your Zaps

Paths by Zapier allows you to add branching logic to your Zaps. This means that you can allow different paths with different actions to run based on set criteria. This builds on what you learned about using Filter by Zapier and takes it one step further to allow you to create multi-step workflow automation pathways that run depending on what you have specified. Let's look at a few examples of how you would use Paths by Zapier:

- You might be an online retailer with an e-commerce store, and you have various products that need to be processed in a slightly different way. Product A might be a digital product that needs to be sent for printing, shipping, and fulfillment with **Printful**. Product B might require assembly prior to shipping, and you need to notify the warehouse team by email, add a card to Trello, and print a shipping note.

- You might have a **Gravity Forms** form on your website for customer service queries, and you allow customers to specify whether their question is related to training, technical issues, or billing. Each support query is dealt with by a different team in the business, so you might want each query to be routed to a different department by sending a Slack message to a department channel and assigning a task in **Asana** to all the members of that team.

In both of these examples, you can use Paths by Zapier to create conditions to allow each pathway to run only if those criteria were satisfied. To help you visualize what this might look like, I've created a simple workflow diagram that represents the second example previously:

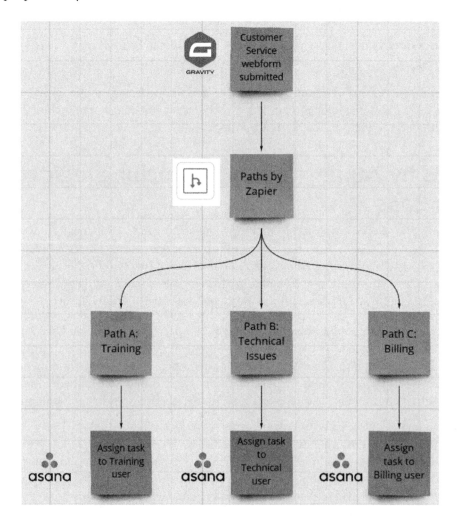

Figure 7.5 – A visualization of a workflow using Paths by Zapier

Paths by Zapier is best used with simple logic; however, once you are more familiar with using it, the two main things to bear in mind are that you can only use Paths by Zapier at the end of a workflow and you are limited to creating three branches to start with. In order to get access to more branches, the account admin user will need to contact Zapier Support. With this being said, you can use multiple Paths by Zapier apps within each path to increase your range.

> **Important note**
>
> Zapier does have a hard limit of 10 branches per path to ensure stability in the Zap editor and prevent long run times with potential time-outs. In addition, Zapier recommends only using three branches with three additional nested paths within each branch. The larger the Zap and the more complex it is, the greater the chance of validation problems and you may not be able to turn your Zap on. Typically, the lower the number of branches, the better the performance of the Zap. In general, the more complex your scenarios, the more risk there is for errors and data corruption. This is a reminder to keep it simple!

Creating complex pathways does require a logical assessment of what conditions are required for each, and it is recommended that you map them out. Here are a few things to consider when thinking about using branching logic:

- *Map out your processes visually*: Refer to *Chapter 2, Preparing to Automate Your Processes*, and use process mapping techniques to visualize your process and strategize the conditional logic prior to creating paths.

- *Plan for the future*: Ask yourself whether there may be a possibility of other conditions being presented later, as this might require you to add additional paths later, bearing in mind the restriction on the number of branches you can add.

This will save you time in the long run if you get it right the first time around.

> **Tip**
>
> If you are not subscribed to a Zapier plan that supports Paths by Zapier, you can use a Filter by Zapier step as a compromise. If your workflow is simple enough, you can replicate a process that would otherwise use Paths by Zapier. You can do this by creating multiple Zaps that run based on the same trigger and placing a filter directly after the trigger step. The filter in each workflow would have the different filter criteria in each Zap, therefore replicating those criteria specified in each branch filter of the Paths by Zapier step. Using this workaround is also appropriate if you need to add more than three unique pathways.

Now let's review how to set up the Paths by Zapier built-in app.

Setting up the Paths by Zapier app

To get started with using Paths by Zapier, add the Paths by Zapier app to the end of your workflow, by either selecting the **Action** step or clicking on the + icon. You will be presented with two pathway options, named **Path A** and **Path B**. This is shown in the following screenshot:

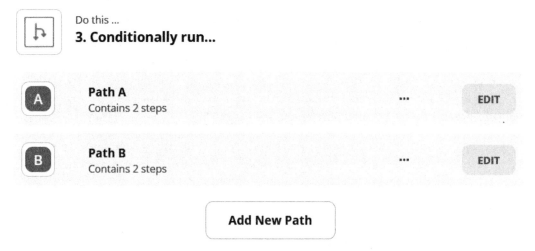

Figure 7.6 – Setting up branches using the Paths by Zapier app

In this section, you will see the following option below the list of path branches:

- **Add New Path**: Clicking on this button will allow you to create one further path branch.

You will also see the following options within each path block:

- **Three dots icon**: Clicking on this icon will show two options in a drop-down menu: **Rename…** and **Delete….** Selecting **Rename…** will allow you to rename the path, and selecting **Delete…** will allow you to delete individual branch paths.
- **Edit**: Clicking on this button will allow you to move on to the next step of the path-building process.

Next, let's review how to customize a path.

Customizing a path

Choose one path to work on first, for example, **Path A**, and click on the **Edit** button in that block to proceed to customize the filter conditions for that path. You will be presented with a pop-up screen as shown in the following screenshot:

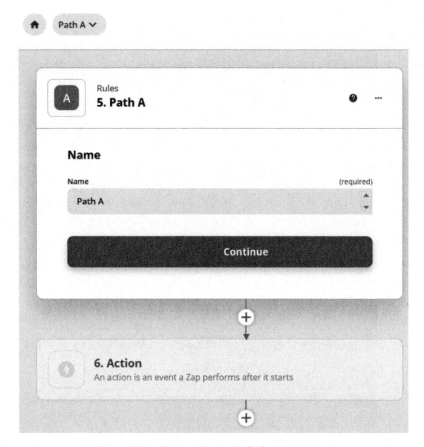

Figure 7.7 – Customizing a Paths by Zapier step

Next, let's take a look at the navigational options from within a path.

Navigating within a path

You will be presented with the following navigational options in the top bar:

- **House icon**: Clicking on this icon will take you back to the main view of the Zap editor showing your Zap steps.

- **Path menu**: Clicking on this menu will present a drop-down menu of paths. You can navigate easily between your paths using this option.

- **Cross icon**: Clicking on this icon closes the popup and takes you back to the main view of the Zap editor.

Now, let's review how to customize a path.

Customizing the first step in the path

The first step of the path now represents a combination of a trigger and a filter for subsequent action steps in the branch.

Work through the following steps to customize your path:

1. In the **Name** section, rename your path. This field is required for the Zap to run. It cannot be left blank.

    As we discussed in *Chapter 3*, *Building Your First Automated Workflow (Zap)*, naming steps in your Zaps will help you to keep track of what each step of your workflow does and makes it easier to find steps and data results from those steps further down your workflow. This is equally important when using Paths by Zapier, as naming each path properly can help you to summarize your filter conditions. Then, click the **Continue** button.

2. Use the instructions we covered in the *Filter by Zapier – applying conditional logic* section to customize your path filter accordingly in the **Rules Setup & Testing** section. Then, click the **Continue** button to test the conditions against example data.

3. Alter your conditions accordingly or click on the **Done Editing** button to continue.

4. Proceed to add one or more action steps.

You should now have a better understanding of how and when to use the Paths by Zapier built-in app. Now, let's take a look at how to use the Delay by Zapier app to add time delays to your Zaps.

Delay by Zapier – adding delays to your Zaps

The Delay by Zapier app allows you to add time delays to subsequent action steps. This can be extremely useful in both simple and more complex workflows where you may want to prevent further action steps from running for a set period of time or until a specific time.

> **Important note**
> The maximum time a delayed task can be held is one month, that is, 31 days.

This app can only be used as an action step and added after a trigger step or between action steps to delay the running of subsequent action steps. The following action events are available to use:

- **Delay For** (action)
- **Delay Until** (action)
- **Delay After Queue** (action)

Let's look at each one of these.

The Delay For action event

This action event waits for a set amount of time before running any further actions in the Zaps. Here are a few examples of how to use the Delay by Zapier **Delay For** action event:

- When a **Typeform** webform has been submitted, send an email with Gmail after a delay of 10 minutes.
- When a new row is added to a **Microsoft Excel** spreadsheet, add new tasks to Microsoft To-Do after a delay of 1 hour.

Let's explore how to set up this action event.

Setting up the Delay For action event

Once you have added an action step either by selecting the **Action** step or clicking on the + icon and chosen **Delay by Zapier** as the app and **Delay For** as the action event, you can then edit the fields in the **Set up action** section as follows:

- **Time Delayed For (value)**: Enter a number with or without a decimal as required by this decimal field type. The minimum delay you can add is 1 minute.
- **Time Delayed For (unit)**: Choose a unit of either minutes, hours, days, or weeks from the drop-down menu, or add dynamic data from previous steps using the **Custom** tab.

These are both required fields and must have values in order for the Zap to run.

An example of this is shown in the following screenshot:

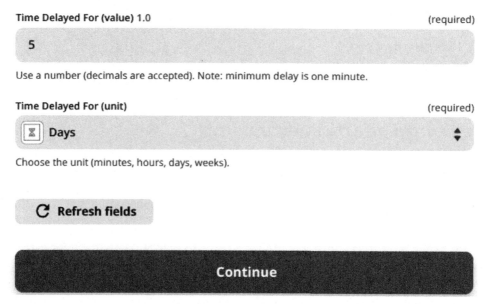

Figure 7.8 – Customizing the Delay For action event

You can then use the **Test action** section to test this step, or **Skip Test**. Proceed to add one or more action steps after your delay step.

You should now be able to use the **Delay For** action event. Next, let's have a look at the **Delay Until** action event.

The Delay Until action event

This action event waits to run any further actions until a time or date you choose. Here are a few examples of how to use the Delay by Zapier **Delay Until** action event:

- When a task is completed in **Asana**, send a Slack message at 2 p.m. that day.

- When an image or video has been added to **Instagram**, send a tweet on Twitter the next day at noon.

Let's explore how to set up this action event.

Setting up the Delay Until action event

Once you have added an action step either by selecting the **Action** step or clicking on the
+ icon and chosen **Delay by Zapier** as the app and **Delay Until** as the action event, you
can then edit the fields in the **Set up action** section as follows:

- **Date/Time Delayed Until**: Use the date/time field type format examples we covered
  in *Chapter 3, Building Your First Automated Workflow (Zap)*, to enter a relative static
  date/time value for this field type or a dynamic date/time value from previous steps.
  For example, you may want to delay until a time specified in your trigger app, such as
  a due date. This is a required field and must have a value in order for the Zap to run.

- **How Should We Handle Dates in The Past?**: This field controls how the delay will
  run if the **Date/Time Delayed Until** field value contains a date/time in the past.
  Choose an option from the drop-down menu to allow the delay task to continue
  if the value is either 15 minutes, 1 hour, or 1 day in the past, or to always continue
  regardless. The default is **Continue if it's up to one day (default)**.

An example of this is shown in the following screenshot:

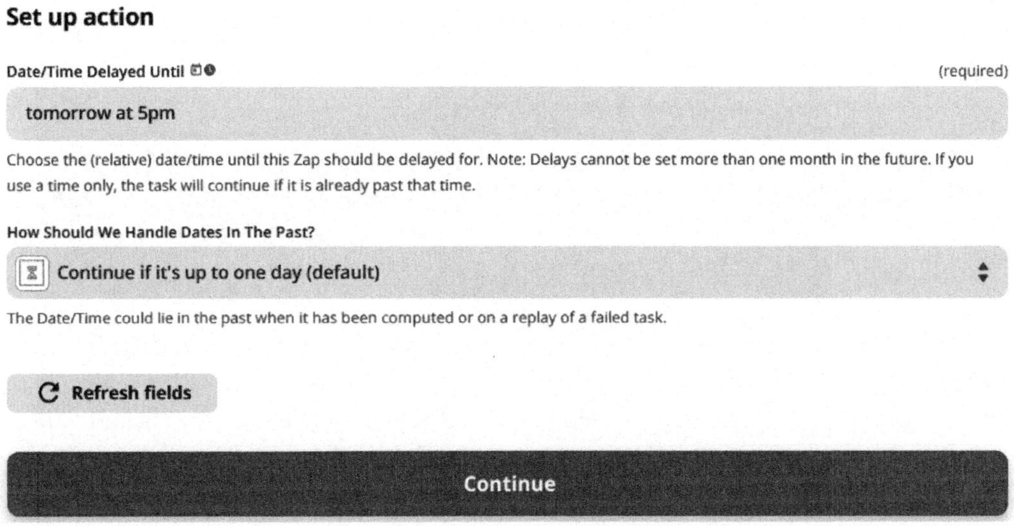

Set up action

Date/Time Delayed Until 🗓❶   (required)

> tomorrow at 5pm

Choose the (relative) date/time until this Zap should be delayed for. Note: Delays cannot be set more than one month in the future. If you
use a time only, the task will continue if it is already past that time.

How Should We Handle Dates In The Past?

> 🛈 Continue if it's up to one day (default)   ⬍

The Date/Time could lie in the past when it has been computed or on a replay of a failed task.

↻ **Refresh fields**

> Continue

Figure 7.9 – Customizing the Delay Until action event

You can then use the **Test action** section to test this step, or **Skip Test**. Proceed to add one or more action steps after your delay step.

> **Important note**
>
> When using times by themselves, if the time has already passed, the delay task will complete immediately, and subsequent actions will run. To prevent this from happening, you could add in a Filter by Zapier step after the Schedule by Zapier **Delay Until** action step where you can specify that you do not want the Zap to continue if the time the Zap triggers is older than the time you specify in your **Delay Until** step.

You should now be able to use the **Delay Until** action event. Next, let's review the **Delay After Queue** action event.

The Delay After Queue action event

This action event waits a set amount of time after other delays in the Zap before running any further actions in the Zaps. This option will only be available to use if there are other delay steps already in the Zap or if tasks in a Zap or multiple Zaps are likely to run in parallel with each other, and you only want them to run in a series. The Zap will be delayed for a set period of time after the last delay in the series.

For example, you might want to send a series of emails to a customer after specified delays when an opportunity changes stage in Salesforce. In this example, you can use the Delay by Zapier **Delay After Queue** action event to run 10 days after all the other delays have completed.

Let's explore how to set up this action event.

Setting up the Delay After Queue action event

Once you have added an action step either by selecting the **Action** step or clicking on the + icon and chosen **Delay by Zapier** as the app and **Delay After Queue** as the action event, you can then edit the fields in the **Set up action** section as follows:

- **Queue Title**: Enter a title of up to 32 characters for the queue using static or dynamic data. This field is optional.

- **Time Delayed For (value)**: Enter a number with or without a decimal as required by this decimal field type. The minimum delay you can add is 1 minute. This is a required field and must have a value in order for the Zap to run.

- **Time Delayed For (unit)**: Choose a unit of either minutes, hours, days, or weeks from the drop-down menu. This is a required field and must have a value in order for the Zap to run.

An example of this is shown in the following screenshot:

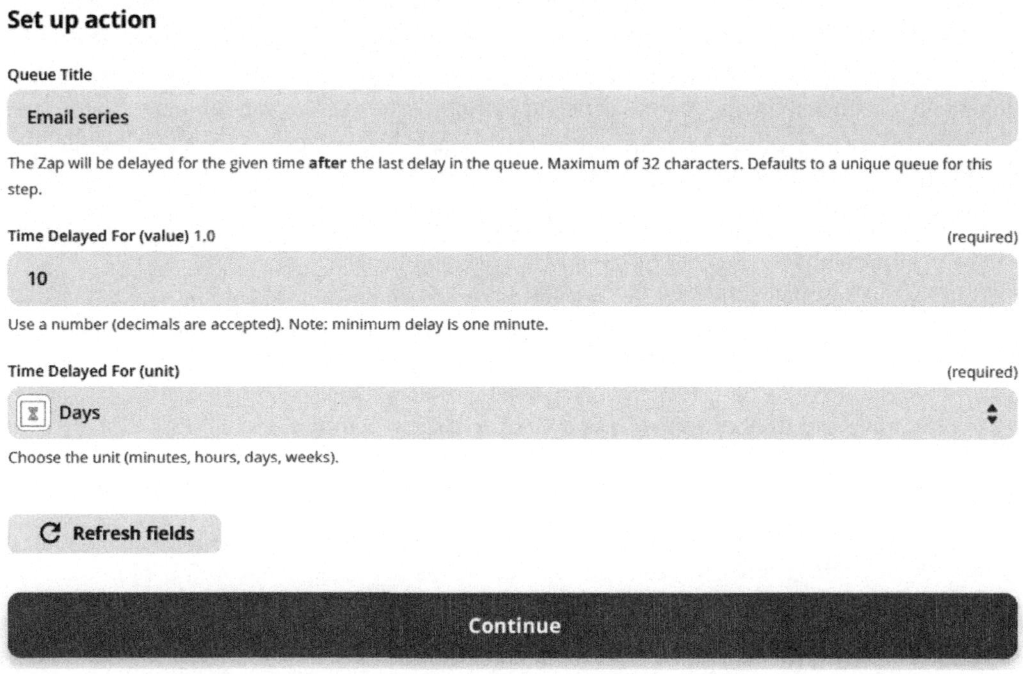

Set up action

Queue Title

> Email series

The Zap will be delayed for the given time **after** the last delay in the queue. Maximum of 32 characters. Defaults to a unique queue for this step.

Time Delayed For (value) 1.0   (required)

> 10

Use a number (decimals are accepted). Note: minimum delay is one minute.

Time Delayed For (unit)   (required)

> ⏳ Days   ▲▼

Choose the unit (minutes, hours, days, weeks).

> C **Refresh fields**

> **Continue**

Figure 7.10 – Customizing the Delay After Queue action event

Use the **Test action** section to test this step and ensure your conditions will be met. Proceed to add one or more action steps after your delay step.

You should now have a better understanding of how and when to use the **Delay After Queue** action event as well as the other Delay by Zapier built-in app action events. Let's now dive into using the Schedule by Zapier app to allow your Zaps to run at scheduled intervals.

Schedule by Zapier – scheduling your Zaps to run at intervals

The Schedule by Zapier app allows you to run a workflow at set times, such as every hour, every day at a certain time, every week on a certain day and time, or every month on a certain day and time. This is useful if you want to automate a series of repetitive tasks at specified times rather than using a traditional event in an app triggering the workflow. This Zapier built-in app can only be used as a trigger step at the start of your workflow, replacing a traditional trigger step. When specifying times in the Schedule by Zapier app, you can use custom values in the formats hh:mm aa, hh:mm, or hhmm, for example, 1:30 pm, 13:30, or 1330.

> **Important note**
>
> When specifying times, your Zaps will trigger based on your account or Zap timezone settings. If no timezone has been specified, the default run time will be UTC (GMT +00:00). Use the instructions in *Chapter 1*, *Introduction to Business Process Automation with Zapier*, to change your account timezone settings and *Chapter 4*, *Managing Your Zaps*, for Zap settings.

You can trigger your workflows to run as follows:

- **Every Hour** (trigger)
- **Every Day** (trigger)
- **Every Week** (trigger)
- **Every Month** (trigger)

Let's look at each one of these.

The Every Hour trigger event

This trigger event can be used to start a workflow every hour on weekdays and weekends, if you choose. This event is the most basic one out of the four scheduling trigger events.

Here are a few examples of how to use the Schedule by Zapier **Every Hour** trigger event:

- Add new tasks to **Basecamp 3** every hour.
- Send a Slack message reminder every hour when calendar events are due.

Let's explore how to set up this trigger event.

Setting up the Every Hour trigger event

Once you have added a trigger step to the start of your workflow by selecting **1. Trigger** and chosen **Schedule by Zapier** as the app and **Every Hour** as the trigger event, you can then edit the fields in the **Set up trigger** section as follows:

- **Trigger On Weekends?**: This field controls whether you want your Zap to be triggered on the weekends or not. Use the Boolean field drop-down menu to choose between **Yes**, if you want it to trigger on Saturdays and Sundays, or **No** if you only want it to trigger from Monday to Friday.

This is shown in the following screenshot:

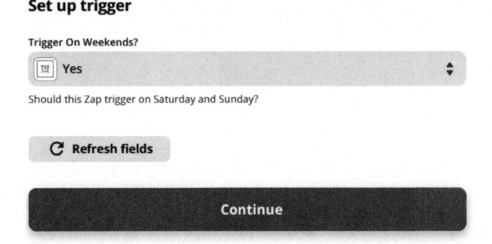

Figure 7.11 – Customizing the Every Hour trigger event

You can then use the **Test trigger** section to test the trigger and retrieve some data to use in your action steps. Proceed to add one or more action steps to your Zap using data from this trigger step.

> **Tip**
> You could use Filter by Zapier to allow your scheduled Zaps to continue if you only wanted them to run during business hours, for example, from 9 a.m. to 5 p.m.

You should now be able to use the **Every Hour** trigger event in a workflow. Next, let's review the **Every Day** trigger event.

The Every Day trigger event

This trigger event can be used to start a workflow every day at a certain time. Here are a few examples of how to use the Schedule by Zapier **Every Day** trigger event:

- Add daily notes to **Zoho Notebook** at 9 a.m. every weekday.

- Post a random GIF from GIPHY to a **Microsoft Teams** channel every day at 11 a.m.

Let's explore how to set up this trigger event.

Setting up the Every Hour trigger event

Once you have added a trigger step to the start of your workflow by selecting **1. Trigger** and chosen **Schedule by Zapier** as the app and **Every Day** as the trigger event, you can then edit the fields in the **Set up trigger** section as follows:

- **Trigger On Weekends?**: As with the **Every Hour** trigger event, this field controls whether your Zap will trigger on the weekend days or not. Use the Boolean field drop-down menu to choose between **Yes** if you want it to trigger on Saturdays and Sundays or **No** if you only want it to trigger from Monday to Friday.

- **Time of Day**: Use this field to specify what time you want your Zap to run at. The drop-down menu offers hourly time options from midnight to 11 p.m. You can also use the **Custom** header option to type in a custom value using the formats hh:mm aa, hh:mm, or hhmm, such as 11:45. This is a required field and must have a value in order for the Zap to run.

This is shown in the following screenshot:

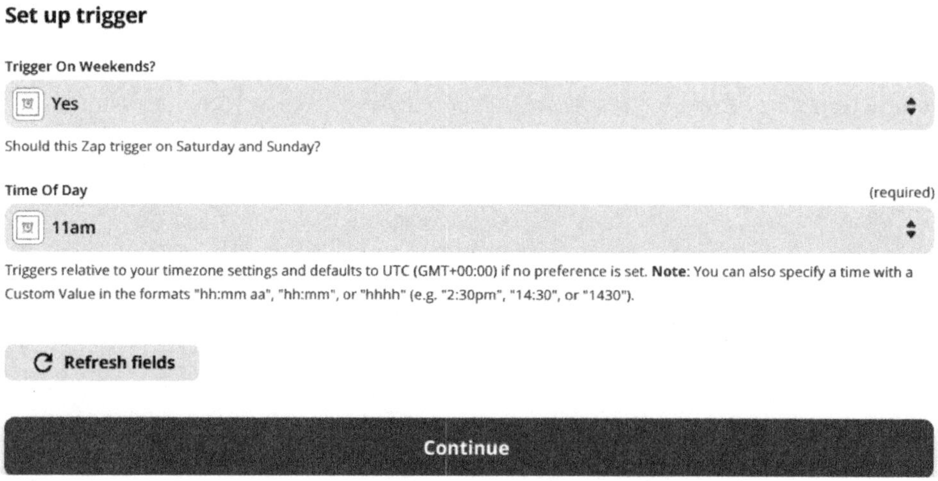

Set up trigger

Trigger On Weekends?

```
🗓  Yes                                                              ⬍
```

Should this Zap trigger on Saturday and Sunday?

Time Of Day   (required)

```
🗓  11am                                                             ⬍
```

Triggers relative to your timezone settings and defaults to UTC (GMT+00:00) if no preference is set. **Note:** You can also specify a time with a Custom Value in the formats "hh:mm aa", "hh:mm", or "hhhh" (e.g. "2:30pm", "14:30", or "1430").

⟳ **Refresh fields**

Continue

Figure 7.12 – Customizing the Every Day trigger event

You can then use the **Test trigger** section to test the trigger and retrieve some data to use in your action steps. Proceed to add one or more action steps to your Zap using data from this trigger step.

You should now be able to use the **Every Day** trigger event in a workflow. Next, let's review the **Every Week** trigger event.

The Every Week trigger event

This trigger event can be used to start a workflow every week on a day and time of your choice. Here are a few examples of how to use the Schedule by Zapier **Every Week** trigger event:

- Add new tasks to **MeisterTask** every week on a Monday at 8 a.m.

- Send an SMS reminder to yourself every week on a Wednesday at 2 p.m.

Let's explore how to set up this trigger event.

Setting up the Every Week trigger event

Once you have added a trigger step to the start of your workflow by selecting **1. Trigger** and chosen **Schedule by Zapier** as the app and **Every Week** as the trigger event, you can then edit the fields in the **Set up trigger** section as follows:

- **Day Of The Week**: This field controls which day of the week your Zap will trigger on. Use the drop-down menu to choose days from **Monday** to **Sunday**.

- **Time of Day**: As with the **Every Day** trigger event, use this field to specify what time you want your Zap to run at. The drop-down menu offers hourly time options from midnight to 11 p.m. You can also use the **Custom** header option to type in a custom value using the formats hh:mm aa, hh:mm, or hhmm, such as 13:30.

Both these fields are required and must have a value in order for the Zap to run.

This is shown in the following screenshot:

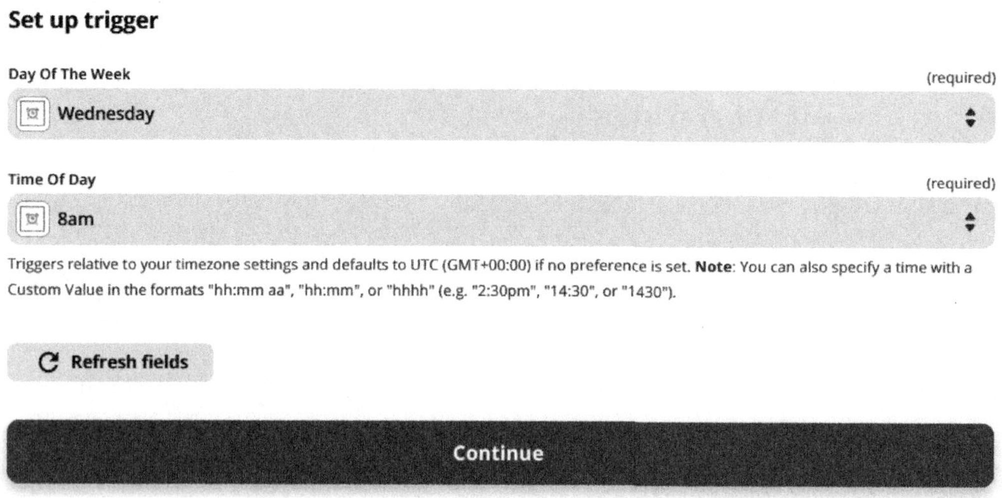

Set up trigger

Day Of The Week   (required)

⌨ Wednesday   ⬍

Time Of Day   (required)

⌨ 8am   ⬍

Triggers relative to your timezone settings and defaults to UTC (GMT+00:00) if no preference is set. **Note**: You can also specify a time with a Custom Value in the formats "hh:mm aa", "hh:mm", or "hhhh" (e.g. "2:30pm", "14:30", or "1430").

C **Refresh fields**

Continue

Figure 7.13 – Customizing the Every Week trigger event

You can then use the **Test trigger** section to test the trigger and retrieve some data to use in your action steps. Proceed to add one or more action steps to your Zap using data from this trigger step.

You should now be able to use the **Every Week** trigger event in a workflow. Next, let's review the **Every Month** trigger event.

The Every Month trigger event

This trigger event can be used to start a workflow every month on a date and time of your choice. Here are a few examples of how to use the Schedule by Zapier **Every Month** trigger event:

- Send a monthly recurring invoice to a customer on the 15th day of every month at 9 a.m.

- Send a reminder email to a customer and a follow-up task in **Todoist** on the first day of every month at 2 p.m.

Let's explore how to set up this trigger event.

Setting up the Every Month trigger event

Once you have added a trigger step to the start of your workflow by selecting **1. Trigger** and chosen **Schedule by Zapier** as the app and **Every Month** as the trigger event, you can then edit the fields in the **Set up trigger** section as follows:

- **Day Of The Month**: This field controls which day of the month your Zap will trigger on. Use the drop-down menu to choose dates from **1** to **31**.

- **Time of Day**: As with the **Every Day** and **Every Week** trigger events, use this field to specify what time you want your Zap to run at. The drop-down menu offers hourly time options from midnight to 11 p.m. You can also use the **Custom** header option to type in a custom value using the formats hh:mm aa, hh:mm, or hhmm, such as 9:15 pm.

Both these fields are required and must have a value in order for the Zap to run.

This is shown in the following screenshot:

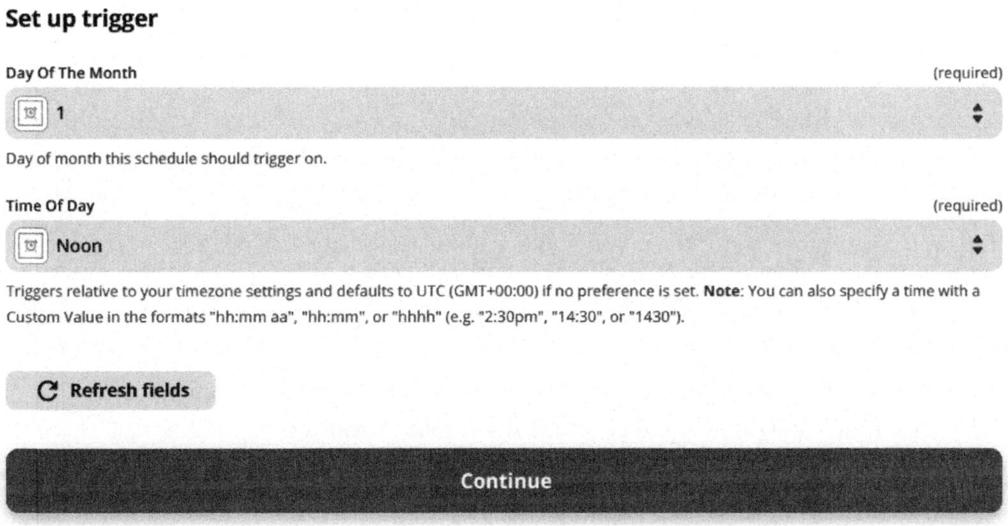

Set up trigger

Day Of The Month   (required)

    [📅] 1   ▲▼

Day of month this schedule should trigger on.

Time Of Day   (required)

    [📅] Noon   ▲▼

Triggers relative to your timezone settings and defaults to UTC (GMT+00:00) if no preference is set. **Note**: You can also specify a time with a Custom Value in the formats "hh:mm aa", "hh:mm", or "hhhh" (e.g. "2:30pm", "14:30", or "1430").

    ↻ **Refresh fields**

    Continue

Figure 7.14 – Customizing the Every Month trigger event

You can then use the **Test trigger** section to test the trigger and retrieve some data to use in your action steps. Proceed to add one or more action steps to your Zap using data from this trigger step.

You should now have a better understanding of how and when to use the **Every Month** trigger event, as well as the other Schedule by Zapier built-in app trigger events.

Now, let's review an example of how to create a multi-step Zap with a schedule, search, filter, and delay.

Exercise – creating a multi-step Zap with a scheduled trigger, search action, filter, path, and delay

You can use one of the processes that you defined in *Chapter 2, Preparing to Automate Your Processes*, to work through the content in this section, if appropriate. Try to incorporate multiple apps in your workflow.

You can perform actions with existing data in your apps at a certain time by using Schedule by Zapier as a trigger, adding a search action step to find existing data in an app, stopping your Zap from running if it doesn't meet certain conditions, delaying your workflow for a specified amount of time, and then adding in branching logic if the scenarios you need to run differ. For example, you might use an Airtable base to collaborate with your **Social Media Manager** (**SMM**) for social media posting. When the SMM adds a post to the base record, you approve it or reject it. You may want to add new posts to a Facebook group and a LinkedIn company page every weekday at 9 a.m, but only if the post has been approved. As Facebook and LinkedIn require slightly different formatting, you might also need to use different logic in your workflows. You also want to reshare the LinkedIn company post on your personal page, but only 2 hours later, as you know your personal page connections are more engaged with your posts at that time.

Here is an example of a workflow you could build to automate this process:

1. *Trigger*: Add the Schedule by Zapier **Every Day** event trigger to run on weekdays at 9 a.m.

2. *Action*: Add a **Find Record** search action to search Airtable base records for the date. Only allow the Zap to continue if a record is found.

3. *Action*: Add a filter with Filter by Zapier to only allow the Zap to continue if the **Approved** field is marked as Yes.

4. *Action*: Add two branches in Path by Zapier where **Path A** will continue only if the **Platform** field is Facebook, and **Path B** will continue only if the **Platform** field is LinkedIn.

5. *Action – Path A*: Add a **Post Message** action in **Facebook Groups**.

6. *Action – Path B*: Add a **Create Company Update** action event in LinkedIn.

7. *Action – Path B*: Add a Delay by Zapier **Delay For** action step where you specify the delay for 2 hours. You could also use the **Delay Until** action event specifying the run time as 11 a.m.

8. *Action – Path B*: Add a **Create Share Update** action event in **LinkedIn**.

Unfortunately, Zapier does not allow sharing of Zap templates with Paths by Zapier steps, so we're unable to share a Zap template with you. Try building out a similar process by repeating this exercise for any appropriate processes that you have documented and that would benefit from automation.

You should now have a better understanding of how and when to use filters, paths, schedules, and delays in your Zaps.

Summary

In this chapter, we introduced four commonly used Zapier built-in apps to help you to add conditional logic and run conditions to your workflows. First, we covered how to use conditional logic in our workflows by using the Filter by Zapier app. Next, we reviewed how to use branching logic with the Paths by Zapier app. Then, we explored how to use time delays in Zaps using the Delay by Zapier app, and how to schedule our workflows to run at specific times by using the Schedule by Zapier app. Lastly, we went through an exercise to demonstrate the use of scheduled triggers, search actions, filters, paths, and delays.

You now have a better understanding of how to use filters, paths, delays, and schedules in your workflow automations.

In the next chapter, you will learn about the four communication-specific built-in Zapier apps; we will give descriptions of their functionality and provide practical tips on how to use them. First, we will cover how to send text messages using the SMS by Zapier app. Then, we will dive into how to trigger workflows on receipt of emails and read emails, as well as how to send emails using the Email by Zapier app. Lastly, we will take a look at using IMAP by Zapier and SMTP by Zapier to retrieve and send emails from mail servers.

8
Built-In Communication Apps

Communicating with your team and clients is an integral part of running any business. Using the digital communication technology that we have available to us can only help to make operations smoother and more productive. Most companies that exist today use email to communicate with their teams, customers, suppliers, and, on a personal level, with friends. Some companies will take things one step further and use mobile phone text messaging for marketing purposes or sending automated reminders for meetings, for example. There are many email messaging and text messaging apps available on the market, many of which integrate with Zapier, so you are able to automate email and text messaging processes, some at a cost. You may, however, want to send simple messages by email or text, at no extra cost to you and in situations where you don't need to retain history. This is where Zapier's four built-in communication apps (**SMS**, **Email**, **IMAP**, and **SMTP**) come into play.

In this chapter, we introduce the four communication-specific built-in Zapier apps, give descriptions of their functionality, and provide practical tips on how to use them. First, we cover how to send text messages using the SMS by Zapier app. Then, we dive into how to trigger workflows on receipt of emails and read emails, as well as how to send emails using the Email by Zapier app. Lastly, we take a look at using IMAP by Zapier and SMTP by Zapier to retrieve and send emails from mail servers.

We will cover the following key topics in this chapter:

- SMS by Zapier – sending text messages

- Email by Zapier – sending and receiving emails

- SMTP by Zapier – sending emails through mail servers

- IMAP by Zapier – retrieving emails from mail servers

Once you have worked through each of these topics, you will know how to send text messages and emails, as well as sending and receiving emails from mail servers.

Technical requirements

To work through the content in this chapter, you will need access to a Zapier account. To build multi-step Zaps, you will need to subscribe to the Zapier Starter plan as a minimum.

SMS by Zapier – sending text messages

Using the SMS by Zapier built-in app, you can send 153-character-length text messages by **SMS (Short Message Service)** through mobile phone cellular networks. This app allows you to send a limited number of SMS messages to specified UK or US numbers that you own or have access to. Although you can't use the app for mass marketing or external reminders, it is useful for sending internal team notifications or reminders to yourself. Here are a few examples of how to use the SMS by Zapier app:

- Get an SMS when you make a sale in your Shopify e-commerce store.

- Get an SMS reminder before a **Google Calendar** meeting event.

- Get a daily SMS with the day's weather prediction using Weather by Zapier.

These are just a few ways to use SMS by Zapier; however; the possibilities are endless.

You can use the SMS by Zapier app in combination with other Zapier built-in apps that we covered in *Chapter 7, Getting Started with Built-In Apps*, as follows:

- Use Filter by Zapier to specify what conditions must be present for messages to be sent, for example, if you wanted to receive an SMS only if you sold a high-value item in your **WooCommerce** e-commerce store.

- Send SMS messages at a specific time using Schedule by Zapier.

- Send SMS messages after a certain period using Delay by Zapier.

SMS by Zapier is included in your Zapier subscription at no extra cost. However, if you want to send SMS messages to a variety of numbers, to international numbers, or in large quantities, you may want to try other apps that integrate with Zapier, such as **Twilio**, **TextMagic,** or **Voodoo SMS**.

Let's explore how to set up this built-in app so that we can start sending our SMS notifications.

Setting up SMS by Zapier

Once you have added an action step and chosen **SMS by Zapier** as the app, you will be asked to sign in to SMS by Zapier the first time you use it. Click on the **Sign in to SMS by Zapier** button and a popup will appear, asking you to verify a number to send messages to, as follows:

- **To Number**: Enter the full phone number with the area and country code (+44 for the UK and +1 for the US, without the +), for example, 4407565901203. This is a required field to enable the app.

- **Confirm via SMS or Call?**: Choose whether to receive a PIN code by SMS or voice call. This field is optional and will default to sending the PIN code by SMS.

- **Confirm PIN**: Use the **Send PIN** button to send the PIN code. Once received, enter the PIN code into the field that appears. This is a required field to enable the app.

This is shown in the following screenshot:

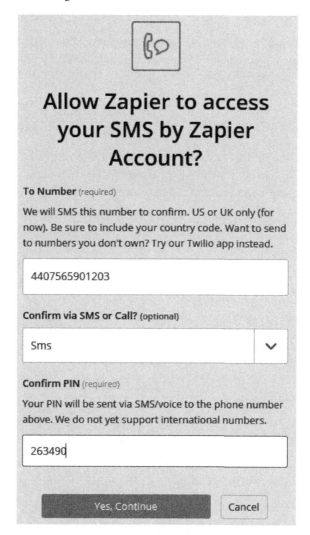

Figure 8.1 – Verifying a phone number in the SMS by Zapier app

Once you have validated your phone number, Zapier will send a confirmation message to you by SMS.

Next, we can proceed to edit the **Set up action** section and fill in the fields as follows:

- **From Number**: Choose from a drop-down list of fixed numbers or select **Random**. When choosing a fixed number, Zapier will attempt to send an SMS from that number; however, if it is unavailable, sending will default to a random number. It is not recommended to choose a custom value, as this may cause the step to error.

- **Message**: Add static text, dynamic data from previous steps, or a combination of both in this field. Messages with over 153 characters will be truncated.

Using our working example from *Chapter 6*, *Creating Multi-Step Zaps and Using Built-In Apps*, we may want to send an SMS to notify us when new deals are added to Pipedrive. We have illustrated how to use static text and dynamic data in the **Message** field in the following screenshot:

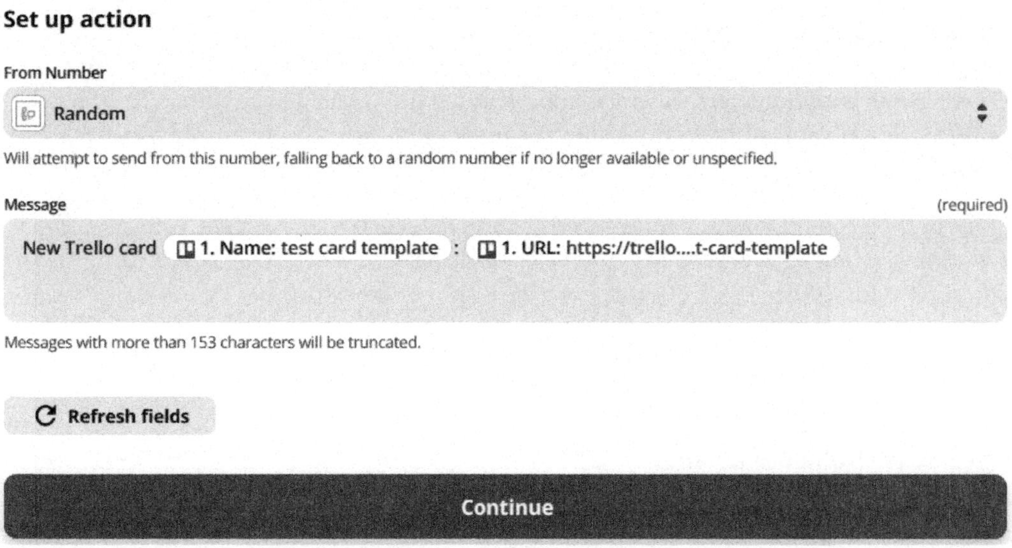

Set up action

From Number

> [○] Random   ▲▼

Will attempt to send from this number, falling back to a random number if no longer available or unspecified.

Message   (required)

> **New Trello card**   [📖] **1. Name: test card template** : [📖] **1. URL: https://trello....t-card-template**

Messages with more than 153 characters will be truncated.

> ↻ **Refresh fields**

> **Continue**

Figure 8.2 – Customizing the Send SMS action event

You can then use the **Test action** section to test this step, or choose **Skip Test**.

Proceed to add one or more action steps to your Zap.

> **Tip**
> For static messages, you can use the **Word Count** function in Microsoft Word or the LEN formula in Microsoft Excel to check how many characters your text message contains. When using dynamic data, to prevent messages from being truncated if they are over 153 characters, you can use the Formatter by Zapier app to transform text, dates/times, and numbers to shorten your data or display it in different ways. For example, you may want to format the Add Time dynamic field value from *Figure 8.2* to be displayed as 07/31/2020. We will cover formatting data with the Formatter by Zapier built-in app in *Chapter 13, Formatting Date and Time, Chapter 14, Formatting Numbers, Chapter 15, Text Formatting Functions in Zapier – Part 1, Chapter 16, Text Formatting Functions in Zapier – Part 2*, and *Chapter 17, Zapier's Utilities Functions*.

You should now have a better understanding of how and when to use the SMS by Zapier built-in app to send SMS messages.

Now let's take a look at how to send and receive emails using the Email by Zapier built-in app.

Email by Zapier – sending and receiving emails

Email by Zapier allows you to send and receive emails to and from a unique `zapiermail.com` email address to use as a trigger or action step. You, therefore, don't have to use your standard email addresses for things such as sending reminders or notifications to yourself or your team or forwarding information to any of your apps using a generic email address.

You can then send outbound emails, and if you've enabled read receipts, you can trigger a workflow when someone opens your sent email. You can also trigger Zaps to run when you receive forwarded emails to the `zapiermail.com` address.

The following trigger and actions events are available to use:

- **New Inbound Email** (trigger)
- **Send Outbound Email** (action)
- **New Read Receipt** (trigger)

Let's look at each one of these.

The New Inbound Email trigger event

This trigger event can be used to start a workflow when a new email has been received. This works by using a unique `zapiermail.com` email address, which you can use as the email recipient. This trigger event is especially handy to use with apps that allow you to create records on receipt of a new email, such as notes, tasks, and saving attachments.

Here are a few examples of how to use the Email by Zapier **New Inbound Email** trigger event:

- Send notes by email to a Slack channel.
- Add new notes to Evernote by email.
- Add new file attachments to **Dropbox** or **Google Drive**.

Let's explore how to set up this trigger event.

Setting up the New Inbound Email trigger event

Once you have added this trigger step to the start of your workflow (to **1. Trigger**) and chosen **Email by Zapier** as the app and **New Inbound Email** as the trigger event, you can then edit the following field in the **Set up trigger** section:

- **Email Address**: This field allows you to customize the unique email address associated with your mailbox. You can use lowercase letters and numbers only. If you want to forward notes to Evernote, you may choose to name the address notes, for example.

This is shown in the following screenshot:

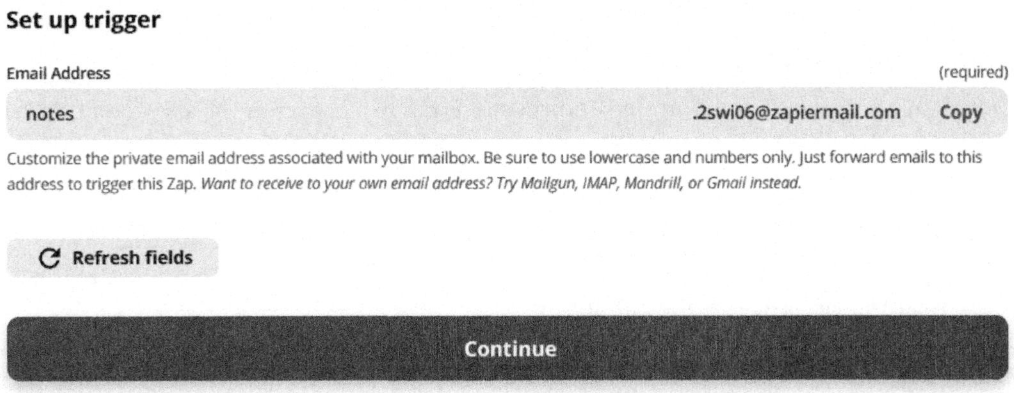

Set up trigger

Email Address	(required)
notes	.2swi06@zapiermail.com Copy

Customize the private email address associated with your mailbox. Be sure to use lowercase and numbers only. Just forward emails to this address to trigger this Zap. *Want to receive to your own email address? Try Mailgun, IMAP, Mandrill, or Gmail instead.*

    C **Refresh fields**

    Continue

Figure 8.3 – Setting up the New Inbound Email trigger event

As illustrated in *Figure 8.3*, our unique mailbox address would be notes.2swi06@zapiermail.com.

You can then click on **Continue** to move on to the **Test trigger** section, where you will be instructed to send an email to your unique email mailbox. Once done, use the **Test Trigger** button and retrieve your test data to use in your action steps.

Proceed to add one or more action steps to your Zap using data from this trigger step.

You should now be able to receive email messages and trigger workflows using the **New Inbound Email** trigger event.

Next, let's take a look at the **Send Outbound Email** action event.

The Send Outbound Email action event

Similar to the SMS by Zapier built-in app, using the Email by Zapier **Send Outbound Email** action event is useful for sending messages, alerts, reminders, and notifications. You can send up to 10 email messages per hour. Here are a few examples of how to use this action event:

- Get an email notification for new Facebook Lead Ad leads.

- Get an email notification when deals in your CRM are lost or won.

- Get an email alert when your Zapier task usage has reached a certain percentage.

Let's explore how to set up this action step.

Setting up the Send Outbound Email action event

Once you have added an action step and chosen **Email by Zapier** as the app and **Send Outbound Email** as the action event, you can then edit the fields in the **Set up action** section as follows:

- **To**: Enter up to five email addresses separated with commas. Use static text or dynamic values from previous steps. This is a required field and must have at least one value in order for the Zap to run.

- **Subject**: Enter a subject for the email using static text or dynamic values from previous steps. This is a required field and must have at least some text in order for the Zap to run.

- **Body (HTML Or Plain)**: Enter the email body using customizable **HTML (Hypertext Markup Language)** or plain text. You can use static text or dynamic values from previous steps. When using plain text, Zapier will attempt to convert it to basic HTML so that it looks more pleasing to the eye; alternatively, you can use free or paid Markdown editor tools such as Haroopad or HackMD to simply and effectively convert plain text to HTML for more customization. This is a required field and must have some character in it in order for the Zap to run.

- **Attachment**: You can attach a file object to the email of up to 10 MB. Attaching plain text content will convert the file to a `.txt` file.

- **From Name**: Enter a name that will be displayed when an email is received. You can use static text or dynamic values from previous steps.

- **Reply To**: Enter an email address that the recipient can reply to.

- **Cc**: Enter up to five email addresses separated with commas as secondary recipients. Use static text or dynamic values from previous steps.

- **Bcc**: Enter up to five email addresses separated with commas as blind secondary recipients. Use static text or dynamic values from previous steps.

- **Force Linebreaks?**: Use this drop-down Boolean field to select the **True** value if you want your emails to be received with line breaks or spacing. Forcing email text to use line breaks and spacing presents the email text with better appearance.

- **Enable Read Receipts?**: Use this drop-down Boolean field to select the **True** value if you want to be notified whether an email sent using this action event is read by the recipient. You must use this in combination with the **New Read Receipt** trigger event (which we will discuss in the next section) and a notification action event, such as an SMS, email, or Slack message, in a separate Zap to enable notifications to be sent.

This is shown in the following screenshot:

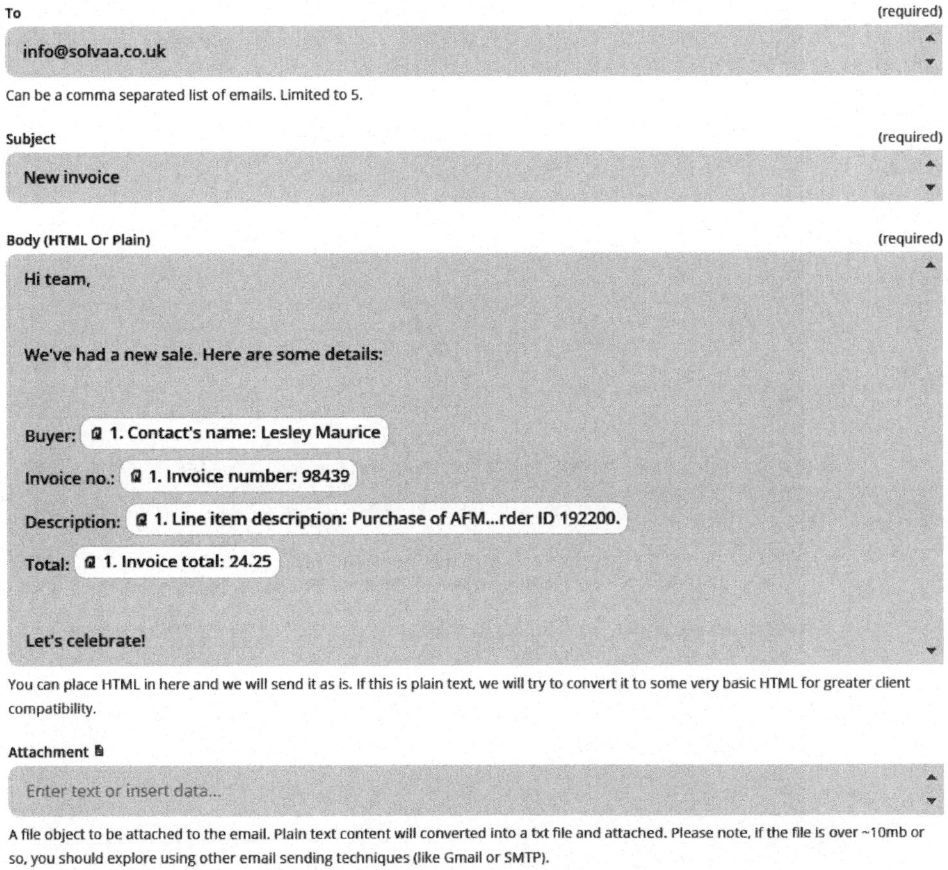

Figure 8.4 – Setting up the Send Outbound Email action event in the Email by Zapier app (1)

The second part of the step customization is shown in the following screenshot:

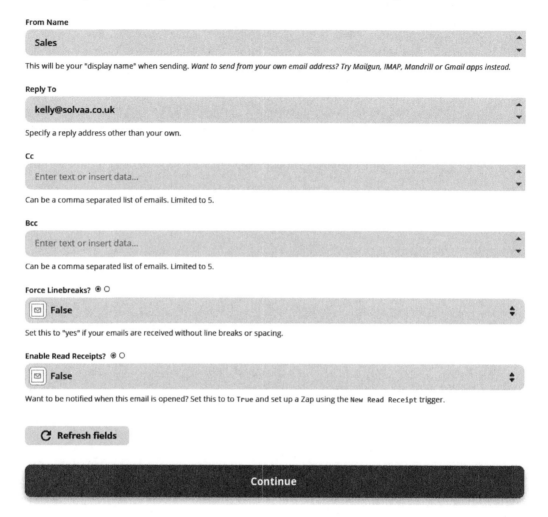

Figure 8.5 – Setting up the Send Outbound Email action event in the Email by Zapier app (2)

You can then use the **Test action** section to test this step, or choose **Skip Test**.

> **Tip**
> You can use other email sending apps such as Gmail, Microsoft Outlook, Mandrill, or SMTP by Zapier if you want to send emails to more than five recipients and if you want to send files larger than 10 MB. If you have multiple recipients being added using dynamic data from previous steps, ensure these values are separated by a comma. You can use Formatter by Zapier to alter such email values to ensure they work with the Send Outbound email action event. We will cover formatting data with the Formatter by Zapier built-in app in *Chapter 13, Formatting Date and Time, Chapter 14, Formatting Numbers, Chapter 15, Text Formatting Functions in Zapier – Part 1, Chapter 16, Text Formatting Functions in Zapier – Part 2*, and *Chapter 17, Zapier's Utilities Functions*.

You should now be able to send email messages using the **Send Outbound Email** action event. Next, let's review the **New Read Receipt** trigger event.

The New Read Receipt trigger event

This trigger event can be used to start a workflow when an email sent using the **Send Outbound Email** action event is opened (if the **Enable Read Receipts** Boolean field is set to **True**). This trigger event is useful if you want to keep an eye on when emails have been opened.

Here are a few examples of how to use the Email by Zapier **New Read Receipts** trigger event:

- Send an SMS message when an email has been read.
- Update an opportunity in Salesforce when an email has been read.

Let's explore how to set up this trigger event.

Setting up the New Read Receipt trigger event

Let's work through the following steps to set up the **New Read Receipt** trigger event:

1. To use this trigger event, you must have a corresponding Zap set up that uses the **Send Outbound Email** action event and has the **Enable Read Receipts** Boolean field set to **True**. You can use the instructions in the *The Send Outbound Email action event* section to create this Zap.

2. Once that is done, send a test email to your own email address and view it. This will allow you to use that test data within the **Test trigger** section of the corresponding **New Read Receipt** trigger step in *step 4*.

3. Add this trigger step to the start of your workflow (to **1. Trigger**) and choose **Email by Zapier** as the app and **New Read Receipt** as the trigger event.

4. Next, you can skip the **Set up trigger** section as there are no fields to customize, and then select **Continue** to use the **Test trigger** section. You can use the **Test Trigger** button and retrieve either static test data or test data from your **Send Outbound Email** action step in the other Zap as we did in *step 2*.

You can now proceed to add one or more action steps to your Zap based on your requirements using data from this trigger step.

You should now have a better understanding of how and when to use the **New Read Receipt** trigger event, as well as the other trigger and action events of the Email by Zapier app. Next, let's cover how to send emails from mail servers using the SMTP by Zapier built-in app.

SMTP by Zapier – sending emails through mail servers

Wikipedia (`https://en.wikipedia.org/wiki/Simple_Mail_Transfer_Protocol`) defines **Simple Mail Transfer Protocol (SMTP)** as "a communication protocol for electronic mail transmission." Simply put, SMTP allows email client apps to send emails. Zapier allows you to connect to many commonly used mail clients apps such as Gmail or Zoho Mail. You may, however, have access to your own mail server and want to send emails independently. You can use SMTP by Zapier for precisely that purpose. SMTP by Zapier acts in a similar way to Email by Zapier; however, you can send emails without volume, recipient, and file size restrictions.

It may be useful to elaborate first of all on what the difference is between a mail client and a mail server. The mail server is the software that runs on a computer server that processes email communications, for example, Microsoft Server Exchange. You can read more about mail servers here: `https://en.wikipedia.org/wiki/Comparison_of_mail_servers`.

The mail client, on the other hand, is the software program that you use to view, write, and send your incoming and outgoing emails. You can see a comparison of mail clients here: `https://en.wikipedia.org/wiki/Comparison_of_webmail_providers`.

To send and receive emails you need both a mail client and a mail server.

The following figure shows a list of a few common SMTP settings that may be useful when you set up your SMTP by Zapier app:

Client	Server	Authentication	Port
Googlemail - Gmail	smtp.gmail.com	SSL	465
Googlemail - Gmail	smtp.gmail.com	StartTLS	587
Outlook.com	smtp-mail.outlook.com	StartTLS	587
Office365.com	smtp.office365.com	StartTLS	587
Yahoo Mail	smtp.mail.yahoo.com	SSL	465
Yahoo Mail Plus	plus.smtp.mail.yahoo.com	SSL	465
Yahoo Mail UK	smtp.mail.yahoo.co.uk	SSL	465
Yahoo Mail Deutschland	smtp.mail.yahoo.com	SSL	465
Yahoo Mail AU/NZ	smtp.mail.yahoo.au	SSL	465
AOL.com	smtp.aol.com	StartTLS	587
AT&T	smtp.att.yahoo.com	SSL	465
NTL @ntlworld.com	smtp.ntlworld.com	SSL	465
BT Connect	smtp.btconnect.com		25
O2 Deutschland	mail.o2online.de		25
T-Online Deutschland	securesmtp.t-online.de	StartTLS	587
1&1 (1and1)	smtp.1and1.com	StartTLS	587
1&1 Deutschland	smtp.1und1.de	StartTLS	587
Verizon	outgoing.verizon.net		587
Zoho Mail	smtp.zoho.com	SSL	465
Mail.com	smtp.mail.com	StartTLS	587
GMX.com	smtp.gmx.com	SSL	465
Net@ddress by USA.NET	smtp.postoffice.net	SSL	465

Figure 8.6 – Common SMTP settings (courtesy of Arclab)

You can get more details from this source: `https://www.arclab.com/en/kb/email/list-of-smtp-and-imap-servers-mailserver-list.html`.

Here are a few examples of how to use the SMTP by Zapier app:

- Send an email to customers when they purchase a product in your e-commerce store.
- Send an email alert for new posts on your Facebook page timeline.

As with SMS by Zapier and the **Send Outbound Email** action event of Email by Zapier, you can use SMTP by Zapier in combination with other Zapier built-in apps such as Filter by Zapier, Schedule by Zapier, and Delay by Zapier.

Let's explore how to set up this built-in app so that you can start sending emails.

Setting up the SMTP by Zapier app

Once you have added an action step chosen **SMTP by Zapier** as the app, you will be asked to sign in to SMTP by Zapier the first time you use it. Click on the **Sign in to SMTP by Zapier** button and a popup will appear, asking you to provide details to allow access to your SMTP by Zapier account, as follows:

- **Host**: Enter the host server that Zapier should connect to. This is a required field, and a valid value must be added in order for the Zap to work.

- **Email/Username**: Enter your SMTP login email address or username credentials. This is a required field, and a valid value must be added in order for the Zap to work.

- **Password**: Enter your SMTP password credentials. This is a required field, and a valid value must be added in order for the Zap to work.

- **Use TLS?**: Use this Boolean field dropdown to select **Yes** or **No** to specify whether you send encrypted emails using **Transport Layer Security** (**TLS**). Check your email client account for this information if you are unsure.

- **Port**: Choose a port number from the number (integer) field drop-down menu. If none is selected, **25** will be used as the default. Many SMTP servers send mail over TLS on port 25.

- **From Email**: Enter an email address to display as the email it is being sent from. Sometimes, adding this email address may fail, and you may need to define a specific **From** address.

This is shown in the following screenshot for a Gmail account:

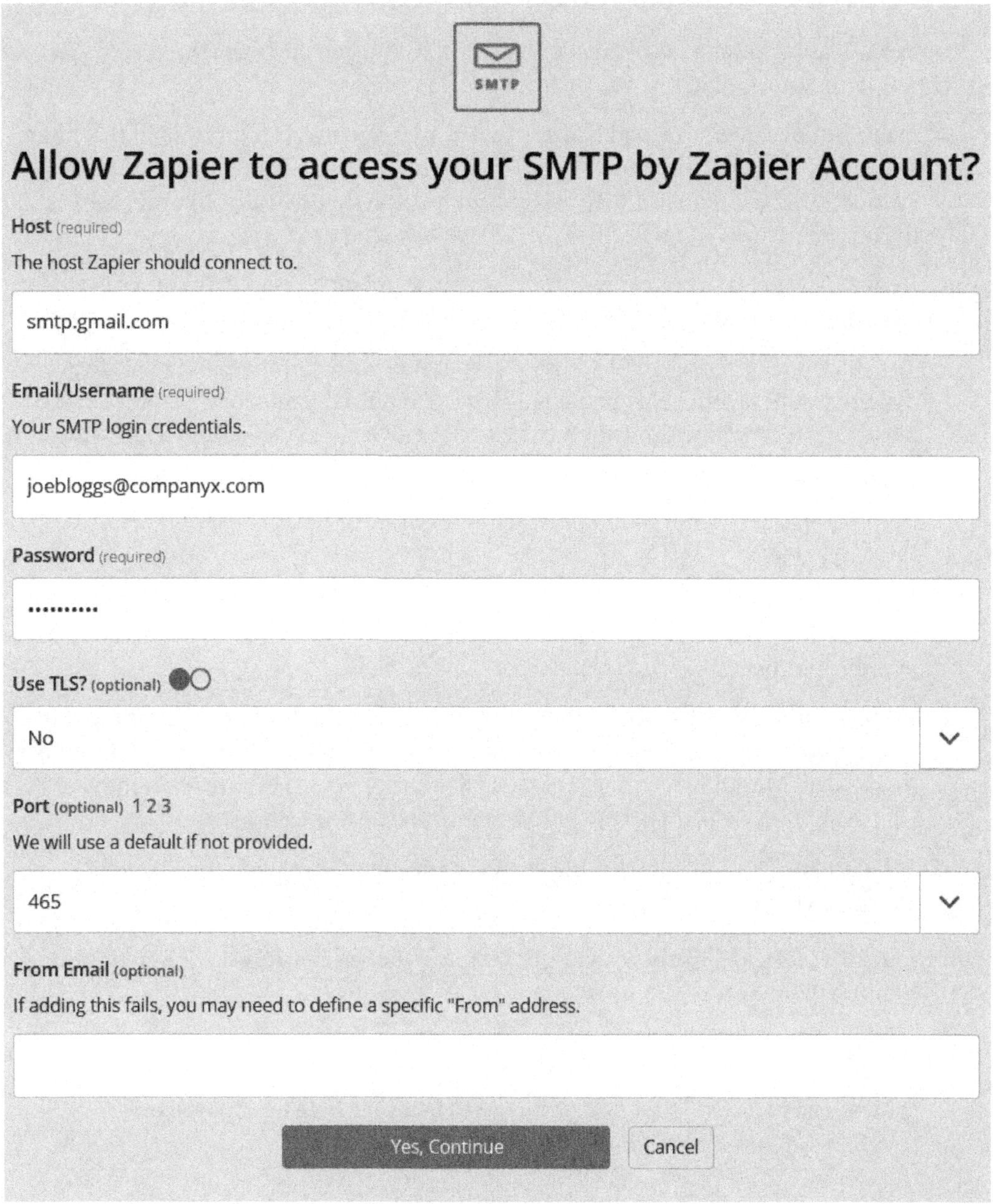

Allow Zapier to access your SMTP by Zapier Account?

Host (required)

The host Zapier should connect to.

> smtp.gmail.com

Email/Username (required)

Your SMTP login credentials.

> joebloggs@companyx.com

Password (required)

> ••••••••••

Use TLS? (optional) ◉○

> No   ⌄

Port (optional) 1 2 3

We will use a default if not provided.

> 465   ⌄

From Email (optional)

If adding this fails, you may need to define a specific "From" address.

>

[Yes, Continue]   [Cancel]

Figure 8.7 – Setting up the SMTP by Zapier app

Once you have clicked on the **Yes, Continue** button, we can proceed to edit the **Set up action** section and fill in the fields as follows:

- **From Name**: Enter a name that will be displayed when an email is received. You can use static text or dynamic values from previous steps.

- **From Email**: Enter an email address that Zapier should attempt to send the email from. Ideally, this email address should match an email address in your SMTP settings. This is a required field and must have at least one value in order for the Zap to run.

- **Reply To**: Enter a specific email address that recipients can reply to other than the from email. Use static text or dynamic values from previous steps.

- **To**: Enter one or more email addresses separated with commas. Use static text or dynamic values from previous steps. This is a required field and must have at least one value in order for the Zap to run.

- **Subject**: Enter a subject for the email using static text or dynamic values from previous steps. This is a required field and must have at least some text in order for the Zap to run.

- **Body**: Enter the email body plain text. You can use static text or dynamic values from the previous steps. This is a required field and must have some character in it in order for the Zap to run.

- **HTML Body**: Enter the email body that you used in the **Body** field duplicated in HTML. You can use static text or dynamic values from previous steps. You can use free or paid Markdown editor tools such as Haroopad or HackMD to simply and effectively convert plain text to HTML for more customization.

- **Attachment**: You can attach a file object to the email. Any plain text content attached will be converted to a `.txt` file.

Once you have selected **Continue**, you can then use the **Test action** section to test this step, or choose **Skip Test**.

> Tip
> Most mail clients will have help documentation giving more information on how to activate IMAP/POP3/SMTP settings.

You should now have a better understanding of how and when to use the SMTP by Zapier app to send emails. Now let's review how to retrieve emails from mail servers using the IMAP by Zapier built-in app.

IMAP by Zapier – retrieving emails from mail servers

Wikipedia (`https://en.wikipedia.org/wiki/Internet_Message_ Access_Protocol`) defines **Internet Message Access Protocol** (**IMAP**) as "*an Internet standard protocol used by email clients to retrieve email messages from a mail server over a TCP/IP connection.*" IMAP allows email client apps to retrieve emails from the server. If you are using an email server other than Gmail, Zoho Mail, or Microsoft Office 365, you can use IMAP by Zapier to retrieve emails from these mail servers. For example, these servers may include Rackspace, Zimbra, or Microsoft Exchange Server.

The following figure shows a list of a few common IMAP settings that will be useful when you set up your IMAP by Zapier app:

Client	Server	Authentication	Port
Googlemail - Gmail	imap.gmail.com	SSL	993
Outlook.com	imap-mail.outlook.com	SSL	993
Office365.com	outlook.office365.com	SSL	993
Yahoo Mail	plus.imap.mail.yahoo.com	SSL	993
Yahoo Mail Plus	plus.imap.mail.yahoo.com	SSL	993
Yahoo Mail UK	imap.mail.yahoo.co.uk	SSL	993
Yahoo Mail Deutschland	imap.mail.yahoo.com	SSL	993
Yahoo Mail AU/NZ	imap.mail.yahoo.au	SSL	993
AOL.com	imap.aol.com	SSL	993
AT&T	imap.att.yahoo.com	SSL	993
NTL @ntlworld.com	imap.ntlworld.com	SSL	993
BT Connect	imap4.btconnect.com		143
O2 Deutschland	imap.o2online.de		143
T-Online Deutschland	secureimap.t-online.de	SSL	993
1&1 (1and1)	imap.1and1.com	SSL	993
1&1 Deutschland	imap.1und1.de	SSL	993
Verizon	incoming.verizon.net		143
Zoho Mail	imap.zoho.com	SSL	993
Mail.com	imap.mail.com	SSL	993
GMX.com	imap.gmx.com	SSL	993
Net@ddress by USA.NET	imap.postoffice.net	SSL	993

Figure 8.8 – Common IMAP server settings (courtesy of Arclab)

You can get more details from this source: `https://www.arclab.com/en/kb/email/list-of-smtp-and-imap-servers-mailserver-list.html`.

The IMAP by Zapier built-in app can be used as a trigger to start workflows based on the following trigger events:

- **New Email** (trigger): This triggers when a new email is received.
- **New Mailbox** (trigger): This triggers when a new mailbox is created.

Let's now explore how to get started using the IMAP by Zapier app.

Setting up the IMAP by Zapier app

Once you have added an action step and chosen **IMAP by Zapier** as the app, you will be asked to sign in to IMAP by Zapier the first time you use it. Click on the **Sign in to IMAP by Zapier** button and a popup will appear, asking you to provide details to allow access to your IMAP by Zapier account, as follows:

- **Host**: Enter the host server that Zapier should connect to. This is a required field, and a valid value must be added in order for the Zap to work.
- **Username**: Enter your IMAP login username credentials. This is a required field, and a valid value must be added in order for the Zap to work.
- **Password**: Enter your IMAP password credentials. This is a required field, and a valid value must be added in order for the Zap to work.
- **Port**: Choose a port number of either `143` or `993` from the number (integer) field drop-down menu. Port number `143` will be used as the default.

This is shown in the following screenshot for a Gmail account:

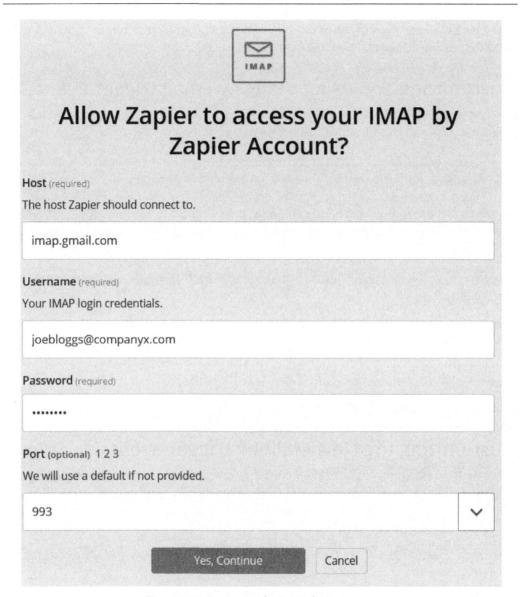

Figure 8.9 – Setting up the IMAP by Zapier app

Then select the **Yes, Continue** button to authenticate the connection.

> **Tip**
> Most mail clients will have help documentation giving more information on how to activate IMAP/POP3/SMTP settings. Check that IMAP is allowed in your mail account settings.

The **New Email** and **New Mailbox** trigger events differ slightly in configuration, and we will cover this next, starting with the **New Email** trigger event.

Customizing and using the New Email trigger event

Once we have authenticated our IMAP connection, we can proceed to edit the **Set up trigger** section and choose which mailbox to use, as follows:

- **Name of Mailbox**: A list of mailbox folders or labels will be brought in from your email account, and you can choose from a drop-down menu which one you want to use. Choose **Inbox** if you want to be notified of all new messages, or specify a folder or label depending on whether you want to be notified of new emails based on how you file them. This is a required field and must have at least one value in order for the Zap to run.

Once you have selected **Continue**, you can then use the **Test trigger** section to test this step, or **Skip Test**.

Here are a few examples of how you can use the IMAP by Zapier **New Email** trigger event:

- Create new Trello cards for new IMAP emails.
- Send Slack channel messages for new IMAP emails.

Now let's have a look at the New Mailbox trigger event.

Customizing the New Mailbox trigger event

Once we have authenticated our IMAP connection, we can proceed to skip the **Set up trigger** section as this will trigger on the creation of any new mailbox in that IMAP account. Once you have selected **Continue**, you can then use the **Test trigger** section to test this step, or choose **Skip Test**.

Here are a few examples of how you can use the IMAP by Zapier **New Mailbox** trigger event:

- Add new rows to a Google Sheets spreadsheet when new IMAP mailboxes are created.
- Send an email when new IMAP mailboxes are created.

You should now have a better understanding of how and when to use the IMAP by Zapier app.

Summary

In this chapter, we helped you get to grips with using the four communication-specific Zapier built-in apps. We covered how to use SMS by Zapier to send text messages as notifications and reminders. Next, we discussed how to use Email by Zapier to trigger workflows on receipt of emails and when emails are read, as well as how to send emails. Lastly, we reviewed how to use IMAP by Zapier to retrieve emails from mail servers, and SMTP by Zapier to send them from mail servers.

You now know how to send text messages and emails, as well as triggering workflows on receipt of emails and reading emails using built-in communication apps by Zapier.

In the next chapter, we will introduce you to a few more of Zapier's range of built-in apps. We will cover specific functions such as how to extract data from emails (using parsing), use RSS feeds in your automations, and compile data into digests.

9
Exploring Built-In Apps for Extracting and Compiling Data

As we discussed in *Chapter 6, Creating Multi-Step Zaps and Using Built-In Apps*, the power of Zapier lies in the functionality that you can take advantage of by using Zapier's built-in apps. In this chapter, we introduce you to built-in apps that extract data from emails, use RSS feeds, and create data digests. We will describe their functionality and provide practical tips on how to use them.

As we covered built-in communication apps in *Chapter 8, Built-In Communication Apps*, we start off with a similar theme by discussing how to extract data from emails using Email Parser by Zapier. Then, we will explore how to use RSS feed readers in automations using RSS by Zapier. After that, we will dive into how to compile data digests with Digest by Zapier. Finally, we will work through an exercise to build a Zap using RSS by Zapier and Digest by Zapier.

We will cover the following key topics in this chapter:

- Email Parser by Zapier – extracting data from emails
- RSS by Zapier – using RSS feed readers
- Digest by Zapier – compiling data in digests
- Exercise – creating a multi-step Zap with an RSS feed digest

Once you have worked through each of these topics, you will know how to parse data from email messages, use RSS feed readers, and compile data in digests.

Technical requirements

To make the most of the content and exercises in this chapter, you will need access to a Zapier account. The Zapier Starter plan will be adequate. You can get access to the Zap templates used in this chapter here: `https://bit.ly/3e5BUkn`. Using the templates will help you to visualize how the process works.

Email Parser by Zapier – extracting data from emails

The Email Parser by Zapier built-in app allows you to extract data from emails that have been forwarded to a unique `@robot.zapier.com` email address. By teaching Email Parser by Zapier to understand patterns in emails that you send to it, it can consistently extract that information for you to use in other steps in your workflow.

Email Parser by Zapier can only be used as a trigger step at the start of your workflow. It is available as the following trigger events:

- **New Email** (trigger)
- **New Mailbox** (trigger)

Let's look at each one of these.

The New Email trigger event

This trigger event can be used to start a workflow when a new email has been received. This works by using a unique `@robot.zapier.com` email address, which you would forward emails to. It is best practice that you set up multiple mailboxes to deal with separate workflows.

Here are a few examples of when to use the Email Parser by Zapier **New Email** trigger event:

- If you receive a summary of information by email after webforms are submitted, you might want to add those details to a CRM such as **Close.io** or **Airtable**.

- If you receive customer payment and billing information by email after a sale is made, you might want to add those details to your accounting app, such as **QuickBooks Online** or Xero.

- If you receive email inquiries to a specific mailbox, you might want to create a task for your team to deal with inquiries in a task management app, such as Trello or Asana.

Let's explore how to set up this trigger event.

Setting up the New Email trigger event

Let's cover how to set up the New Email trigger event, as follows:

1. Once you have added this trigger step to the start of your workflow (to **1. Trigger**), and chosen **Email Parser by Zapier** as the app and **New Email** as the trigger event, you can select **Continue**.

2. In the **Choose Account** section, click on the **Sign in to Email Parser by Zapier** button to create a new Email Parser by Zapier account.

3. A new pop-up window will be displayed. To sign in using your Zapier account credentials, select the **Log in with your Zapier account** button. To use an alternative username and password, enter these details in the boxes provided and select the **Login** button. This is shown in the following screenshot:

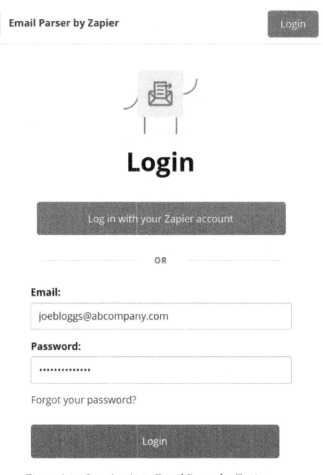

Figure 9.1 – Logging in to Email Parser by Zapier

4. Allow Zapier to connect to Email Parser by Zapier by clicking on the **Authorize** button. You can also click on the **Cancel** button to cancel.

5. On the next screen, further authentication is required, so click the **Authorize** button. Once authorized, you will be redirected back to the trigger step.

Before we can customize the trigger step, we need to create a new mailbox in your Email Parser by Zapier account. Let's take a look at how to do this next.

Setting up mailboxes in the Email Parser by Zapier account and mapping templates

We now need to create a mailbox, forward an email template, map our data, and alter the settings. To illustrate this, we will use the example of a webform submission where we want to extract the name, email address, service, and inquiry details. Let's get started by working through each of the following steps:

1. Navigate to `parser.zapier.com` and sign in to your Email Parser by Zapier account either by logging in with your Zapier account or adding separate login details.

2. Click on the orange **Create Mailbox** button to create a new mailbox. A new mailbox address will be provided, as shown in the following screenshot:

Email Parser by Zapier

We're waiting...

Send an email to l41004xt@robot.zapier.com!

Refresh page to look for new email.   auto refresh in 9 seconds.

Skip waiting.

Figure 9.2 – Email Parser by Zapier mailbox creation

3. Copy the mailbox address provided and send an example of an email that you want to parse to the mailbox. You can refresh the page to look for new emails by clicking on the **Refresh page to look for new email.** button or auto-refresh will happen every 10 seconds. Alternatively, click on the **Skip waiting** link to skip.

4. Once a new email has been received, use these steps to correctly parse information from your email:

- **Address**: Change your mailbox name by changing the prefix. Use a name that identifies the process but is unique and hard to guess, for example, abcompanywebform. You can also leave the mailbox name as it was.

- **Initial Template**: This field will show the data from the email you forwarded to the mailbox. Label the data you want to consistently parse from emails forwarded to this mailbox, by highlighting the text and naming it. This is shown in the following screenshot:

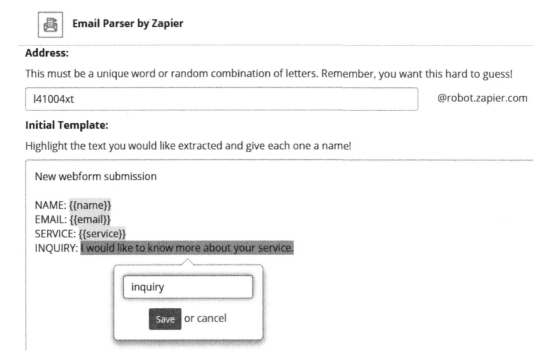

Figure 9.3 – Formatting the Email Parser by Zapier mailbox Address and Initial Template

- **Body Source**: Use the drop-down menu to select whether you want Email Parser to extract content from plain text (**Always use plain text body content**), HTML (**Always use HTML body content**), or whatever the best content is (**Use the best body content available**). The latter is the default and is recommended. This is important for consistently extracting data.

- **Parser Engine**: Use the drop-down menu to choose which parser engine to use. Choose between **Classic (v1, legacy)**, **Experimental (v2)**, and **Best Match (v1 + v2)**. The latter is the default and is recommended.

5. Select the **Save Address and Template** button to save and proceed or **Delete Mailbox** to delete the mailbox and start again.

Now let's review how to help Zapier intelligently parse data from your emails.

Adjusting Email Parser mailbox templates for the best results

Email Parser by Zapier works best with consistent formats of information, such as data presented on the same lines with the same spacing between lines. If the parser engine extracts information incorrectly, you can teach it the correct formats by reporting inaccuracies and editing additional templates. It is recommended that you send a few example emails to the parser mailbox, check the consistency of extracted information, and edit the template or report inaccuracies. You can do this as follows:

1. From the main mailbox dashboard, click on the **View Emails** link of the appropriate mailbox.

   The emails sent will be shown in list order with the email address they were sent from and when they were sent. You can either delete the emails by checking the **Delete** box and clicking on the **Delete Selected E-mails** button, or **Show** or **Hide** content using the appropriate link.

2. To review the accuracy of data for any email, click on the **Show** link.

3. Choose from the following four data view options:

   - **extracted**: Click on the **extracted** link to show the parsed data from the email.
   - **original**: Click on the **original** link to show the original email data forwarded to the parser.
   - **template**: Click on the **template** link to show the labeled data from the original template.
   - **output**: Click on the **output** link to show parsed data output with the data labels and extracted data.

An example is shown in the following screenshot:

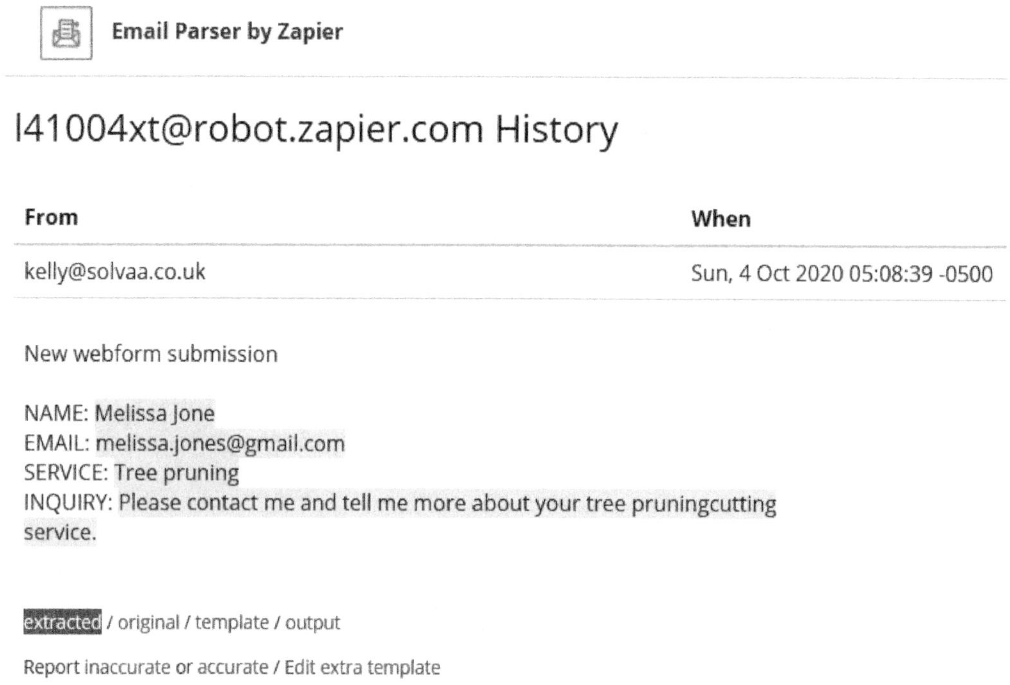

 Email Parser by Zapier

l41004xt@robot.zapier.com History

From	When
kelly@solvaa.co.uk	Sun, 4 Oct 2020 05:08:39 -0500

New webform submission

NAME: Melissa Jone
EMAIL: melissa.jones@gmail.com
SERVICE: Tree pruning
INQUIRY: Please contact me and tell me more about your tree pruningcutting service.

extracted / original / template / output

Report inaccurate or accurate / Edit extra template

Figure 9.4 – Reviewing email history in Email Parser by Zapier

4. Notify the parser engine of whether the extracted text was incorrect, by clicking on the **inaccurate** link, or correct, by clicking on the **accurate** link.

5. Click on the **Edit extra template** link to add an additional template to the mailbox parser data.

> **Tip**
> Unless your email data is straightforward and basic, ensuring Email Parser by Zapier works consistently can be a case of trial and error with remapping data and changing settings to teach the parser engine to extract data correctly. If you have more complex data to extract, consider using a dedicated parser app such as **Docparser** or **Mailparser**.

Now that we have created the mailbox and tested and adjusted the settings, let's complete the setup of the trigger step.

Completing the setup of the trigger step

Navigate back to your Zap in the Zap editor, and from there, complete the setup of the trigger step by editing the field in the **Set up trigger** section as follows:

- **Mailbox**: This field allows you to select which mailbox you want to use. Use the drop-down option to choose from the list of mailboxes that you have created.

This is shown in the following screenshot:

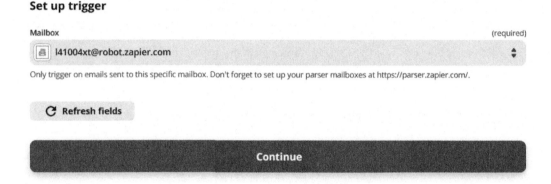

Figure 9.5 – Customizing the New Email trigger event

You can then select **CONTINUE**, and in the **Test trigger** section, click on the **Test Trigger** button and retrieve your test data to use in your action steps. If you have not yet sent a test email to your parser engine mailbox, you will be instructed to send one.

Proceed to add one or more action steps to your Zap using data from this trigger step.

You should now be able to use the **New Email** trigger event. Next, let's take a look at the **New Mailbox** trigger event.

The New Mailbox trigger event

This trigger event can be used to start a workflow when a new mailbox is added to your Email Parser by Zapier account. This trigger event is useful if you and your team are collaborating on Zapier, and you want to keep an eye on when mailboxes are being created.

Here are a couple of examples of how to use the Email Parser by Zapier **New Mailbox** trigger event:

- Send a message to Microsoft Teams when a new mailbox is created.
- Send an email when a new mailbox is added.

Let's explore how to set up this trigger event.

Setting up the New Mailbox trigger event

Once you have added this trigger step to the start of your workflow (to **1. Trigger**), choose **Email Parser by Zapier** as the app and **New Mailbox** as the trigger event. Then select **Continue** to use the **Test trigger** section. Use the **Test Trigger** button to retrieve test data.

Proceed to add one or more action steps to your Zap using data from this trigger step.

You should now have a better understanding of how and when to use the **New Mailbox** trigger event, as well as the **New Email** trigger event of the Email by Zapier built-in app.

Next, let's cover how to use the RSS by Zapier built-in app to use RSS feed data in your automations.

RSS by Zapier – using RSS feed readers

It can be overwhelming trying to keep on top of all the content that gets pushed our way, and we risk missing out on crucial new content. **Really Simple Syndication** (shortened to **RSS**) feeds update whenever the website publishes a new blog post or page. This is really useful as you can use this information to sift through what you want to see and be updated on new content. Most websites have RSS feeds in the format of `site.com/feed` or `site.com/rss`. Often, they will display in an `_Feeds` link in the footer bar. Private feeds often require you to use login credentials to access them. For more information on how to find the RSS feed for almost any website, check out this article: `https://zapier.com/blog/how-to-find-rss-feed-url/`.

The RSS by Zapier built-in app allows you to use RSS feed updates as a trigger, which, by then adding a notification action step such as an email, SMS, or Slack message, will give you an update on new content. You can also create your own custom RSS feed with the app.

Here are a few examples of how you can use RSS by Zapier:

- Share new blog posts from your own website on your social media channels.

- Add new articles from your favorite websites to a Google Sheets spreadsheet or **Knack**.

- Get an email when a new blog article is published on your competitor's website.

RSS by Zapier can be used as both a trigger and action step and is available as the following events:

- **New Item in Feed** (trigger)
- **New Items in Multiple Feeds** (trigger)
- **Create Item in Feed** (action)

Let's explore how to set up each of these in turn.

The New Item in Feed trigger event

The **New Item in Feed** trigger event can be used to start a workflow when new content is released from a specific website.

Let's explore how to set up this trigger event.

Setting up the New Item in Feed trigger event

Once you have added this trigger step to the start of your workflow (to **1. Trigger**), and chosen **RSS by Zapier** as the app and **New Item in Feed** as the trigger event, you can select **Continue**. You can then edit the fields in the **Set up trigger** section as follows:

- **Feed URL**: This field allows you to choose the RSS feed URL that you want to be notified of when new feed items are available. Establish the correct RSS feed format to use by exploring or searching on the relevant website. The format is normally `site.com/feed` or `site.com/rss`. This is a required field and must have a value in order for the Zap to run.

- **Username**: If the RSS feed is private, enter username credentials to enable access. You can type in static text, map in dynamic data from previous steps, or use a combination.

- **Password**: If the RSS feed is private, type in password credentials to enable access.

- **What Triggers a New Feed Item**: This drop-down field allows you to choose what type of data triggers the event. The default option is **Different Guid/URL (recommended)**, and it is recommended that you use this. Choose **Different Content** or **Anything is Different** as advanced options if you understand the ins and outs of RSS feed functionality.

These are shown in the following screenshot:

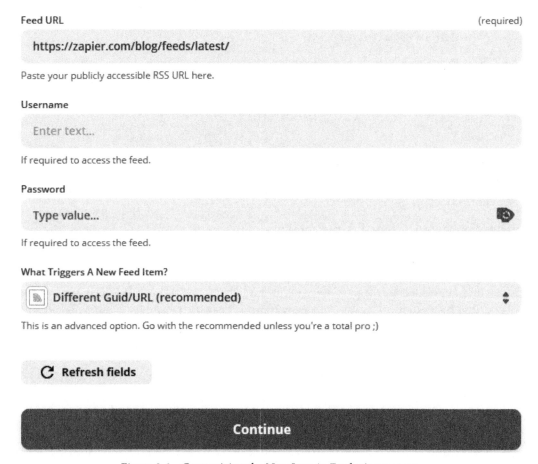

Figure 9.6 – Customizing the New Item in Feed trigger event

You can then select **CONTINUE**, and in the **Test trigger** section, use the **Test Trigger** button to retrieve your test data to use in your action steps.

Proceed to add one or more action steps to your Zap using data from this trigger step.

> Tip
> If you only want to see certain new items, such as posts from zoho.com, then you can add a conditional logic step with Filter by Zapier.

You should now be able to use the **New Item in Feed** trigger event. Next, let's take a look at the **New Items in Multiple Feeds** trigger event.

The New Items in Multiple Feeds trigger event

The **New Items in Multiple Feeds** trigger event can be used to start a workflow when new content is released from up to 10 websites. This saves you from having to set up multiple Zaps to trigger for each RSS feed.

Let's explore how to set up this trigger event.

Setting up the New Items in Multiple Feeds trigger event

Once you have added this trigger step to the start of your workflow (to **1. Trigger**), and chosen **RSS by Zapier** as the app and **New Items in Multiple Feeds** as the trigger event, you can select **Continue**. You can then edit the fields in the **Set up trigger** section as follows:

- **Feed URLs**: These fields allow you to choose the RSS feed URLs that you want to be notified of when new feed items are available. Establish the correct RSS feed format to use by exploring or searching on the relevant website. The format is normally site.com/feed or site.com/rss. Add one URL per field, and additional fields will appear once you start typing, for you to add a maximum of 10 URLs. Delete any URLs by clicking on the **x** button at the end of the field. This is a required field and must have a value in order for the Zap to run.

- **What Triggers a New Feed Item**: This drop-down field allows you to choose what type of data triggers the event. The default option is **Different Guid/URL (recommended)**, and it is recommended that you use this. Choose **Different Content** or **Anything is Different** as advanced options if you understand the ins and outs of RSS feed functionality.

These are shown in the following screenshot:

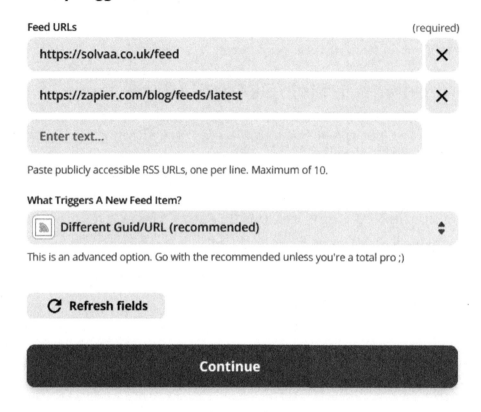

Figure 9.7 – Customizing the New Items in Multiple Feeds trigger event

You can then select **CONTINUE**, and in the **Test trigger** section, use the **Test Trigger** button to retrieve your test data to use in your action steps.

Proceed to add one or more action steps to your Zap using data from this trigger step.

You should now be able to use the **New Items in Multiple Feeds** trigger event. Next, let's take a look at the **Create Item in Feed** action event.

The Create Item in Feed action event

The **Create Item in Feed** action event allows you to create a bespoke feed and host it on a website with a shareable link. This is best used in combination with one of the trigger events **New Item in Feed** or **New Items in Multiple Feeds**.

Let's explore how to set up this action event.

Setting up the Create Item in Feed action event

Use the **Create Item in Feed** action event once you have set up your trigger step.

Once you have added an action step either by selecting the **Action** step or clicking on the + icon, and have chosen **RSS by Zapier** as the app and **Create Item in Feed** as the action event, you can then edit the fields in the **Set up action** section as follows:

- **Feed URL**: This field allows you to create and customize your unique and private RSS feed URL. Zapier generates the prefix, and you can customize the suffix by adding a combination of letters, numbers, and hyphens. Do not add spaces or symbols. You can also copy the URL by clicking the **Copy** button so that you can store it somewhere for quick reference, for example, in your Evernote notes. This is a required field and must have a value in order for the Zap to run.

- **Feed Title**: Enter the title of your new feed. You can enter static text, dynamic data mapped from previous steps, or a combination. If left blank, the title will default to **A Feed Called X** where **X** is the prefix that you entered in the **Feed URL** field.

- **Max Records**: Enter a number for the maximum number of records you want returned in the feed. The maximum is 50, however, adding a number to this field allows you to reduce the number. You can enter static text, dynamic data mapped from previous steps, or a combination into this integer field.

- **Item Title**: Enter a title for the item to publish. Type in static content, map dynamic content from previous steps in your Zap, or a combination. This is a required field and must have a value in order for the Zap to run.

- **Source URL**: Provide details of a source URL where the feed item is permanently hosted. This is a required field and must have a value in order for the Zap to run.

- **Content**: Provide details of the content of the feed item in either plain text or HTML format. You can type in static content, map dynamic content from previous steps in your Zap, or a combination. This is a required field and must have a value in order for the Zap to run.

- **Automatically Truncate Messages Over 10KB?**: Use this Boolean field to select whether you want Zapier to truncate data in your **Content** field if it is over 10 KB. Choose **Yes** to truncate the message or **No** to generate an error message if the data is too large.

- **Author Name**: Add the name of the author by typing in static content, mapping dynamic content from previous steps in your Zap, or a combination.

- **Author Email**: Add the author's email address by typing in static content, mapping dynamic content from previous steps in your Zap, or a combination.

- **Author Link**: Add a link to the author by typing in static content, mapping dynamic content from previous steps in your Zap, or a combination. This could be a link to the author's bio or website, for example.

- **Media URL**: Add a raw media URL to allow the downloading of files such as podcast files, images, or videos, for example. You can type in static content, map dynamic content from previous steps in your Zap, or a combination.

- **Media MIME Type**: Specify the media MIME type (a two-part identifier for file formats) of the URL you added in the **Media URL** field. If left blank, Zapier will default it to audio/mpeg. More details about MIME types can be found on Wikipedia: https://en.wikipedia.org/wiki/Media_type. You can type in static content, map dynamic content from previous steps in your Zap, or a combination.

- **Media Length In Bytes**: Some media players require a valid length. If left blank, this field defaults to 0. You can type in static content, map dynamic content from previous steps in your Zap, or a combination.

- **Pubdate**: Provide details of the publishing date of the feed item. The most popular term to use is "now," however, you can use any compatible date/time format in this field. You can type in static content, map dynamic content from previous steps in your Zap, or a combination. Feed items are not ordered by **Pubdate**, but by the date they were inserted instead.

An example is shown in the following three screenshots, using data mapped from a **New Item in Feed** trigger event:

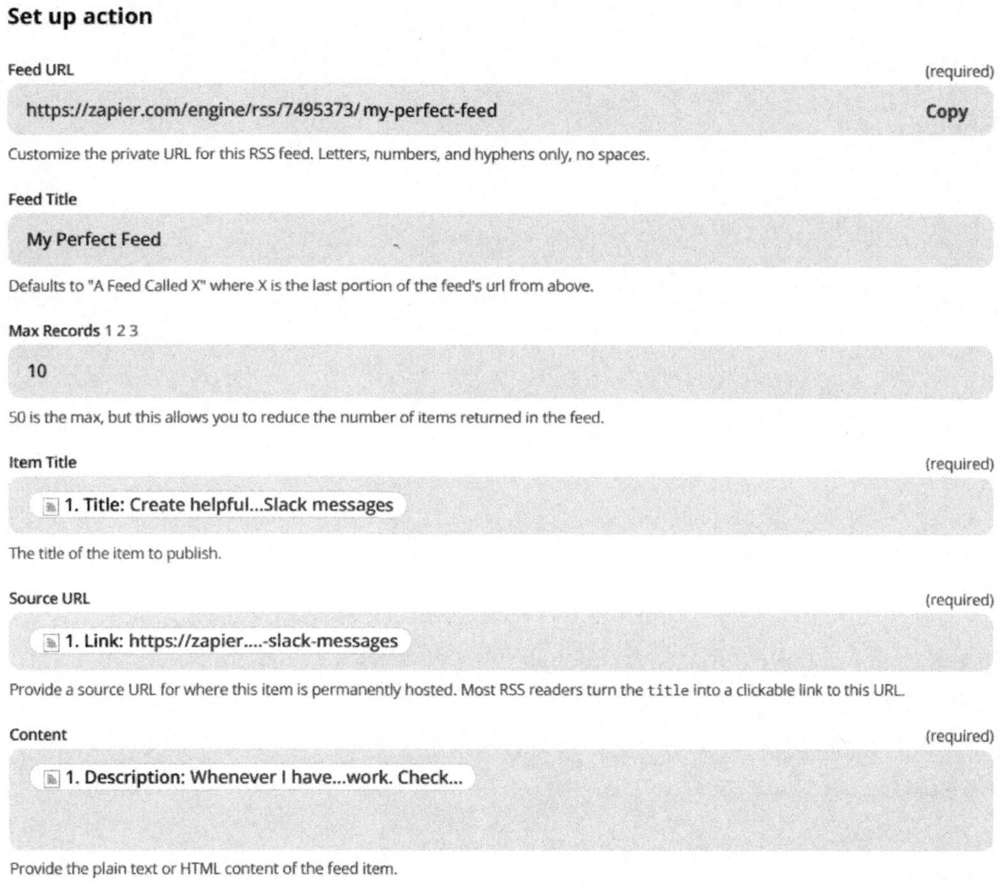

Set up action

Feed URL   (required)

https://zapier.com/engine/rss/7495373/ my-perfect-feed   Copy

Customize the private URL for this RSS feed. Letters, numbers, and hyphens only, no spaces.

Feed Title

My Perfect Feed

Defaults to "A Feed Called X" where X is the last portion of the feed's url from above.

Max Records 1 2 3

10

50 is the max, but this allows you to reduce the number of items returned in the feed.

Item Title   (required)

📄 1. Title: Create helpful...Slack messages

The title of the item to publish.

Source URL   (required)

📄 1. Link: https://zapier....-slack-messages

Provide a source URL for where this item is permanently hosted. Most RSS readers turn the `title` into a clickable link to this URL.

Content   (required)

📄 1. Description: Whenever I have...work. Check...

Provide the plain text or HTML content of the feed item.

Figure 9.8 – Customizing the Create Item in Feed action event (1)

The second part of the action step is shown in the following screenshot:

Automatically Truncate Messages Over 10KB? ⊚ ○

> 📄 Yes   ⬍

Use this field to control whether Zapier will truncate data over the 10kb limit (select Yes), or generate an error if the data is too large (select No). See our Help for more information.

Author Name

> 📄 1. Raw Author: tyler.robertson...yler Robertson)

Author Email

> Enter text or insert data...

Author Link

> Enter text or insert data...

Media URL

> Enter text or insert data...

Specify a raw download URL for your podcast file, image, or other media file.

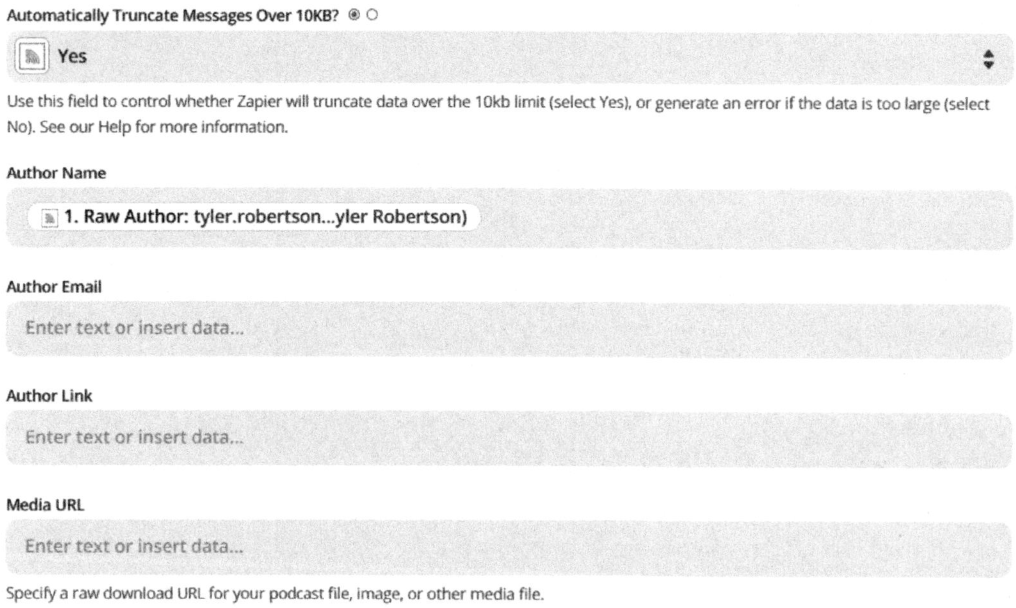

Figure 9.9 – Customizing the Create Item in Feed action event (2)

The third part of the action step is shown in the following screenshot:

Media MIME Type

> Enter text or insert data...

What is the MIME type for your raw file? Defaults to audio/mpeg.

Media Length In Bytes

> Enter text or insert data...

Some players require a valid length. Defaults to 0.

Pubdate 📅①

> 📄 1. Pub Date: Mon, 19 Jul 2021 16:00:00 GMT

Most people would put "now", but you can change it to something like "tomorrow" or "next week monday at 7pm" or "2013-08-23 12:00:00 +0800"! *Note, we do not order by pubdate, just by order inserted.*

> ↻ **Refresh fields**

> **Continue**

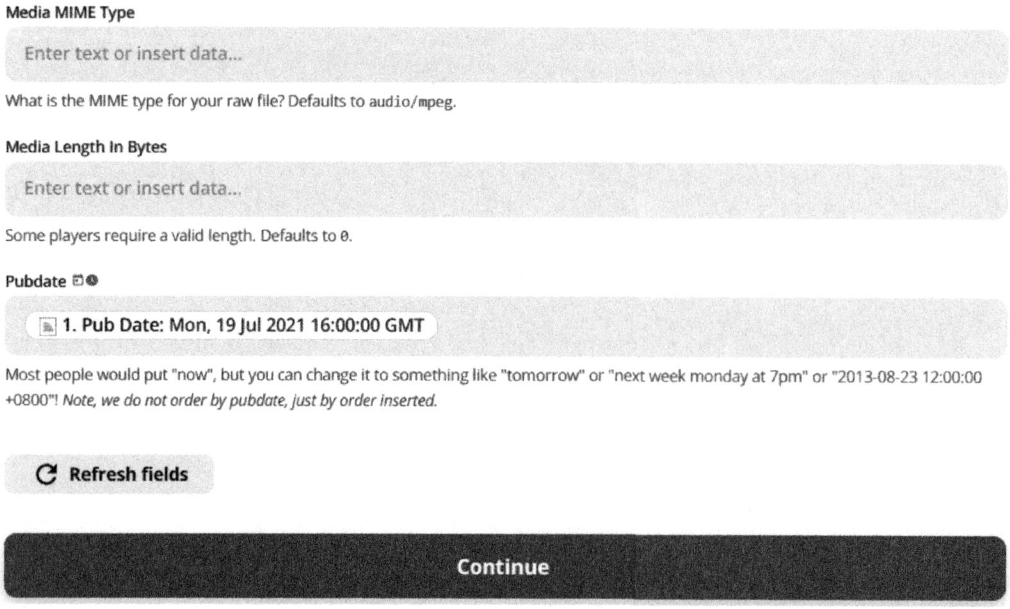

Figure 9.10 – Customizing the Create Item in Feed action event (3)

Click on the **Continue** button, and you can then use the **Test trigger** section to test this step or **Skip Test**.

The following screenshot shows an example of what the feed will look like:

Figure 9.11 – An example of the result of using a Create Item in Feed action event

Proceed to add one or more action steps or turn on your Zap.

You should now have a better understanding of how and when to use the RSS by Zapier built-in app with its various triggers and actions.

Now let's cover how to use the Digest by Zapier built-in app to compile data in digests.

Digest by Zapier – compiling data in digests

The Digest by Zapier built-in app allows you to capture data from multiple workflow trigger events and compile the data into single summaries that can be used in other action events. This is really useful if you have several notifications that you want to receive a summary of at one time rather than as they happen. If you don't want to be disturbed on certain days with regular notifications, turn them off and just receive a summary at times you specify. Conversely, some of your apps may not send you notifications of certain events, and in this case, you might want reports of certain occurrences at a regular time. You can also search for existing digest data to use in your workflows.

Here are a few examples of how you can use this built-in app:

- Send a weekly email to management with a summary of all sales invoices created over that week.

- Send an email with a periodic summary at 10 a.m. and 3 p.m. of all Slack notifications you have received that day.

- Send a Slack message with a list of **Teamwork Projects** tasks that you have been assigned during that week.

- Send a Microsoft Teams message with a weekly summary of social media mentions.

This app can only be used as an action or search action step, and the following events are available to use:

- **Append Entry and Schedule Digest** (action)
- **Release Existing Digest** (action)
- **Find Digest** (search action)

Bear in mind that once data is released from a digest using either of the action steps, the digest is cleared and will collate new digest data as events occur.

Let's look at each one of these.

The Append Entry and Schedule Digest action event

The **Append Entry and Schedule Digest** action event allows you to aggregate data from your trigger app, append it to the end of a list of other collected data from the trigger app, and then schedule it to run at a time that you specify.

To illustrate using Digest by Zapier, we will use the example of creating a summary of sales invoices created in Xero over a period.

Let's explore how to set up this action event.

Setting up the Append Entry and Schedule Digest action event

Use the **Append Entry and Schedule Digest** action event once you have set up your trigger step, with the relevant trigger data you want to push to Digest by Zapier.

Once you have added an action step either by selecting the **Action** step or clicking on the + icon, and have chosen **Digest by Zapier** as the app and **Append Entry and Schedule Digest** as the action event, you can then edit the fields in the **Set up action** section as follows:

- **Title**: Enter a descriptive title for the digest. This will help you to identify the digest when you use it in other Digest by Zapier events. For example, we could give the digest a title of New Sales Invoice Summary.

- **Entry**: In this field, type in static text, map dynamic data from previous steps, or use a combination of both that you want to be included in the digest. For example, we might want to include the invoice number, date, currency, and amount in the digest.

- **Frequency**: This field controls how often Zapier will deliver the digest. Choose from **Daily**, **Weekly**, **Monthly**, **Threshold (when a certain number of entries is reached)**, and **Manual (pair with separate "Release Digest" Zap)**. The choice of frequency determines additional fields that are displayed.

All these three fields are required and must have a value in order for the Zap to run.

Let's take a look at the different **Frequency** field options.

Frequency: Daily

The **Daily** option in the **Frequency** field drop-down menu is the default for this field. Once selected, the following fields will appear:

- **Time Of Day**: Use this field to specify what time you want the digest data to be released. The drop-down menu offers hourly time options from midnight to 11 p.m. You can also use the **Custom** header option to type in a custom value using the formats hh:mm aa, hh:mm, or hhmm, such as 11:45, or map a dynamic value from a previous step. This is a required field and must have a value in order for the Zap to run.

- **Trigger On Weekends?**: This field controls whether your digest will be released on weekend days or not. Use the Boolean field drop-down menu to choose between **Yes**, if you want it to trigger on Saturdays and Sundays, or **No** if you only want it to trigger from Monday to Friday.

These are shown in the following screenshot:

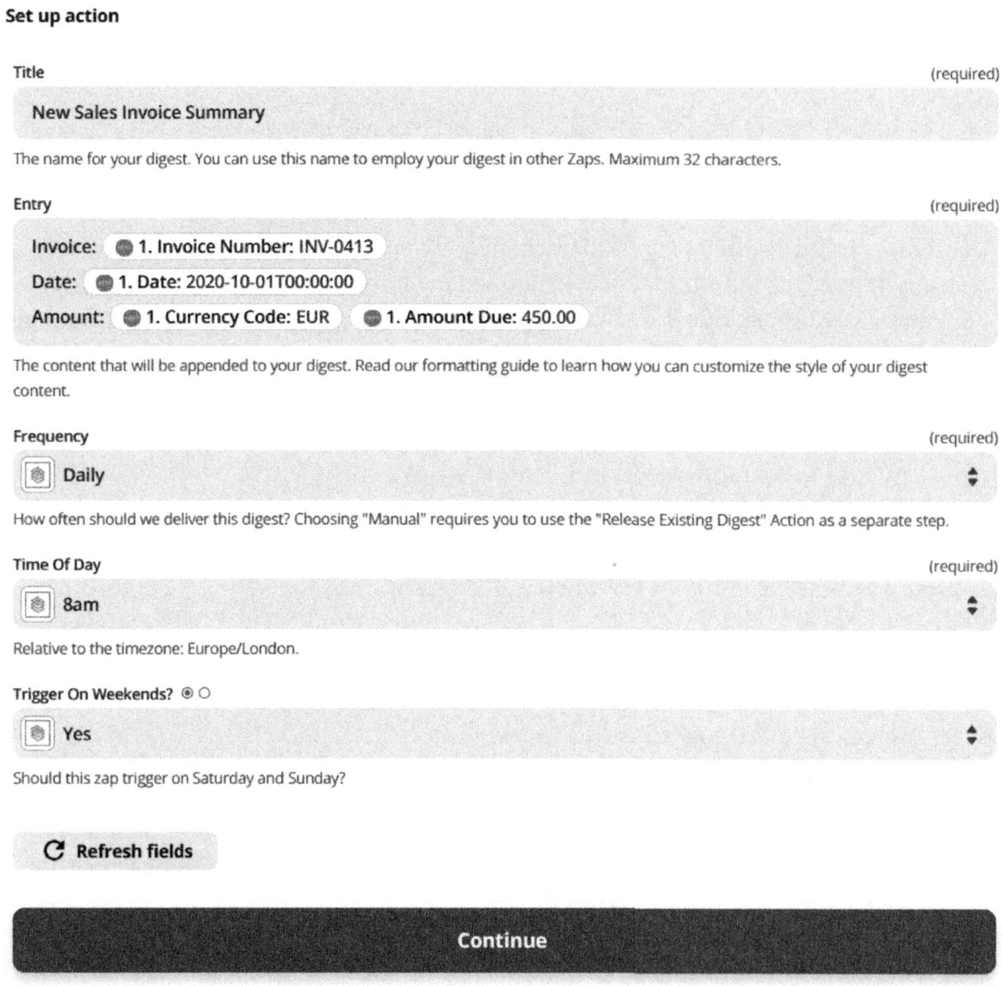

Set up action

Title   (required)

New Sales Invoice Summary

The name for your digest. You can use this name to employ your digest in other Zaps. Maximum 32 characters.

Entry   (required)

Invoice: ● 1. Invoice Number: INV-0413

Date: ● 1. Date: 2020-10-01T00:00:00

Amount: ● 1. Currency Code: EUR   ● 1. Amount Due: 450.00

The content that will be appended to your digest. Read our formatting guide to learn how you can customize the style of your digest content.

Frequency   (required)

🏶 Daily   ↕

How often should we deliver this digest? Choosing "Manual" requires you to use the "Release Existing Digest" Action as a separate step.

Time Of Day   (required)

🏶 8am   ↕

Relative to the timezone: Europe/London.

Trigger On Weekends? ⊙ ○

🏶 Yes   ↕

Should this zap trigger on Saturday and Sunday?

↻ **Refresh fields**

Continue

Figure 9.12 – Customizing the Daily Frequency field option in the Append Entry and Schedule Digest action event

Click on the **CONTINUE** button, and you can then use the **Test action** section to test this step or **Skip Test**.

Proceed to add one or more action steps so that you receive your digest summaries and then turn on your Zap.

Let's review the **Weekly** option next.

Frequency: Weekly

When you select the **Weekly** option in the **Frequency** field dropdown, the following fields will appear:

- **Day Of The Week**: This field controls which day of the week you want the digest data to be released. Use the drop-down menu to choose days from **Monday** to **Friday**.

- **Time Of Day**: Use this field to specify what time you want your digest to be released. The drop-down menu offers hourly time options from midnight to 11 p.m. You can also use the **Custom** header option to type in a custom value using the formats hh:mm aa, hh:mm, or hhmm, such as 11:45, or map a dynamic value from a previous step.

Both of these fields are required and must have a value in order for the Zap to run.

These are shown in the following screenshot:

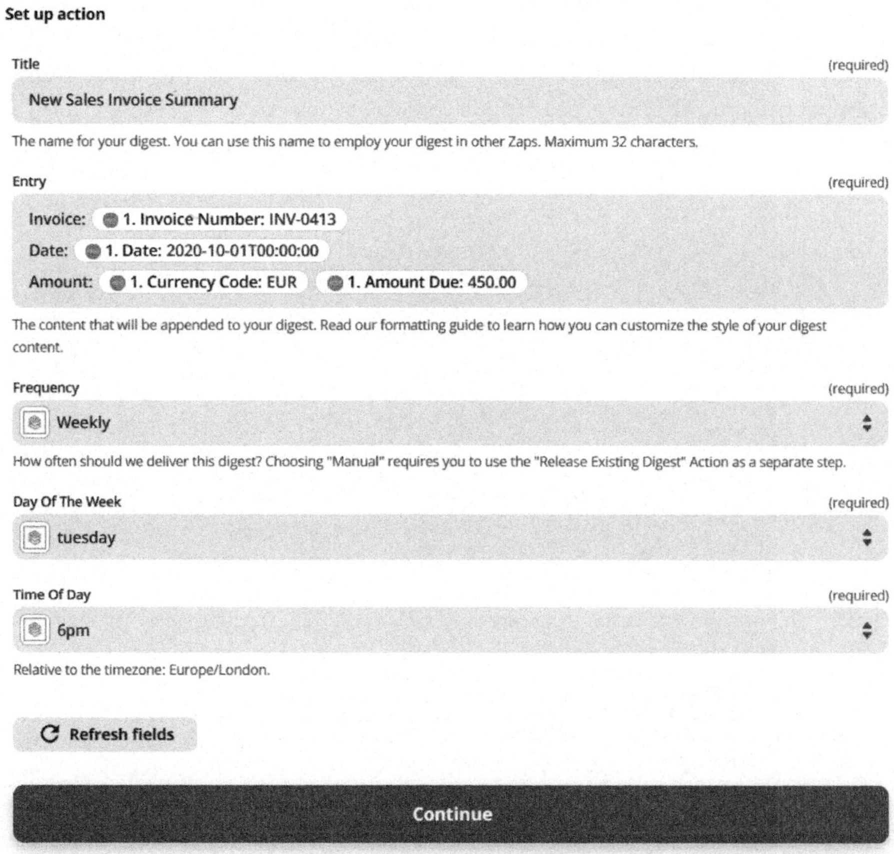

Figure 9.13 – Customizing the Weekly Frequency field option in the Append Entry and Schedule Digest action event

Click on the **CONTINUE** button, and you can then use the **Test action** section to test this step or **Skip Test**.

Proceed to add one or more action steps so that you receive your digest summaries and then turn on your Zap.

Let's explore the **Monthly** option next.

Frequency: Monthly

When you select the **Monthly** option in the **Frequency** field dropdown, the following fields will appear:

- **Day Of The Month**: This field controls which day of the month you want the digest data to be released. Use the drop-down menu to choose dates from **1** to **31**.

- **Time Of Day**: Use this field to specify what time you want your digest data to be released. The drop-down menu offers hourly time options from midnight to 11 p.m. You can also use the **Custom** header option to type in a custom value using the formats hh:mm aa, hh:mm, or hhmm, such as 9:15 p.m.

Both of these fields are required and must have a value in order for the Zap to run.

These are shown in the following screenshot:

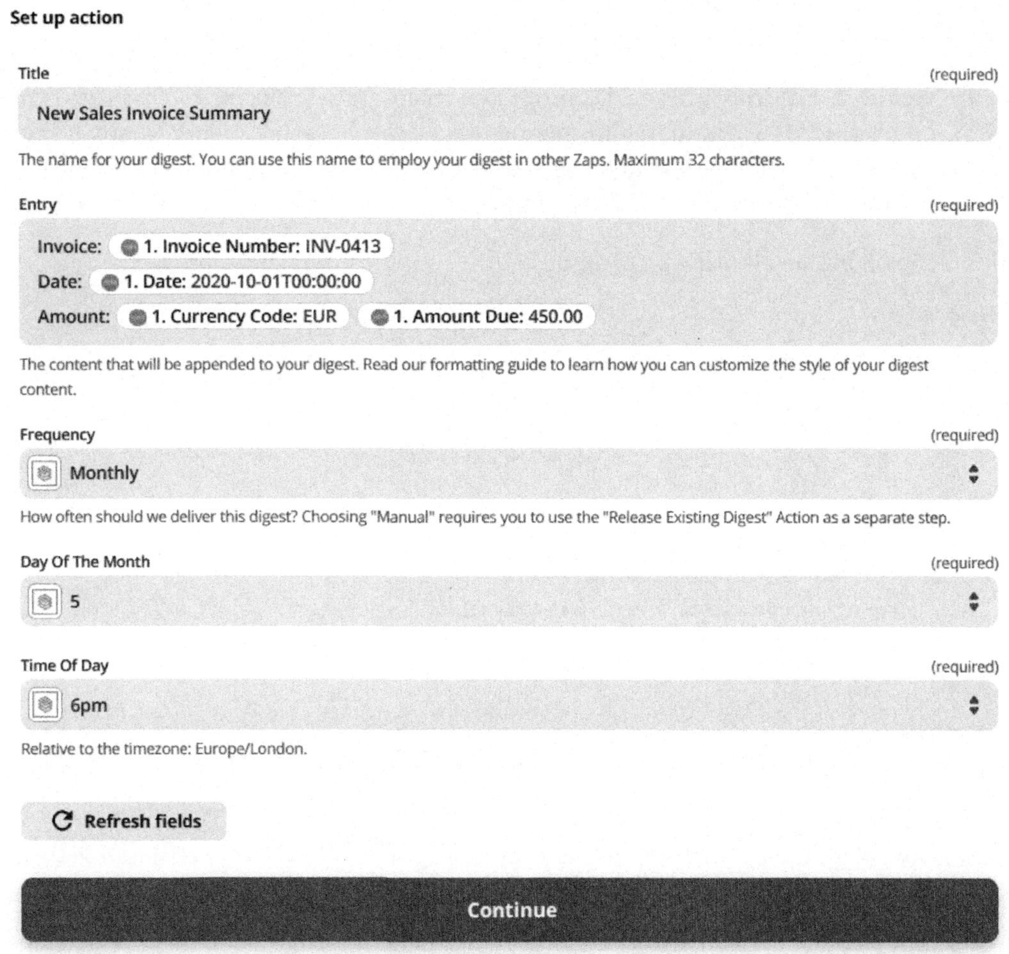

Set up action

Title   (required)

> New Sales Invoice Summary

The name for your digest. You can use this name to employ your digest in other Zaps. Maximum 32 characters.

Entry   (required)

> Invoice: ⬤ 1. Invoice Number: INV-0413
> Date: ⬤ 1. Date: 2020-10-01T00:00:00
> Amount: ⬤ 1. Currency Code: EUR   ⬤ 1. Amount Due: 450.00

The content that will be appended to your digest. Read our formatting guide to learn how you can customize the style of your digest content.

Frequency   (required)

> 🔘 Monthly   ⬍

How often should we deliver this digest? Choosing "Manual" requires you to use the "Release Existing Digest" Action as a separate step.

Day Of The Month   (required)

> 🔘 5   ⬍

Time Of Day   (required)

> 🔘 6pm   ⬍

Relative to the timezone: Europe/London.

> C⟳ **Refresh fields**

> **Continue**

Figure 9.14 – Customizing the Monthly Frequency field option in the Append Entry and
Schedule Digest action event

Click on the **CONTINUE** button, and you can then use the **Test action** section to test this step or **Skip Test**.

Proceed to add one or more action steps so that you receive your digest summaries and then turn on your Zap.

Let's take a look at the **Threshold (when a certain number of entries is reached)** option next.

Frequency: Threshold (when a certain number of entries is reached)

When you select the **Threshold (when a certain number of entries is reached)** option, the following field will appear:

- **Number Of Entries**: This field controls how many entries the digest will collate before it is released. The maximum time period to hold the digest is 1 month from the first entry, so if the number has not been reached in this time, the digest will automatically be released. This field is required and must have a value in order for the Zap to run.

This is shown in the following screenshot:

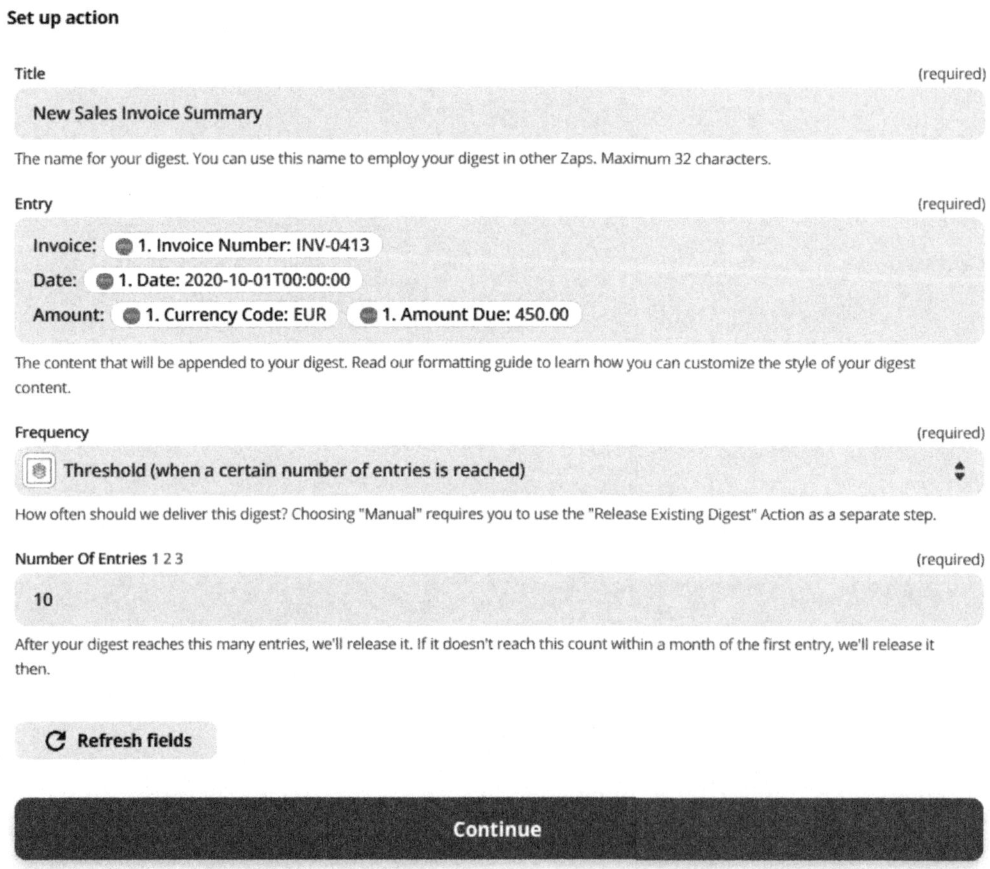

Set up action

Title   (required)

New Sales Invoice Summary

The name for your digest. You can use this name to employ your digest in other Zaps. Maximum 32 characters.

Entry   (required)

Invoice: ● 1. Invoice Number: INV-0413

Date: ● 1. Date: 2020-10-01T00:00:00

Amount: ● 1. Currency Code: EUR   ● 1. Amount Due: 450.00

The content that will be appended to your digest. Read our formatting guide to learn how you can customize the style of your digest content.

Frequency   (required)

[⊞] Threshold (when a certain number of entries is reached)   ⬍

How often should we deliver this digest? Choosing "Manual" requires you to use the "Release Existing Digest" Action as a separate step.

Number Of Entries 1 2 3   (required)

10

After your digest reaches this many entries, we'll release it. If it doesn't reach this count within a month of the first entry, we'll release it then.

⟳ **Refresh fields**

Continue

Figure 9.15 – Customizing the Threshold (when a certain number of entries is reached) Frequency field option in the Append Entry and Schedule Digest action event

Click on the **CONTINUE** button, and you can then use the **Test action** section to test this step or **Skip Test**.

Proceed to add one or more action steps so that you receive your digest summaries and then turn on your Zap.

Let's review the **Manual (pair with separate "Release Digest" Zap)** option next.

Frequency: Manual (pair with separate "Release Digest" Zap)

When you select the **Manual (pair with separate "Release Digest" Zap)** option in the **Frequency** field dropdown, no further fields appear.

This is shown in the following screenshot:

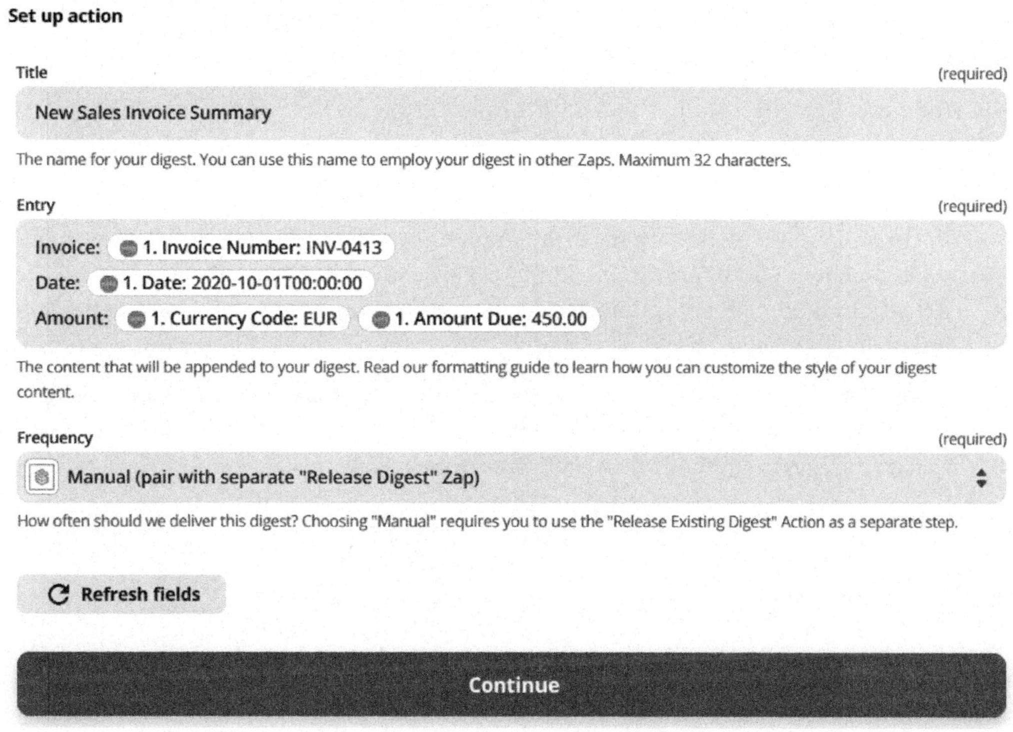

Set up action

Title   (required)

    New Sales Invoice Summary

The name for your digest. You can use this name to employ your digest in other Zaps. Maximum 32 characters.

Entry   (required)

    Invoice: ⊙ 1. Invoice Number: INV-0413
    Date: ⊙ 1. Date: 2020-10-01T00:00:00
    Amount: ⊙ 1. Currency Code: EUR   ⊙ 1. Amount Due: 450.00

The content that will be appended to your digest. Read our formatting guide to learn how you can customize the style of your digest content.

Frequency   (required)

    ⊜   Manual (pair with separate "Release Digest" Zap)   ⇕

How often should we deliver this digest? Choosing "Manual" requires you to use the "Release Existing Digest" Action as a separate step.

    ↻ Refresh fields

    Continue

Figure 9.16 – Customizing the Manual (pair with separate "Release Digest" Zap) Frequency field option in the Append Entry and Schedule Digest action event

Click on the **CONTINUE** button, and you can then use the **Test action** section to test this step or **Skip Test**.

> **Important note**
> This field option works alongside a **Release Existing Digest** action event,
> which you must set up in your existing Zap as one of the subsequent steps or in
> a separate Zap in order for your digest to be released.

Proceed to add the **Release Existing Digest** action step or turn your Zap on.

Now let's discuss how to set up the **Release Existing Digest** action event.

The Release Existing Digest action event

The **Release Existing Digest** action event works in conjunction with the **Manual (pair with separate "Release Digest" Zap)** option in the **Frequency** field dropdown of the **Append Entry and Schedule Digest** action event. It allows the digest that has been manually set to release at a certain point.

This action event can be used in the same Zap as an **Append Entry and Schedule Digest** action event or in a separate Zap. Here are a couple of examples of when either situation is appropriate:

- **In the same Zap**: If you want to delay the release of your digest for a set period of time, such as 12 hours, you can add in a Delay by Zapier **Delay For** action step, the **Release Existing Digest** action step, and a notification action step (such as the **Send Email** action event of Email by Zapier).

- **In another Zap**: If you want your digest to release after another, unrelated trigger event, such as an opportunity closing in your CRM, you can use the **Release Existing Digest** action event and a notification action step.

Let's explore how to set up this action event.

Setting up the Release Existing Digest action event

Use the **Release Existing Digest** action event once you have set an action step either in this Zap or another Zap that involves the **Append Entry and Schedule Digest** action event.

Once you have added an action step either by selecting the **Action** step or clicking on the + icon, and have chosen **Digest by Zapier** as the app and **Release Existing Digest** as the action event, you can then edit the fields in the **Set up action** section as follows:

- **Digest**: This field controls which digest to use in the step. From the dropdown, choose from a list of digests created. Alternatively, use the **Custom** option to enter the name of the digest by typing it in, or map in a dynamic date from previous steps.

This is shown in the following screenshot:

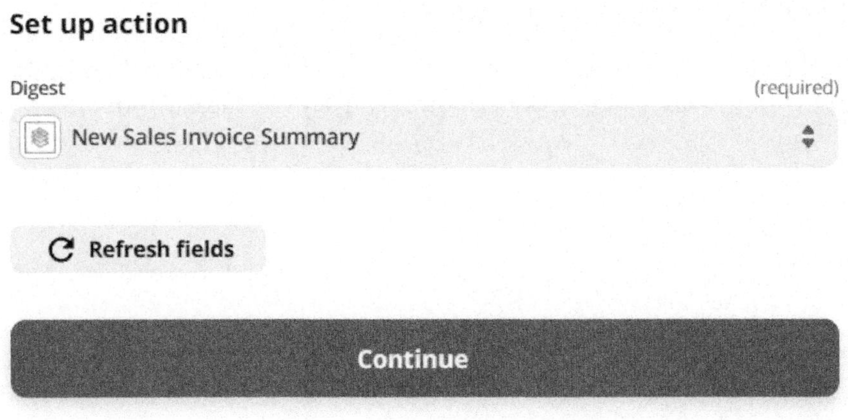

Set up action

Digest   (required)

New Sales Invoice Summary

C Refresh fields

Continue

Figure 9.17 – Customizing the Release Existing Digest action event

Click on the **CONTINUE** button, and you can then use the **Test action** section to test this step or **Skip Test**.

Proceed to add one or more action steps so that you receive your digest summaries and then turn on your Zap.

Next, let's discuss how to set up the **Find Digest** search action event.

The Find Digest search action event

The **Find Digest** search action event is handy to use when you want to periodically retrieve all the existing data in a digest. For example, you might want to check the digest for data every day (using a Schedule by Zapier trigger) and send an email notification with the results. You could also add in a subsequent step to release the data, after passing a filter with certain conditions, such as if it was the fifteenth day of the month.

Let's explore how to set up this action event.

Setting up the Find Digest action event

Use the **Find Digest** search action event once you have set up a trigger step.

Once you have added an action step either by selecting the **Action** step or clicking on the + icon, and have chosen **Digest by Zapier** as the app and **Find Digest** as the action event, you can then edit the fields in the **Set up action** section as follows:

- **Digest**: This field controls which digest to use in the step. From the dropdown, choose from a list of digests created. Alternatively, use the **Custom** option to enter the name of the digest by typing it in, or map in dynamic data from previous steps.

This is shown in the following screenshot:

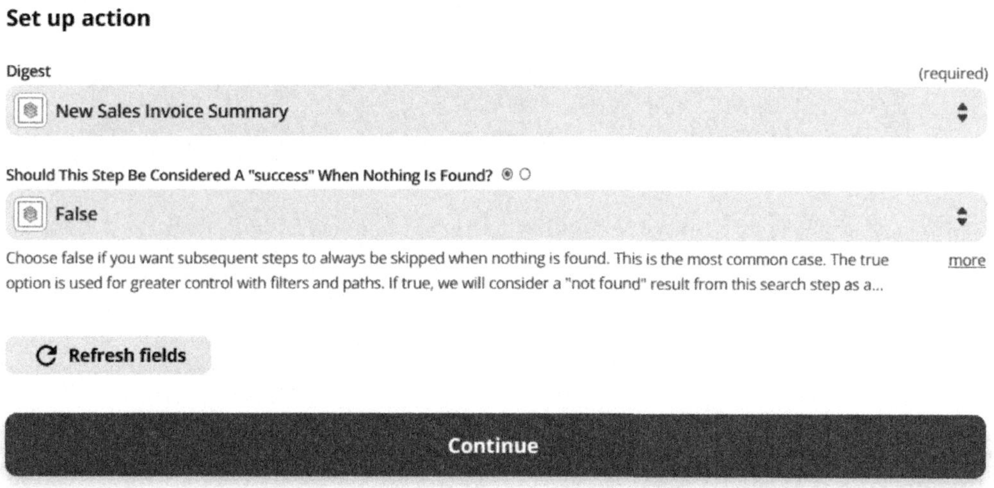

Set up action

Digest   (required)

| 🔅 | New Sales Invoice Summary | ⬍ |

Should This Step Be Considered A "success" When Nothing Is Found? ⦿ ○

| 🔅 | False | ⬍ |

Choose false if you want subsequent steps to always be skipped when nothing is found. This is the most common case. The true   more
option is used for greater control with filters and paths. If true, we will consider a "not found" result from this search step as a...

↻ **Refresh fields**

Continue

Figure 9.18 – Customizing the Find Digest search action event

Click on the **CONTINUE** button, and you can then use the **Test action** section to test this step or **Skip Test**.

Proceed to add one or more action steps and then turn on your Zap.

You should now have a better understanding of how and when to use the Digest by Zapier built-in app.

Now, let's review an example of how to create a Zap that creates a digest of an RSS feed.

Exercise – creating a multi-step Zap with an RSS feed digest

You can use one of the processes that you defined in *Chapter 2, Preparing to Automate Your Processes*, to work through the content in this section, if appropriate. Try to incorporate multiple apps in your workflow.

You might want to create a monthly digest of your three favorite blogs. You want to receive the summary on the first of the month at 9 a.m. in a Slack message, and to add a task to MeisterTask so that you don't forget to read them. If you don't mark your task as complete after 7 days, you want to receive another reminder in Slack.

Here is an example of a simple workflow you could build to automate this process:

1. *Trigger*: Add the RSS by Zapier **New Items in Multiple Feeds** event trigger and specify the blogs that you want to receive feed updates for.

2. *Action*: Add a Digest by Zapier **Append Entry and Schedule Digest** action event and specify **Frequency** as **Monthly**, **Day Of The Month** as **1**, and **Time** as **9am**.

3. *Action*: Add a Slack **Send Direct Message** action event to yourself.

4. *Action*: Add a MeisterTask **Create Task** action event.

5. *Action*: Add a Delay by Zapier **Delay For** action step where you specify the delay for 7 days.

6. *Action*: Add a **Find Task** search action to search MeisterTask for the task created in *step 4*.

7. *Action*: Add a filter with Filter by Zapier to only allow the Zap to continue if the task is still open.

8. *Action*: Add a Slack **Add Reminder** action event to remind yourself that you haven't read your digest yet.

You can get access to a copy of this Zap template here: `https://bit.ly/3e5BUkn`.

Try building out a similar process by repeating this exercise for any appropriate processes that you have documented and would benefit from automation.

You should now have a better understanding of how and when to use email parsing, RSS feeds, and digests in your Zaps.

Summary

In this chapter, we introduced you to a few more of Zapier's range of built-in apps. We covered how to extract data from emails using Email Parser by Zapier, and then we explored how to use RSS feed readers in your automations using RSS by Zapier. Then, we discussed how to compile data digests with Digest by Zapier. Lastly, we covered an exercise to create a digest of an RSS feed.

You now know how to extract or parse data from emails, use RSS feeds in your automations, and collate data into digests.

In the next chapter, you will learn about a variety of Zapier's other built-in apps. We will cover how to initiate one-off automation from any page on the internet, how to shorten URLs, and how to translate and detect text in different languages. We will also discuss how to retrieve and score a lead's company information, how to use data on weather conditions, and how to use astrological predictions in your automations.

10
Other Useful Built-In Apps by Zapier

In this chapter, we will continue looking at more built-in functionality that Zapier has to offer with its range of built-in apps. We will cover descriptions of their functionality and provide practical tips on how to use them.

First, we will explore how to use the Zapier Chrome extension (previously called Push by Zapier) to initiate one-off automation from any page on the internet, and how to shorten URLs with URL Shortener by Zapier. Then, we will discuss how to translate text from different languages using Translate by Zapier, and how to score lead information using Lead Score by Zapier. Lastly, we will cover how to use data on weather conditions using Weather by Zapier, and how to use astrological predictions using Retrograde by Zapier.

We will cover the following key topics in this chapter:

- Zapier Chrome extension – triggering one-off automations from any web page
- URL Shortener by Zapier – shortening URLs in your Zaps
- Translate by Zapier – translating text
- Lead Score by Zapier – scoring and retrieving lead information
- Weather by Zapier – using weather conditions in your Zaps
- Retrograde by Zapier – using astrological predictions in your Zaps

Once you have worked through each of these topics, you will know how to initiate one-off workflows from any web page, shorten URLs, translate text, score and retrieve lead information, and use weather conditions and astrological predictions in your Zaps.

Technical requirements

To get the most out of the content and exercises in this chapter, you will need access to a Zapier account. The Zapier Starter plan will be adequate.

Zapier Chrome extension – triggering one-off automations from any web page

The Zapier Chrome extension built-in app, previously called **Push by Zapier**, uses a **Google Chrome extension** to trigger one-off automations from anywhere on the web manually. There are hundreds, probably thousands, of ways you can use this app to add productivity to your day. Here are a few examples of how you can use the Zapier Chrome extension built-in app with content extracted from your Google Chrome browser:

- Create a new task in Teamwork Projects to review content in an article you came across while browsing the internet.

- Send a Slack message when you receive a new email.

- Add data to a new row in a Smartsheet when you see content you might want to share with your audience.

The Zapier Chrome extension can be used as a trigger step at the start of your workflow, replacing a traditional trigger step, but only once you have installed the Google Chrome extension, as follows:

- **New Push** (trigger)

First, let's review how to add the Google Chrome extension to your browser.

Setting up the Google Chrome extension on your browser

The first thing we need to do to use the Zapier Chrome extension built-in app is to install the Google Chrome extension in our browser. Follow these steps to install the extension:

1. From your Google Chrome browser window, navigate to `https://chrome.google.com/webstore/detail/zapier/ngghlnfmdgnpegcmbpgehkbhkhkbkjpj`.

2. Click on the **Add to Chrome** button.

3. In the popup that appears, click on **Add extension** to authenticate the installation.

4. Pin your Zapier Chrome extension to your browser view by clicking on the puzzle piece icon and then the pin icon next to the Zapier Chrome extension in the drop-down menu. This will ensure it is easy to trigger your workflows at any point.

The next thing you need to do is to set up your workflows. Click on the **Zapier Chrome extension** icon in your browser to reveal a drop-down window with the following options:

- **Settings** (cogwheel icon): Selecting this icon will allow you to change the extension settings.

- **Actions tab**: This tab shows some instructions on how to use the extension and links to a few pre-built Zap templates to get you started. Clicking on any of these will take you to the Zap editor to use the template. Alternatively, you can click on the **Create Zap** button to create a Zap from scratch in the Zap editor. You will also be shown the connected email address associated with your Zapier account, and once you have built some Zapier Chrome extension Zaps that have been turned on, they will be shown in a list, allowing you to select one to use.

- **Suggested tab**: This tab shows some suggested workflows for you to try. You can click on the **Allow Access** button to retrieve workflow suggestions based on your browser history. A popup will appear asking you to authorize the access. Click on the **Allow** button to accept. This is very useful as it is a list of pre-built Zaps personalized to you and will give you ideas on how to get started with using Push by Zapier. You can also click on the **More workflows** button to be taken to the Zapier **Explore** page.

Choose one of the options to start building your Zap in the Zap editor.

Now let's explore how to set up each of the trigger events.

The New Push trigger event

The **New Push** trigger event allows you to retrieve details of the active browser tab's title and URL when the button is pushed for this Zap in the Zapier Chrome extension and add static data in specified custom fields that you can then use in your action steps. The time the event occurred will also be retrieved. For example, you might want to assign a task to a member of your team, give the task a title, and add notes of what they need to do. We will use this example to demonstrate how to set up the **New Push** trigger event.

Setting up the New Push trigger event

Once you have added a trigger step to the start of your workflow by selecting **1. Trigger** and chosen **Zapier Chrome extension** as the app and **New Push** as the trigger event, click on the **Continue** button. Then, edit the form fields in the **Set up trigger** section as follows:

1. Type a descriptive field name into each field.

2. Rearrange the field order by hovering your cursor over the six dots icon to the left, and drag and drop to reposition.

3. Remove unnecessary fields by using the **X** icon on the right.

   The form fields section is required and must have a value in order for the Zap to run. You must enter at least one field value.

   Using the example described earlier, this is shown in the following screenshot:

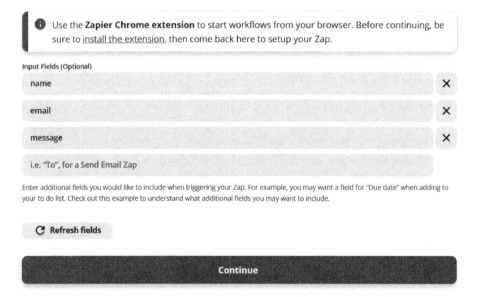

Figure 10.1 – Customizing the New Push trigger event

4. Click on the **Continue** button to proceed.

5. In the **Test trigger** section, use the **Test Trigger** button to pull through some sample data to use and initiate your Zap from the Zapier Chrome extension. You can then add action steps to your Zap, and once complete, turn your Zap on.

6. Navigate to the **Zapier Chrome extension** in your browser to reveal a list of Zaps created. The Zap you just started making will be displayed. If you have not named the Zap, it will be labeled TESTING with the Zap ID. Click on the Zap name to reveal the field labels and enter the relevant details. Click on the **Send** button to activate the push. Once successful, the text will be highlighted in green with a green tick icon.

The details screen is shown in the following screenshot:

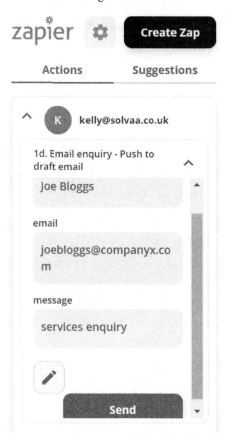

Figure 10.2 – Using the Zapier Chrome extension in the browser with the New Push trigger event

Adjust your Zap as required.

> **Tip**
> Use the timestamp data retrieved to add a due date to your task action steps.
> We will discuss using and formatting dates and times in more detail in *Chapter 13, Formatting Date and Time*, and *Chapter 22, Tips, Tricks, and Best Practices to Enhance Your Productivity*.

You should now have a better understanding of how and when to use the Zapier Chrome extension built-in app.

Now, let's review how to use the URL Shortener by Zapier built-in app to shorten URLs.

URL Shortener by Zapier – shortening URLs in your Zaps

If you want to make long and untidy **Uniform Resource Locator** (**URL**) strings shorter and easier on the eye, you can use the **URL Shortener by Zapier** built-in app to do this. This is especially useful if you have text length restrictions in the app you're sending the URL to and if you want the URL to be displayed in a neater format. URLs are generated with a `zpr.io/` prefix and a unique alphanumeric suffix. This works similar to shortened URLs generated using **Bitly**.

Here are a few examples of when you can use the URL Shortener by Zapier app:

- Sending a shortened URL in an SMS or when you post a tweet to Twitter. They both have text limit restrictions.
- Sending an email to a customer with a link to a web page with a long URL.
- Adding the shortened URLs of new blog articles to Airtable.

URL Shortener by Zapier can only be used as an action step and is available as the following action event:

- **Shorten URL** (action)

Let's explore how to set up and use this action event.

Setting up the Shorten URL action event

Use the **Shorten URL** action event once you have set up your trigger step.

Once you have added an action step, by either selecting the **Action** step or clicking on the + icon, and chosen **URL Shortener by Zapier** as the app and **Shorten URL** as the action event, you can then edit the following field in the **Set up action** section:

- **URL**: Use this field to enter either a static URL value, a dynamic value from previous steps, or a combination of both. This is a required field and must have a value in order for the Zap to run.

An example of this is shown in the following screenshot:

Set up action

URL   (required)

    1. Link: https://example...blog/some-post/

Include http:// or https://.

C **Refresh fields**

Continue

Figure 10.3 – Customizing the Shorten URL action event

Click on the **Continue** button. You can then use the **Test action** section to test this step to generate the shortened URL. This is shown in the following screenshot:

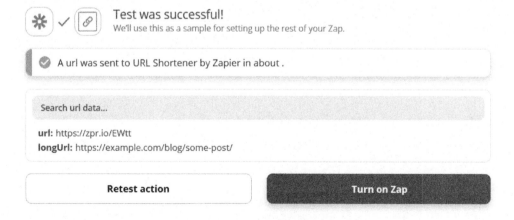

Test was successful!
We'll use this as a sample for setting up the rest of your Zap.

A url was sent to URL Shortener by Zapier in about .

Search url data...

url: https://zpr.io/EWtt
longUrl: https://example.com/blog/some-post/

Retest action   **Turn on Zap**

Figure 10.4 – An example of a shortened URL result using URL Shortener by Zapier

Proceed to add one or more action steps after your **Shorten URL** step.

You should now have a better understanding of how and when to use the URL Shortener built-in app.

Now, let's discuss how to use the Translate by Zapier built-in app to translate text into different languages and detect a language in some text.

Translate by Zapier – translating text

The Translate by Zapier built-in app allows you to translate text into over 100 different languages. It can also be used to detect a language in a set of text.

Here are a few examples of how you can use this app:

- Translating a received email from German to English and adding the translated text to your **Customer Relationship Management (CRM)**
- Detecting the language on a web page and raising a ticket in **Zendesk** for specific members in your multilingual team to address

This app can only be used as an action step, and the following action events are available to use:

- **Translate Text** (action)
- **Detect Language** (action)

Let's look at each of these.

The Translate Text action event

The **Translate Text** action event allows you to translate words, phrases, and web pages of up to 1,000 characters into over 100 languages.

Let's explore how to set up this action event.

Setting up the Translate Text action event

Use the **Translate Text** action event once you have set up your trigger step.

Once you have added an action step, by either selecting the **Action** step or clicking on the + icon, and chosen **Translate by Zapier** as the app and **Translate Text** as the action event, you can then edit the fields in the **Set up action** section as follows:

- **Source Language**: If you know the language of the source text you are using, choose a language from the drop-down list. You can also map in a dynamic field from previous steps. This is useful if you have stated the language in previous steps, for example, if you have this data on a Google Sheets spreadsheet or in a CRM. You can also leave the field blank and Zapier will detect the source language.

- **Text**: In this field, type in static text, map dynamic data from previous steps, or use a combination of both that you want to be translated. Any text over 1,000 characters will be trimmed in the result. This is a required field and must have a value in order for the Zap to run.

- **Target Language**: This field controls which language you want the text to be translated to. Choose a language from the drop-down list or map in a dynamic field from previous steps. This is a required field and must have a value in order for the Zap to run.

For example, we may want to translate a Zapier blog post description from Latin to Swahili. This is shown in the following screenshot:

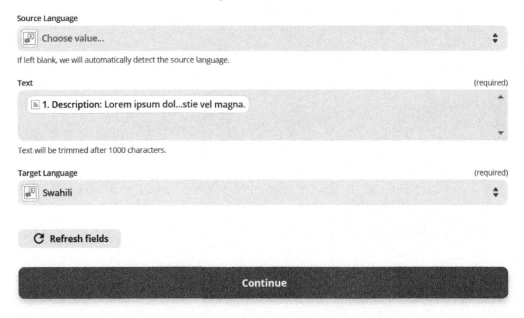

Figure 10.5 – Customizing the Translate Text action event

Click on the **Continue** button, and you can then use the **Test action** section to test this step, or **Skip Test**.

Proceed to add one or more action steps or turn on your Zap.

Now, let's discuss how to detect a language in text using the **Detect Language** action event.

The Detect Language action event

The **Detect Language** action event allows you to detect one of up to 100 languages in a set of text.

Let's explore how to set up this action event.

Setting up the Detect Language action event

Use the **Detect Language** action event once you have set up your trigger step.

Once you have added an action step, by either selecting the **Action** step or clicking on the + icon, and chosen **Translate by Zapier** as the app and **Detect Language** as the action event, you can then edit the following field in the **Set up action** section:

- **Text**: In this field, type in static text, map dynamic data from previous steps, or use a combination of both that you want to be translated. This is a required field and must have a value in order for the Zap to run.

Using the same example of text in Latin, this is shown in the following screenshot:

Figure 10.6 – Customizing the Detect Language action event

Click on the **Continue** button, and you can then use the **Test action** section to test this step, or **Skip Test**.

The result will display the language Zapier assumes it to be and produce a confidence score.

Proceed to add one or more action steps or turn on your Zap.

You should now have a better understanding of how and when to use the Translate by Zapier built-in app.

Next, let's review how to use the Lead Score by Zapier built-in app to score and retrieve information on your leads.

Lead Score by Zapier – scoring and retrieving lead information

The **Lead Score by Zapier** built-in app allows you to gather information from the web about a contact and their associated company using their email address. The search also produces a customer fit qualification score based on various data points. The app uses data from MadKudu.com, a data enrichment service that as a stand-alone service can be quite pricey for small businesses and start-ups. With the Lead Score by Zapier app, you can perform up to 500 free searches per month using this service. However, if you're likely to need a higher number of searches, you can sign up for a paid plan on MadKudu.com, and use the Zapier-**MadKudu** integration instead of Lead Score by Zapier.

The most common reasons you would want to use Lead Score by Zapier are for enriching contact data, lead prioritization, and qualification, therefore allowing you to make better decisions on which leads to follow up with first and understand your contacts better. This will allow you to create more applicable communications and better experiences for your leads and customers. Lead Score by Zapier saves you the hassle of manually searching for this data, and can give you access to additional data that might not be shown in your CRM's native contact and associated company search data, for example, in Salesforce or **HubSpot**.

Here are a few examples of how you can use the Lead Score by Zapier built-in app:

- If a new lead submits a webform, you may want to find out more details about the contact's company, company size, and location.
- When a new contact is added to your CRM, enrich the contact data and get a customer qualification score.
- When a new subscriber is added to your email marketing tool **Klaviyo**, retrieve more personal information on the contact.

Lead Score by Zapier is used as a search action step with the following action event:

- **Find Person and Company Information** (search action)

Let's review how to use this search action event.

The Find Person and Company Information search action event

The **Find Person and Company Information** search action event allows you to search MadKudu.com for data on contacts and associated companies using an email address.

Let's explore how to set up this search action event.

Setting up the Find Person and Company Information search action event

Use the **Find Person and Company Information** search action event once you have set up your trigger step.

Once you have added an action step, by either selecting the **Action** step or clicking on the + icon, and chosen **Lead Score by Zapier** as the app and **Find Person and Company Information** as the action event, you can then edit the fields in the **Set up action** section as follows:

- **Email**: In this field, type in static text, map dynamic data from previous steps, or use a combination of both that you want to be translated in an email format, for example, joe@company.com. This is a required field and must have a value in order for the Zap to run.

- **Should This Step Be Considered A "success" When Nothing Is Found**: Use this Boolean field to select **True** or **False** from the drop-down menu, enter text, or insert data from previous steps for this step to be considered a "success" if nothing is found in the search. The default for this field is **False**, which you should choose if you want the Zap to stop running at this point if nothing is found, as this is the most common use case. This means that all subsequent steps will be skipped. Use the **True** option if you want to allow the Zap to continue and subsequent steps to run. You can then add more control to your workflows by adding Filter by Zapier or Paths by Zapier conditional logic for more control and allowing those steps to pass or stop based on whether the search returned a result or not.

For example, we may want to retrieve information associated with the email address `joebloggs@zapier.com`. This is shown in the following screenshot:

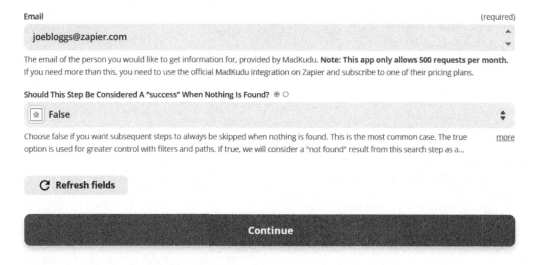

Figure 10.7 – Customizing the Find Person and Company Information search action event

Click on the **Continue** button, and you can then use the **Test action** section to test this step, or **Skip Test**.

The following screenshot shows an example of data returned for `joebloggs@zapier.com`:

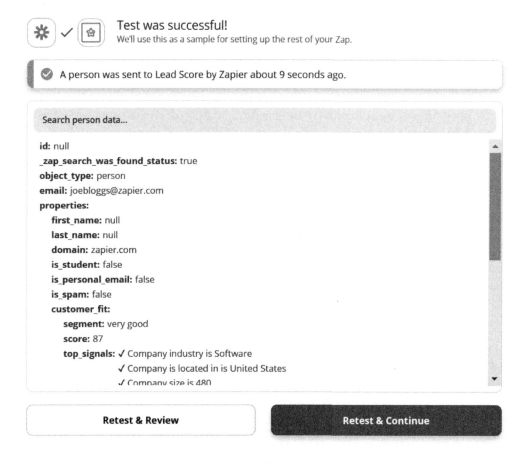

Figure 10.8 – An example of data retrieved by the Lead Score by Zapier search action

You can proceed to add one or more action steps or turn on your Zap.

The search results produce a list of properties, as follows:

- **Person properties**: `first_name`, `last_name`, `domain`, `is_student`, `is_personal_email`, `is_spam`, `customer_fit`, `segment`, `score`, `top_signals`, and `grade_emoji`.

- **Company properties**: `name`, `domain`, `location`, `state`, `state_code`, `country`, `country_code`, `employees`, and `industry`.

> **Tip**
> When you have limitations on API calls to your software, such as a CRM where you can only create or change a fixed number of properties in a certain time period, it would be useful to turn on the **True** option for **Should This Step Be Considered A "success" When Nothing Is Found** to stop your Zap running. Then add filter conditions in the next step.

You should now have a better understanding of how and when to use the Lead Score by Zapier built-in app.

Now, let's cover how to use the Weather by Zapier built-in app to use weather conditions in your workflows.

Weather by Zapier – using weather conditions in your Zaps

The **Weather by Zapier** built-in app gives you access to weather conditions in a specified area, based on latitude and longitude coordinates. You can use it to get daily weather notifications and only to trigger if it will rain that day (for your local area based on your Zapier timezone settings). You can also search for current weather conditions and tomorrow's forecast for a specified location. This app is handy to use personally or if you and your team work outdoors, for example, if you work in the construction, landscaping, or dog walking industries. Weather by Zapier is best used with a notification action in subsequent steps, such as sending an email or SMS.

> **Important note**
> The Weather by Zapier app uses the timezone settings specified in your account to run accurate triggers and search actions. Ensure that your timezone settings have been adjusted accordingly.

Weather by Zapier can be used as both a trigger and an action step and is available as the following events:

- **Will It Rain Today?** (trigger)
- **Today's Forecast** (trigger)
- **Get Current Weather** (search action)
- **Get Tomorrow's Forecast** (search action)

Let's explore how to set up each of these in turn.

The Will It Rain Today? trigger event

The **Will It Rain Today?** trigger event can be used to start a workflow when the weather forecast shows that it is due to rain on that day. The app checks the weather forecast for the day at around 7 a.m. (based on your timezone settings) and only triggers if rain is forecast.

Here are a few examples of how you can use the **Will It Rain Today?** trigger event:

- Send an SMS to yourself if it is going to rain today.

- If your team works outdoors, send an email to them if it is going to rain today.

Let's explore how to set up this trigger event.

Setting up the Will It Rain Today? trigger event

Once you have added this trigger step to the start of your workflow (to **1. Trigger**) and chosen **Weather by Zapier** as the app and **Will It Rain Today?** as the trigger event, you can select **Continue**. You can then edit the fields in the **Set up trigger** section as follows:

- **Latitude**: Enter a decimal value for the latitude of the location you want to check. You can use `https://www.latlong.net/` to find the latitude if you don't know it. This is a required field and must have a value in order for the Zap to run.

- **Longitude**: Enter a decimal value for the longitude of the location you want to check. You can use `https://www.latlong.net/` to find the longitude if you don't know it. This is a required field and must have a value in order for the Zap to run.

- **Units**: This drop-down field allows you to choose to display the forecast results in **Celsius** or **Fahrenheit**. The default is **Fahrenheit**.

Using the example of Paris, France, this is shown in the following screenshot:

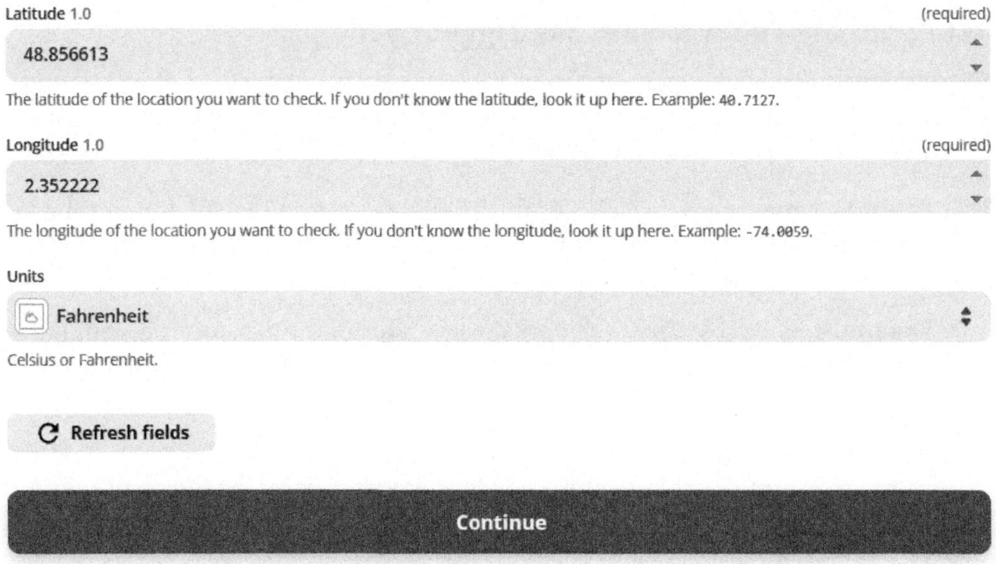

Latitude 1.0   (required)

48.856613

The latitude of the location you want to check. If you don't know the latitude, look it up here. Example: 40.7127.

Longitude 1.0   (required)

2.352222

The longitude of the location you want to check. If you don't know the longitude, look it up here. Example: -74.0059.

Units

🌡 Fahrenheit

Celsius or Fahrenheit.

C **Refresh fields**

Continue

Figure 10.9 – Customizing the Will It Rain Today? trigger event

You can then select **Continue**, and in the **Test trigger** section, use the **Test Trigger** button to retrieve your test data to use in your action steps.

You can use a wide variety of data retrieved from your trigger step, such as precipitation intensity and probability, high and low temperatures, wind speed, and UV index.

Proceed to add one or more action steps to your Zap using data from this trigger step.

You should now be able to use the **Will It Rain Today?** trigger event. Next, let's take a look at the **Today's Forecast** trigger event.

The Today's Forecast trigger event

The **Today's Forecast** trigger event can be used to start a workflow with the forecast for the day. The app checks the weather forecast for the day around 7 a.m. in your local time (based on your timezone settings) and only triggers if rain is forecast.

Here are a few examples of how you can use the **Today's Forecast** trigger event:

- Send a Slack channel message with the forecast for the day.
- Send a tweet on Twitter with a sun emoji when the forecast shows it will be sunny (use Filter by Zapier to specify the conditions).

Let's explore how to set up this trigger event.

Setting up the Today's Forecast trigger event

Once you have added this trigger step to the start of your workflow (to **1. Trigger**) and chosen **Weather by Zapier** as the app and **Today's Forecast** as the trigger event, you can select **Continue**. You can then edit the fields in the **Set up trigger** section as follows:

- **Latitude**: Enter a decimal value for the latitude of the location you want to check. You can use `https://www.latlong.net/` to find the latitude if you don't know it. This is a required field and must have a value in order for the Zap to run.

- **Longitude**: Enter a decimal value for the longitude of the location you want to check. You can use `https://www.latlong.net/` to find the longitude if you don't know it. This is a required field and must have a value in order for the Zap to run.

- **Units**: This drop-down field allows you to choose to display the forecast results in **Celsius** or **Fahrenheit**. The default is **Fahrenheit**.

You can then select **Continue** and in the **Test trigger** section, use the **Test Trigger** button to retrieve your test data to use in your action steps.

You can use a wide variety of data retrieved from your trigger step, such as a summary of the forecast, humidity, precipitation intensity and probability, high and low temperatures, wind speed, and UV index.

Proceed to add one or more action steps to your Zap using data from this trigger step.

You should now be able to use the **Today's Forecast** trigger event. Next, let's take a look at the **Get Current Weather** search action event.

The Get Current Weather search action event

The **Get Current Weather** search action event is ideal to use when you need to know the weather right now or at a specific time of day.

Here are a few examples of how you can use the **Get Current Weather** action search event:

- When you're due to have a meeting, send a notification with the weather forecast.

- When you want to check the weather at a point in time, rather than using a Google search, use Zapier Chrome extension to trigger a workflow to check the weather and send you an SMS.

Let's explore how to set up this search action event.

Setting up the Get Current Weather search action event

Use the **Get Current Weather** search action event once you have set up your trigger step.

Once you have added an action step, by either selecting the **Action** step or clicking on the + icon, and chosen **Weather by Zapier** as the app and **Get Current Weather** as the action event, you can then edit the fields in the **Set up action** section as follows:

- **Latitude**: Enter a decimal value for the latitude of the location you want to check. You can use `https://www.latlong.net/` to find the latitude if you don't know it. This is a required field and must have a value in order for the Zap to run.

- **Longitude**: Enter a decimal value for the longitude of the location you want to check. You can use `https://www.latlong.net/` to find the longitude if you don't know it. This is a required field and must have a value in order for the Zap to run.

- **Units**: This drop-down field allows you to choose to display the forecast results in **Celsius** or **Fahrenheit**. The default is **Fahrenheit**.

- **Should This Step Be Considered A "success" When Nothing Is Found**: Use this Boolean field to select **True** or **False** from the drop-down menu, enter text, or insert data from previous steps for this step to be considered a "success" if nothing is found in the search. The default for this field is **False**, which you should choose if you want the Zap to stop running at this point if nothing is found, as this is the most common use case. This means that all subsequent steps will be skipped. Use the **True** option when you want to allow the Zap to continue and subsequent steps to run. You can then add more control to your workflows by adding Filter by Zapier or Paths by Zapier conditional logic for more control and allowing those steps to pass or stop based on whether the search returned a result or not.

Using the example of London, United Kingdom, this is shown in the following screenshot:

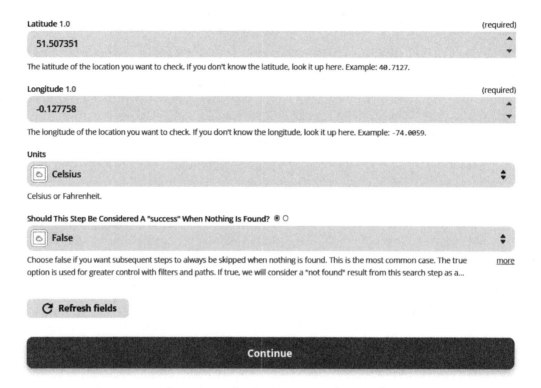

Figure 10.10 – Customizing the Get Current Weather search action event

Click on the **Continue** button, and you can then use the **Test action** section to test this step, or **Skip Test**.

The following screenshot shows the result of some example data:

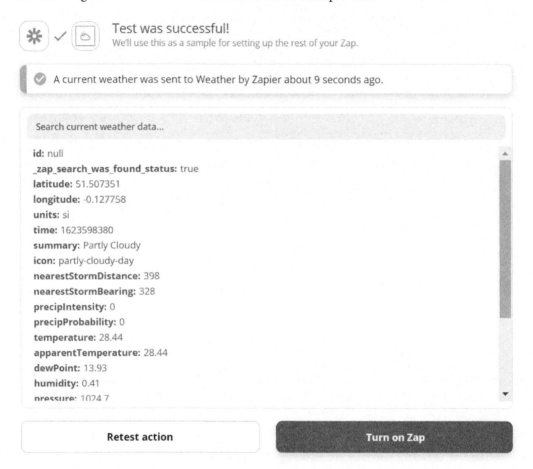

Figure 10.11 – An example of data retrieved from a Get Current Weather search action

You can proceed to add one or more action steps or turn on your Zap.

You should now be able to use the **Get Current Weather** search action event. Next, let's take a look at the **Tomorrow's Forecast** search action event.

The Tomorrow's Forecast search action event

The **Tomorrow's Forecast** search action event is ideal to use when you need to know the weather forecast for the next day.

Here are a few examples of how you can use the **Tomorrow's Forecast** action search event:

- Send an email with tomorrow's job list to your team along with the weather forecast.
- Use Schedule by Zapier to trigger an automation to check tomorrow's weather at 5 p.m. every day and send you an SMS.

Let's explore how to set up this search action event.

Setting up the Tomorrow's Forecast search action event

Use the **Tomorrow's Forecast** search action event once you have set up your trigger step.

Once you have added an action step, either by selecting the **Action** step or clicking on the + icon, and chosen **Weather by Zapier** as the app and **Tomorrow's Forecast** as the action event, you can then edit the fields in the **Set up action** section as follows:

- **Latitude**: Enter a decimal value for the latitude of the location you want to check. You can use `https://www.latlong.net/` to find the latitude if you don't know it. This is a required field and must have a value in order for the Zap to run.

- **Longitude**: Enter a decimal value for the longitude of the location you want to check. You can use `https://www.latlong.net/` to find the longitude if you don't know it. This is a required field and must have a value in order for the Zap to run.

- **Units**: This drop-down field allows you to choose to display the forecast results in **Celsius** or **Fahrenheit**. The default is **Fahrenheit**.

- **Should This Step Be Considered A "success" When Nothing Is Found**: Use this Boolean field to select **True** or **False** from the drop-down menu, enter text, or insert data from previous steps for this step to be considered a "success" if nothing is found in the search. The default for this field is **False**, which you should choose if you want the Zap to stop running at this point if nothing is found, as this is the most common use case. This means that all subsequent steps will be skipped. Use the **True** option when you want to allow the Zap to continue and subsequent steps to run. You can then add more control to your workflows by adding Filter by Zapier or Paths by Zapier conditional logic for more control and allowing those steps to pass or stop based on whether the search returned a result or not.

Click on the **Continue** button, and you can then use the **Test action** section to test this step, or **Skip Test**.

You can proceed to add one or more action steps or turn on your Zap.

You should now have a better understanding of how and when to use the Weather by Zapier app.

Next, let's discuss how to use the Retrograde by Zapier built-in app to use astrological predictions in your automations.

Retrograde by Zapier – using astrological predictions in your Zaps

You can use the Retrograde by Zapier built-in app to trigger your workflows based on Mercury retrograde astrological predictions. You can choose to trigger your workflows when Mercury enters or leaves retrograde or to trigger once a day when Mercury is in retrograde.

The following is a list of trigger event options that Retrograde by Zapier has available:

- **Mercury enters Retrograde** (trigger): This event triggers once Mercury enters retrograde.

- **Mercury in Retrograde** (trigger): This event triggers once per day when Mercury is in retrograde.

- **Mercury leaves Retrograde** (trigger): This event triggers once Mercury leaves retrograde.

Each of the triggers is similar in setup; however, they all return slightly different data. Let's explore how to set up and use these trigger events.

Setting up a Retrograde by Zapier trigger event

Once you have added a trigger step to the start of your workflow (to **1. Trigger**) and chosen **Retrograde by Zapier** as the app and either **Mercury enters Retrograde**, **Mercury in Retrograde**, or **Mercury leaves Retrograde** as the trigger event, you can select **Continue**. As there are no fields to edit, in the **Test trigger** section, use the **Test Trigger** button to retrieve your test data to use in your action steps.

Proceed to add one or more action steps to your Zap using data from this trigger step.

Now, let's review the type of data returned by each of the trigger events.

Data retrieved for the Mercury enters Retrograde trigger event

The following screenshot shows an example of data returned by the **Mercury enters Retrograde** trigger event:

Figure 10.12 – Example data returned by the Mercury enters Retrograde trigger event

Next, let's discuss the type of data returned by the **Mercury in Retrograde** trigger events.

Data retrieved for the Mercury in Retrograde trigger event

The following screenshot shows an example of data returned by the **Mercury in Retrograde** trigger event:

Figure 10.13 – Example data returned by the Mercury in Retrograde trigger event

Next, let's discuss the type of data returned by the **Mercury leaves Retrograde** trigger event.

Data retrieved for the Mercury leaves Retrograde trigger event

The following screenshot shows an example of data returned by the **Mercury leaves Retrograde** trigger event:

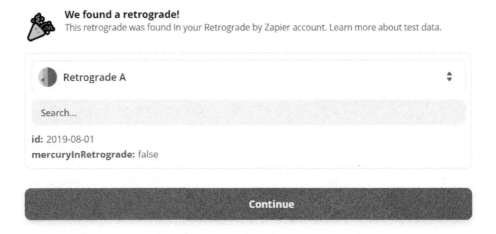

Figure 10.14 – Example data returned by the Mercury leaves Retrograde trigger event

You should now have a better understanding of how and when to use the Retrograde by Zapier app.

Summary

In this chapter, we learned about a few more of Zapier's range of built-in apps. We covered specific functions such as how to use Zapier Chrome extension to initiate a one-off automation from any page on the internet, how to shorten URLs with URL Shortener by Zapier, and how to translate and detect text from different languages using Translate by Zapier. We also discussed how to retrieve and score lead information using Lead Score by Zapier, how to use data on weather conditions using Weather by Zapier, and how to use astrological predictions using Retrograde by Zapier in your automations.

You now know how to kick off one-off automations from your web browser, shorten URLs, and translate text. You also know how to retrieve lead and score information and use weather conditions and astrological predictions in your automations.

In the next chapter, you will learn about more advanced built-in apps. We will review how to use webhooks, JavaScript, and Python code in our Zaps, as well as how to store data.

11
Advanced Built-In Apps by Zapier

The power of Zapier lies in using the extensive functionality made available in the built-in apps, all without using code. You can accomplish a vast array of automations using these apps. However, you will find that there will be times that you may want to achieve something with your Zaps that won't be possible using the standard no-code built-in app functionality or through an existing integration in Zapier. When this happens, it is time to use webhooks and code in your Zaps, thus opening up even more possibilities to automate your manual and repetitive tasks with Zapier. You can use Webhooks by Zapier and Code by Zapier, respectively, to accomplish this.

It is also useful to know about one of the other built-in apps that will help when you want to store and retrieve small datasets. You can use Storage by Zapier to store reference data each time a Zap runs and then share it with other Zaps by retrieving it.

In this chapter, you will have an overview of the more advanced built-in apps by Zapier that allow you to use webhooks (Webhooks by Zapier), and JavaScript or Python code (Code by Zapier) in your Zaps, as well as storing and retrieving data (Storage by Zapier). These three apps are categorized by Zapier as **Developer Tools**, and as these are advanced topics, we will only provide a brief overview of their functionality, without going into too much detail. We will, however, provide you with some use cases and further references.

This chapter will be most useful for Zapier users with a higher level of technical skill, such as software and web developers. A good understanding of concepts around the use of APIs and programming languages such as Python and JavaScript would be beneficial. The content that we will cover will, however, give the non-technical user an introduction to what is possible with these built-in apps.

We will cover the following key topics in this chapter:

- Webhooks by Zapier – Using webhooks in your Zaps
- Code by Zapier – Using JavaScript or Python code in your Zaps
- Storage by Zapier – Saving and storing data

Once you have reviewed each of these topics, you will understand how to use webhooks and code in your Zaps, as well as how to save and store data.

Technical requirements

To make the most of the content and exercises in this chapter, you will need access to a Zapier account. The Zapier Free plan will be adequate. You will need the Zapier Starter plan to create multi-step workflows and to use the Webhooks by Zapier built-in app.

Webhooks by Zapier – Using webhooks in your Zaps

In *Chapter 1, Introduction to Business Process Automation with Zapier*, we introduced how integrations work to request data from one application, producing a response in another. The information requests are usually in the form of creating new resources, retrieving existing ones, editing/updating existing resources, or deleting existing resources. In **HTTP (Hypertext Transfer Protocol** – the foundation for how data is passed along on the internet) terms, these requests are denoted as the following methods:

- POST: Used to create a new resource
- GET: Used to retrieve an existing resource
- PUT: Used to edit or update an existing resource
- DELETE: Used to delete an existing resource

As you already know, the API integrations that have been created between Zapier and other apps have specific trigger, action, and search events that you can use in your Zaps.

For triggers, event changes in apps are identified by either using a polling method or by using webhooks, which then cause the trigger step in your Zaps to run. Whereas the polling method involves repeatedly checking for new information at scheduled intervals, with webhooks, you provide the app with a URL that your originating app constantly monitors for new events, thus receiving information in real time. Webhooks are an instant, and therefore a much more efficient, way of communicating event information. This means that Zaps using webhooks trigger much quicker than other Zaps where the trigger step uses the polling method. Webhooks can also be used for action and search events using the HTTP methods we described previously.

Essentially, webhooks either accept data to trigger a workflow in Zapier or send data to a specified URL when an event happens.

Although, in most cases, the integrations built with Zapier cover the most commonly requested events users may need, often, the app's API allows for many more events, therefore increasing flexibility. Once you have reviewed the app's API documentation to assess what other events are possible, you can then use webhooks (if they are available for use) using the Webhooks by Zapier built-in app to take advantage of these options. The app's API documentation will also normally give clear instructions on how to authenticate or authorize the webhook connection and how to configure it. For example, Trello's API documentation page can be found at `https://developer.atlassian.com/cloud/trello/guides/rest-api/webhooks/`.

The Webhooks by Zapier built-in app can be used with the following trigger and action events:

- **Retrieve Poll** (trigger): This trigger event polls a URL and searches for new entries.
- **Catch Hook** (trigger): This instant trigger event waits for a new POST, GET, or PUT notification to a URL provided by Zapier.
- **Catch Raw Hook** (trigger): This instant trigger event waits for a new POST, GET, or PUT notification to a URL provided by Zapier. This is a more detailed version of the Catch Hook trigger event and supplies the request body as unparsed data and includes headers.
- **Custom Request** (action): This action event sends off a custom request by providing raw data.
- **POST** (action): This action event sends a single request to create a new resource.
- **GET** (action): This action event sends a single request to retrieve an existing resource.
- **PUT** (action): This action event sends a single request to update an existing resource.

Here are a few examples of when you can use Webhooks by Zapier to achieve more in your automations and not be limited by existing Zapier trigger, action, and search events:

- You may want to create a new company in **Freshdesk** when an opportunity is won in Salesforce. The Freshdesk integration with Zapier has a **Create Company** action event that only allows certain details to be added when a new company is created (**Name**, **Description**, **Notes**, and **Domain**), and there is no available action event to update the company. If you have set up custom fields in Freshdesk, you may want your new company to be updated with custom field data such as **Customer Status** or **Product Type**. The Freshdesk API allows PUT requests to update the company (https://developers.freshdesk.com/api/#update_company), and you can therefore use Webhooks by Zapier to do this using the PUT action event.

- You may want to kick off a workflow when a new task is assigned to a specific user in Asana. The Asana integration with Zapier has a **New Task in Project** trigger event that only allows you to trigger for specific projects. There are no trigger events available that allow you to capture all projects or just tasks for a specific user. The Asana API, however, allows you to retrieve information from specific user task lists (https://developers.asana.com/docs/get-tasks-from-a-user-task-list), and you can therefore use Webhooks by Zapier to do this using the **Retrieve Poll** trigger event.

Using webhooks is also useful if your app or business tool does not support a Zapier integration. Webhooks allow developers who are familiar with your tools to create requests between different tools without the need to understand new API documentation. For example, when a new user signs up to create a free trial account, you could create a POST request to create a new contact in your CRM and accounting system. If the integration with Zapier does not support a specific trigger, action, or search event that you need, it is always worth reviewing the API documentation to assess whether it is possible using webhooks.

Zapier has created a few very useful help documents to help you get started with webhooks. You can find out more about webhooks in general at https://zapier.com/help/doc/how-get-started-webhooks-zapier, and how to use webhooks in Zapier at https://zapier.com/blog/what-are-webhooks/.

> **Important note**
> Webhooks by Zapier is a Premium app and can only be used with the Zapier Starter plan or higher.

You should now have a better understanding of how and when to use the Webhooks by Zapier built-in app.

Next, let's review how to use the Code by Zapier built-in app.

Code by Zapier – Using JavaScript or Python code in your Zaps

The next step up from using webhooks in your Zaps is to use code when you can't achieve what you need to with the no-code built-in apps or Webhooks by Zapier. You can write custom code in either the JavaScript or Python programming languages and use it in your Zaps with Code by Zapier to either trigger the workflow or perform various tasks to totally transform and customize your data.

The Code by Zapier built-in app can be used as the following trigger and action events:

- **Run JavaScript** (trigger): This trigger event allows you to use JavaScript to start a workflow.

- **Run Python** (trigger): This trigger event allows you to use Python to start a workflow.

- **Run JavaScript** (action): This action event allows you to run JavaScript as an action step in your Zap.

- **Run Python** (action): This action event allows you to run Python as an action step in your Zap.

Here are a few examples of when you can use Code by Zapier to achieve more in your automations and not be limited by existing Zapier trigger, action, and search events:

- You may want to retrieve detailed information about a contact in Pipedrive, such as all the phone numbers associated with the contact, once your workflow has triggered. You may then want to manipulate those phone numbers to remove the area code, all in one step. The Pipedrive integration with Zapier has a **Find Person** search action event that only allows for one phone number to be retrieved. The Pipedrive API allows requests for information on a person (`https://developers.pipedrive.com/docs/api/v1/#!/Persons/getPerson`), and you can therefore use Code by Zapier to do this using the **Run JavaScript** or **Run Python** action events.

- Your customer records in **Dear Inventory** may have multiple addresses and contacts associated with them, and you might want to update them all at one time. The Dear Inventory integration with Zapier has an **Update Customer** action event that only allows you to update one address and one contact at a time. The Dear Inventory API allows you to update the customer record with multiple addresses and contacts in one go (`https://dearinventory.docs.apiary.io/#reference/customer/customer`), and you can therefore use Code by Zapier to do this using the **Run JavaScript** or **Run Python** action events.

Zapier has created a few very useful help documents to help you get started with Code by Zapier:

`https://zapier.com/help/doc/how-get-started-code-zapier`

`https://zapier.com/help/create/code-webhooks/use-python-code-in-zaps`

`https://zapier.com/help/doc/code-examples`

You should now have a better understanding of how and when to use the Code by Zapier built-in app.

Next, let's review how to use the Storage by Zapier built-in app.

Storage by Zapier – Saving and storing data

There may be many scenarios where it would be useful to be able to store small sets of data for use in your workflows. The Storage by Zapier built-in app allows you to save and retrieve small data values. You can, therefore, store reference data each time a Zap runs and then share it with other Zaps by retrieving it.

Storage by Zapier does not operate with user accounts. Instead, you must specify a **Secret Storage Key** in the format of a **Universally Unique Identifier** (**UUID4**), which acts much like a password, to identify and group storage data. You would then use this secret storage key to identify where to add data to and retrieve data from. You can, therefore, have multiple storage keys that identify your storage locations.

You can store individual values or lists of values. You can also use **child values** (nested values of data) if you want to store and retrieve several values related to a unique identifier, for example, the name and email address of a specific contact.

The Storage by Zapier built-in app can be used as the following action and search action events:

- **Set Child Value** (action): This action event allows you to set one or multiple child values that are stored at a specified key.

- **Set Value** (action): This action event allows you to set a value stored at a specified key.

- **Increment Value** (action): This action event allows you to incrementally add a value at a specified key.

- **Pop Value From List** (action): This action event allows you to remove a value from a list of values. If the list is empty, however, it will return a default value that you define.

- **Push Value Onto List** (action): This action event allows you to push a value onto an existing list of values.

- **Remove All Values** (action): This action event allows you to remove all values from a Storage by Zapier connected account.

- **Remove Child Value** (action): This action event allows you to remove one or multiple child values stored at a specified key.

- **Remove Value** (action): This action event allows you to remove a value or a list of values stored at a specified key.

- **Set Multiple Values** (action): This action event allows you to set multiple values stored at specified keys.

- **Set Value If** (action): This action event allows you to conditionally set a value stored at a specified key if the stored value matches a previously defined value.

- **Get Child Value** (search action): This search action event allows you to retrieve a child value stored at a specified key. You can also create a new child value if none has been stored.

- **Get Value** (search action): This search action event allows you to retrieve a value stored at a specified key. You can also create a new value if none has been stored.

- **Get All Values** (search action): This search action event allows you to retrieve all values stored.

- **Get List Values** (search action): This search action event allows you to retrieve all values from a list and format the output as one value.

- **Get Multiple Values** (search action): This search action event allows you to retrieve multiple values stored at specified keys.

- **Get Secret** (search action): This search action event allows you to retrieve your secret storage key as a value so that it can be used in a Code by Zapier step.

- **Get or Set a Child Value** (search action): This search action event allows you to retrieve or create a child value.

- **Get or Set a Value** (search action): This search action event allows you to retrieve or create a value.

Here are a few examples of how you can use Storage by Zapier:

- You may want to keep a running tally of various key performance indicators and analytics, such as how many new leads have been added to your CRM in a day or how many sales you have made in a week. You can use the **Increment Value** action event to add the values to different keys cumulatively, and then in a separate Zap use the **Remove Value** action event with a Schedule by Zapier trigger event to erase the value periodically (every day or month, for example). You can then display the values in a dashboard reporting tool such as Databox or Geckoboard.

- You may want to store the name and email address of every new user who subscribes to your email list. You can use the **Set Child Value** action event and specify the user ID as the Secret Storage Key and the name and email address as child values. Then, you can use the **Get Child Value** search action event in a separate Zap to retrieve those values.

Zapier has created useful help documents to help you get started with Storage by Zapier:

https://zapier.com/help/doc/how-get-started-storage-zapier

You can also access your storage data by using Code by Zapier steps in your workflows, as described in the following Zapier help document:

https://zapier.com/help/doc/using-storage-zapier-values-code-steps

> **Important note**
> When using the **Get Secret** search action, bear in mind that this will expose your secret key and should be used with caution.

You should now have a better understanding of how and when to use the Storage by Zapier built-in app.

Summary

In this chapter, we discussed three advanced built-in apps by Zapier. We began by reviewing how to use webhooks in your Zaps with Webhooks by Zapier. Then, we covered how to use JavaScript or Python code with Code by Zapier. Lastly, we explored how to use Storage by Zapier to store and retrieve data.

You now understand what the Webhooks by Zapier, Code by Zapier, and Storage by Zapier built-in apps can be used for.

In the next chapter, you will learn about the two built-in apps that can be used for managing your Zapier account: App Status by Zapier and Zapier Manager. We will cover how to use App Status by Zapier to get notifications of integration issues and review the various trigger, action, and search action events that Zapier Manager has for managing errors and changes in your Zapier account.

12
Managing Your Zapier Account with Built-In Apps

Once you have got to grips with the inner workings of Zapier and you have created several Zaps, you will want to know that your automations are running smoothly in the background as you conduct your daily business. You will also want to know straight away when problems occur, such as when your connected apps are experiencing downtime, there are errors with your Zaps, or changes occur in your Zapier account. Thankfully, Zapier has created two built-in apps that will help you keep on top of these situations. In general, when using the trigger events from these built-in apps, you can use various action steps as alerts, such as sending an email, SMS, or Slack message, or adding a task or activity to your tasks management app or CRM.

In this chapter, we discuss the two built-in apps that can be used for managing your Zapier account. We will start by covering App Status by Zapier to get notifications of integration issues. Then, we will review Zapier Manager for managing issues and changes in your Zapier account. Finally, we will cover some use cases.

This chapter will be most useful for those users who are responsible for the administration of systems within the business and where there is a critical need to keep an eye on system maintenance. This is especially important when multiple users in a team are creating automations, specifically in Team and Company plan accounts, and monitoring the administrative aspect of Zapier accounts using automations is beneficial. It is worth mentioning, however, that even single user account owners will benefit from some alert notification Zaps being created, such as those related to errors and task usage.

We will cover the following key topics in this chapter:

- App Status by Zapier – Getting notifications of integration incidents
- Zapier Manager – Managing errors and account changes
- Use cases

Once you have worked through each of these topics, you will know how to set up workflows to manage notifications of app integration incidents, as well as how to manage errors and changes in your Zapier account.

Technical requirements

To make the most of the content and exercises in this chapter, you will need access to a Zapier account. The Zapier Free plan will be adequate. Some examples included in this chapter involve multi-step workflows, for which you will need a Starter plan or higher. For the *Events for Team and Company account user management* section, you will need to use a Team or Company account.

App Status by Zapier – Getting notifications of integration incidents

In *Chapter 5, Troubleshooting and Handling Zap Errors,* we discussed how to manage status alerts of your connected apps by monitoring the Zapier **Status** page and creating alert workflows. This is where we introduced the App Status by Zapier built-in app.

The App Status by Zapier built-in app can only be used as a trigger step and is available as the following trigger event:

- **New or Updated App Incident** (trigger)

This event will trigger on new, updated, and resolved app status incidents from the apps you specify.

Here are a few examples of when you could use this app:

- Send an email when there is a new, updated, or resolved incident with Mailchimp.
- Add a new task to **Wrike** when there is a new incident with **Zoho Campaigns** and Zoho CRM.

Refer to the *Setting up an app status alert workflow with the App Status by Zapier built-in app* section in *Chapter 5, Troubleshooting and Handling Zap Errors*, for a detailed explanation of how to use this built-in app to create alert notifications of new, updated, and resolved incidents with public apps that you specify. We also discussed there how to create your alert Zaps using pre-built Zap templates directly from the Zapier **Status** page.

You should now have a better understanding of how and when to use the App Status by Zapier built-in app.

Next, let's cover how to use the Zapier Manager built-in app to manage errors and account changes in your Zapier account.

Zapier Manager – Managing errors and account changes

We introduced the Zapier Manager built-in app in *Chapter 5, Troubleshooting and Handling Zap Errors*, where we discussed how to use it to manage error alerts such as errors with Zaps, Zaps being turned off, or tasks being halted.

You can also use Zapier Manager to notify yourself and your team about new public apps being added to Zapier, changes to your account such as new folders or Zaps being created, task usage limits being reached, or new Zapier invoices being released. You can search for a Zap or public app, as well as turning Zaps on or off. If you are using a Team account, you can use Zapier Manager to invite a new user to your Zapier team or notify you of new team members being added.

The Zapier Manager built-in app can be used with several trigger, action, and search events, which we have categorized as follows:

1. Managing Zap errors and alerts:

- **New Zap Error** (trigger)
- **Zap Turned Off** (trigger)
- **New Halted Task** (trigger)

2. Managing apps, Zaps, and folders:

- **New Public App** (trigger)
- **Find App** (search action)
- **New Folder** (trigger)
- **New Zap** (trigger)
- **Turn Zap On/Off** (action)
- **Find Zap** (search action)

3. Zapier account administration:

- **Task Usage Limit Reached** (trigger)
- **New Invoice** (trigger)

4. Team and Company account user management:

- **New Team Member** (trigger)
- **Create Team Invitation** (action)

Let's look at each of these in turn.

Events for managing Zap errors and alerts

In *Chapter 5, Troubleshooting and Handling Zap Errors,* we discussed how to use the Zapier Manager built-in app to manage error alerts using each of the three trigger events as follows:

- **New Zap Error** (trigger)
- **Zap Turned Off** (trigger)
- **New Halted Task** (trigger)

Here are a few examples of when to use these trigger events:

- **New Zap Error**: When an error occurs in a Zap, post a message to **Twist**.
- **Zap Turned Off**: When a Zap is turned off, add a task to **Podio**.
- **New Halted Task**: When a task is halted, send an SMS.

In *Chapter 5, Troubleshooting and Handling Zap Errors*, refer to the *Setting up an error alert workflow with the Zapier Manager built-in app* section for a detailed explanation of how to use this built-in app to create alerts for errors with Zaps, Zaps being turned off, or tasks being halted.

Let's now review how to use the various trigger, action, and search action events for managing apps, Zaps, and folders in your Zapier account.

Events for managing app, Zaps, and folders

In *Chapter 4, Managing your Zaps*, we discussed managing your connected apps, and the importance of adequately naming your Zaps and sorting them into folders to maintain a clutter-free and organized Zapier account. With this in mind, you might want to know when new public apps have been connected to Zapier, and when new folders and Zaps are created if your team shares a Zapier account. You may also want to search for information on an app or a Zap, as well as turning a Zap on or off in certain scenarios.

The six Zapier Manager built-in app trigger, action, and search action events that can be used for these purposes are as follows:

- **New Public App** (trigger)
- **Find App** (search action)
- **New Folder** (trigger)
- **New Zap** (trigger)
- **Turn Zap On/Off** (action)
- **Find Zap** (search action)

Let's look at each one of these.

The New Public App trigger event

The **New Public App** trigger event can be used to start a workflow when Zapier announces that a new public app has been integrated with the platform. Keeping on top of these alerts is useful if you use certain apps in your business that do not currently integrate with Zapier.

Here are a few examples of how you can use this trigger event:

- Send an email when a new public app has been announced.
- Send a Twitter message when a new public app has been released on the Zapier platform.

Let's explore how to set up this trigger event.

Setting up the New Public App trigger event

Once you have added this trigger step to the start of your workflow (to **1. Trigger**) and chosen **Zapier Manager** as the app and **New Public App** as the trigger event, you can select **Continue**. You can then edit the fields in the **Set up trigger** section as follows:

- **Category**: From the alphabetical drop-down list, choose the app category you want your trigger to fire on. You can select **All** if you want to be notified of all apps, or alternatively, specify the category. Categories are based on the information you find in the app ecosystem directory, `https://zapier.com/apps`. Add one category per field, and additional fields will appear once you have confirmed the category in each field. Delete any field lines by clicking on the **X** button at the end of the field. You can also type a static value into each field.

This is shown in the following screenshot:

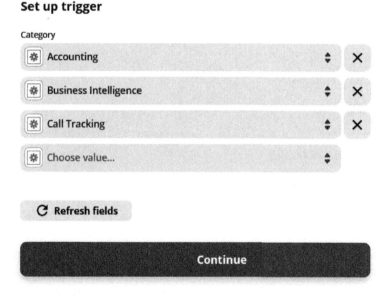

Figure 12.1 – Customizing the New Public App trigger event

You can then select **Continue**, and in the **Test trigger** section, use the **Test Trigger** button to retrieve your test data to use in your action steps.

The trigger extracts the following data that can be used in your action steps:

- App ID
- App title

- Description of the app
- App site URL
- App page URL on Zapier
- Listed categories

Proceed to add one or more action steps to your Zap using data from this trigger step.

You should now be able to use the **New Public App** trigger event. Next, let's take a look at the **Find App** search action event.

The Find App search action event

The **Find App** search action event is handy to use when you want to retrieve information about a public app. For example, say you want to watch an app, such as **Cascade**, for changes to the categories it is listed in. In this case, you could set **Schedule by Zapier** as the trigger to fire every 4 weeks, then use the **Find App** search action to find the information on the Cascade app, and thereafter add the data to a Google Sheets spreadsheet.

Let's explore how to set up this action event.

Setting up the Find App search action event

Use the **Find App** search action event once you have set up a trigger step.

Once you have added an action step either by selecting the **Action** step or clicking on the + icon and have chosen **Zapier Manager** as the app and **Find App** as the action event, you can then edit the fields in the **Set up action** section as follows:

- **Name**: Enter the name of the app by either typing in static data, using the **Custom** tab to map in dynamic data from previous steps, or a combination of both.

- **Should This Step Be Considered A "success" When Nothing Is Found**: Use this Boolean field to select **True** or **False** from the drop-down menu, enter text, or insert data from previous steps for this step to be considered a "success" if nothing is found in the search. The default for this field is **False**, which you should choose if you want the Zap to stop running at this point if nothing is found, as this is the most common use case. This means that all subsequent steps will be skipped. Use the **True** option when you want to allow the Zap to continue and subsequent steps to run. You can then add more control to your workflows by adding Filter by Zapier or Paths by Zapier conditional logic for more control and allowing those steps to pass or stop based on whether the search returned a result or not.

This is shown in the following screenshot:

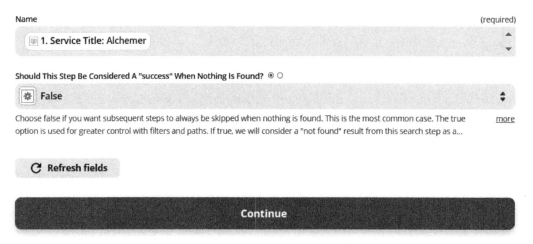

Figure 12.2 – Customizing the Find App search action event

Click on the **Continue** button, and you can then use the **Test action** section to test this step or go for **Skip Test**.

Proceed to add one or more action steps and then turn on your Zap.

You should now be able to use the **Find App** search action event. Next, let's take a look at the **New Folder** trigger event.

The New Folder trigger event

The **New Folder** trigger event can be used to start a workflow when a new folder is added to your Zapier account or accounts you have access to. This is especially useful if several people in your team use the same account and you want to know when new folders are being created and what Zaps they contain, or if you want to record this information somewhere.

Here are a few examples of how you can use this trigger event:

- Send a group chat message in **Chatwork** when a new folder is created.
- Add a new row to a Google Sheets spreadsheet when a new folder is created.

Let's explore how to set up this trigger event.

Setting up the New Folder trigger event

Once you have added this trigger step to the start of your workflow (to **1. Trigger**) and chosen **Zapier Manager** as the app and **New Folder** as the trigger event, you can select **Continue**. You can then edit the fields in the **Set up trigger** section as follows:

- **Account**: If you are a member of multiple Team or Company accounts, use the drop-down menu to stipulate which account you want to receive alerts for. These accounts will be denoted by the name of the account, for example, "Joe Bloggs' Team." If you only have access to one account, choose the relevant account (normally denoted by "Personal Account," if not a Team or Company account). You can also use the **Custom** tab to then type in a static value. If this field is left blank, the trigger will fire for new folders created in all the Zapier accounts you have access to.

    This is shown in the following screenshot:

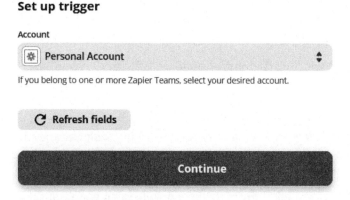

Figure 12.3 – Customizing the New Folder trigger event

You can then select **Continue**, and in the **Test trigger** section, use the **Test Trigger** button to retrieve your test data to use in your action steps.

The trigger extracts the following data that can be used in your action steps:

- Folder ID
- Folder title
- Whether the folder has been shared or not
- The email address of the user that created the folder

Proceed to add one or more action steps to your Zap using data from this trigger step.

You should now be able to use the **New Folder** trigger event. Next, let's take a look at the **New Zap** trigger event.

The New Zap trigger event

The **New Zap** trigger event can be used to start a workflow when a new Zap is added to your Zapier account or accounts you have access to. As with the **New Folder** trigger event, this is especially useful if several people in your team use the same account and you want to know when new Zaps are being created, or if you want to record this information somewhere.

Here are a few examples of how you can use this trigger event:

- Send an email when a new Zap is created.
- Add a new record in Airtable when a new Zap is created.

Let's explore how to set up this trigger event.

Setting up the New Zap trigger event

Once you have added this trigger step to the start of your workflow (to **1. Trigger**) and chosen **Zapier Manager** as the app and **New Zap** as the trigger event, you can select **Continue**. You can then edit the fields in the **Set up trigger** section as follows:

- **Account**: If you are a member of multiple Team or Company accounts, use the drop-down menu to stipulate which account you want to receive alerts for. These accounts will be denoted by the name of the account, for example, "Joe Bloggs' Team." If you only have access to one account, choose the relevant account (normally denoted by "Personal Account," if not a Team or Company account). You can also use the **Custom** tab to then type in a static value. If this field is left blank, the trigger will fire for new Zaps created in all the Zapier accounts you have access to.

- **Folder**: Choose a folder from a drop-down list that you want the trigger to fire on. You can also use the **Custom** tab to then type in a static value. If this field is left blank, the trigger will fire on all new Zaps created.

This is shown in the following screenshot:

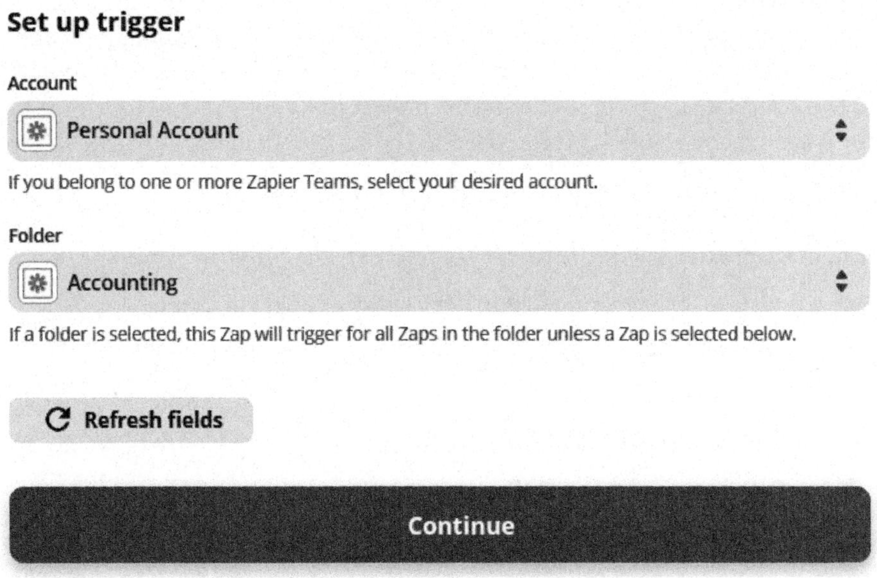

Set up trigger

Account

| ❋ Personal Account | ⇕ |

If you belong to one or more Zapier Teams, select your desired account.

Folder

| ❋ Accounting | ⇕ |

If a folder is selected, this Zap will trigger for all Zaps in the folder unless a Zap is selected below.

↻ Refresh fields

Continue

Figure 12.4 – Customizing the New Zap trigger event

You can then select **Continue**, and in the **Test trigger** section, use the **Test Trigger** button to retrieve your test data to use in your action steps.

The trigger extracts the following data that can be used in your action steps:

- Folder root ID
- Zap title
- Zap URL
- Zap Task History URL
- Whether the Zap has been paused or not
- Whether the Zap is on or off (state)
- The email address of the last user to edit the Zap
- The date and time the Zap was last live
- The date and time the Zap was last paused

Proceed to add one or more action steps to your Zap using data from this trigger step.

You should now be able to use the **New Zap** trigger event. Next, let's take a look at the **Turn Zap On/Off** action event.

The Turn Zap On/Off action event

The **Turn Zap On/Off** action event is useful to use when you want to turn a Zap on or off when a specific trigger event occurs. Turning a Zap off, for example, might be useful in combination with one of the error trigger events such as **New Zap Error**. You might want to turn the Zap off and then create a task in your project management tool to tell your team to assess the issue. Once the task has been completed, you can then turn the Zap back on again.

Here are a few examples of how you can use this trigger event:

- When a Zap error occurs, turn the Zap off and add a task in MeisterTask.
- When a task has been completed in MeisterTask, turn a Zap on.

Let's explore how to set up this action event.

Setting up the Turn Zap On/Off action event

Use the **Turn Zap On/Off** action event once you have set up a trigger step.

Once you have added an action step either by selecting the **Action** step or clicking on the + icon and chosen **Zapier Manager** as the app and **Turn Zap On/Off** as the action event, you can then edit the fields in the **Set up action** section as follows:

- **Desired Zap State**: From the drop-down list, choose a status to transition the Zap to. The options are **Turn Zap Off**, **Turn Zap On**, and **Toggle Zap State**. If you choose **Toggle Zap State**, the status of the Zap will change depending on its current state. For example, if it is on, this action event will turn it off and vice-versa. You can also use the **Custom** tab to then type in a static value, use a dynamic value from previous steps, or use a combination. Bear in mind that if you are using static or dynamic values instead of the drop-down list, the recognized values for this field are Turn Zap Off = **0**, Turn Zap On = **1**, and Toggle Zap State = **2**. This is a required field and must have a value for the step to run successfully.

- **Account**: If you are a member of multiple Team or Company accounts, use the drop-down menu to stipulate which account you want to receive alerts for. These accounts will be denoted by the name of the account, for example, "Joe Bloggs' Team." If you only have access to one account, choose the relevant account (normally denoted by "Personal Account," if not a Team or Company account). You can also use the **Custom** tab to then type in a static value, use a dynamic value from previous steps, or use a combination.

- **Folder**: Choose a folder from a drop-down list. You can also use the **Custom** tab to then type in a static value, use a dynamic value from previous steps, or a combination.

- **Zap**: Specify a Zap from a drop-down list. You can also use the **Custom** tab to then type in a static value, use a dynamic value from previous steps, or a combination. This is a required field and must have a value for the step to successfully run.

This is shown in the following screenshot:

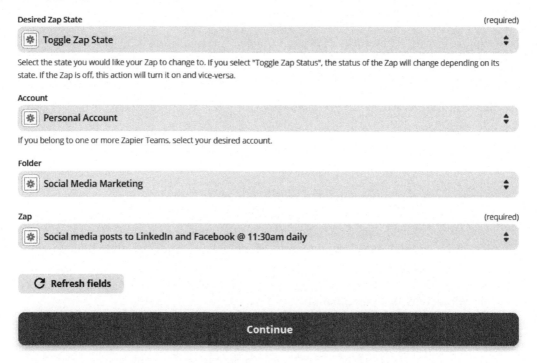

Figure 12.5 – Customizing the Turn Zap On/Off action event

Click on the **Continue** button, and you can then use the **Test action** section to test this step or **Skip Test**.

Proceed to add one or more action steps and then turn on your Zap.

You should now be able to use the **Turn Zap On/Off** action event. Next, let's take a look at the **Find Zap** search action event.

The Find Zap search action event

The **Find Zap** search action event is handy to use when you want to retrieve information about a specific Zap. For example, you might want to use this to watch for when changes are made to the Zap, such as if the Zap is moved to another folder.

Here are a few examples of how you can use this search action event:

- Schedule a maintenance check on a specific Zap weekly using Schedule by Zapier, search to retrieve data on the Zap, and add it to a new record in Airtable.

- When a task is halted, search for more information on the Zap and send a Slack message to your team.

Let's explore how to set up this action event.

Setting up the Find Zap search action event

Use the **Find Zap** search action event once you have set up a trigger step.

Once you have added an action step either by selecting the **Action** step or clicking on the + icon and chosen **Zapier Manager** as the app and **Find Zap** as the action event, you can then edit the fields in the **Set up action** section as follows:

- **Account**: If you are a member of multiple Team or Company accounts, use the drop-down menu to stipulate which account you want to receive alerts for. These accounts will be denoted by the name of the account, for example, "Joe Bloggs' Team." If you only have access to one account, choose the relevant account (normally denoted by "Personal Account," if not a Team or Company account). You can also use the **Custom** tab to then type in a static value, use a dynamic value from previous steps, or a combination.

- **Name**: Enter the name of the Zap by either typing in static data, using the **Custom** tab to map in dynamic data from previous steps, or a combination of both. This is a required field and must have a value for the step to successfully run.

- **Should This Step Be Considered A "success" When Nothing Is Found**: Use this Boolean field to select **True** or **False** from the drop-down menu, enter text, or insert data from previous steps for this step to be considered a "success" if nothing is found in the search. The default for this field is **False**, which you should choose if you want the Zap to stop running at this point if nothing is found, as this is the most common use case. This means that all subsequent steps will be skipped. Use the **True** option when you want to allow the Zap to continue and subsequent steps to run. You can then add more control to your workflows by adding Filter by Zapier or Paths by Zapier conditional logic for more control and allowing those steps to pass or stop based on whether the search returned a result or not.

This is shown in the following screenshot:

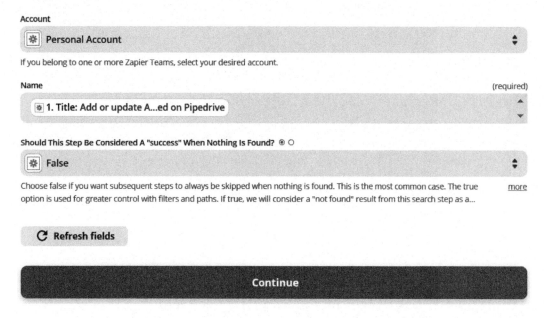

Figure 12.6 – Customizing the Find Zap search action event

Click on the **Continue** button, and you can then use the **Test action** section to test this step or **Skip Test**.

Proceed to add one or more action steps and then turn on your Zap.

You should now be able to use the **Find Zap** search action event.

Let's now review how to use the various trigger events that can be used for Zapier account administration.

Events for Zapier account administration

Keeping an eye on your account from an administration perspective is handy to identify when changes happen or urgent attention is required. You may want to know when your task limit on your current plan is soon to be reached so that you have an idea of when to upgrade your pricing plan. This ensures continuity of service with your automations, as your tasks may be held back if you reach your account task limit unexpectedly. Equally, if a member of your team has upgraded your account to a higher pricing plan, you may want to be alerted when a new invoice has been generated.

The two Zapier Manager built-in app trigger events that can be used for these purposes are as follows:

- **Task Usage Limit Reached** (trigger)
- **New Invoice** (trigger)

Let's look at each one of these.

The Task Usage Limit Reached trigger event

The **Task Usage Limit Reached** trigger event can be used to start a workflow when your Zapier account task usage has hit a specified threshold of either a percentage or number of tasks in relation to your allocated task amount denoted by your Zapier pricing plan.

Here are a few examples of how you can use this trigger event:

- Send an SMS to yourself if your task usage has reached 70% of the limit.
- Send an email to your team if your task usage has hit 950 of a 1,000 task limit.

Let's explore how to set up this trigger event.

Setting up the Task Usage Limit Reached trigger event

Once you have added this trigger step to the start of your workflow (to **1. Trigger**) and chosen **Zapier Manager** as the app and **Task Usage Limit Reached** as the trigger event, you can select **Continue**. You can then edit the fields in the **Set up trigger** section as follows:

- **Account**: If you are a member of multiple Team or Company accounts, use the drop-down menu to stipulate which account you want to receive alerts for. These accounts will be denoted by the name of the account, for example, "Joe Bloggs' Team." If you only have access to one account, choose the relevant account (normally denoted by "Personal Account," if not a Team or Company account). You can also use the **Custom** tab to then type in a static value. If this field is left blank, the trigger will fire for task usage limits reached in all the Zapier accounts you have access to.

- **Usage Threshold (Percent)**: Use this drop-down menu to select a percentage ranging from 10 to 90, specified in increments of 10. You can also type in static text, map dynamic data from previous steps (using the **Custom** tab), or use a combination of both. The trigger will fire when your task usage hits this percentage of included tasks of your pricing plan. The default is 80% if you do not specify a value.

- **Usage Threshold (Task)**: Use this number field to type in a numeric value less than your total number of included tasks as per your pricing plan. The trigger will fire when your task usage hits this amount. If you have also specified a percentage in the **Usage Threshold (Percent)** field, the trigger will fire on whichever amount occurs first.

This is shown in the following screenshot:

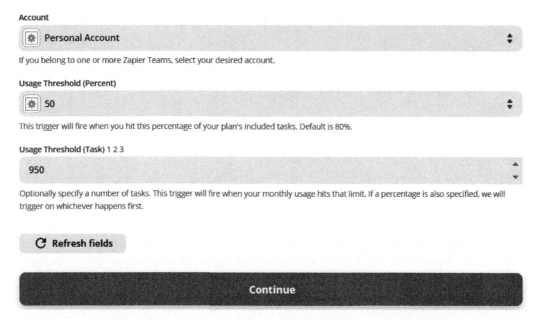

Figure 12.7 – Customizing the Task Usage Limit Reached trigger event

You can then click on **Continue,** and in the **Test trigger** section, use the **Test Trigger** button to retrieve your test data to use in your action steps.

The trigger extracts the following data that can be used in your action steps:

- ID
- Task count
- Task limit
- Percent
- Time remaining before billing date (and task count renewal)

Proceed to add one or more action steps to your Zap using data from this trigger step.

You should now be able to use the **Task Usage Limit Reached** trigger event. Next, let's take a look at the **New Invoice** trigger event.

The New Invoice trigger event

The **New Invoice** trigger event can be used to start a workflow when a new invoice is generated in your Zapier account, or in one that you have access to on a Team or Company account. This is useful if you want to be notified of any new upgrades to your Zapier pricing plan, or if you want to alert your accounting team of a new invoice being created.

Here are a few examples of how you can use this trigger event:

- Send a Microsoft Teams message when a new invoice is generated thus alerting you of a pricing plan change.
- Send an email to your accounting team when a new invoice is generated.

Let's explore how to set up this trigger event.

Setting up the New Invoice trigger event

Once you have added this trigger step to the start of your workflow (to **1. Trigger**) and chosen **Zapier Manager** as the app and **New Invoice** as the trigger event, you can select **Continue**. You can then edit the fields in the **Set up trigger** section as follows:

- **Account**: If you are a member of multiple Team or Company accounts, use the drop-down menu to stipulate which account you want to receive alerts for. These accounts will be denoted by the name of the account, for example, "Joe Bloggs' Team." If you only have access to one account, choose the relevant account (normally denoted by "Personal Account," if not a Team or Company account). You can also use the **Custom** tab to then type in a static value. If this field is left blank, the trigger will fire for new invoices generated in all the Zapier accounts you have access to.

You can then select **Continue**, and in the **Test trigger** section, use the **Test Trigger** button to retrieve your test data to use in your action steps.

The trigger extracts the following data that can be used in your action steps:

- Invoice ID
- Date the invoice was created
- Invoice amount
- Amount due
- Invoice URL

Proceed to add one or more action steps to your Zap using data from this trigger step.

You should now be able to use the **New Invoice** trigger event. Let's now review how to use the trigger and action events for managing Team and Company account users.

Events for Team and Company account user management

If you have a Team or Company Zapier account, you will most certainly want to make it easier for yourself to monitor new users being added and to create new user account invitations automatically. The two Zapier Manager built-in app trigger events that can be used for these purposes are as follows:

- **New Team Member** (trigger)
- **Create Team Invitation** (action)

Let's look at each one of these.

The New Team Member trigger event

The **New Team Member** trigger event can be used to start a workflow when a new user is added to your Zapier Team account. This is especially useful if you or members of your team want to be alerted when new team members have been added as users.

Here are a few examples of how you can use this trigger event:

- Send an SMS to yourself when a new team member is added.
- Send an email to your team when a new team member is added.

Let's explore how to set up this trigger event.

Setting up the New Team Member trigger event

Once you have added this trigger step to the start of your workflow (to **1. Trigger**) and chosen **Zapier Manager** as the app and **New Team Member** as the trigger event, you can select **Continue**. You can then edit the fields in the **Set up trigger** section as follows:

- **Account**: If you are a member of multiple Team or Company accounts, use the drop-down menu to stipulate which account you want to receive alerts for. These accounts will be denoted by the name of the account, for example, "Joe Bloggs' Team." If you only have access to one account, choose the relevant account (normally denoted by "Personal Account," if not a Team or Company account). You can also use the **Custom** tab to then type in a static value. If this field is left blank, the trigger will fire for new users added in all the Zapier accounts you have access to.

This is shown in the following screenshot:

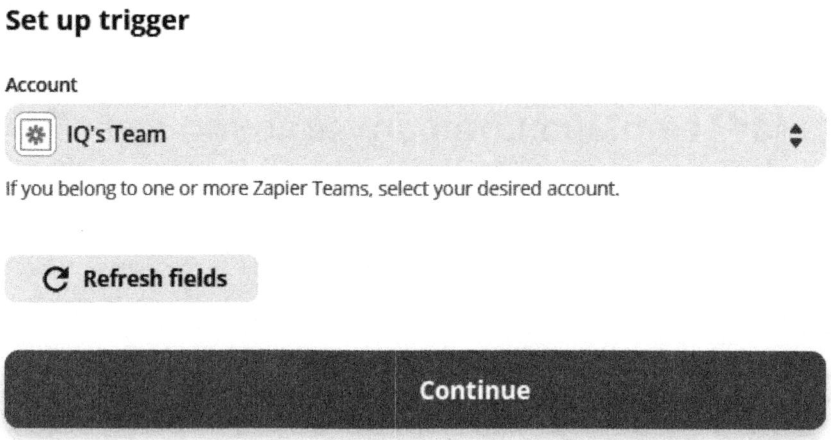

Set up trigger

Account

| ✱ IQ's Team | ⬍ |

If you belong to one or more Zapier Teams, select your desired account.

↻ **Refresh fields**

Continue

Figure 12.8 – Customizing the New Team Member trigger event

You can then select **Continue,** and in the **Test trigger** section, use the **Test Trigger** button to retrieve your test data to use in your action steps.

The trigger extracts the following data that can be used in your action steps:

- User ID
- User email address
- User's name
- Team name

Proceed to add one or more action steps to your Zap using data from this trigger step.

You should now be able to use the New Team Member trigger event. Next, let's take a look at the Create Team Invitation action event.

The Create Team Invitation action event

The **Create Team Invitation** action event allows you to add a new user to your Team or Company Zapier account. Zapier will send an email invitation to the user, asking them to accept the invitation and access the account within 30 days.

An example of how to use this action event would be when a new employee onboarding task is completed in ClickUp; you could add a new user to Zapier and send an email to your team.

Let's explore how to set up this action event.

Setting up the Create Team Invitation action event

Use the **Create Team Invitation** action event once you have set up your trigger step, with the relevant trigger data you want to push to Zapier Manager.

Once you have added an action step either by selecting the **Action** step or clicking on the + icon and chosen **Zapier Manager** as the app and **Create Team Invitation** as the action event, you can then edit the fields in the **Set up action** section as follows:

- **Invitee Email**: Enter an email address either using a typed in static value, dynamic data from previous steps (using the **Custom** tab), or a combination of both. This is a required field and must have a value for the Zap to continue.

- **Team**: If you are a member of multiple Team or Company accounts, use the drop-down menu to stipulate which account you want to receive alerts for. If you only have access to one account, choose the relevant account. You can also choose dynamic values from previous steps using the **Custom** tab.

This is shown in the following screenshot:

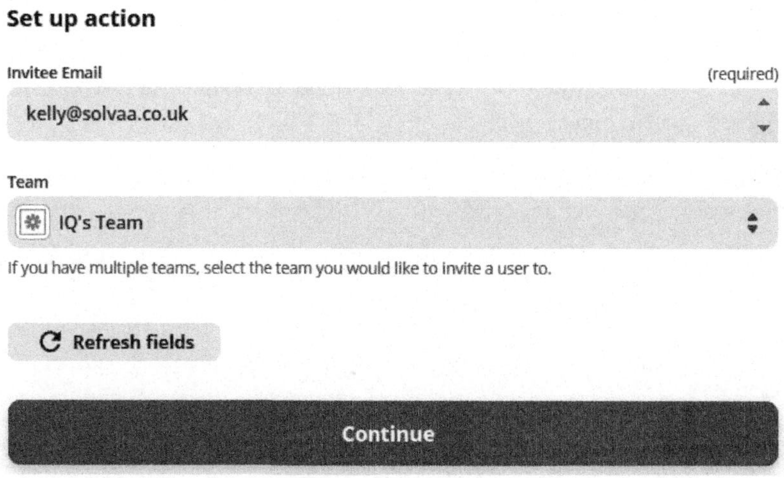

Set up action

Invitee Email   (required)

    kelly@solvaa.co.uk

Team

    ✳ IQ's Team

If you have multiple teams, select the team you would like to invite a user to.

    ↻ **Refresh fields**

    Continue

Figure 12.9 – Customizing the Create Team Invitation action event

Click on the **Continue** button, and you can then use the **Test action** section to test this step or go for **Skip Test**.

Proceed to add one or more action steps to your Zaps, if required, and then turn on your Zap.

You should now have a better understanding of how and when to use the **Create Team Invitation** action event, as well as all the other trigger, action, and search action events of the Zapier Manager built-in app.

Next, let's look at a few scenarios where you can use App Status by Zapier and Zapier Manager to manage your Zapier account.

Use cases

As mentioned earlier in the chapter, having automations set up to manage various aspects of your Zapier account is most suited to situations when multiple users are accessing Zapier on Team and Company accounts and many processes are being automated. System administrators certainly will want to keep a handle on what is happening in the account to monitor task usage and errors, as well as automatically taking action based on certain criteria.

The most common scenarios would involve creating alerts with your favorite notification tools, such as email or Slack, that trigger on any of the trigger events in either App Status by Zapier or Zapier Manager. Zap errors, halted tasks, and Zaps being turned off, as well as app status alerts, would be the most common for maintenance purposes. However, if you're in a team, knowing when another team member creates a new folder or, more specifically, a new Zap, would be useful. You can then action other steps, such as adding information to a Google Sheets spreadsheet.

For example, it would be handy to turn high-task usage Zaps off using the **Turn Zap On/Off** action when you reach 90% of your task limit. You would use the **Task Usage Limit Reached** trigger to start the workflow and select a specific high-usage Zap to turn off. You could then restart the workflow when your task usage refreshes the next month, being triggered by the **New Invoice** trigger.

You can get more inspiration here: `https://zapier.com/blog/updates/1594/new-zapier-manager-automate-your-automations`.

You should now have a better understanding of how and when to use App Status by Zapier and Zapier Manager to help manage your Zapier account.

Summary

In this chapter, we discussed the two built-in apps that can be used for managing your Zapier account that we introduced in *Chapter 5, Troubleshooting and Handling Zap Errors*. We began with reviewing App Status by Zapier to get notifications of integration issues, and then we covered the various trigger, action, and search action events that Zapier Manager has for managing errors and changes in your Zapier account.

You now know how to use App Status by Zapier and Zapier Manager to get alerts of app integration problems and manage issues and alterations in your Zapier account.

In the next chapter, you will learn how to manipulate dates and times with the versatile Formatter by Zapier built-in app. We will cover how to convert and adjust date and time values into different formats, as well as how to add and subtract time.

Section 3: Using the Features of the Formatter by Zapier Built-In App

In this section, you will gain an understanding of the extensive functionality and practical uses of the Formatter by Zapier app. You will learn how to format dates, times, text, numbers, and other actions.

This section comprises the following chapters:

- Chapter 13, *Formatting Date and Time*
- Chapter 14, *Formatting Numbers*
- Chapter 15, *Text Formatting Functions in Zapier – Part 1*
- Chapter 16, *Text Formatting Functions in Zapier – Part 2*
- Chapter 17, *Zapier's Utilities Functions*

13
Formatting Date and Time

The data that appears in your Zaps may not always be presented in the format that you need it in. You may often find that you need to change the format of that data so that it can be viewed in a certain way or so that it is compatible with the data formats required by your other apps. For example, say a new subscriber joins your newsletter but they have entered their name in lowercase; perhaps you may want to capitalize the first letter. Or, a date might be shown in an American format but you might want to change it to an internationally recognized format instead. You may also want to strip out text that is presented in HTML format, or use a spreadsheet-type formula to calculate something. All of this, and more, is possible without using code, and by using Zapier's extremely versatile Formatter by Zapier built-in app to manipulate a huge array of values into formats you prefer or need for a specific purpose.

In this chapter, we will first introduce the Formatter by Zapier built-in app, with its range of functionality to manipulate dates and times, numbers, text, and various other values. With a primary focus on formatting dates and times, we will cover the basics of how to adjust date and time values in your Zaps. Then, we will discuss how to use the date and time your Zap runs in the rest of your action steps in the Zap. After that, we will explore how to use the Formatter by Zapier built-in app to add and subtract time, and finally, we will dive into formatting date and time values using this built-in app.

We will cover the following key topics in this chapter:

- An introduction to the Formatter by Zapier built-in app
- The basics of adjusting date and time values using Zapier
- Using the date and time your Zap runs in fields
- Manipulating dates and times with Formatter by Zapier

Once you have worked through each of these topics, you will have a better understanding of the different action events available for use with the Formatter by Zapier built-in app. You will also know how to adjust date and time values in your Zaps, use the date and time your Zap runs, and how to add or subtract time and manipulate date and time data using the Formatter by Zapier built-in app.

Technical requirements

To make the most of the content and exercises in this chapter, you will need access to a Zapier account. The Zapier Starter plan will be required for you to create multi-step workflows using the Formatter by Zapier built-in app.

An introduction to the Formatter by Zapier built-in app

When creating your workflow automations, you may sometimes find that the data you retrieve from one app isn't recognized in another app, or you may want to change this data in some other way to present it differently. Having the ability to manipulate data values in this way without using code is of course a huge benefit. Zapier allows you to do this using a built-in app called Formatter by Zapier.

The Formatter by Zapier app is by far the most versatile and useful built-in app by Zapier. The functionality is so extensive that we will cover this app and each of its action events in four separate chapters.

The Formatter by Zapier built-in app can only be used as an action step and has the following action events:

- **Date/Time**: This action event allows you to convert date and time values to different formats (including timezones) and add or subtract time. We cover date and time formatting using the Formatter by Zapier built-in app in this chapter.

- **Numbers**: This action event allows you to manipulate numbers, phone numbers, and currencies, and use spreadsheet-type formulas and math operations. We cover number formatting using the Formatter by Zapier built-in app in *Chapter 14, Formatting Numbers*.

- **Text**: You can extensively format text using this action event. You can adjust title case, uppercase, and lowercase, find and replace text, trim whitespace, count words and adjust length, and pluralize text. We will cover these functions in *Chapter 15, Text Formatting Functions in Zapier – Part 1*. You can also create superhero names, split and truncate text, extract patterns, URLs, phone numbers, numbers, and email addresses, convert Markdown to HTML, convert text to ASCII, use Default Value and URL Encode / Decode, and remove HTML tags. We will discuss these functions in *Chapter 16, Text Formatting Functions in Zapier – Part 2*.

- **Utilities**: The **Utilities** action event allows you to create and customize line items, convert text to line items and vice versa, use lookup tables and picklists, and import .csv files. We cover the **Utilities** action event in the Formatter by Zapier built-in app in *Chapter 17, Zapier's Utilities Functions*.

You should now have a better understanding of the different action events and functionality of the Formatter by Zapier built-in app.

Before we get into the details of how to manipulate date and time values with Formatter by Zapier, let's review the basics of how to adjust time and date values in your Zaps.

The basics of adjusting date and time values using Zapier

Before we dive in to using the Formatter by Zapier built-in app for manipulating date and time values, it is useful to know how you can adjust date and time values in your Zaps on a basic level.

In *Chapter 3, Building Your First Automated Workflow (Zap)*, we introduced you to the **Date/Time** field type. When you are presented with this type of field in your action steps, you can use a **field modifier**, either standalone or after a static or dynamic date or time value, to adjust the date/time.

Field modifiers must consist of the following three variables:

- A plus (+) or minus (-) sign, to signify adding or subtracting time.

- A number.

- A unit of time, in either seconds (second, seconds, or s), minutes (minute, minutes, or m), hours (hour, hours, or h), days (day, days, or d), months (month or months), or years (year, years, or y). You can either use the abbreviation or the full spelling in singular or plural.

For example, if you need to create an invoice in your accounting app and want the **Date** and **Due Date** fields to be populated with values of 1 day from the day the Zap ran and 1 month from the date a deal was due to close in your CRM, respectively, you would use modifiers as shown in the following screenshot:

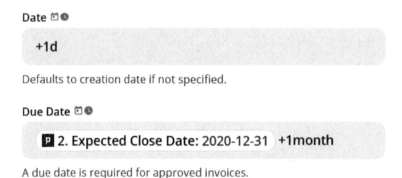

Figure 13.1 – Using date/time field modifiers in your Zaps

Here are a few examples of modifiers that you can use:

- +1h: 1 hour after the date/time the Zap has run or after the date/time value in the field

- -2days: 2 days before the date/time the Zap has run or before the date/time value in the field

- +5y: 5 years after the date/time the Zap has run or after the date/time value in the field

- +30s: 30 seconds after the date/time the Zap has run or after the date/time value in the field

- -10minutes: 10 minutes before the date/time the Zap has run or before the date/time value in the field

When using modifiers after a static or dynamic value, such as in the **Due Date** field shown in *Figure 13.1*, you must ensure there is a space between the date/time value and the modifier.

You can also add multiple modifiers either standalone or after a date/time value. In these circumstances, you must leave a space between them, for example, +1month -5days.

You should now have a better understanding of how to adjust time and date values using Zapier.

Now let's explore how to insert the date and time your Zap runs into fields in your action steps.

Using the date and time your Zap runs in fields

There may be times that you want to insert the date and time that your Zap triggers in one or more fields in your action steps. For example, you might want to record the date and time when a new row of data was added to a Google Sheets spreadsheet. This is easily achieved by entering {{zap_meta_human_now}} into a field, and when the Zap runs, this command will output a human-readable string in the format MM/DD/YY hh:mm AM/PM, such as 11/01/20 07:40 PM.

This command can be used in **Date/Time** field types and text fields where you can type in a static value. The command uses the timezone settings specified in your Zapier account or the Zap settings. If no timezone has been specified, the timestamp will default to **Universal Time Coordinated** (**UTC**). We discussed how to adjust your account timezone settings in *Chapter 1, Introduction to Business Process Automation with Zapier*, and individual Zap timezone settings in *Chapter 4, Managing Your Zaps*.

Once you have entered the command into a field, the string will not show the timestamp data while you are creating or editing your Zap. It will be displayed in the action app that you specified only after the Zap has triggered and run. This is shown in the following screenshot:

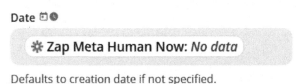

Figure 13.2 – Using the date and time your Zap runs in your action steps

You can also use the following timestamps accordingly:

- `{{zap_meta_utc_iso}}`: It is advisable to use this command if you need a string that can be read by other apps and APIs, that is, a machine-readable string as opposed to the standard, human-readable string. This command ignores your timezone settings and will produce an ISO-8601 timestamp in UTC, such as `2020-11-01T08:19:12+00:00`. ISO-8601 is an internationally recognized time standard, which you can read more about here: `https://en.wikipedia.org/wiki/ISO_8601`.

- `{{zap_meta_timestamp}}`: This command should be used when an app or API requires a timestamp format in Unix time. Unix time is widely used in computer hardware and software operating systems, as well as digital file formats, and is denoted by the number of seconds since 1st January 1970, for example, `1591537509`. You can read more about Unix time here: `https://en.wikipedia.org/wiki/Unix_time`.

- `{{zap_meta_[timezone]_iso}}`: Substitute `[timezone]` with the three- to five-letter timezone abbreviation format you want to use. For example, `{{zap_meta_est_iso}}` is for **Eastern Standard Time (EST)**, and `{{zap_meta_gmt_iso}}` is for **Greenwich Mean Time (GMT)**. You can read more about timezone abbreviations here: `https://en.wikipedia.org/wiki/List_of_time_zone_abbreviations`.

Working with timezones in your Zaps can be tricky, often involving trial and error to get your data correct and accepted by your various apps. You can read further about tips for handling timezone data on the Zapier website: `https://zapier.com/blog/format-datetimes/`.

> **Important note**
>
> Not all timezone abbreviations are compatible with the `{{zap_meta_[timezone]_iso}}` command. The most common American timezones as well as some European and Asia-Pacific timezones are generally compatible. It is advisable to perform some testing with the command, in advance.

You should now have a better understanding of how to use the time and date that your Zap runs in your action steps.

Next, let's take a look at how to use the Formatter by Zapier built-in app to manipulate dates and times.

Manipulating dates and times with Formatter by Zapier

Now that you've learned about how to adjust dates and times and how to insert the date and time that your Zap ran into your action steps, we will take this a step further and explore how to manipulate dates and times more extensively with the Formatter by Zapier built-in app.

There may be many occasions where you need to transform date and time values from either your trigger or action steps by adding or subtracting time, or displaying the date or time in a certain format. You can use Formatter by Zapier to accomplish this.

For manipulating dates and times, Formatter by Zapier can only be used as an action step and is available as the following action event:

- **Date / Time** (action)

  When using this action event, you can use the following **Date / Time** transform options found within the **Set up action** section:

  - **Add/Subtract Time**
  - **Format**

Before we explore how to set up each of these transform options in turn, let's cover how to use custom date formats.

Using custom date formats

When you want to transform a date or time using the Formatter by Zapier **Date / Time** transform options, you can either select the format or style you want to use from a drop-down list or specify a custom format that is not listed. As Zapier may not always recognize the format you want to convert from, you can also use custom formats to specify the format to convert from.

The following table shows a list of date and time token formats that Zapier recognizes, and these tokens can be used in any combination to produce the format you want:

Time variable	Custom token	Example output
Sub-second	SSS	000, 001, 002 … to 999
	SS	00, 01, 02 … to 99
	S	0, 1, 2 … to 9
Second	ss	00, 01, 02 … to 59
	s	0, 1, 2 … to 59
Minute	mm	00, 01, 02 … to 59
	m	0, 1, 2 … to 59
Hour	HH	00, 01, 02 … to 24
	H	0, 1, 2 … to 24
	hh	01, 02, 03 … to 12
	h	1, 2, 3 … to 12
Month	MMMM	January, February, March … to December
	MMM	Jan, Feb, Mar … to Dec
	MM	01, 02, 03 … to 12
	M	1, 2, 3 … to 12
Year	YYYY	2018, 2019, 2020, and so on
	YY	18, 19, 20, and so on
Day of the year	DDDD	001, 002, 003 … to 365
	DDD	1, 2, 3 … to 365
Day of the month	DD	01, 02, 03 … to 31
	D	1, 2, 3 … to 31
Day of the week	dddd	Monday, Tuesday, Wednesday … to Sunday
	ddd	Mon, Tue, Wed … to Sun
	d	1, 2, 3 … to 7
AM/PM	A	AM, PM
	a	am, pm
Timezone	ZZ	-07:00, -06:00 … +06:00, +07:00
	Z	-0700, -0600 … +0600, +0700
Unix timestamp	X	1347360521

Figure 13.3 – A table showing date and time custom formats accepted by Zapier

The data in *Figure 13.3* has been sourced from this Zapier help article: `https://zapier.com/help/create/format/modify-date-formats-in-zaps#customize-date-time-options`.

Using the data from *Figure 13.3*, we may want to convert the time stamp `2020-11-01T09:15:30` to `09:15 November 1 20`. For this, we would use the token format `HH:mm MMMM D YY`.

Next, let's dive into using Formatter by Zapier to add and subtract time.

Adding or subtracting time

Adding or subtracting time to or from a timestamp value is extremely useful when you want times to be displayed differently in your consequent action steps.

Here are a couple of examples of when you can use the Formatter by Zapier **Date / Time** action event with the **Add/Subtract Time** transform option:

- When an opportunity is marked as won in Salesforce CRM, create an invoice in QuickBooks Online with a due date 1 month from the close date.

- When a **Facebook Messenger** message is received, create a Trello card with a due time 1 hour from the time the message was received.

Let's explore how to set up the **Add/Subtract Time** transform option.

Setting up the Date/Time action event with the Add/Subtract Time transform option

Use the **Date / Time** action event once you have set up your trigger step.

Once you have added an action step either by selecting the **Action** step or clicking on the + icon, choosing **Formatter by Zapier** as the app and **Date / Time** as the action event, you can edit the fields in the **Set up action** section as follows:

- **Transform**: From the drop-down menu, select the **Add/Subtract Time** option.

- **Input**: Use this field to enter the date value you would like to manipulate. This can be either a static URL value, a dynamic value from previous steps, or a combination of both, to specify the **Input** value. For accuracy, the **Input** value must be in an accepted date/time format. Although this is not a required field, the formatter function will not return a result if there is no value.

- **Expression**: Use this field to specify the amount of time you want to add to or subtract from the value indicated in the **Input** field, for example, `+1h`, `-3days`, or `+2 months`. Either enter a static URL value, a dynamic value from previous steps, or a combination of both. For accuracy, the input must be in an accepted date/time format, as we discussed in the *The basics of adjusting date and time values using Zapier* section. This is a required field and must have a value in order for the Zap to run.

- **To Format**: Specify the format you want the date/time output to be displayed as. Either select a date/time format from the drop-down menu, or add a custom format under the **Custom** tab. You can use the custom date formats that we discussed in the *Using custom date formats* section.

- **From Format**: Zapier will attempt to read the format of the **Input** value. If Zapier gets it wrong, you can use this field to specify the exact format. Either select a date/time format from the drop-down menu, or add a custom format under the **Custom** tab. You can use the custom date formats that we discussed in the *Using custom date formats* section.

This is shown in the following screenshot:

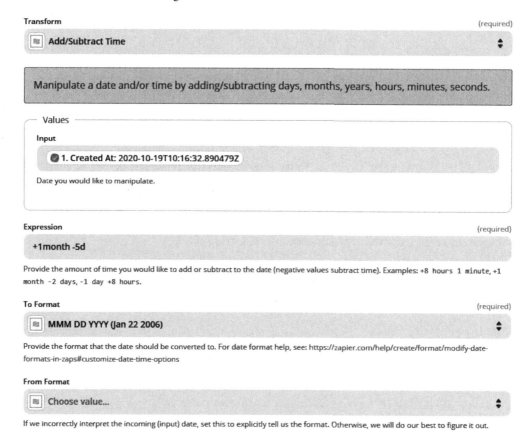

Figure 13.4 – Using the Formatter by Zapier Date / Time action event to add or subtract time

Click on the **Continue** button. You can then use the **Test action** section to test this step to generate the altered date/time format. The result from the scenario in *Figure 13.4* is shown in the following screenshot:

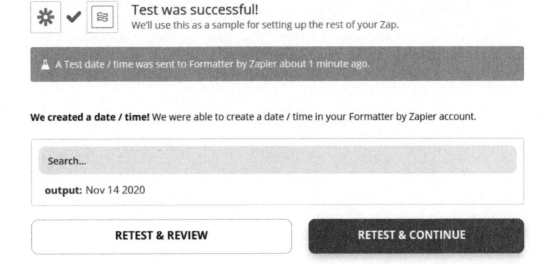

Figure 13.5 – An example of the altered time format when using the Date / Time action event to add or subtract time

Proceed to add one or more action steps after your **Date / Time** action step.

You should now have a better understanding of how to add or subtract time from date and time values using the Formatter by Zapier built-in app.

Now, let's cover how to use the Formatter by Zapier built-in app to format date and time values.

Formatting dates and times

Formatting dates and times from your trigger or actions steps may often be required when time formats between the apps you are using in your Zaps are different. You may also want to display your time formats in a more readable style, such as the date without hours, minutes, and seconds.

Here are a couple of examples of when you can use the Formatter by Zapier Date / Time action event with the **Format** transform option:

- When a task is marked as complete in Asana, convert the format of the completed date and time and create a new meeting in Google Calendar.

- When a Microsoft Outlook email is received, change the display of the date received to a more readable format, for example, `29 Jan 2020`.

Let's explore how to set up the **Format** transform option.

Setting up the Date / Time action event with the Format transform option

Use the **Date / Time** action event once you have set up your trigger step.

Once you have added an action step either by selecting the **Action** step or clicking on the + icon, choosing **Formatter by Zapier** as the app and **Date / Time** as the action event, you can then edit the fields in the **Set up action** section as follows:

- **Transform**: From the drop-down menu, select the **Format** option.

- **Input**: Use this field to enter the date value you would like to manipulate. This can be either a static URL value, a dynamic value from previous steps, or a combination of both, to specify the **Input** value. For accuracy, the input must be in an accepted date/time format. Although this is not a required field, the formatter function will not return a result if there is no value.

- **To Format**: Specify the format you want the date/time output to be displayed as. Either select a date/time format from the drop-down menu or add a custom format under the **Custom** tab. You can use the custom date formats that we discussed in the *Using custom date formats* section. This is a required field and a value is needed in order for the step to run successfully.

- **To Timezone**: From the drop-down list, specify the timezone you want the date/time output that is displayed to be relevant to. You can also map in a custom value from a previous step. The default for this field is **UTC**.

- **From Format**: Zapier will attempt to read the format of the input value. If Zapier gets it wrong, you can use this field to specify the exact format. Either select a date/time format from the drop-down menu or add a custom format under the **Custom** tab. You can use the custom date formats that we discussed in the *Using custom date formats* section.

- **From Timezone**: From the drop-down list, specify the timezone related to your input value. You can also map in a custom value from a previous step. The default for this field is **UTC**.

This is shown in the following screenshot:

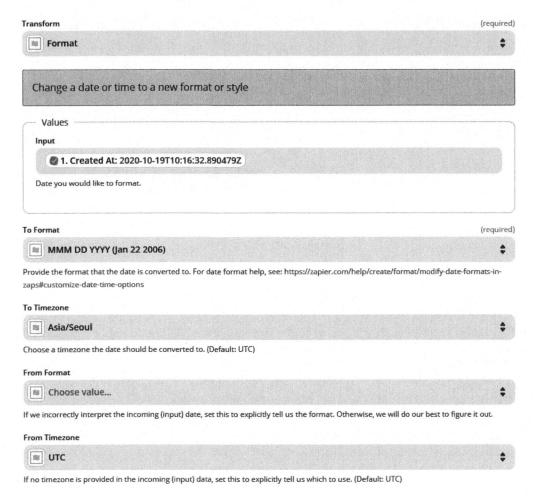

Figure 13.6 – Using the Formatter by Zapier Date / Time action event to add or subtract time

Click on the **Continue** button. You can then use the **Test action** section to test this step to generate the altered date/time format. The result from the scenario in *Figure 13.6* is shown in the following screenshot:

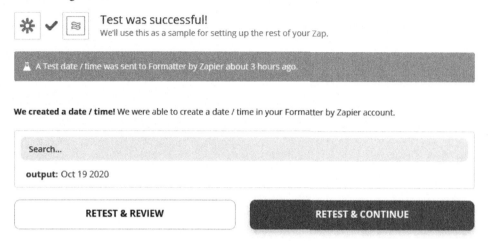

Figure 13.7 – An example of the altered time format when using the Date / Time action event to format dates and times

Proceed to add one or more action steps after your **Date / Time** action step.

You should now have a better understanding of how to format dates and times using the Formatter by Zapier built-in app.

Summary

In this chapter, we introduced the functionality of the Formatter by Zapier app, to allow you to manipulate dates and times, numbers, text, and other types of data. Thereafter, the primary focus for the content in this chapter was regarding manipulating dates and times. We covered the basics of how to adjust date and time values in your Zaps. After that, we discussed how to use the date and time that your Zap runs in your action steps. Then, we explored how to use the Formatter by Zapier built-in app to add and subtract time. Lastly, we discussed how to format date and time values using the Formatter by Zapier built-in app.

You now understand what action events Formatter by Zapier offers. You also now know how to adjust date and times in your Zaps and use the date and time your Zap runs. Lastly, you now know how to use the Formatter by Zapier built-in app to add or subtract time and convert date and time values into different formats.

In the next chapter, you will learn how to use the Formatter by Zapier built-in app to manipulate numbers, phone numbers, and currencies, and how to use spreadsheet-type formulas and math operations.

14
Formatting Numbers

You might often find that numerical data values do not usually appear in the way you want them to be displayed visually or in the way your other apps will accept them. There might be several scenarios where this will be the case. For example, a lead may enter a contact phone number when they submit an inquiry form, but that format may not be recognized by your SMS app. Or, if your team submits timesheets, you may need to calculate their overtime payments before sending them a summary by email. You might also want to add a space, period, or comma to a number or transform a number into a specific currency format. As you can imagine, there are many possible situations when you might need to adjust a number, and that is where the Formatter by Zapier **Numbers** action event comes in.

In this chapter, we will dive into using the Formatter by Zapier built-in app to manipulate a range of number formats. We will begin with an introduction to using Zapier to transform numerical values. Next, we will explore how to format numbers, currencies, and phone numbers. Then, we will cover how to use the Formatter by Zapier built-in app to perform basic mathematical operations. Lastly, we will examine how to use spreadsheet-style formulas to perform calculations.

We will cover the following key topics in this chapter:

- Using Zapier to transform numerical values

- Formatting numbers with Formatter by Zapier

- Formatting currencies with Formatter by Zapier

- Formatting phone numbers with Formatter by Zapier

- Performing mathematical operations with Formatter by Zapier

- Using spreadsheet-style formulas with Formatter by Zapier

Once you have worked through each of these topics, you will have a better understanding of the different number-transforming events available for use with the Formatter by Zapier built-in app. You will know how to adjust numbers, currencies, and phone numbers, as well as how to perform math operations and use spreadsheet-style formulas in your Zaps.

Technical requirements

To make the most of the content in this chapter, you will need access to a Zapier account. The Zapier Starter plan will be required for you to create multi-step workflows using the Formatter by Zapier built-in app.

Using Zapier to transform numerical values

Formatter by Zapier can easily be used to transform numerical values from one format to another. There might be several scenarios in which you need to transform your data, such as when a value is not accepted in some of your apps, when you want to display the format differently, or if you need to make calculations.

For manipulating numbers, Formatter by Zapier can only be used as an action step and is available as the following action event:

- **Numbers** (action)

When using this action event, you can use the following **Numbers** transform options found within the **Set up action** section of your action step:

- **Format Number**
- **Format Currency**
- **Format Phone Number**
- **Perform Math Operation**
- **Spreadsheet-Style Formula**

Let's get started by exploring how to transform general number formats.

Formatting numbers with Formatter by Zapier

Changing the format of a number can be very useful when you want to adjust the way decimal marks, thousands separators, and spaces are displayed. In general, these situations might arise when data from one app is presented in one format, and you want to change it to be displayed in another way. Zapier has a solution to this problem. You can use the Formatter by Zapier **Numbers** action event with the **Format Number** transform option to adjust the format of numbers.

Here are a few examples of when you can use this transform option:

- When you want to change the format of a number using a period as a decimal mark, such as 1000.00, to use a comma as the decimal mark, such as 1000,00.

- When you want to change the format of a number using groupings with a comma, such as 1,000,000, to use spaces, such as 1 000 000.

- When you want to change the format of a number where no thousands separators are present, such as 1000000, to have separators with commas, such as 1,000,000.

Essentially, this transform option can be used to change a number to a new style, however, it does not allow you to perform the rounding or padding of a number.

Let's explore how to set up the Format Number transform option.

Setting up the Numbers action event with the Format Number transform option

Use the **Numbers** action event once you have set up your trigger step.

Once you have added an action step either by selecting the **Action** step or clicking on the + icon and chosen **Formatter by Zapier** as the app and **Numbers** as the action event, you can then edit the fields in the **Set up action** section as follows:

- **Transform**: From the drop-down menu, select the **Format Number** option. This is a required field and must have a value in order for the Zap to run.

- **Input**: Use this field to enter the number format you want to manipulate. You can either enter a static value, a dynamic value from previous steps (using the **Custom** tab), or a combination of both, to specify the **Input** value. Although this is not a required field, the formatter function will not return a result if there is no value.

- **Input Decimal Mark**: This field is used to specify the character that denotes the decimal or fractional part of the number value in the **Input** field. Use the drop-down options to select either **Comma** or **Period**. Under the **Custom** tab, you can also use a dynamic value from previous steps with the characters , or ., respectively. This is a required field and must have a value in order for the Zap to run.

- **To Format**: Specify the format you want the number output to be displayed in. Select a format from the drop-down menu, where you can either use the comma character, period character, or space for the thousands separator with either a comma or period character for the decimal mark. These format options are **Comma for grouping & period for decimal**, **Period for grouping & comma for decimal**, **Space for grouping & period for decimal**, and **Space for grouping & comma for decimal**. Alternatively, add a dynamic value from previous steps under the **Custom** tab that matches the format code options **0**, **1**, **2**, or **3**. This is a required field and must have a value in order for the Zap to run.

An example is shown in the following screenshot where we want to convert the input value containing a period as the decimal mark, and the output required has a space for the thousands separator and a comma for the decimal:

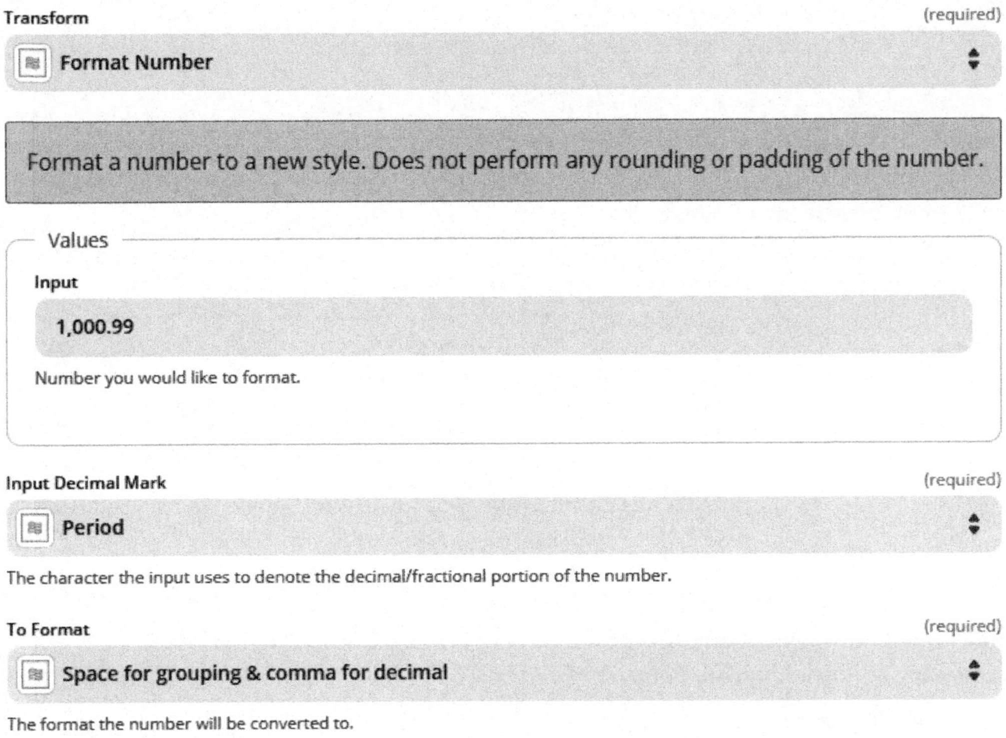

Transform (required)

▦ **Format Number** ↕

Format a number to a new style. Does not perform any rounding or padding of the number.

Values

Input

1,000.99

Number you would like to format.

Input Decimal Mark (required)

▦ **Period** ↕

The character the input uses to denote the decimal/fractional portion of the number.

To Format (required)

▦ **Space for grouping & comma for decimal** ↕

The format the number will be converted to.

Figure 14.1 – Using the Formatter by Zapier Numbers action event to format a number

Click on the **Continue** button. You can then use the **Test action** section to test this step to generate the altered number format. The result from the scenario in *Figure 14.1* is shown in the following screenshot:

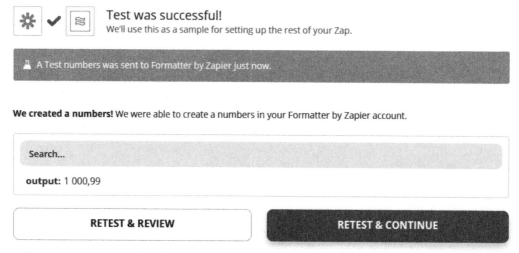

Figure 14.2 – An example of the altered numerical value when using the Numbers action event to format a number

Proceed to add one or more action steps after your **Numbers** action step.

You should now have a better understanding of how to format numbers with the Formatter by Zapier built-in app.

Next, let's dive into formatting currency values.

Formatting currencies with Formatter by Zapier

Whether you work with single or multiple currencies in your business, it's likely that at some point or another, you might need to convert numerical values into a currency format appropriate to your (or another) **locale** or to be displayed in a certain way. You can do this easily using the Formatter by Zapier **Numbers** action event with the **Format Currency transform option**.

Here are a couple of examples of when you can use this transform option:

- When you want to change the format of a number such as 1,000.23 to a German (Germany) locale format with the comma as the decimal mark, displayed in Euros with the currency symbol at the start and currency shortcode at the end, such as €1.000,23 EUR.

- When you want to change the format of a number such as 1000.23 to an English (United States) locale format with the period as the decimal mark, displayed in US Dollars with the currency symbol at the start, with no thousands grouping, such as $1000.23.

Before we dive into setting up an action step with the **Format Currency** transform option, let's review some useful information about country locales and currency formats.

Understanding country locales and currency formatting

When working with currencies, it's useful to know that most countries have a specific format in which they display their currencies. For example, many European countries use a comma for the decimal mark, whereas the United States uses a period.

Currencies can be formatted using Zapier following **Unicode** character guidelines for displaying number patterns. According to Wikipedia, Unicode is defined as *"an information technology (IT) standard for the consistent encoding, representation, and handling of text expressed in most of the world's writing systems."*

The most common Unicode characters used in currency pattern formatting are as follows:

- **.**: Using . in a pattern specifies where the decimal mark should be placed.

- **,**: Using , in a pattern specifies where the thousands separator should be placed.

- **0**: Using 0 in a pattern specifies that there is "zero padding." Therefore, if the input number is too short, a zero will be placed there.

- **#**: Using # in a pattern specifies that there is "no padding." Therefore, if the input number is too short a zero, no value will be placed there.

- **¤**: Using ¤ in a pattern specifies where the currency symbol or code should be placed. If multiple symbols are used in sequence, the currency is displayed slightly differently. For example, for Euro in the English (United Kingdom) locale, ¤ equals €, ¤¤ equals EUR, and ¤¤¤ equals euros.

You can therefore put together a string of Unicode characters to convert currencies to the format you would like them to be displayed in.

More information on Unicode number patterns, including some example pattern formats, can be found here: http://www.unicode.org/reports/tr35/tr35-numbers.html#Number_Format_Patterns.

Next, let's explore how to set up the **Format Currency** transform option.

Setting up the Numbers action event with the Format Currency transform option

Use the **Numbers** action event once you have set up your trigger step.

Once you have added an action step either by selecting the **Action** step or clicking on the + icon, and chosen **Formatter by Zapier** as the app and **Numbers** as the action event, you can then edit the fields in the **Set up action** section as follows:

- **Transform**: From the drop-down menu, select the **Format Currency** option. This is a required field and must have a value in order for the Zap to run.

- **Input**: Use this field to enter the number that you want to transform to a currency format. You can either enter a static value, a dynamic value from previous steps (using the **Custom** tab), or a combination of both, to specify the **Input** value. Although this is not a required field, the formatter function will not return a result if there is no value.

- **Currency**: Specify the currency you want the number output to be displayed as. Select a format from a comprehensive list in the drop-down menu, or add the **ISO** (an international standard) 4217 three-character currency code under the **Custom** tab. Details of currency codes can be found here: `https://en.wikipedia.org/wiki/ISO_4217`. This is a required field and must have a value in order for the Zap to run.

- **Currency Locale**: Specify the currency locale you want the number output to be displayed as. Select a format from a shortlist of commonly used currency locales in the drop-down menu, or add the ISO 639 language code and ISO 3166 country code in the format en_US for English (United States). Details of language codes can be found here: `https://en.wikipedia.org/wiki/ISO_639`. Details of country codes can be found here: `https://en.wikipedia.org/wiki/ISO_3166`. This is a required field and must have a value in order for the Zap to run.

- **Currency Format**: Specify the format you want the currency output to be displayed in by selecting a Unicode pattern format from the drop-down menu. Alternatively, add a custom format under the **Custom** tab by either entering a static value in Unicode pattern format, a dynamic value from previous steps, or a combination of both. Use the Unicode characters from the *Understanding country locales and currency formatting* section as guidance. This is a required field and must have a value in order for the Zap to run.

An example is shown in the following screenshot:

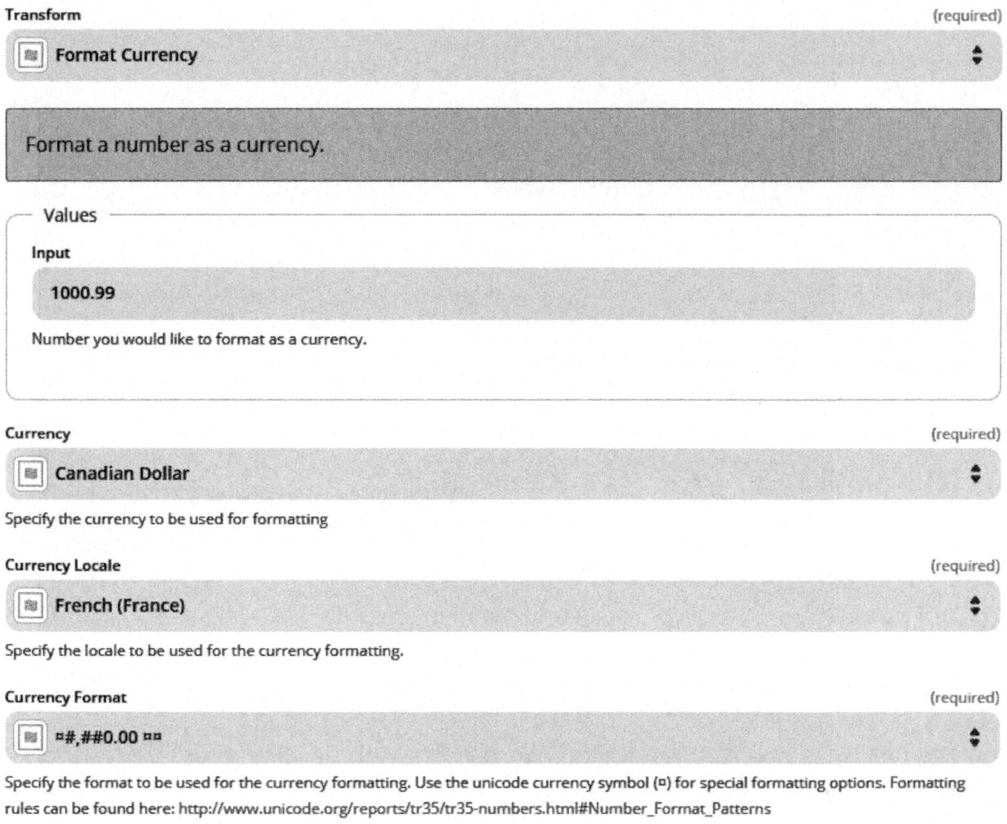

Transform (required)

> **Format Currency** ⬍

Format a number as a currency.

Values

Input

> 1000.99

Number you would like to format as a currency.

Currency (required)

> **Canadian Dollar** ⬍

Specify the currency to be used for formatting

Currency Locale (required)

> **French (France)** ⬍

Specify the locale to be used for the currency formatting.

Currency Format (required)

> ¤#,##0.00 ¤¤ ⬍

Specify the format to be used for the currency formatting. Use the unicode currency symbol (¤) for special formatting options. Formatting rules can be found here: http://www.unicode.org/reports/tr35/tr35-numbers.html#Number_Format_Patterns

Figure 14.3 – Using the Formatter by Zapier Numbers action event to format currencies

Click on the **Continue** button. You can then use the **Test action** section to test this step to generate the altered currency format. The result from the scenario in *Figure 14.3* is shown in the following screenshot:

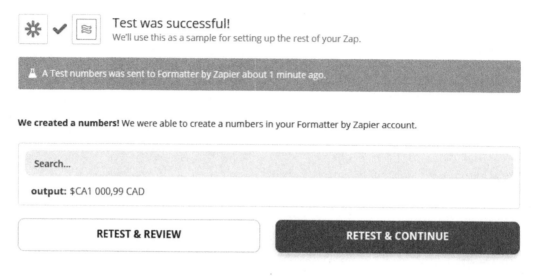

Figure 14.4 – An example of the altered value when using the Numbers action event to format a currency

Proceed to add one or more action steps after your **Numbers** action step.

You should now have a better understanding of how to format currencies with the Formatter by Zapier built-in app.

Next, let's review the basics of how to transform phone numbers.

Formatting phone numbers with Formatter by Zapier

Telephone communication is not dead! Second to email, communicating with prospects, customers, and suppliers via the telephone is an important part of any business. Being able to automate your telephone communications is a bonus. You may want to automatically send an SMS or voicemail to a prospect when they first make contact with you. However, sometimes the telephone numbers that our contacts supply us with aren't always in the format that we can use in other apps. Therefore, having the ability to automatically adjust and manipulate telephone numbers is crucial when you use multiple apps for communicating by telephone. That is where the Formatter by Zapier **Numbers** action event with the **Format Phone Number** transform option comes in.

Here are a few examples of when you can use this option:

- When you receive a lead with a cellphone number, and you want to change it to an internationally recognized format so that you can send an automated SMS using Twilio.

- When a new customer signs up to your service and provides a phone number, and you want to change it to a format that is recognized by a voicemail drop app, such as **Slybroadcast**.

- When a new contact is added to your CRM, and you want to change the format of the contact phone number they provided to one that is recognized by your CRM calling module.

Next, let's review how to set up the **Format Phone Number** transform option.

Setting up the Numbers action event with the Format Phone Number transform option

Use the **Numbers** action event once you have set up your trigger step.

Once you have added an action step either by selecting the **Action** step or clicking on the + icon, and chosen **Formatter by Zapier** as the app and **Numbers** as the action event, you can then edit the fields in the **Set up action** section as follows:

- **Transform**: From the drop-down menu, select the **Format Phone Number** option. This is a required field and must have a value in order for the Zap to run.

- **Input**: Use this field to enter the number that you want to transform to another phone number format. You can either enter a static value, a dynamic value from previous steps (using the **Custom** tab), or a combination of both, to specify the **Input** value. Although this is not a required field, the formatter function will not return a result if there is no value.

- **To Format**: Specify the format you want the number output to be displayed in. Select a format from a list of commonly used phone number formats in the drop-down menu. Alternatively, add a dynamic value from previous steps under the **Custom** tab that matches the format code options 0, 1, 2, to 8. This is a required field and must have a value in order for the Zap to run.

- **Phone Number Country Code**: Specify the country code that you want the phone number output to be displayed with. Select from a list of commonly used formats in the drop-down menu, enter a static value for the 2-letter ISO country code under the **Custom** tab, or a dynamic value from previous steps. Details of ISO country codes can be found here: `https://countrycode.org/`. For example, choosing **United States** (country code US) will produce a phone number where the first two characters are +1. If left blank, the country code will not be displayed in the output.

- **Validate Phone Number?**: Use this Boolean field to specify whether you want the converted phone number to be checked for validity in the country code specified in the **Phone Number Country Code** field. Use the drop-down menu to select **Yes** or **No**. Alternatively, add a custom format under the **Custom** tab by either entering a static value or a dynamic value from previous steps matching the format **true** or **false**, respectively. Set to **No** when testing or if only formatting is required. If the number is invalid, the number specified in the **Input** field will be output unformatted. The default for this field is **Yes**.

An example is shown in the following screenshot:

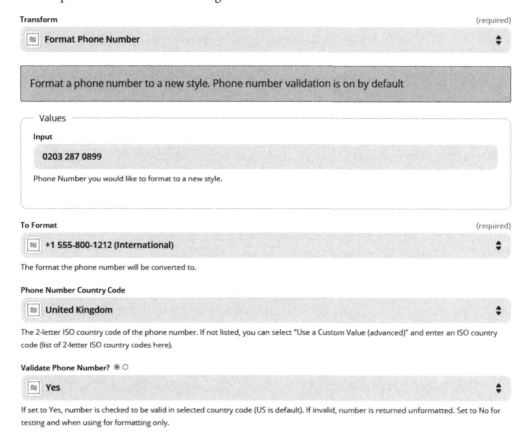

Figure 14.5 – Using the Formatter by Zapier Numbers action event to format phone numbers

Click on the **Continue** button. You can then use the **Test action** section to test this step to generate the altered phone number format. The result from the scenario in *Figure 14.5* is shown in the following screenshot:

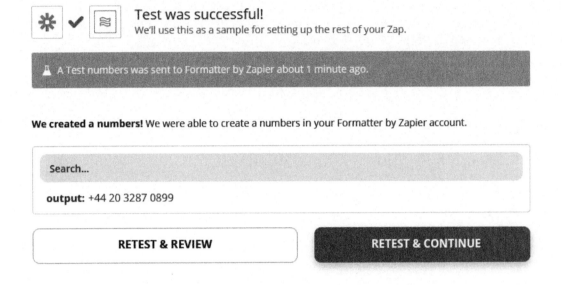

Figure 14.6 – An example of the output value when using the Numbers action event to format a phone number

Proceed to add one or more action steps after your **Numbers** action step.

You should now have a better understanding of how to format phone numbers with the Formatter by Zapier built-in app.

Next, let's take a look at how to perform basic math operations.

Performing mathematical operations with Formatter by Zapier

There are most likely situations where you are consistently manually performing basic mathematical functions on a regular basis. You might want to add two or three values together or convert a number to a percentage. Thankfully, Formatter by Zapier allows you to perform standard math operations using multiple values.

Using the **Numbers** action event and the **Perform Math Operation** transform option, Formatter by Zapier allows you to perform the following basic mathematical operations:

- **Add**
- **Subtract**
- **Multiply**
- **Divide**
- **Make Negative**

Here are a few examples of when you can use this transform option:

- When your customer fills out an order form on **Google Forms** with an order amount for red balls and an order amount for yellow balls, and you want to calculate the total order amount.
- When your team members submit an expense claim form with **FastField Mobile Forms** for travel and subsistence and you want to deduct the value from their monthly allowance.
- When a lead engages with you by email, and you want to add a pre-defined engagement point value to a lead score.

Next, let's review how to set up the Perform Math Operation transform option.

Setting up the Numbers action event with the Perform Math Operation transform option

Use the **Numbers** action event once you have set up your trigger step.

Once you have added an action step either by selecting the **Action** step or clicking on the + icon, and chosen **Formatter by Zapier** as the app and **Numbers** as the action event, you can then edit the fields in the **Set up action** section as follows:

- **Transform**: From the drop-down menu, select the **Perform Math Operation** option. This is a required field and must have a value in order for the Zap to run.

- **Operation**: Specify the math operation that you want to perform. Select an operation from the list in the drop-down menu, and choose from the **Add**, **Subtract**, **Multiply**, **Divide**, and **Make Negative options**. Alternatively, add a dynamic value from the previous steps under the **Custom** tab that matches the format code options of add, sub, mul, div, or neg, respectively. This is a required field and must have a value in order for the Zap to run.

- **Input**: Use this field to enter the values you want to use in the calculation on multiple lines. You can either enter static values, dynamic values from previous steps, or a combination of both. Although this is not a required field, the formatter function will not return a result if there is no value.

An example is shown in the following screenshot where we want to multiply the values 9 and 10:

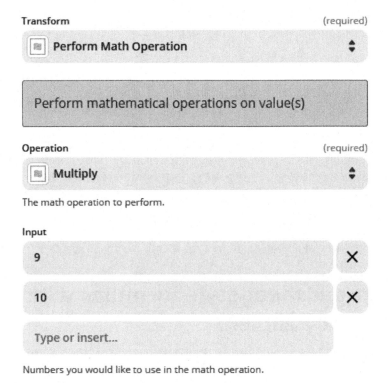

Figure 14.7 – Using the Formatter by Zapier Numbers action event to perform a math operation

Click on the **Continue** button. You can then use the **Test action** section to test this step to generate the output from the math operation. The result from the scenario in *Figure 14.7* is shown in the following screenshot:

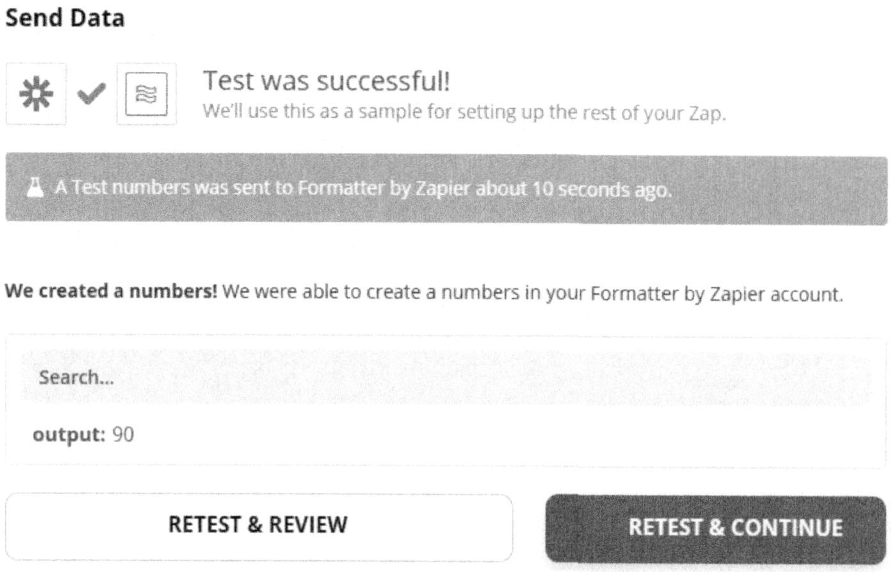

Send Data

Test was successful!
We'll use this as a sample for setting up the rest of your Zap.

A Test numbers was sent to Formatter by Zapier about 10 seconds ago.

We created a numbers! We were able to create a numbers in your Formatter by Zapier account.

Search...

output: 90

RETEST & REVIEW   RETEST & CONTINUE

Figure 14.8 – An example of the output value when using the Numbers action event to perform math operations

Proceed to add one or more action steps after your **Numbers** action step.

You should now have a better understanding of how to perform basic mathematical operations with the Formatter by Zapier built-in app.

Next, let's explore how to use spreadsheet-type formulas in your Zaps.

Using spreadsheet-style formulas with Formatter by Zapier

If you need to do more than using the five basic mathematical operations that we just discussed, you can use complex spreadsheet-style fomulas in your Zaps instead. You can do this using the Formatter by Zapier **Numbers** action event **Spreadsheet-Style Formula** transform option.

Here are a few examples of when you can use this transform option:

- When you want to calculate the average of several numbers, such as 8, 12, and 13 to get 11, using the AVERAGE(number, [number, …]) formula.

- When you want to output the largest number from a list of values, such as 1, 9, and 53 to get 53, using the MAX(number, [number, …]) formula.

- When you want to produce a random number between 0 and 1, such as 0.512453, using the RAND() formula.

Next, let's review how to set up the **Spreadsheet-Style Formula** transform option.

Setting up the Numbers action event with the Spreadsheet-Style Formula transform option

Use the **Numbers** action event once you have set up your trigger step.

Once you have added an action step either by selecting the **Action** step or clicking on the + icon, and chosen **Formatter by Zapier** as the app and **Numbers** as the action event, you can then edit the fields in the **Set up action** section as follows:

- **Transform**: From the drop-down menu, select the **Spreadsheet-Style Formula** option. This is a required field and must have a value in order for the Zap to run.

- **Formula**: Use this field to specify the formula with the values that you want to be calculated. Add static values for the formula and numeric values, or dynamic values mapped from previous steps under the **Custom** tab. This is a required field and must have a value in order for the Zap to run.

Zapier has created a handy reference document with various formulas that can be used with Formatter by Zapier: https://zapier.com/help/create/format/understand-spreadsheet-style-formula-functions.

An example is shown in the following screenshot where we want to divide the sum of values 2 and 4 by 3:

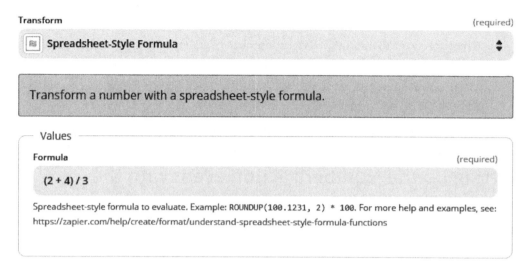

Figure 14.9 – Using the Formatter by Zapier Numbers action event to perform
a spreadsheet-style operation

Click on the **Continue** button. You can then use the **Test action** section to test this step to generate the output. The result from the scenario in *Figure 14.9* is shown in the following screenshot:

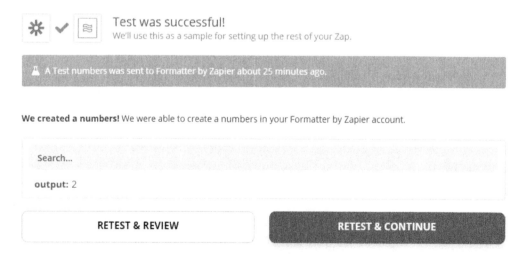

Figure 14.10 – An example of the output value when using the Numbers action event to perform
spreadsheet-style operations

Proceed to add one or more action steps after your **Numbers** action step.

You should now have a better understanding of how to use spreadsheet-style formulas.

Summary

In this chapter, we covered how to use the Formatter by Zapier built-in app to manipulate a variety of number formats. We started by introducing how to use Zapier for the general formatting of numbers. Then, we covered how to format numbers, currencies, and phone numbers in more detail. Next, we explored how to use the Formatter by Zapier built-in app to perform basic mathematical operations. Lastly, we examined how to use spreadsheet-style formulas to perform calculations.

You now know how to use the Formatter by Zapier built-in app to transform numerical values such as numbers, currencies, and phone numbers, as well as how to perform basic math operations and use spreadsheet-style formulas to perform calculations.

In the next chapter, you will learn how to use some of the functionality of the Formatter by Zapier built-in app to format text. We will explore adjusting title case, uppercase, and lowercase, finding and replacing text, trimming whitespace, counting words, adjusting the length of a string of text, and pluralizing text.

15
Text Formatting Functions in Zapier – Part 1

So far, in this book, we've covered two important functions of the versatile Formatter by Zapier built-in app. In *Chapter 13, Formatting Date and Time*, we discussed how to use Formatter by Zapier to manipulate dates and times. In *Chapter 14, Formatting Numbers*, we covered how to use it to transform numbers. As covered in those two topics, being able to transform text into a variety of different formats is incredibly useful. For example, the name of a contact may be displayed in full (as a first name and surname), and you may want to split out the first name so that you can personalize an email rather than using the contact's full name. Or you might want to extract an email address from a block of text to be able to add that to your marketing automation software. You might also want to truncate text to a specified character length when sharing a summary of content on Twitter. There are many possibilities for when you might need to adjust text, and that is where the Formatter by Zapier **Text** action event comes in. Users familiar with Microsoft Excel will see similarities between this Zapier functionality and text transformation formula usage in Microsoft Excel spreadsheets.

In this chapter, we continue with the focus on the versatile Formatter by Zapier built-in app, and you will learn how to use some of the extensive functionality available to format text. First, we will discuss how to use Zapier to transform text values in general. Next, we will explore capitalizing text, applying title case, uppercase, and lowercase, and pluralizing words. Then, we will cover finding the position of and replacing text, counting characters and words, and removing whitespace.

We will cover the following key topics in this chapter:

- Using Zapier to transform text values
- Capitalizing the first letter of every word
- Applying title case to a string of words
- Converting all the characters in a string of text to uppercase
- Converting all the characters in a string of text to lowercase
- Pluralizing words
- Finding the first position of specified text
- Replacing characters, words, or phrases
- Counting the number of characters in a string of text
- Counting the number of words in a string of text
- Removing whitespace

Once you have worked through each of these topics, you will have a better understanding of some of the different text transforming functions available for use with the Formatter by Zapier built-in app. You will know how to use Zapier to adjust text to various formats.

Technical requirements

To get the most out of the content in this chapter, you will need access to a Zapier account. The Zapier Starter plan will be required for you to create multi-step workflows using the Formatter by Zapier built-in app.

Using Zapier to transform text values

Formatter by Zapier can easily be used to transform text values from one format to another. There might be several scenarios in which you need to transform your data, such as when you want to display the format differently or if you need to extract a certain type of data from a block of text.

For manipulating text, Formatter by Zapier can only be used as an action step and is available as the following action event:

- **Text** (action)

When using this action event, you can use the following **Text** transform options found within the **Set up action** section of your action step, listed in the **Transform** drop-down menu:

- **Capitalize**
- **Convert Markdown to HTML**
- **Convert to ASCII**
- **Default Value**
- **Extract Email Address**
- **Extract Number**
- **Extract Pattern**
- **Extract Phone Number**
- **Extract URL**
- **Find**
- **Length**
- **Lowercase**
- **Pluralize**
- **Remove HTML tags**
- **Replace**
- **Split Text**
- **Superhero Name**
- **Titlecase**
- **Trim Whitespace**
- **Truncate**
- **Uppercase**
- **URL Decode**

- **URL Encode**
- **Word Count**

We will cover the **Convert Markdown to HTML, Convert to ASCII, Default Value, Extract Email Address, Extract Number, Extract Pattern, Extract Phone Number, Extract URL, Split Text, Superhero Name, Truncate, URL Decode,** and **URL Encode** text transform options in *Chapter 16, Text Formatting Functions in Zapier – Part 2*.

Let's get started with exploring how to capitalize the first letter of every word.

Capitalizing the first letter of every word

If you're a stickler for formatting text correctly, you'll most likely want to ensure that, where appropriate, words in a bunch of text display capital letters at the start of the word. This is especially important when addressing people by name or displaying business names and addresses on invoices. You can capitalize the first letter of every word in a string of text using the Formatter by Zapier **Text** action event with the **Capitalize** transform function. For example, if the string of text was this is a test, the transformed text would be This Is A Test. Microsoft Excel users will recognize the similarity of this Zapier functionality to the PROPER formula in a Microsoft Excel spreadsheet to capitalize text.

Here are a few examples of when you can use this transform option:

- When new contacts sign up for your newsletter, it is common that they may add their name in all-lowercase, such as kelly instead of Kelly. You might want to make their name look as it should when you address them in emails. So, when a new subscriber is added to Mailchimp, for example, you can transform their name to its formal setting.

- You might collect client billing addresses by asking them to complete a webform. It might be the case that they add the address in all-lowercase, such as 99 hollow avenue, washington. Before adding the data to your accounting system, you might want to capitalize the first letter of each word in the address, so that it reads 99 Hollow Avenue, Washington.

Next, let's review how to set up an action step with the **Capitalize** transform option.

Setting up the Text action event with the Capitalize transform option

Use the **Text** action event once you have set up your trigger step.

Once you have added an action step, by either selecting the **Action** step or clicking on the + icon, and chosen **Formatter by Zapier** as the app and **Text** as the action event, you can then edit the fields in the **Set up action** section as follows:

- **Transform**: From the drop-down menu, select the **Capitalize** option. This is a required field and must have a value for the Zap to run.

- **Input**: Use this field to enter the text of which you want to transform the first character of every word. You can enter either a static value, a dynamic value from previous steps, or a combination of both to specify the **Input** value. Although this is not a required field, the formatter function will not return a result if there is no value.

An example is shown in the following screenshot:

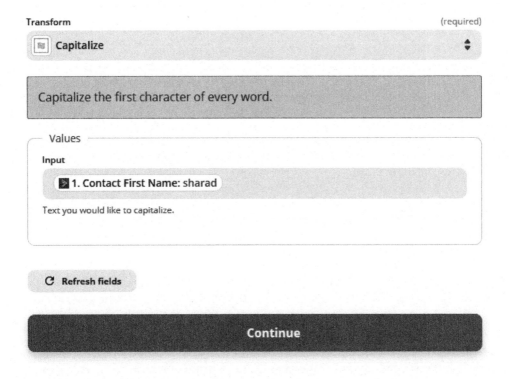

Figure 15.1 – Using the Formatter by Zapier Text action event to capitalize text

Click on the **Continue** button. You can then use the **Test action** section to test this step to generate the altered capitalized text. The result from the scenario in *Figure 15.1* is shown in the following screenshot:

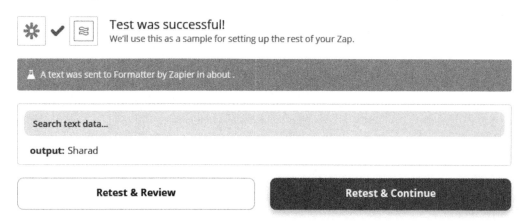

Figure 15.2 – An example of the altered value when using the Text action event to capitalize text

Proceed to add one or more action steps after your **Text** action step.

> **Tip**
> If you want to only capitalize the first letter of major words and leave the first letter of words such as articles, conjunctions, and prepositions, for example, "a" or "the," in lowercase, then use the Titlecase transform function.

You should now have a better understanding of how to use the **Capitalize** transform function. Next, let's take a look at how to apply title case to a string of words with the **Titlecase** transform function.

Applying title case to a string of words

Following on from the Capitalize transform function, there may be times where you only want to capitalize the first letter of each word in a string of text if it isn't an article, conjunction, or preposition, in other words, any nouns, pronouns, verbs, adjectives, and adverbs, as well as the first word in a title or subtitle. This is known as title case, where all major words have the first letter capitalized, and all minor words have the first letter remain as lowercase. It is commonly used in titles of books, songs, movies, and blog articles. In this case, you should use the Formatter by Zapier Text action event with the Titlecase transform function. For example, if the string of text were `this is an example of the best test to use`, the transformed text would be `This Is an Example of the Best Test to Use`.

Here are a few examples of when you can use this transform option:

- When your blog writers add a new draft blog post to your **WordPress** website, and you want to ensure the format of the post title is always consistently in title case. You can use the **Titlecase** transform option to alter the format of the title and then update the blog post accordingly with the WordPress action event.

- You might manage your **YouTube** video publishing schedule in a Google Sheets spreadsheet or project management tool such as ClickUp. The schedule may include the title of the YouTube video, which you might want to consistently be posted in title case. You can use the **Titlecase** transform option to alter the format of the title and then add the corrected title when you post the new video to YouTube.

Next, let's review how to set up an action step with the **Titlecase** transform option.

Setting up the Text action event with the Titlecase transform option

Use the **Text** action event once you have set up your trigger step.

Once you have added an action step, by either selecting the **Action** step or clicking on the + icon, and chosen **Formatter by Zapier** as the app and **Text** as the action event, you can then edit the fields in the **Set up action** section as follows:

- **Transform**: From the drop-down menu, select the **Titlecase** option. This is a required field and must have a value in order for the Zap to run.

- **Input**: Use this field to enter the text that you want to transform to title case. You can enter either a static value, a dynamic value from previous steps, or a combination of both to specify the **Input** value. Although this is not a required field, the formatter function will not return a result if there is no value.

An example is shown in the following screenshot:

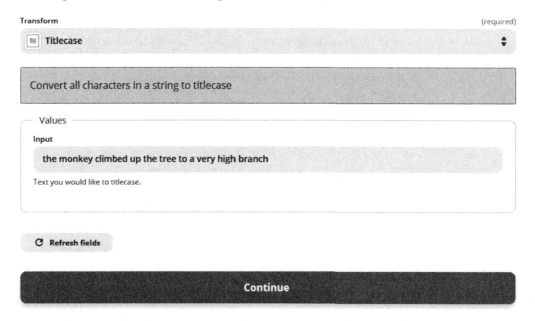

Figure 15.3 – Using the Formatter by Zapier Text action event to change text to title case

Click on the **Continue** button. You can then use the **Test action** section to test this step to generate the altered text. The result from the scenario in *Figure 15.3* is shown in the following screenshot:

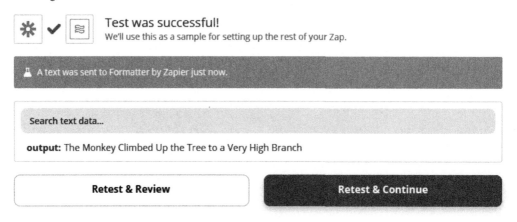

Figure 15.4 – An example of the altered value when using the Text action event to change to title case

Proceed to add one or more action steps after your **Text** action step.

You should now have a better understanding of how to use the **Titlecase** transform function. Next, let's explore how to convert all the characters in a string of text to uppercase with the **Uppercase** transform function.

Converting all the characters in a string of text to uppercase

Most of us know that typing our text messages or emails in capital letters could be interpreted as raising your virtual "voice" or emphasizing a point. It's best to use this sparingly. There may, however, be other times when it's necessary to have text displayed in capital letters. The original text may be in all-lowercase or a mixture of upper and lowercase. In order to alter a string of text so that it is displayed in uppercase only, you can use the Formatter by Zapier **Text** action event with the **Uppercase** transform function. For example, if the string of text were `wunderlust factory`, the transformed text would be `WUNDERLUST FACTORY`. Microsoft Excel users will recognize the similarity of this Zapier functionality to the `UPPER` formula in a Microsoft Excel spreadsheet to convert text to uppercase.

Here are a few examples of when you can use this transform option:

- When leads fill out a form on your website, you might want the lead's company name to be displayed entirely in uppercase in your **Customer Relationship Management (CRM)**. You can use the **Uppercase** transform option to alter the format of the company name to uppercase and then add the lead's details to the CRM with the new company name format.

- You might want to upload a copy of a document to **Google Drive** when you receive it by email as an attachment. You might also prefer to have all your filenames in a consistent uppercase format. You can use the **Uppercase** transform option to alter the format of the title of the file to uppercase before uploading it to Google Drive.

Next, let's review how to set up an action step with the **Uppercase** transform option.

Setting up the Text action event with the Uppercase transform option

Use the **Text** action event once you have set up your trigger step.

Once you have added an action step, by either selecting the **Action** step or clicking on the + icon, and chosen **Formatter by Zapier** as the app and **Text** as the action event, you can then edit the fields in the **Set up action** section as follows:

- **Transform**: From the drop-down menu, select the **Uppercase** option. This is a required field and must have a value for the Zap to run.

- **Input**: Use this field to enter the text that you want to transform into capital letters. You can enter either a static value, a dynamic value from previous steps, or a combination of both to specify the **Input** value. Although this is not a required field, the formatter function will not return a result if there is no value.

An example is shown in the following screenshot:

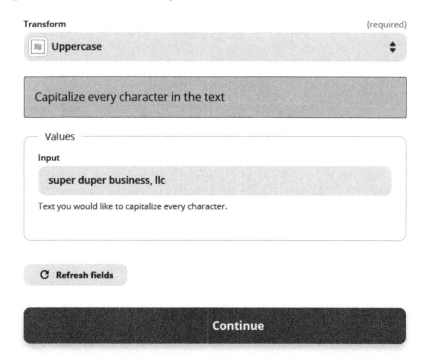

Figure 15.5 – Using the Formatter by Zapier Text action event to change text to capital letters

Click on the **Continue** button. You can then use the **Test action** section to test this step to generate the altered text in uppercase. The result from the scenario in *Figure 15.5* is shown in the following screenshot:

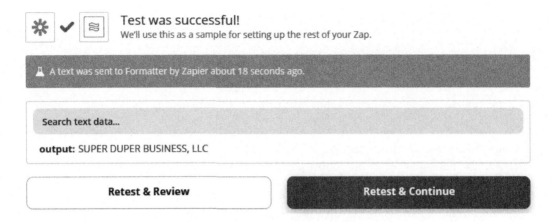

Figure 15.6 – An example of the altered value when using the Text action event
to change all the text to uppercase

Proceed to add one or more action steps after your **Text** action step.

You should now have a better understanding of how to use the **Uppercase** transform function. Next, let's discuss how to convert all the characters in a string of text to lowercase with the **Lowercase** transform function.

Converting all the characters in a string of text to lowercase

Conversely to the **Uppercase** transform option, there may be occasions where you want to do the opposite, and change text that is purely uppercase or a combination of upper and lowercase to lowercase only. You can use the Formatter by Zapier **Text** action event with the **Lowercase** transform function. For example, if the string of text were The Ice-cream Parlour, the transformed text would be the ice-cream parlour. Microsoft Excel users will recognize the similarity of this Zapier functionality to the LOWER formula in a Microsoft Excel spreadsheet to convert text to lowercase.

Here are a few examples of when you can use this transform option:

- When your contacts make a purchase through your Shopify website, you might want to generate unique user aliases for them to use in your other apps. If you use their name in the alias, you might want to make it lowercase for consistency.

- You might be using **Google Docs** to create contracts for your prospects from a template when they book a consultation call with you through Calendly. You might want to have all Google Docs filenames in a consistent lowercase format based on the name of the client and the date the document was created.

Next, let's review how to set up an action step with the **Lowercase** transform option.

Setting up the Text action event with the Lowercase transform option

Use the **Text** action event once you have set up your trigger step.

Once you have added an action step, by either selecting the **Action** step or clicking on the + icon, and chosen **Formatter by Zapier** as the app and **Text** as the action event, you can then edit the fields in the **Set up action** section as follows:

- **Transform**: From the drop-down menu, select the **Lowercase** option. This is a required field and must have a value for the Zap to run.

- **Input**: Use this field to enter the text that you want to transform into lowercase letters. You can enter either a static value, a dynamic value from previous steps, or a combination of both to specify the **Input** value. Although this is not a required field, the formatter function will not return a result if there is no value.

An example is shown in the following screenshot:

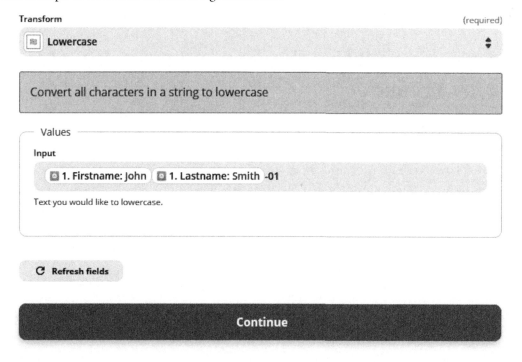

Figure 15.7 – Using the Formatter by Zapier Text action event to change the text to lowercase letters

Click on the **Continue** button. You can then use the **Test action** section to test this step to generate the altered text in lowercase. The result from the scenario in *Figure 15.7* is shown in the following screenshot:

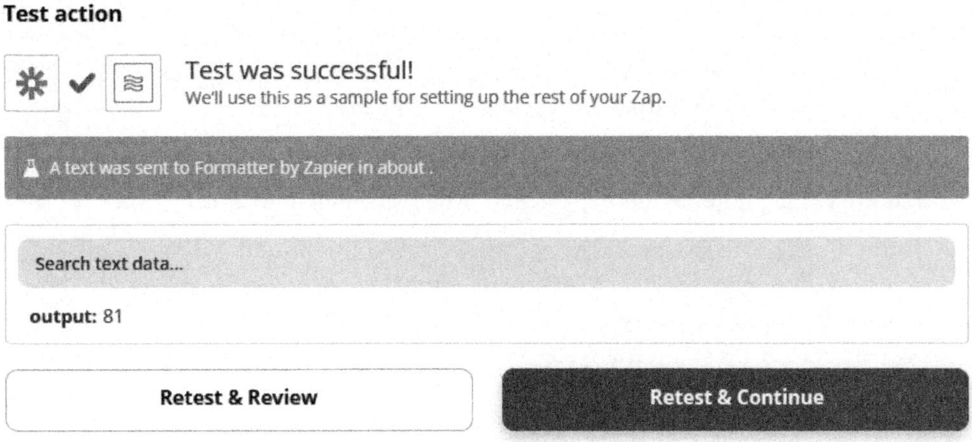

Test action

Test was successful!
We'll use this as a sample for setting up the rest of your Zap.

A text was sent to Formatter by Zapier in about .

Search text data...

output: 81

| Retest & Review | Retest & Continue |

Figure 15.8 – An example of the altered value when using the Text action
event to change all the text to lowercase

Proceed to add one or more action steps after your **Text** action step.

You should now have a better understanding of how to use the **Lowercase** transform function. Next, let's cover how to pluralize words using the **Pluralize** transform function.

Pluralizing words

It is sometimes handy to convert a word from a singular format to a plural format. You can change any English word to plural using the Formatter by Zapier **Text** action event with the **Pluralize** transform function.

Here is an example of when you can use this transform option.

You might have an e-commerce store that uses the WooCommerce platform. When customers buy from you, you might want to follow up purchases with an email on a more personal level, with text formatted to read better. Let's say your customer purchases six red t-shirts but your WooCommerce site lists the product as `red t-shirt`; you could use the **Pluralize** transform function to change the text to `red t-shirts` based on how many the customer ordered. Your email will then read better, with `6 red t-shirts`.

Next, let's review how to set up an action step with the **Pluralize** transform option.

Setting up the Text action event with the Pluralize transform option

Use the **Text** action event once you have set up your trigger step.

Once you have added an action step, by either selecting the **Action** step or clicking on the + icon, and chosen **Formatter by Zapier** as the app and **Text** as the action event, you can then edit the fields in the **Set up action** section as follows:

- **Transform**: From the drop-down menu, select the **Pluralize** option. This is a required field and must have a value in order for the Zap to run.

- **Input**: Use this field to enter the text that you want to pluralize. You can enter either a static value, a dynamic value from previous steps, or a combination of both to specify the **Input** value. Although this is not a required field, the formatter function will not return a result if there is no value.

An example is shown in the following screenshot:

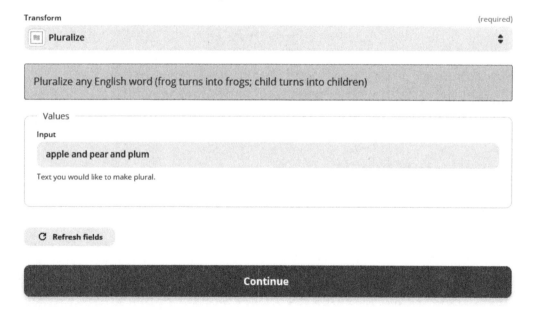

Figure 15.9 – Using the Formatter by Zapier Text action event to pluralize text

Click on the **Continue** button. You can then use the **Test action** section to test this step to generate the altered pluralized text. The result from the scenario in *Figure 15.9* is shown in the following screenshot:

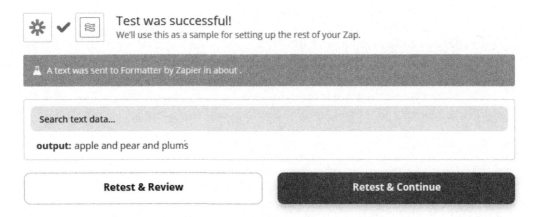

Figure 15.10 – An example of the altered value when using the Text action event to pluralize text

Proceed to add one or more action steps after your **Text** action step.

> **Note**
> The **Pluralize** transform function generally works best for a single word. If multiple words are presented, generally the last word in the string will be pluralized.

You should now have a better understanding of how to use the **Pluralize** transform function. Next, let's take a look at how to find the first position of a specified text value with the **Find** transform function.

Finding the first position of specified text

You might, on occasion, want to know in what numerical position a word first appears in a string of text. You can use the Formatter by Zapier **Text** action event with the **Find** transform function to find the first numerical position of a word or phrase in a string of text. A number will be returned representing the character position of the first letter of the word or phrase. For example, if you wanted to find the position of the word green in a string of text such as green is a wonderful color, the returned value would be 0. If the string of text were isn't green a wonderful color?, the returned value would be 6. If the search term does not exist in the string of text, the value that is returned would be -1. You can also skip a number of characters that you do not want to be included in the search. For example, if the text string is plum and apple and pear and plum, we can ignore the first position of the word plum by skipping the first four or more characters in the string during the search. This returns a result of position 28 for the start of the second occurrence of the word plum in the string.

Here is an example of when you can use this transform option:

- You have a team of blog writers that write blog posts based on a topic and **SEO** (short for **search engine optimization**) information that you add to a Microsoft Excel spreadsheet. When your bloggers upload the new post to WordPress, you might want to use the **Find** transform function to locate the first position of your SEO keyphrase and then be notified by email of that position.

Next, let's review how to set up an action step with the **Find** transform option.

Setting up the Text action event with the Find transform option

Use the **Text** action event once you have set up your trigger step.

Once you have added an action step, by either selecting the **Action** step or clicking on the + icon, and chosen **Formatter by Zapier** as the app and **Text** as the action event, you can then edit the fields in the **Set up action** section as follows:

- **Transform**: From the drop-down menu, select the **Find** option. This is a required field and must have a value in order for the Zap to run.

- **Input**: Use this field to enter the text that you want to search for the numerical position of a value that you enter in the **Find** field. You can enter either a static value, a dynamic value from previous steps, or a combination of both to specify the **Input** value. Although this is not a required field, the formatter function will not return a result if there is no value.

- **Find**: Use this field to enter the word or phrase that you want to search for in the text from the **Input** field. You can enter either a static value, a dynamic value from previous steps, or a combination of both to specify this value. Although this is not a required field, the formatter function will not return a result if there is no value.

- **Skip Characters**: Use this field to enter how many characters you might want to skip when searching for the value entered in the **Find** field. You can enter either a static value, a dynamic value from previous steps, or a combination of both to specify this value. This field can be left blank. Use this field when you don't want to find the position of the first word but only subsequent words.

An example is shown in the following screenshot:

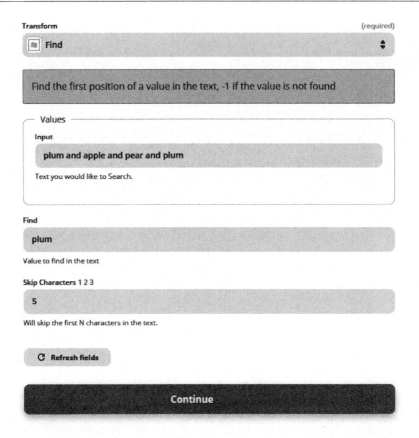

Figure 15.11 – Using the Formatter by Zapier Text action event to find the numerical position of a word

Click on the **Continue** button. You can then use the **Test action** section to test this step to generate the numerical position of the word. The result from the scenario in *Figure 15.11* is shown in the following screenshot:

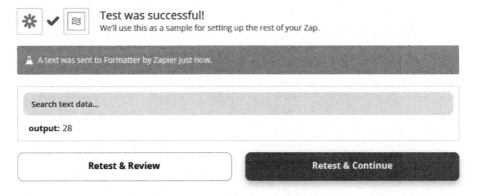

Figure 15.12 – An example of the altered value when using the Text action event to pluralize text

Proceed to add one or more action steps after your **Text** action step.

You should now have a better understanding of how to use the **Find** transform function. Next, let's explore how to replace characters, words, or phrases with the **Replace** transform function.

Replacing characters, words, or phrases

You've probably used the find and replace function many times before when editing a document in **Microsoft Word** or Google Docs, a spreadsheet in Microsoft Excel or Google Sheets, or a database such as Smartsheet or Airtable. It does what the name says – finds something and then replaces it with something else. Zapier uses similar functionality, allowing you to find and replace words and phrases in text strings. You can use the Formatter by Zapier **Text** action event with the **Replace** transform function to achieve this. Microsoft Excel users will recognize the similarity of this Zapier functionality to the REPLACE or SUBSTITUTE formulas in a Microsoft Excel spreadsheet to find and replace text.

The **Replace** transform function also allows you to find special characters using special character syntax as follows:

- **Space characters**: The [:space:] syntax is used to match space (\s) characters.
- **Tab characters**: The [:tab:] syntax is used to match tab (\t) characters.
- **Newline characters**: The [:newline:] syntax is used to match newline (\n) characters, which are those used to identify the end of a line of text or the start of a new line.
- **Carriage-return characters**: The [:return:] syntax is used to match carriage-return (\r) characters, which are those that denote the start of the current line (at the left margin).

Here is an example of when you can use this transform option.

You might ask clients to submit reviews via a **Typeform** webform. After the form has been submitted, you might want to search the body of the testimonial for a certain word or phrase and replace it with another before uploading it to your WordPress website as a new post.

Next, let's review how to set up an action step with the **Replace** transform option.

Setting up the Text action event with the Replace transform option

Use the **Text** action event once you have set up your trigger step.

Once you have added an action step, by either selecting the **Action** step or clicking on the + icon, and chosen **Formatter by Zapier** as the app and **Text** as the action event, you can then edit the fields in the **Set up action** section as follows:

- **Transform**: From the drop-down menu, select the **Replace** option. This is a required field and must have a value in order for the Zap to run.

- **Input**: Use this field to enter the text that you want to search for a word or phrase and replace it with another. You can enter either a static value, a dynamic value from previous steps, or a combination of both to specify the **Input** value. Although this is not a required field, the formatter function will not return a result if there is no value.

- **Find**: Use this field to enter the word or phrase that you want to search for in the text from the **Input** field. You can enter either a static value, a dynamic value from previous steps, or a combination of both to specify this value. This is a required field and must have a value in order for the Zap to run. This field supports special character syntax. For example, to find spaces, use the [:space:] syntax.

- **Replace**: Use this field to enter the word or phrase that you want to replace the value from the **Find** field with. You can enter either a static value, a dynamic value from previous steps, or a combination of both to specify this value. Although this is not a required field, the formatter function will not return a result if there is no value.

An example is shown in the following screenshot:

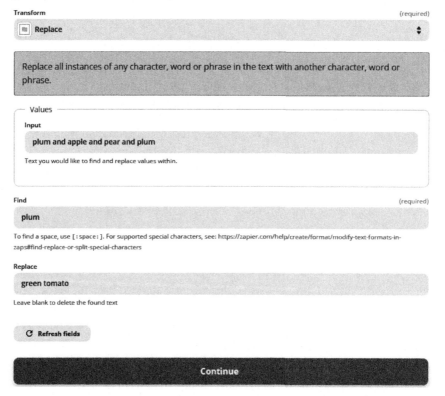

Figure 15.13 – Using the Formatter by Zapier Text action event to find and replace text

Click on the **Continue** button. You can then use the **Test action** section to test this step to find and replace any text. The result from the scenario in *Figure 15.13* is shown in the following screenshot:

Test action

Test was successful!
We'll use this as a sample for setting up the rest of your Zap.

A text was sent to Formatter by Zapier in about .

Search text data...

output: green tomato and apple and pear and green tomato

Retest & Review   Retest & Continue

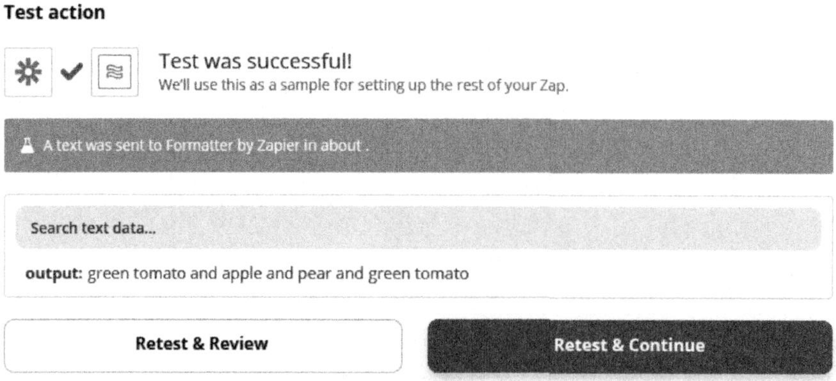

Figure 15.14 – An example of the altered value when using the Text action event to find and replace text

Proceed to add one or more action steps after your **Text** action step.

You should now have a better understanding of how to use the **Replace** transform function. Next, let's discuss how to count the number of characters in a string of text using the **Length** transform function.

Counting the number of characters in a string of text

Having the ability to automatically count the number of characters in a string of text can be very useful in a number of scenarios. This is especially important if the apps involved in action steps have character limitations. One example of this would be the character limitations for tweets on Twitter. You can use the Formatter by Zapier **Text** action event with the **Length** transform function to check the character length in a string of text before passing the text to other action steps. Microsoft Excel users will recognize the similarity of this Zapier functionality to the LEN formula in a Microsoft Excel spreadsheet to count the number of characters in a string of text.

Here are a few examples of when you can use this transform option:

- You might reshare content on various social media channels; however, a piece of content might be too long to share on platforms such as Twitter. You could use the **Length** transform function to count the character length and then use Filter by Zapier to stop your workflow from continuing if the character length is over 280.

- You might want to check the number of characters in the body of a new WordPress blog post before adding the value to Airtable.

- You might want to reshare your social media posts by SMS for some clients who don't use social media, using Twilio or Voodoo SMS, for example. Most SMS platforms have character length restrictions, so you could use the **Length** transform function to count the character length before stopping the workflow with Filter by Zapier.

Next, let's review how to set up an action step with the **Length** transform option.

Setting up the Text action event with the Length transform option

Use the **Text** action event once you have set up your trigger step.

Once you have added an action step, by either selecting the **Action** step or clicking on the + icon, and chosen **Formatter by Zapier** as the app and **Text** as the action event, you can then edit the fields in the **Set up action** section as follows:

- **Transform**: From the drop-down menu, select the **Length** option. This is a required field and must have a value for the Zap to run.

- **Input**: Use this field to enter the text that you want to perform a character length count on. You can enter either a static value, a dynamic value from previous steps, or a combination of both to specify the **Input** value. Although this is not a required field, the formatter function will not return a result if there is no value.

- **Ignore Whitespace**: Use this Boolean field to choose whether you want to ignore all whitespace characters including spaces, tabs, and newlines. Select **True** to ignore whitespace and **False** to include whitespace. Although this is not a required field, the default if neither option is selected is to include whitespace.

An example is shown in the following screenshot:

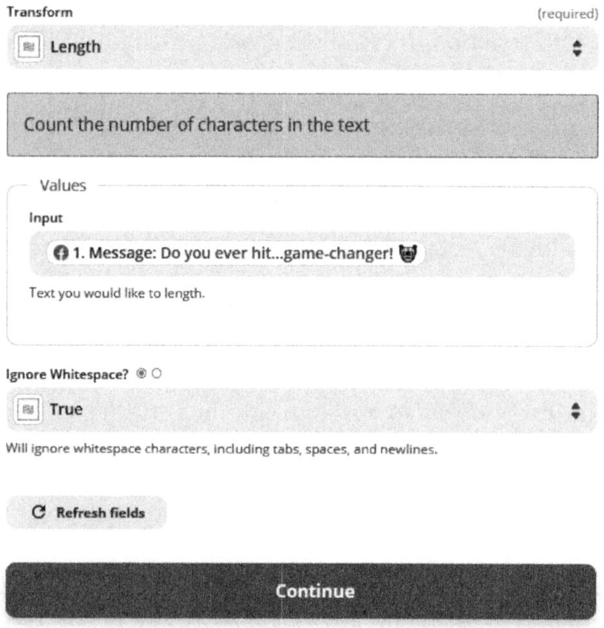

Transform   (required)

▥ Length   ▲▼

Count the number of characters in the text

Values

Input

🜲 1. Message: Do you ever hit...game-changer! 🎭

Text you would like to length.

Ignore Whitespace? ⦿ ○

▥ True   ▲▼

Will ignore whitespace characters, including tabs, spaces, and newlines.

↻ Refresh fields

Continue

Figure 15.15 – Using the Formatter by Zapier Text action event to count the number of characters

Click on the **Continue** button. You can then use the **Test action** section to test this step to count the number of characters. The result from the scenario in *Figure 15.15* is shown in the following screenshot:

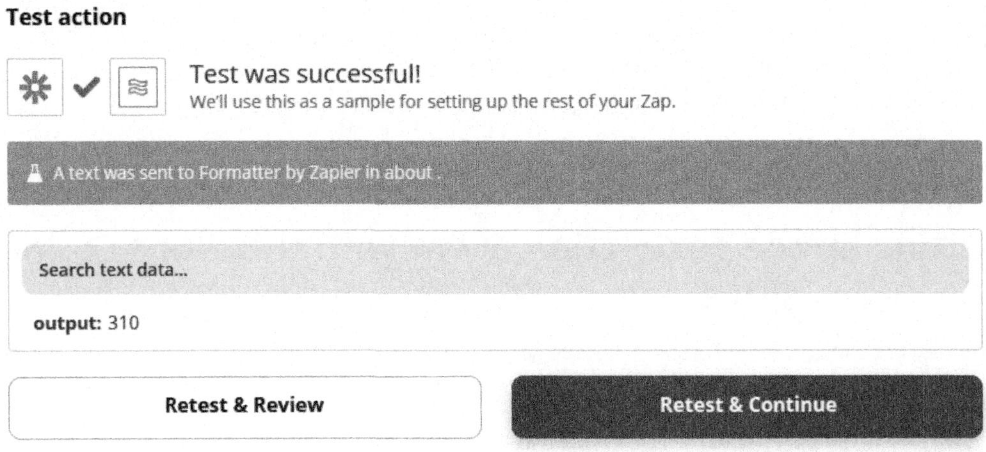

Test action

Test was successful!
We'll use this as a sample for setting up the rest of your Zap.

A text was sent to Formatter by Zapier in about .

Search text data...

output: 310

Retest & Review   Retest & Continue

Figure 15.16 – An example of the returned value when using the Text action event to count the number of characters

Proceed to add one or more action steps after your **Text** action step.

> **Tip**
> Use the **Length** transform function in the same workflow as the **Truncate** transform function to reduce the length of strings of texts if they are more than a certain character length, such as for tweets.

You should now have a better understanding of how to use the **Length** transform function. Next, let's cover how to count the number of words in a string of text with the **Word Count** transform function.

Counting the number of words in a string of text

As with counting characters in a string of text, it is often handy to be able to count the number of words. This is especially useful when dealing with documents and copywriting scenarios. You can use the Formatter by Zapier **Text** action event with the **Word Count** transform function to achieve this.

Here are a few examples of when you can use this transform option:

- You might want to check the number of words in the body of a new WordPress blog post before adding the value to Knack.

- You might handle your customer service desk queries in Freshdesk and want to compare the number of words in each ticket update with the time between updates by adding the figures to a Google Sheets spreadsheet.

Next, let's review how to set up an action step with the **Word Count** transform option.

Setting up the Text action event with the Word Count transform option

Use the **Text** action event once you have set up your trigger step.

Once you have added an action step, by either selecting the **Action** step or clicking on the + icon, and chosen **Formatter by Zapier** as the app and **Text** as the action event, you can then edit the fields in the **Set up action** section as follows:

- **Transform**: From the drop-down menu, select the **Word Count** option. This is a required field and must have a value in order for the Zap to run.

- **Input**: Use this field to enter the text in which you want to count the number of words contained. You can enter either a static value, a dynamic value from previous steps, or a combination of both to specify the **Input** value. Although this is not a required field, the formatter function will not return a result if there is no value.

An example is shown in the following screenshot:

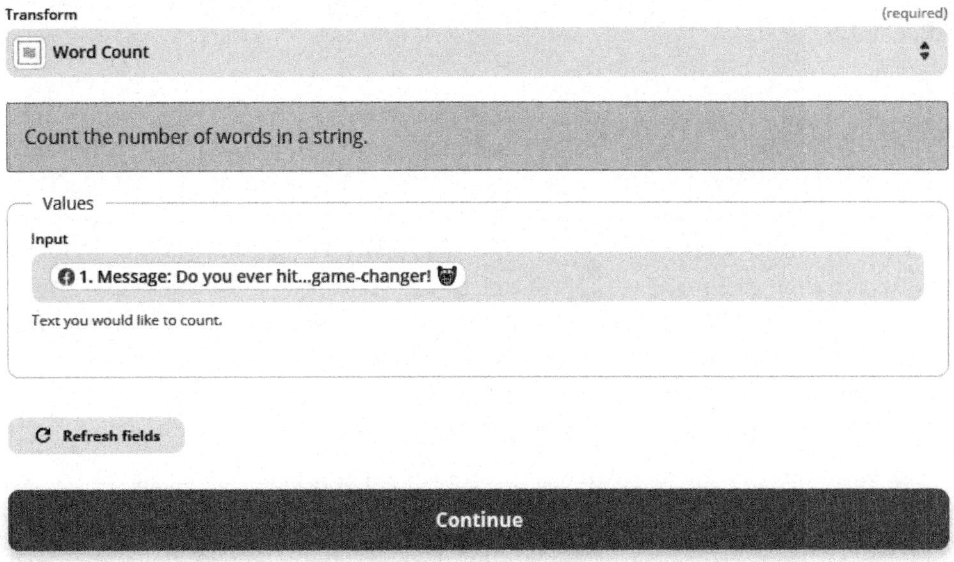

Figure 15.17 – Using the Formatter by Zapier Text action event
to count the number of words in a string of text

Click on the **Continue** button. You can then use the **Test action** section to test this step to return a value defining the number of words in the text string. The result from the scenario in *Figure 15.17* is shown in the following screenshot:

Test action

Test was successful!
We'll use this as a sample for setting up the rest of your Zap.

A text was sent to Formatter by Zapier in about .

Search text data...

output: 81

Retest & Review   **Retest & Continue**

Figure 15.18 – An example of the value returned when using
the Text action event to count the number of words

Proceed to add one or more action steps after your **Text** action step.

You should now have a better understanding of how to use the **Word Count** transform function. Next, let's explore how to remove whitespace using the **Trim Whitespace** transform function.

Removing whitespace

Sometimes strings of text may not have been edited in the way we need to be able to use them in other steps in our workflows. This is often the case when certain apps present data in a certain way with blank character spacing before or after the text. In these scenarios, if you want to alter the format of the text so that no whitespace exists at the beginning or end of a string of text, you can use the Formatter by Zapier **Text** action event with the **Trim Whitespace** transform function to achieve this. Microsoft Excel users will recognize the similarity between using this Zapier functionality and the TRIM formula in a Microsoft Excel spreadsheet to remove whitespace from a string of text.

Here is an example of when you can use this transform option:

- You might ask job seekers to send in applications by completing a webform. There might be formatting issues with the webform, presenting the data with large whitespace blocks before or after the body of parts of the form submission data. You can use the **Trim Whitespace** transform function to remove the whitespace prior to adding the application to your task management app such as ClickUp.

Next, let's review how to set up an action step with the **Trim Whitespace** transform option.

Setting up the Text action event with the Trim Whitespace transform option

Use the **Text** action event once you have set up your trigger step.

Once you have added an action step, by either selecting the **Action** step or clicking on the + icon, and chosen **Formatter by Zapier** as the app and **Text** as the action event, you can then edit the fields in the **Set up action** section as follows:

- **Transform**: From the drop-down menu, select the **Trim Whitespace** option. This is a required field and must have a value in order for the Zap to run.

- **Input**: Use this field to enter the text that you want to remove whitespace from. You can enter either a static value, a dynamic value from previous steps, or a combination of both to specify the **Input** value. Although this is not a required field, the formatter function will not return a result if there is no value.

An example is shown in the following screenshot:

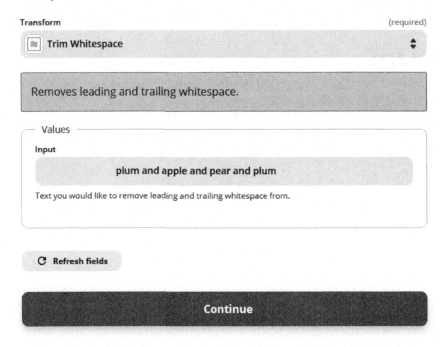

Figure 15.19 – Using the Formatter by Zapier Text action event to trim whitespace

Click on the **Continue** button. You can then use the **Test action** section to test this step to return a value without leading and trailing whitespace. The result from the scenario in *Figure 15.19* is shown in the following screenshot:

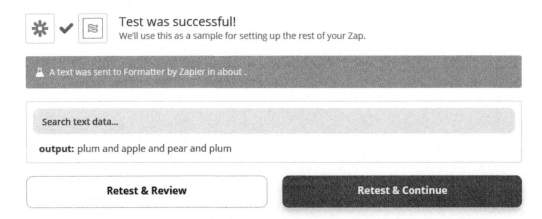

Figure 15.20 – An example of the value returned when using the Text action event to trim whitespace

Proceed to add one or more action steps after your **Text** action step.

You should now have a better understanding of how to use the **Trim Whitespace** transform function.

Summary

In this chapter, we continued our focus on the versatile Formatter by Zapier built-in app and the extensive functionality available to format text. First, we covered how to use Zapier to transform text values in general. Next, we explored capitalizing text, applying title case, uppercase, and lowercase, and pluralizing words. Lastly, we explored finding the position of and replacing text, counting characters and words, truncating text, and removing whitespace.

You now know how to use the Formatter by Zapier built-in app to transform text values in a number of different ways, including capitalizing, applying title case, uppercase, and lowercase, pluralizing words, finding the position of and replacing text, counting characters and words, and removing whitespace.

In the next chapter, you will continue to learn how to use more functionality of the Formatter by Zapier built-in app to format text. We will explore how to create a superhero name, split text into segments, truncate text, and extract patterns, URLs, phone numbers, numbers, and email addresses. We will also briefly discuss the more advanced functions to convert Markdown to HTML, convert to ASCII, URL Encode and Decode, using default values, and removing HTML tags.

16

Text Formatting Functions in Zapier – Part 2

In *Chapter 15, Text Formatting Functions in Zapier – Part 1*, we introduced several of the Formatter by Zapier built-in app text transform options. In this chapter, we continue to discuss the functionality that Zapier has available to format text.

First, we will explore how to create a superhero name, split text into segments, and truncate text. Then, we will cover how to remove HTML to leave plain text and how to assign a default value. After that, we will discuss the possibilities of how to extract email addresses, numbers, URLs, and phone numbers from blocks of text. Lastly, we will briefly discuss the more advanced functions of how to extract patterns, convert HTML to Markdown and vice versa, convert text to ASCII, and finally, encode and decode URLs.

We will cover the following key topics in this chapter:

- Converting a name into the name of a superhero
- Splitting characters or words into segments
- Truncating text to a specified character length

- Removing HTML to leave plain text

- Assigning a default value

- Extracting data from blocks of text

- Advanced text formatting features

Once you have worked through each of these topics, you will have a better understanding of the different text transforming functions available for use with the Formatter by Zapier built-in app. You will know how to use Zapier to adjust text to various formats.

Technical requirements

To make the most of the content in this chapter, you will need access to a Zapier account. The Zapier Starter plan will be required for you to create multi-step workflows using the Formatter by Zapier built-in app.

Converting a name into the name of a superhero

So far in this book, we've covered plenty of useful but formal formatting functions that can be used for various business cases. Zapier is not all just about being formal. Sometimes, you might want to have a bit of fun and be playful with text formatting. Zapier can convert any name or a short string of text into a randomly chosen name of a superhero by using the Formatter by Zapier **Text** action event with the **Superhero Name** transform function. For example, if the name that you wanted to convert was Kelly Goss, the transformed text might be Space Fury. This text transform function is great to use when you want to do something fun and outside of the norm with your data.

Here are a few examples of when you can use this transform option:

- You might want new subscribers to be randomly assigned superhero names that you will address them by in your email communications. So, when John Smith signs up to your email newsletter in **Autopilot**, you can refer to him in the future as Scarlet Flame.

- You might like to have a bit of fun with your staff and decide to assign all new staff members with a superhero name when they are added as users to Asana. You could then send them an email to welcome them to the Asana team and let them know their new superhero name.

Next, let's review how to set up an action step with the **Superhero Name** transform option.

Setting up the Text action event with the Superhero Name transform option

Use the **Text** action event once you have set up your trigger step.

Once you have added an action step either by selecting the **Action** step or clicking on the + icon and chosen **Formatter by Zapier** as the app and **Text** as the action event, you can then edit the fields in the **Set up action** section as follows:

- **Transform**: From the drop-down menu, select the **Superhero Name** option. This is a required field and must have a value in order for the Zap to run.

- **Input**: Use this field to enter the text of the name or word string that you want to transform into a superhero name. You can either enter a static value, a dynamic value from previous steps, or a combination of both to specify the **Input** value. Although this is not a required field, the formatter function will not return a result if there is no value.

An example is shown in the following screenshot:

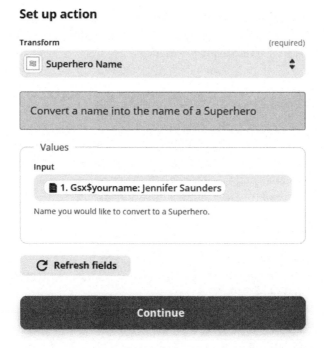

Figure 16.1 – Using the Formatter by Zapier Text action event to transform words into a superhero name

Click on the **Continue** button. You can then use the **Test action** section to test this step to generate the superhero name. The result from the scenario in *Figure 16.1* is shown in the following screenshot:

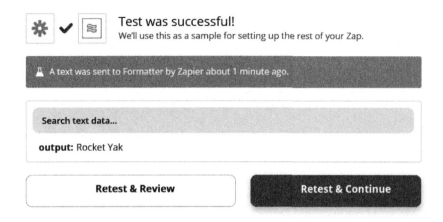

Figure 16.2 – An example of the altered value when using the Text action event to convert words to a superhero name

Proceed to add one or more action steps after your **Text** action step.

You should now have a better understanding of how to use the **Superhero Name** transform function. Next, let's take a look at how to split characters or words into segments with the **Split Text** transform function.

Splitting characters or words into segments

Being able to manipulate text with a splitting function is possibly one of the most versatile functions of all the Formatter by Zapier text transform options. There will be many occasions where data is presented as a string of text and you will want to extract one or more words from that string to then use in other parts of your workflows. A common example of this is the need to use either the first and last name when only the full name is presented. You can use the Formatter by Zapier **Text** action event with the **Split Text transform function** to split the word string to return the two values.

You can use words or characters to split text, and the **Split Text** transform function allows you to split words or strings of words that are separated by special characters using special character syntax as follows:

- **Space characters**: The `[:space:]` syntax is used to match space (`\s`) characters.
- **Tab characters**: The `[:tab:]` syntax is used to match tab (`\t`) characters.

- **Newline characters**: The `[:newline:]` syntax is used to match newline (`\n`) characters, which are those used to identify the end of a line of text or start of a new line.
- **Carriage-return characters**: The `[:return:]` syntax is used to match carriage-return (`\r`) characters, which are those that denote the start of the current line (at the left margin).

Here are a few examples of when you can use this transform option:

- When a new lead fills out a webform, you might have a field for them to enter their full name instead of separate fields for first and last name. If you wanted to use their first name only in an email or add their first and last name as individual fields to your CRM, you could use the **Split Text** transform function accordingly.
- You might use an e-sign app that does not integrate with Zapier but you receive an email confirmation once the document has been signed with the title of the document as the subject. Once that document is signed, you might want to search for data in a row on a Google Sheets spreadsheet using the signee's company name, which you have strategically placed as the first word in the document name. You can use the **Split Text** transform function to split out the first word in the string in the email subject.

Let's review how to set up an action step with the **Split Text** transform option.

Setting up the Text action event with the Split transform option

Use the **Text** action event once you have set up your trigger step.

Once you have added an action step either by selecting the **Action** step or clicking on the **+** icon and chosen **Formatter by Zapier** as the app and **Text** as the action event, you can then edit the fields in the **Set up action** section as follows:

- **Transform**: From the drop-down menu, select the **Split Text** option. This is a required field and must have a value in order for the Zap to run.
- **Input**: Use this field to enter the string of text that you want to split. You can either enter a static value, a dynamic value from previous steps, or a combination of both to specify the **Input** value. Although this is not a required field, the formatter function will not return a result if there is no value.

- **Separator**: Use this field to enter the word, character, or syntax that you want to use as the splitting value from the **Input** field. You can either enter a static value, a dynamic value from previous steps, or a combination of both to specify this value. This field supports special character syntax. For example, to split text separated by spaces, use the [:space:] syntax. Although this is not a required field, if left blank the default is the [:space:] syntax.

- **Segment Index**: Use this drop-down field to select which segment of split text you want to return. The options are **First, Second, Last, Second to Last, All (as Line-items)**, and **All (as Separate Fields)**. The values returned when using **All (as Line-items)** can be used in steps where line items are supported, for example, in invoicing apps. You can either enter a static value, a dynamic value from previous steps, or a combination of both to specify this value. Although this is not a required field, if left blank, the **First** index will be returned.

An example is shown in the following screenshot, where we want to extract all values as separate items that have been separated by spaces:

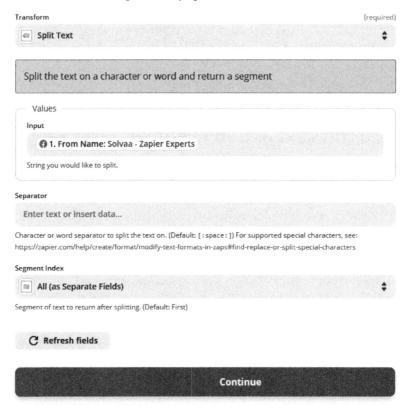

Figure 16.3 – Using the Formatter by Zapier Text action event to split text separated by spaces

Click on the **Continue** button. You can then use the **Test action** section to test this step to split out text in a string of words. The result from the scenario in *Figure 16.3* is shown in the following screenshot:

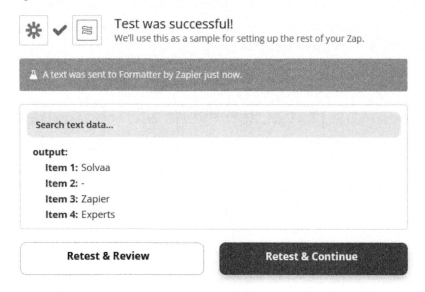

Figure 16.4 – An example of the altered value when using the Text action event to split a string of text separated by spaces

Proceed to add one or more action steps after your **Text** action step.

You should now have a better understanding of how to use the **Split Text** transform function. Next, let's discuss how to truncate text to a specified character length using the **Truncate** transform function.

Truncating text to a specified character length

There may be times that you want to reduce the character length of a block of text so that you can use it as a summary, or you might have restrictions on the number of characters. A typical example of this is when posting content on social media where you have a fixed character length, such as reposting a Facebook post (which could have over 60,000 characters) to Twitter, which has a maximum character length of 280. You can use the Formatter by Zapier **Text** action event with the **Truncate** transform function to reduce the number of characters in a block of text and optionally replace the last three characters with ....

Here are a few examples of when you can use this transform option:

- When you publish a new blog post on WordPress, truncate the blog post content to produce a teaser summary suitable to use on social media.

- When you post a new Facebook post, truncate it to a shorter character length and repost it on Twitter and LinkedIn.

Let's review how to set up an action step with the **Truncate** transform option.

Setting up the Text action event with the Truncate transform option

Use the **Text** action event once you have set up your trigger step.

Once you have added an action step either by selecting the **Action** step or clicking on the + icon and chosen **Formatter by Zapier** as the app and **Text** as the action event, you can then edit the fields in the **Set up action** section as follows:

- **Transform**: From the drop-down menu, select the **Truncate** option. This is a required field and must have a value in order for the Zap to run.

- **Input**: Use this field to enter the text that you want to truncate. You can either enter a static value, a dynamic value from previous steps, or a combination of both to specify the **Input** value. Although this is not a required field, the formatter function will not return a result if there is no value.

- **Max Length**: Use this number field to enter a number value for the maximum number of characters you want the word string to be truncated to. You can either enter a static value, a dynamic value from previous steps, or a combination of both to specify this value. This is a required field and must have a value in order for the Zap to run.

- **Skip Characters**: Use this number field to specify how many of the characters at the beginning of the word string that you want to skip. For example, if the string of words began with `This is an example: Today's weather is hot and sunny.` and you wanted to truncate the words `This is an example:`, you would enter the number `19` to skip those characters. You can either enter a static value, a dynamic value from previous steps, or a combination of both to specify this value.

- **Append Ellipsis**: Use this drop-down boolean field to select either **True** or **False** as to whether you want to shorten the text at the end by three characters and replace them with .... You can either use the dropdown or enter a static value, a dynamic value from previous steps, or a combination of both to specify this value.

An example is shown in the following screenshot where we want to truncate a long Facebook post to 250 characters and append ellipses:

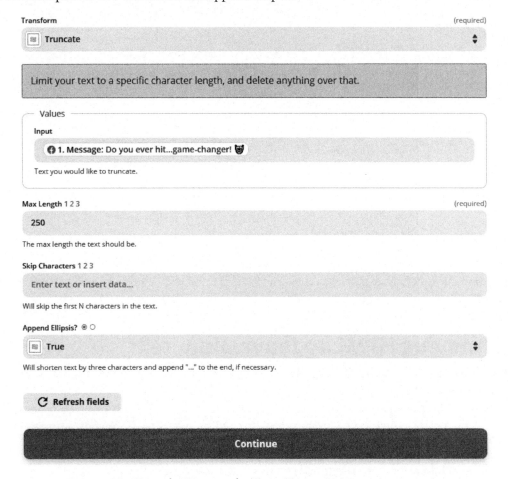

Figure 16.5 – Using the Formatter by Zapier Text action event to truncate text

Click on the **Continue** button. You can then use the **Test action** section to test this step to truncate characters in a string of words. The result from the scenario in *Figure 16.5* is shown in the following screenshot:

Figure 16.6 – An example of the altered value when using the Text action event to truncate and append ellipses to a string of text

Proceed to add one or more action steps after your **Text** action step.

You should now have a better understanding of how to use the **Truncate** transform function. Next, let's cover how to remove HTML from blocks of text using the **Remove HTML** transform function.

Removing HTML to leave plain text

As **HTML** (short for **HyperText Markup Language**) is used to customize the way data is displayed on the web, such as on websites, digital documents, and emails, there will be occasions when you will want to view just the plain text without any coding. You can use the Formatter by Zapier **Text** action event with the **Remove HTML** transform function to achieve this by stripping out all the HTML coding to leave just the plain text behind.

Here are a few examples of when you can use this transform option:

- When you want to extract the body of an email, but the data is only presented in HTML.

- When you publish a new blog post on WordPress, and you want to remove any HTML before posting a teaser summary on social media.

Let's review how to set up an action step with the **Remove HTML** transform option.

Setting up the Text action event with the Remove HTML transform option

Use the **Text** action event once you have set up your trigger step.

Once you have added an action step either by selecting the **Action** step or clicking on the + icon and chosen **Formatter by Zapier** as the app and **Text** as the action event, you can then edit the fields in the **Set up action** section as follows:

- **Transform**: From the drop-down menu, select the **Remove HTML** option. This is a required field and must have a value in order for the Zap to run.

- **Input**: Use this field to enter the text that you want to truncate. You can either enter a static value, a dynamic value from previous steps, or a combination of both to specify the **Input** value. Although this is not a required field, the formatter function will not return a result if there is no value.

An example is shown in the following screenshot:

Figure 16.7 – Using the Formatter by Zapier Text action event to remove HTML from a block of text

Click on the **Continue** button. You can then use the **Test action** section to test this step to remove HTML from a block of text. The result from the scenario in *Figure 16.7* is shown in the following screenshot:

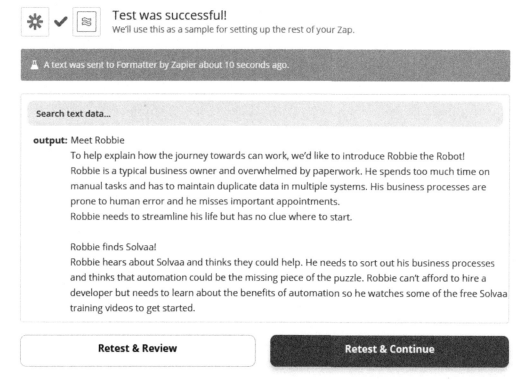

Figure 16.8 – An example of the altered value when using the Text action event to remove HTML

Proceed to add one or more action steps after your **Text** action step.

You should now have a better understanding of how to use the **Remove HTML** transform function. Next, let's cover how to assign a default value.

Assigning a default value

You might encounter situations where data has not been entered for whatever reason, therefore leaving a field blank. In some cases, this lack of data may cause problems later in your workflows. To prevent problems later down the line, you might want to conditionally assign a value that acts as the default where data might be missing from a specific field. You can use the Formatter by Zapier **Text** action event with the **Default Value** transform function to achieve this by assigning a default value when a field contains no data.

Here are a few examples of when you can use this transform option:

- When new deals are created in Zoho CRM, but an owner has not been assigned, you may want to automatically assign these deals to a specific user who can then reassign the deal to a member of the team.

- When new cards are created in Trello but members have not been assigned, you may want to automatically assign these cards to a manager who then assigns the card to someone in the team.

Let's review how to set up an action step with the **Default Value** transform option.

Setting up the Text action event with the Default Value transform option

Use the **Text** action event once you have set up your trigger step.

Once you have added an action step either by selecting the **Action** step or clicking on the + icon and chosen **Formatter by Zapier** as the app and **Text** as the action event, you can then edit the fields in the **Set up action** section as follows:

- **Transform**: From the drop-down menu, select the **Default Value** option. This is a required field and must have a value in order for the Zap to run.

- **Input**: Use this field to enter the text that you want to truncate. You can either enter a static value, a dynamic value from previous steps, or a combination of both to specify the **Input** value. If a line-item value is entered, a line-item field will be returned. Although this is not a required field, the formatter function will not return a result if there is no value.

- **Default Value**: Use this field to enter the default value to use if the data in the **Input** field is blank. You can either enter a static value, a dynamic value from previous steps, or a combination of both to specify the **Default Value**. This field supports the [:space:], [:tab:], [:newline:], and [:return:] special character syntaxes. This is a required field and must have a value in order for the Zap to run.

An example is shown in the following screenshot where if a new Trello card does not have a member assigned, a senior staff member will be assigned in later steps by using their user ID as the default value:

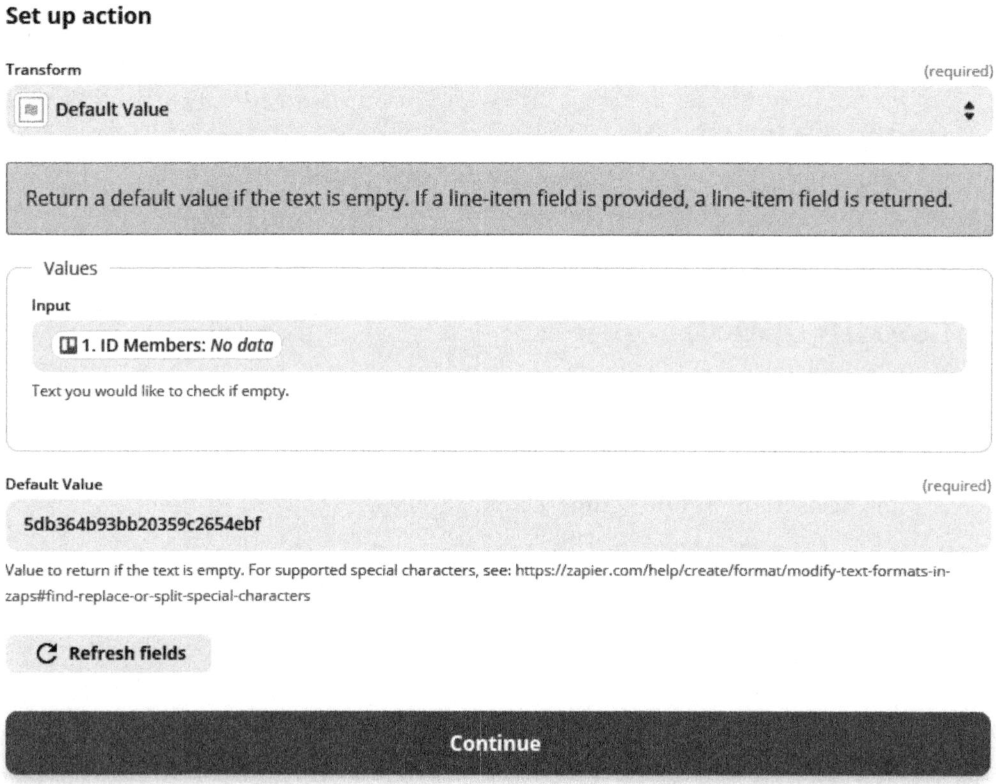

Set up action

Transform   (required)

| 📄 **Default Value** | ⬍ |

Return a default value if the text is empty. If a line-item field is provided, a line-item field is returned.

Values

Input

📖 **1. ID Members:** *No data*

Text you would like to check if empty.

Default Value   (required)

5db364b93bb20359c2654ebf

Value to return if the text is empty. For supported special characters, see: https://zapier.com/help/create/format/modify-text-formats-in-zaps#find-replace-or-split-special-characters

↻ **Refresh fields**

Continue

Figure 16.9 – Using the Formatter by Zapier Text action event to assign a default value

Click on the **Continue** button. You can then use the **Test action** section to test this step to assign a default value if a text field is empty. The result from the scenario in *Figure 16.9* is shown in the following screenshot:

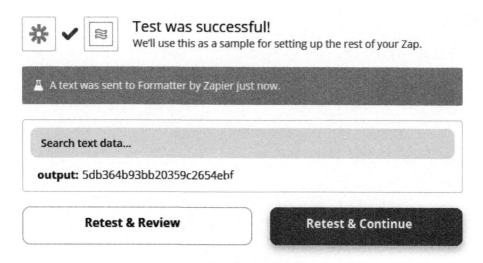

Figure 16.10 – An example of the altered value when using the Text action event to assign a default value

Proceed to add one or more action steps after your **Text** action step.

You should now have a better understanding of how to use the **Default Value** transform function. Next, let's cover how to extract email addresses, numbers, URLs, and phone numbers from blocks of text using the **Extract** transform functions.

Extracting data from blocks of text

Another brilliant feature of the Formatter by Zapier **Text** action is the ability to extract data from block of text. This is especially useful if you have large strings of text and you want to return the first expressed value of an email address, number, phone number, or URL.

For example, your webform may not integrate with Zapier, but you receive a confirmation email with the submission details. The form asks the person submitting to add three email addresses, and you only want to extract the first email address entered. Alternatively, you may want to retrieve a phone number, URL, or number from this webform submission. You can use the Formatter by Zapier **Text** action event with the following transform functions to achieve this:

- **Extract Email Address**
- **Extract Number**
- **Extract URL**
- **Extract Phone Number**

To illustrate how to use each of these transform functions, we will use the following trigger data highlighted in the following screenshot:

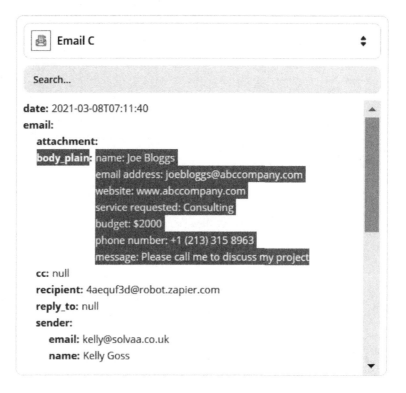

Figure 16.11 – Trigger data that will be used to illustrate extracting data from blocks of text

Now let's dive into each of these transform functions in turn.

Extracting an email address from a block of text

When using the **Extract Email Address** transform function, the formatter will search for a string of letters, numbers, and certain symbols commonly used in email addresses, such as a plus sign, period, or dashes, that precede an @ symbol and a site domain name, such as solvaa.co.uk. For example, joe-bloggs1@abccompany.com. It will not recognize disjunct email address strings with spaces, such as Joe Bloggs at abccompany dot com.

Let's review how to set up an action step with the **Extract Email Address** transform option.

Setting up the Text action event with the Extract Email Address transform option

Use the **Text** action event once you have set up your trigger step.

Once you have added an action step either by selecting the **Action** step or clicking on the + icon and chosen **Formatter by Zapier** as the app and **Text** as the action event, you can then edit the fields in the **Set up action** section as follows:

- **Transform**: From the drop-down menu, select the **Extract Email Address** option. This is a required field and must have a value in order for the Zap to run.

- **Input**: Use this field to enter the text that you want to extract the first email address from a block of text. You can either enter a static value, a dynamic value from previous steps, or a combination of both to specify the **Input** value. Although this is not a required field, the formatter function will not return a result if there is no value.

An example is shown in the following screenshot:

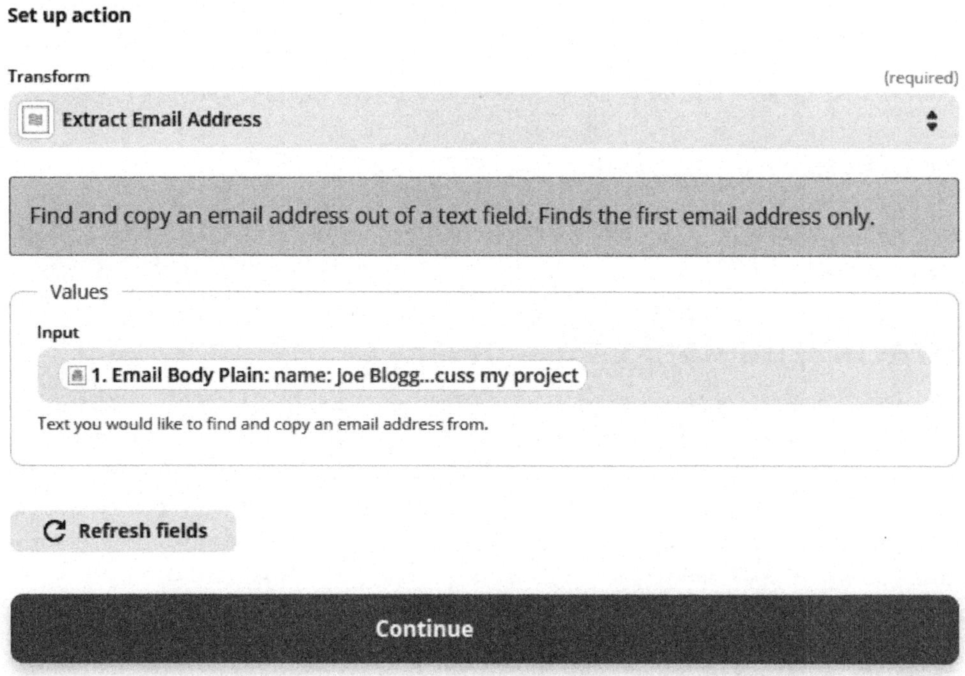

Set up action

Transform   (required)

🗊 **Extract Email Address**   ♦

Find and copy an email address out of a text field. Finds the first email address only.

┌─ Values ───┐
│ Input   │
│   🗊 1. Email Body Plain: name: Joe Blogg...cuss my project   │
│ Text you would like to find and copy an email address from.   │
└───┘

C **Refresh fields**

Continue

Figure 16.12 – Using the Formatter by Zapier Text action event to extract an email address from a block of text

Click on the **Continue** button. You can then use the **Test action** section to test this step to extract an email address from a block of text. The result of the scenario in *Figure 16.12* is shown in the following screenshot:

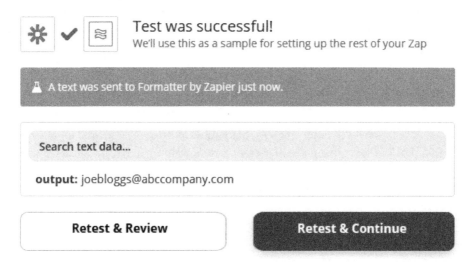

Test was successful!
We'll use this as a sample for setting up the rest of your Zap

🧪 A text was sent to Formatter by Zapier just now.

Search text data...

output: joebloggs@abccompany.com

Retest & Review   **Retest & Continue**

Figure 16.13 – An example of the returned value when using the Text action event to extract an email address from a block of text

Proceed to add one or more action steps after your **Text** action step.

Next, let's discuss how to extract numbers from blocks of text using the **Extract Number** transform function.

Extracting numbers from blocks of text

When using the **Extract Number** transform function, the formatter will search for a single digit or a string of numbers in one row. The numbers in a string can be separated by a period as a decimal separator or one or more commas indicating groupings of digits. Number strings separated by spaces and symbols such as dashes are not recognized in full; only the first number of a set of numbers in the string would be recognized. For example, an acceptable string would be 1,758,000.82, whereas 1-758-000-82 is not acceptable.

Let's review how to set up an action step with the **Extract Number** transform option.

Setting up the Text action event with the Extract Number transform option

Use the **Text** action event once you have set up your trigger step.

Once you have added an action step either by selecting the **Action** step or clicking on the + icon and chosen **Formatter by Zapier** as the app and **Text** as the action event, you can then edit the fields in the **Set up action** section as follows:

- **Transform**: From the drop-down menu, select the **Extract Number** option. This is a required field and must have a value in order for the Zap to run.

- **Input**: Use this field to enter the block of text containing the number that you want to extract. You can either enter a static value, a dynamic value from previous steps, or a combination of both to specify the **Input** value. Although this is not a required field, the formatter function will not return a result if there is no value.

An example is shown in the following screenshot:

Figure 16.14 – Using the Formatter by Zapier Text action event to extract a number from a block of text

Click on the **Continue** button. You can then use the **Test action** section to test this step to extract a number from a block of text. The result from the scenario in *Figure 16.14* is shown in the following screenshot:

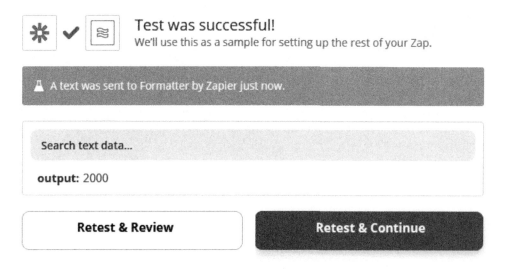

Figure 16.15 – An example of the returned value when using the Text action event to extract a number from a block of text

Proceed to add one or more action steps after your **Text** action step.

> **Important note**
> From the trigger data shown in *Figure 16.11*, if the phone number was displayed first, the value returned would be 1 from the phone number.

Next, let's explore how to extract URLs from blocks of text using the **Extract URL** transform function.

Extracting URLs from blocks of text

When using the **Extract URL** transform function, the formatter will search for a string of letters, numbers, and dashes followed by a period and then a recognized **Top-Level Domain (TLD)** name such as one ending in .com, .org, .co.uk, or .com.au, for example. You can find out more about TLDs here: https://en.wikipedia. org/wiki/Top-level_domain. The formatter also recognizes the https:// and http:// prefixes as well as subdomains, folders, and query parameters. Therefore, an accepted string example would be https://solvaa.co.uk/?s=zapier. It will not recognize disjunct URL strings with spaces, such as solvaa dot com.

Let's review how to set up an action step with the **Extract URL** transform option.

Setting up the Text action event with the Extract URL transform option

Use the **Text** action event once you have set up your trigger step.

Once you have added an action step either by selecting the **Action** step or clicking on the + icon and chosen **Formatter by Zapier** as the app and **Text** as the action event, you can then edit the fields in the **Set up action** section as follows:

- **Transform**: From the drop-down menu, select the **Extract URL** option. This is a required field and must have a value in order for the Zap to run.

- **Input:** Use this field to enter the block of text containing the URL that you want to extract. You can either enter a static value, a dynamic value from previous steps, or a combination of both to specify the **Input** value. Although this is not a required field, the formatter function will not return a result if there is no value.

An example is shown in the following screenshot:

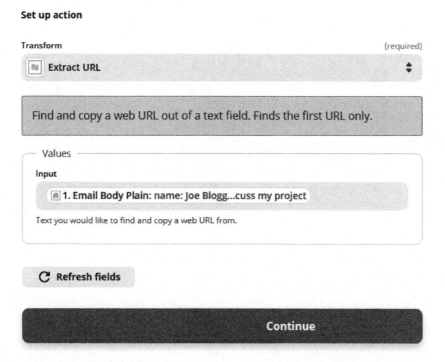

Figure 16.16 – Using the Formatter by Zapier Text action event to extract a URL from a block of text

Click on the **Continue** button. You can then use the **Test action** section to test this step to extract a URL from a block of text. The result from the scenario in *Figure 16.16* is shown in the following screenshot:

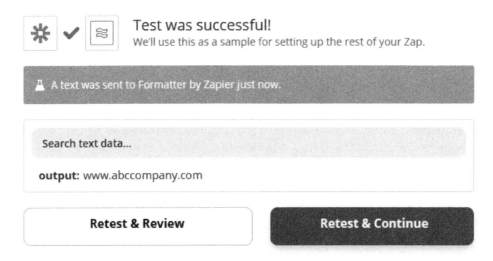

Figure 16.17 – An example of the returned value when using the Text action event to extract a URL from a block of text

Proceed to add one or more action steps after your **Text** action step.

Next, let's take a look at how to extract phone numbers from blocks of text using the **Extract Phone Number** transform function.

Extracting phone numbers from blocks of text

When using the **Extract Phone Number** transform function, the formatter will search a 10-digit phone number in groupings of 3-3-4 digits or 4-3-3 digits with or without a country code or extension number. The numbers can be separated by hyphens, periods, or spaces. Area codes in parentheses are recognized. Extension numbers are recognized when a number follows x, ext, or extension. For example, an acceptable phone number string would be +44 (758) 592-0332, whereas 44 758 592 0332 is not accepted as a phone number format.

Let's review how to set up an action step with the **Extract Phone Number** transform option.

Setting up the Text action event with the Extract Phone Number transform option

Use the **Text** action event once you have set up your trigger step.

Once you have added an action step either by selecting the **Action** step or clicking on the + icon and chosen **Formatter by Zapier** as the app and **Text** as the action event, you can then edit the fields in the **Set up action** section as follows:

- **Transform**: From the drop-down menu, select the **Extract Phone Number** option. This is a required field and must have a value in order for the Zap to run.

- **Input**: Use this field to enter the block of text containing the phone number that you want to extract. You can either enter a static value, a dynamic value from previous steps, or a combination of both to specify the **Input** value. Although this is not a required field, the formatter function will not return a result if there is no value.

- **Phone Number Format**: Use this drop-down field to select which phone number format you want to use for the search. The options are **North American Number Plan (NANP) e.g. (123) 456-7890, International e.g. (12) 34-56-78-90, Universal 1 (includes NANP and some International)**, and **Universal 2 (includes NANP and some International)**. The default used in searches is **Universal 1**, which will recognize most NANP and international numbers. Choose one of the other options for more specific searches if this proves unreliable.

An example is shown in the following screenshot:

Set up action

Transform   (required)

| Extract Phone Number | ⬍ |

> ℹ️ Find and copy a complete phone number out of a text field. Finds the first phone number only.

Values

Input

📄 1. Email Body Plain: name: Joe Blogg...cuss my project

Text you would like to find and copy a phone number from.

Phone Number Format

| Universal 1 (includes NANP and some International) | ⬍ |

Phone Number Fo...   Custom

🔍 Search ...

◯ **North American Number Plan (NANP) e.g. (123) 456-7890**
na

◯ **International e.g. (12) 34-56-78-90**
in

◉ **Universal 1 (includes NANP and some International)**
uni1

◯ **Universal 2 (includes NANP and more International)**
uni2

Clear

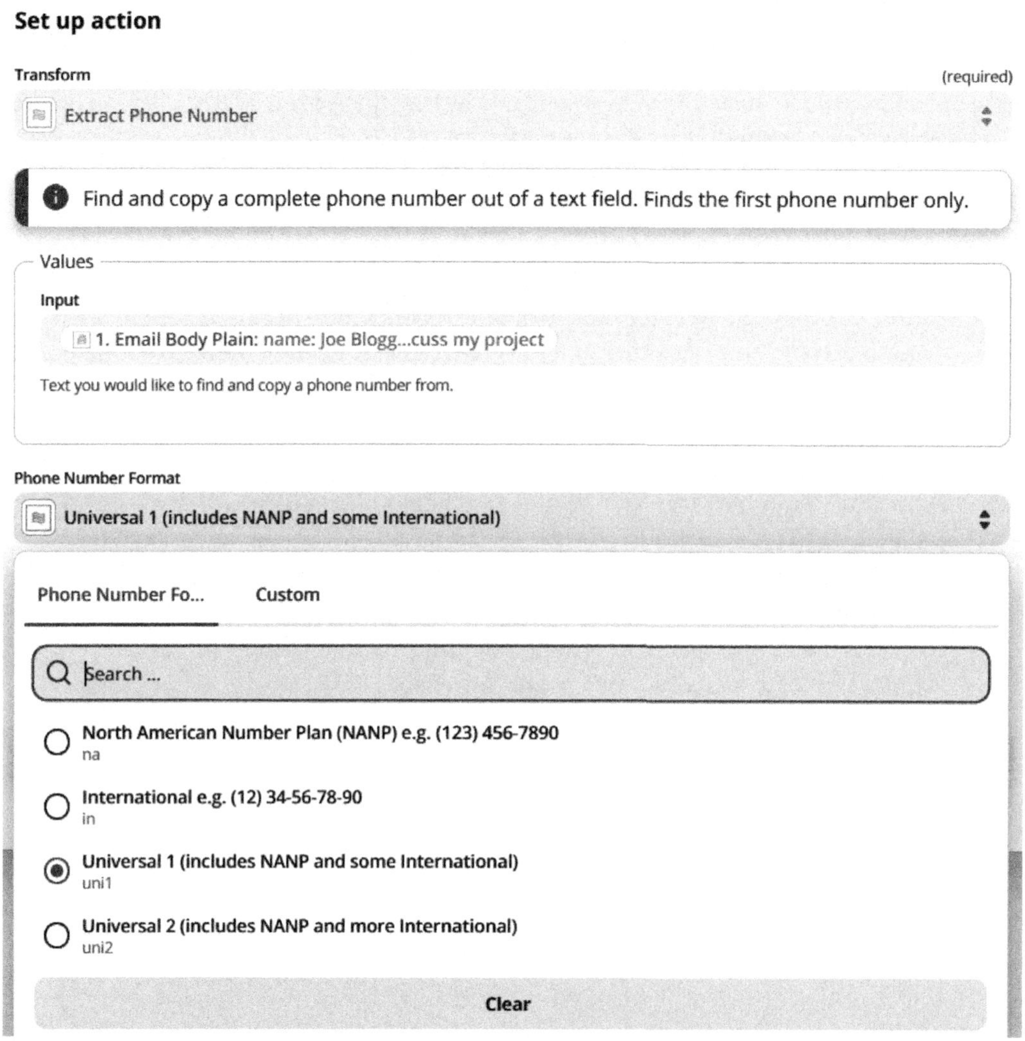

Figure 16.18 – Using the Formatter by Zapier Text action event to extract a number from a block of text

Click on the **Continue** button. You can then use the **Test action** section to test this step to extract a phone number in Universal 1 format from a block of text. The result from the scenario in *Figure 16.18* is shown in the following screenshot:

Figure 16.19 – An example of the returned value when using the Text action event to extract a number from a block of text

Proceed to add one or more action steps after your **Text** action step.

You should now have a better understanding of how to extract data from blocks of text using the **Extract Email Address**, **Extract Number**, **Extract URL** and **Extract Phone Number** transform functions. Next, let's review the advanced text formatting features that Zapier has to offer.

Advanced text formatting features

As you have learned so far, the Formatter by Zapier built-in app allows you to manipulate text in many versatile ways without having any knowledge of coding or any technical background whatsoever. There are, however, a few transform functions that allow you to manipulate text using programming languages. As these are advanced topics, we will only provide a brief overview of their functionality, without going into too much detail.

The following transform options can be used to manipulate text with programming languages:

- **Extract Pattern**: You can use this transform option when you need to extract partial data from a field with more specificity than the other **Extract** transform options we have covered. This allows you to use Python regular expressions (regexes). You can find out more about Python regexes here: `https://developers.google.com/edu/python/regular-expressions`.

- **Convert HTML to Markdown**: You can use this transform option when you want to convert **Hypertext Markup Language (HTML)** to **Markdown**, a markup language used to add formatting elements to plain text. You can find out more about Markdown here: `https://en.wikipedia.org/wiki/Markdown`.

- **Convert Markdown to HTML**: You can use this transform option to do the reverse of the preceding, converting Markdown to HTML.

- **Convert to ASCII**: You can use this transform option when you want to convert plain text to **ASCII (American Standard Code for Information Interchange)**. You can find out more about ASCII here: `https://en.wikipedia.org/wiki/ASCII`.

- **URL Encode**: You can use this transform option when you want to encode plain text to a machine-readable format. You can find out more about **URL encoding** here: `https://en.wikipedia.org/wiki/Percent-encoding`.

- **URL Decode**: You can use this transform option to do the reverse of the preceding and decode data to a human-readable plain text format.

You should now have a better understanding of how to use the various advanced text formatting features of the Formatter by Zapier built-in app.

Summary

In this chapter, we continued the focus on the versatile Formatter by Zapier built-in app and the extensive functionality available to format text. First, we explored how to create a superhero name, split text into segments, truncate text, remove HTML, and use a default value. Then, we covered how to extract data from text, specifically how to extract URLs, phone numbers, numbers, and email addresses. Lastly, we briefly discussed the more advanced functions of how to extract patterns, convert Markdown to HTML and vice versa, convert to ASCII, and encode or decode URLs.

You now know how to use the Formatter by Zapier built-in app to transform text values in a number of different ways, including creating a superhero name, splitting text into segments, truncating text, removing HTML, using default values, and extracting URLs, phone numbers, numbers, and email addresses. You also understand that the Formatter by Zapier built-in app can be used for more advanced functions, such as extracting patterns, converting Markdown to HTML or vice versa, converting to ASCII, and URL encoding and decoding.

In the next chapter, you will learn how to use the **Utilities** functions within the Formatter built-in app. We will cover line item creation and customization, converting text to line items and vice versa, using lookup tables and picklists, and importing CSV files.

17
Zapier's Utilities Functions

So far, we have discussed using the Formatter by Zapier built-in app to perform a variety of actions to transform dates and times, numbers, and text. There are a few other helpful transform functions we have not yet explored, and these are categorized under the Utilities action event. In this chapter, we conclude our exploration of the features of the Formatter by Zapier built-in app by covering the functionality of the Utilities action event.

First, we will give an overview of the Formatter by Zapier Utilities action event and the transform functions available. Then, we will cover how to import data from CSV files and use them in your Zaps, how to use lookup tables to store and help you find related data, and how to pick data from a list of values based on the position in the list. Finally, we will introduce line-items and explore the various transform functions related to using line-items in your automations. This will include converting text to line-items and vice versa, as well as line-item creation and customization.

We will cover the following key topics in this chapter:

- Introducing the Formatter by Zapier Utilities action event
- Importing data from CSV files
- Using lookup tables for related data

- Picking data from a list
- Manipulating line-items

Once you have worked through each of these topics, you will have a better understanding of the different Utilities transform functions available for use with the Formatter by Zapier built-in app. You will know how to use Zapier to import data from CSV files, use lookup tables, pick data from a list, and work with line-items.

Technical requirements

To make the most of the content in this chapter, you will need access to a Zapier account. The Zapier Starter plan will be required for you to create multi-step workflows using the Formatter by Zapier built-in app.

Introducing the Formatter by Zapier Utilities action event

As we have discovered so far, Formatter by Zapier can easily be used to transform a wide range of values from one format to another. We have explored how to manipulate dates and times, numbers, and text into different formats. You might want to upload data from CSV files to use in your automations, find related data such as user IDs linked to a user's email address, select a value in a specific position in a list such as the first or last, or you might need to manipulate data in the form of line-items, commonly used in invoicing and e-commerce apps. To account for these requirements, Zapier has created a grouping of these functions in the Formatter by Zapier built-in app, which can only be used as an action step and is available as the following action event:

- **Utilities** (action)

When using this action event, you can use the following **Utilities** transform options found within the **Set up action** section of your action step, listed in the **Transform** drop-down menu:

- **Import CSV File**
- **Line Itemizer (Create/Append/Prepend)**
- **Line-item to Text**
- **Lookup Table**

- **Pick from List**

- **Text to Line-Item**

We will review each of these functions in turn.

You should now have a better understanding of the basics of the Formatter by Zapier built-in app **Utilities** action event. Next, let's explore how to import CSV files using the **Import CSV File** transform option.

Importing data from CSV files

Wouldn't it be handy to be able to automatically extract data from spreadsheet files so that you can use it in your Zaps? Well, Zapier allows you to do this. For example, you might receive a summary of the day's transactions in a CSV file by email, and you want to pull this data straight into your accounting software. Zapier can help you extract data from a CSV file and present it in a string of text and as **line-items** by using the Formatter by Zapier **Utilities** action event with the **Import CSV File** transform function.

Here are a few examples of when you can use this transform option:

- You might use an Excel spreadsheet to record details of sales and associated lead-to-sales conversion times. A CSV copy of this is forwarded to you by email every day at 5 p.m. from your CRM, and you normally have to extract the data you want and manually share it with your team. You could extract that data from that CSV using the **Import CSV File** transform function and forward the most important parts of the day's data to your Slack channel for your sales team to see.

- You might have access to a report file (via a publicly accessible URL) that allows you to download the data in the form of a CSV. The report file provides you with information about your daily sales transactions from your till system. The file clears all data and refreshes at midnight. Using the **Import CSV File** transform function, you could extract the data in the CSV and automatically create invoices in your accounting system on a daily basis (with a Schedule by Zapier trigger).

In *Chapter 3, Building Your First Automated Workflow (Zap)*, we introduced and discussed file field types. The principles aligned with these field types and what is accepted by them applies to the **Import CSV File** transform option input. Essentially, the Formatter by Zapier built-in app can only import a CSV file object from an app, such as when it is an attachment in a Gmail email, or from a publicly accessible URL that points to a CSV file such as a Microsoft Excel or Smartsheet sheet. The **File** field also accepts text that would be converted into a `.txt` file.

Next, let's review how to set up an action step with the **Import CSV File** transform option.

Setting up the Utilities action event with the Import CSV File transform option

To illustrate how to use each of the **Import CSV File** transform functions, we will use the example of receiving a CSV file by email with sales for the day. The following screenshot shows an example of a CSV file with data:

	A	B	C
1	Fruit	Quantity	Cost
2	Apples	1	0.5
3	Bananas	4	0.7
4	Pears	12	0.6

Figure 17.1 – Data in a CSV file that will be used to illustrate using the Import CSV File transform function

Use the **Utilities** action event once you have set up your trigger step.

Once you have added an action step either by selecting the **Action** step or clicking on the + icon, and have chosen **Formatter by Zapier** as the app and **Utilities** as the action event, you can then edit the fields in the **Set up action** section as follows:

- **Transform**: From the drop-down menu, select the **Import CSV File** option. This is a required field and must have a value in order for the Zap to run.

- **CSV File**: Use this field to map the CSV file you want to extract data from. You can enter a dynamic value from previous steps to specify the file to use. In our example, we would use the attachment value from our email trigger step. This is a required field and must have a value in order for the Zap to run.

- **Force First Row As Header Row**: Use this drop-down Boolean field to select either **Yes** or **No** as to whether you want to force the formatter to recognize the first row as a header row. By default, it will try to determine whether a header row exists. When testing, if it has not worked to detect the header row, you can force it by selecting the **Yes** option.

- **Type Of CSV File**: Use this drop-down field to select the type of CSV file. The options are **Detect Automatically**, **Comma Delimited**, **Semicolon Delimited**, **Excel Comma Delimited**, **Excel Tab Delimited**, **On Column**, and **Text File (no csv parsing)**. By default, the Formatter will attempt to detect the type of file. When testing, if it has not worked to detect the file type, you can force it by selecting the appropriate file option.

Data imports are limited to around 150 KB, which is the equivalent of approximately 1,000 rows, which might cause some limitations for some users.

An example is shown in the following screenshot:

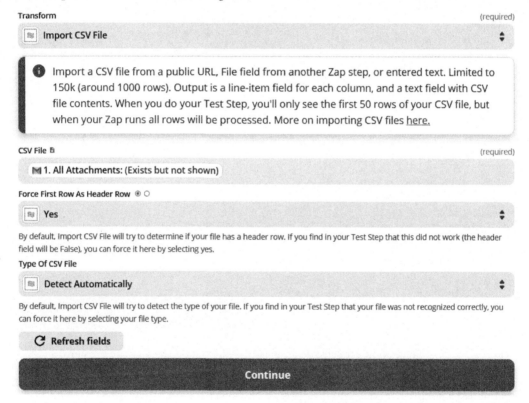

Figure 17.2 – Using the Formatter by Zapier Utilities action event to import data from a CSV file

Click on the **Continue** button. You can then use the **Test action** section to test this step to extract the data from the CSV file. The result from the scenario in *Figure 17.2* is shown in the following screenshot:

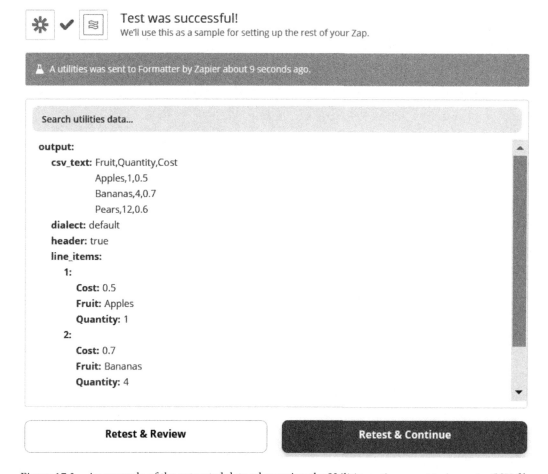

Figure 17.3 – An example of the extracted data when using the Utilities action event to import a CSV file

Proceed to add one or more action steps after your **Utilities** action step. You can either use the text field presented in the csv_text output or the line-items presented in the line_items output (specifically for apps that support line-items) or both. We will discuss line-items in more detail in the *Manipulating line-items* section.

> **Important note**
> When testing your action step, bear in mind that you will only see a limited number of rows (normally 50) of your CSV file, however, when your Zap runs in real time, all the data in the file will be processed.

You should now have a better understanding of how to import CSV files using the **Import CSV File** transform function.

Next, let's explore how to use lookup tables to store and help you find related data using the **Lookup Table** transform function.

Using lookup tables

The more you work with Zapier to connect your apps and automate your processes, the more you will find that commonly used key values in your various apps are represented differently. For example, if you sell online courses, passing data between your shopping cart **ThriveCart** and your course platform **Kajabi** could be a challenge as products are recorded with different IDs in each of the systems. This is where the Formatter by Zapier **Utilities** action event with the transform function **Lookup Table** is useful. You can use this transform function to store related search keys and matching result data, such as product names and their respective IDs, so that you can use them in other steps in your workflows. Microsoft Excel users are likely to be quite familiar with this type of functionality, which is comparable to the VLOOKUP function. Bear in mind that the main difference to consider is that in Microsoft Excel this function is case-insensitive whereas in Zapier it is case-sensitive.

Here are a couple of examples of when you can use this transform option:

- Let's say that when a deal or opportunity hits a certain stage in your pipeline in your CRM, you want to assign a card to the deal owner in your task management app. In this case, your users have different identifiers in your CRM to your task management app. For example, your sales manager, John, might be identified by name as John Smith in Pipedrive and J A Smith in Trello. Users are also identified by unique IDs in most systems, so in this case, John has a user ID of 125869 in Pipedrive and a user ID of 51f8a8cd179ff019a67e95312 in Trello. We can assign John as the member to the card using his Trello user ID. Therefore, we can use a lookup table in the Formatter by Zapier **Utilities** action event to list all the Pipedrive user names and their associated Trello user IDs of the users for who we might need this data. We would then use the username in Pipedrive as the search key to return the user ID for Trello.

- You might use a scheduling and appointment booking app such as **Acuity Scheduling** and need to pass your sales data to your accounting app, QuickBooks Online. As the names and IDs of the products are different in the two systems, you can use a lookup table in the Formatter by Zapier **Utilities** action event to record the search data you need. You can record the Acuity Scheduling product name as the search key and the QuickBooks Online product ID as a value to be returned.

Next, let's review how to set up an action step with the **Lookup Table** transform option.

Setting up the Utilities action event with the Lookup Table transform option

Use the **Utilities** action event once you have set up your trigger step.

Once you have added an action step either by selecting the **Action** step or clicking on the + icon, and have chosen **Formatter by Zapier** as the app and **Utilities** as the action event, you can then edit the fields in the **Set up action** section as follows:

- **Transform**: From the drop-down menu, select the **Lookup Table** option. This is a required field and must have a value in order for the Zap to run.

- **Lookup Key**: Use this field to map in the search key value of the data you want to search for in the lookup table. You can either enter a static value, a dynamic value from previous steps, or a combination of both to specify this value. This field supports line-items. Although this is not a required field, the formatter function will not return a result if there is no value.

- **Lookup Table**: This table is comprised of two columns. In the left column, enter the data you want to use as the search reference. This is the data that Zapier will use to match against the search value in the **Lookup Key**, for example, the user name. This column only accepts static text being entered. It is also case-sensitive and will only return an exact match with the **Lookup Key** value. In the right column, enter the data that you want to be returned from the search, for example, the corresponding user ID. You can either enter a static value, a dynamic value from previous steps, or a combination of both to specify the value in this column.

- **Fallback Value**: Enter a default value to use if the **Lookup Key** value does not match any of the search reference data in the left column. This is especially useful if the **Lookup Key** value is empty.

An example is shown in the following screenshot:

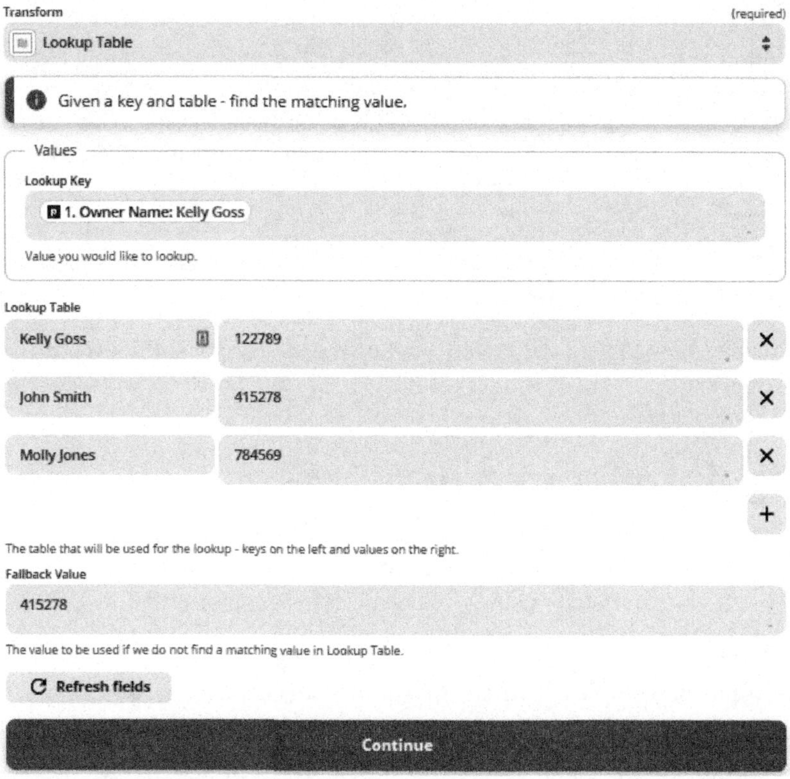

Figure 17.4 – Using the Formatter by Zapier Utilities action event to find related data in a lookup table

Click on the **Continue** button. You can then use the **Test action** section to find reference data in a lookup table. The result from the scenario in *Figure 17.4* is shown in the following screenshot:

Figure 17.5 – An example of the matching data retrieved from the lookup table when using the Utilities action event

Proceed to add one or more action steps after your **Utilities** action step.

> **Tip**
> Although there is only one field for the **Lookup Key**, you can retrieve and find multiple values from the **Lookup Table** if your search key is in line-item format. You can also have multiple steps using this function in one Zap. This is ideal if you need to use various search criteria to find related data.

You should now have a better understanding of how and when to use lookup tables using the **Lookup Table** transform function.

Next, let's discuss how to pick data from a list of values using the **Pick from List** transform function.

Picking data from a list

Have you ever wanted to run a quiz or assign a random result to your participants? Or perhaps you need to assign a support query to a member of your team based on a priority rating. You can easily do this by using the Formatter by Zapier **Utilities** action event with the **Pick from List** transform function to choose a value from a list based on its position.

Here are a couple of examples of when you can use this transform option:

- You might create a single-question fun Q&A that you push out on social media to engage your audience with and drive traffic to your website. You ask them to complete one question in Google Forms, such as "What is your birth month?" and then randomly assign them an "inner mythical beast" based on their answer. You can pick a random result from a list of "inner mythical beast" values, such as Unicorn, Dragon, Pheonix, Kraken, and Pegasus, then display the result on a page on your website.

- You might have a list of team members that you assign help desk requests to. The team could be assigned the requests by randomly picking their names from a list. Alternatively, you might want to assign the requests to specific users based on a priority rating. For example, Jim the customer service assistant is assigned level 0 requests, Jenny the supervisor is assigned level 1 requests, and June the manager is assigned all level 2 ratings. You can create a list with Jim, Jenny, and June, in that order to pick which person to route a request to.

Let's review how to set up an action step with the **Pick from List** transform option.

Setting up the Utilities action event with the Pick from List transform option

Use the **Utilities** action event once you have set up your trigger step.

Once you have added an action step either by selecting the **Action** step or clicking on the + icon, and have chosen **Formatter by Zapier** as the app and **Utilities** as the action event, you can then edit the fields in the **Set up action** section as follows:

- **Transform**: From the drop-down menu, select the **Pick from List** option. This is a required field and must have a value in order for the Zap to run.

- **Operation**: Use this drop-down field to specify the position of the value you want to find in the **Input** fields. The options are **Choose First**, **Choose Last**, or **Choose Random**. These will choose the first or last positions, or a randomly selected position, respectively, in the list of **Input** fields. You can also enter a static value, a dynamic value from previous steps, or a combination of both, to specify the n-th position in the list, if you select the **Custom** option. Bear in mind that the first position will be 0, the second 1, the third 2, and so on. You can also use negative numbers to select from the end of the list, such as -1 for the last, -2 for the second last, and so on. This is a required field and must have a value in order for the Zap to run.

- **Input**: Use this field to map in the values of the data that you want to return. As you enter a value in one field line, another will appear just below. Add in the values in the order you want to set them. You can remove lines by clicking on the **X** button at the end of the line. You can either enter a static value, a dynamic value from previous steps, or a combination of both to specify this value. Although this is not a required field, the formatter function will not return a result if there is no value.

- **Fallback Value**: Enter a default value to use if the **Operation** value does not match any position in the **Input** section.

An example is shown in the following screenshot:

Transform   (required)

| ▦ | **Pick from list** | ⬍ |

> ⓘ   Pick the first, last, random, or n-th value that is not empty.

Operation   (required)

| 3 | ⬍ |

Value to choose.

Input

| Elephant | ✕ |

| Giraffe | ✕ |

| Lion | ✕ |

| Cheetah | ✕ |

| Enter text or insert data... | |

Values you would like to choose from.

Default

| Lion | |

Optional default value to use if no item could be choosen.

↻ **Refresh fields**

Continue

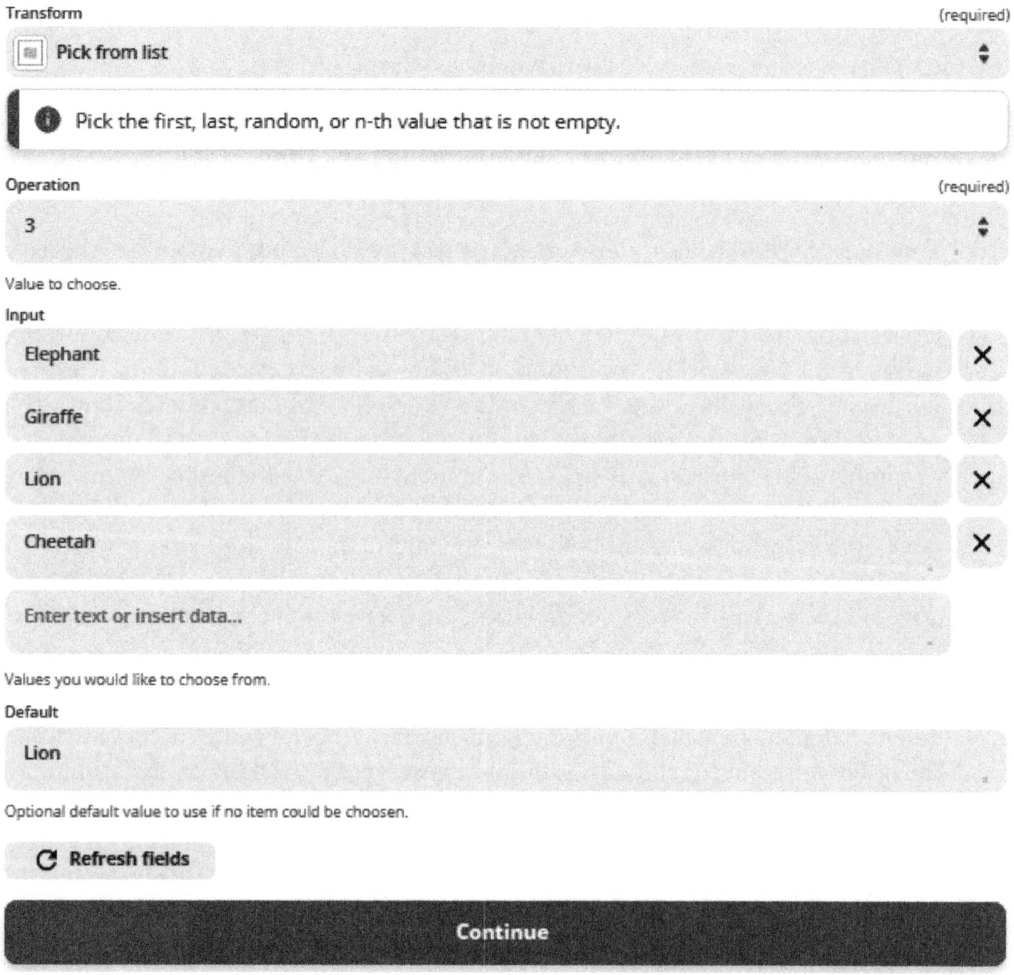

Figure 17.6 – Using the Formatter by Zapier Utilities action event to pick a value from a list

Click on the **Continue** button. You can then use the **Test action** section to pick a value from a list. The result from the scenario in *Figure 17.6* is shown in the following screenshot:

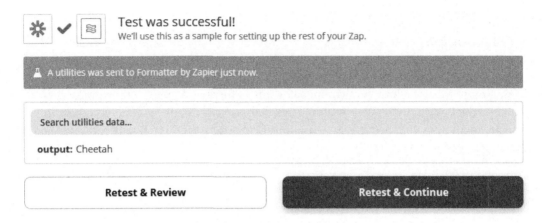

Figure 17.7 – An example of the data returned when picking from a list

Proceed to add one or more action steps after your **Utilities** action step.

You should now have a better understanding of how and when to use the **Pick from List** transform function.

Next, let's cover how to manipulate data in or convert data to line-item format.

Manipulating line-items

Line-items are blocks of data that have multiple items associated with them and are used in a special field within Zapier. They are essentially objects containing what is commonly known as an **array** of objects. The use of line-item data is very common in e-commerce, payment processing, and accounting apps, such as Shopify, PayPal, and Xero, where you often have multiple lines of data in an order or invoice, like itemized lines on a paper receipt. For example, in one order, a customer might purchase a first product, such as two medium t-shirts priced at $9.99 each, and a second product, such as one large t-shirt priced at $10.99. They might also have paid for shipping at $7.50, and a coupon of $5.00 off was applied to the entire order. The details for each individualized item consist of the product name, description, quantity, and price, and these details are normally shown as one line on an invoice. You can also think of each line as a row in a spreadsheet where the details are displayed in columns. One invoice can therefore consist of multiple lines with specific details related to that line.

The content in this section might be most useful for users in bookkeeping or accounting roles that deal with financial transactions, as well as those in operations roles around shipping and logistics.

Understanding line-items

When you map data into your fields in your action steps in your Zaps, you usually have one piece of text data, represented individually or as a string of text. Line-items are complex in the sense that they often contain several bits of data clumped together, and having more than one line-item complicates things further. As you can imagine, when data bunched into line-items or multiple line-items exists in one app that you want to transfer to another app, being able to use line-item automation is a huge time-saver so that you don't need to enter all those details manually.

You can quickly identify data that is presented as line-items as an item with rows of data, as shown in the following screenshot:

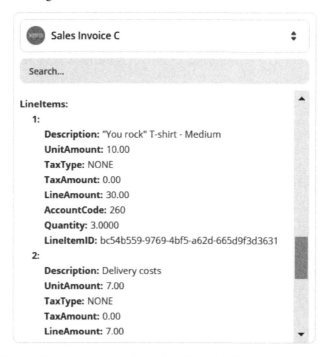

Figure 17.8 – An example of how line-item data is displayed in rows

The data is also labeled with the words **Line Items**, as shown in the following screenshot:

Figure 17.9 – An example of how line-item data is labeled

There are a few apps that integrate with Zapier that offer **line-item support**, and the following are a few examples:

- *Accounting apps*: **QuickBooks Online**, Xero
- *CRM apps*: **Keap**
- *E-commerce apps*: **ShipStation**, Shopify, WooCommerce
- *Invoicing apps*: **Harvest**, **Wave**, **Zoho Invoice**
- *Payment processing apps*: **Chargify**, **PayPal**
- *Other apps*: Google Sheets
- *Zapier built-in apps*: Formatter by Zapier

Many of Zapier's Formatter action events and transform functions support the use of line-items, so that you can manipulate multiple rows of text, numbers, dates, and times with line-item data in one action.

It is, of course, much simpler if the apps you are transferring data between all support line-items, but as only a few apps do, there is often the need to manipulate data to either create line-items or change line-items back into text field data. Therefore, to use line-items, both your trigger app and action app(s) must support their use. If one or the other doesn't, you can use Formatter by Zapier with the **Utilities** action event to transform line-item data to make it compatible to use with apps that either require data in line-item format or support it. We can use the following transform functions:

- **Text to Line-item**
- **Line-item to Text**
- **Line Itemizer (Create/Append/Prepend)**

Let's review how to convert text to line-items using the **Text to Line-item** transform function.

Converting text to line-items

By using the Formatter by Zapier built-in app with the **Utilities** action event and the **Text to Line-item** transform option, you can easily convert a grouping of different **comma-delimited text** variables into line-items. Comma-delimited text is also known as **comma-separated text**. These are values that are normally separated by a comma, such as `Apple, Pear, Kiwi` or `Apple,Pear,Kiwi`.

You might want to perform this action when you have data in text format and want to create line-items to use in other apps that support line-item usage. In the preceding example, the text would be transformed to `["Apple","Pear","Kiwi"]`.

Here are a few examples of when you can use this transform option:

- Your CRM might have multiple product listings, quantities, and prices associated with your deals, and when a deal hits a certain stage in the pipeline, you might want to create an invoice in your accounting system. Your CRM doesn't support line-items so the product information in the deal is presented as text. You can use the **Text to Line-item** transform function to change the text to line-items to be able to generate invoices in your accounting system, QuickBooks Online.

- You might take orders for special products using a webform embedded in your website. Once an order comes through, you want to convert each part of the order to line-items so that you can create separate lines in a Google spreadsheet. You can use the **Text to Line-item** transform function to do that.

Let's discuss how to set up an action step with the **Text to Line-item** transform option.

Setting up the Utilities action event with the Text to Line-item transform option

Use the **Utilities** action event once you have set up your trigger step.

Once you have added an action step either by selecting the **Action** step or clicking on the + icon, and have chosen **Formatter by Zapier** as the app and **Utilities** as the action event, you can then edit the fields in the **Set up action** section as follows:

- **Transform**: From the drop-down menu, select the **Text to Line-item** option. This is a required field and must have a value in order for the Zap to run.

- **Input**: Use this field to map in the comma-separated text values that you want to convert to line-items. You can either enter a static value, a dynamic value from previous steps, or a combination of both, to specify this value. Although this is not a required field, the formatter function will not return a result if there is no value.

An example is shown in the following screenshot:

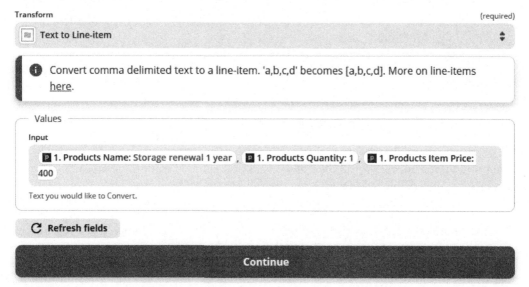

Figure 17.10 – Using the Formatter by Zapier Utilities action event to change text to line-items

Click on the **Continue** button. You can then use the **Test action** section to transform comma-separated text to line-item arrays. The result from the scenario in *Figure 17.10* is shown in the following screenshot:

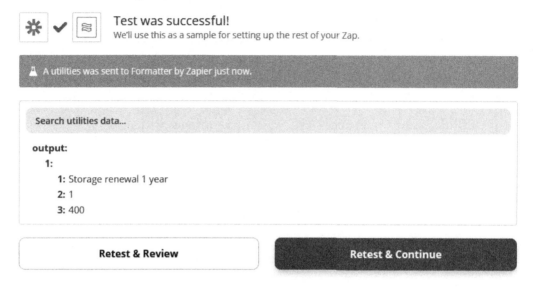

Figure 17.11 – An example of the data returned when transforming text to line-items

The output shown in *Figure 17.11* is displayed as one line-item with three rows of data.

Proceed to add one or more action steps after your **Utilities** action step.

You should now have a better understanding of how and when to use the **Text to Line-item** transform function.

Next, let's cover how to reverse this action and convert line-items to text using the **Line-item to Text** transform function.

Converting line-items to text

We've just discussed how to convert comma-delimited text to line-items. There will be scenarios where you want to do the opposite, in that you will want to change line-item data into comma-delimited text. We can use the Formatter by Zapier built-in app with the **Utilities** action event and the transform option **Line-item to Text** to do just that.

In the same action step, we can also split the resulting text into separate fields in the same way the **Split Text** transform function works, as discussed in *Chapter 16, Text Formatting Functions in Zapier – Part 2*.

For example, you might raise invoices in your accounting app, Xero, for products that you sell. You also include delivery charges on the invoice as a separate invoice line. Once the invoice has been created, you want to send a message in Slack to your team with the details of the product sold and not the delivery charge.

Let's use this example to illustrate how to use and set up an action step with the **Line-item to Text** transform option.

Setting up the Utilities action event with the Line-item to Text transform option

Use the **Utilities** action event once you have set up your trigger step.

Once you have added an action step either by selecting the **Action** step or clicking on the + icon, and have chosen **Formatter by Zapier** as the app and **Utilities** as the action event, you can then edit the fields in the **Set up action** section as follows:

- **Transform**: From the drop-down menu, select the **Line-item to Text** option. This is a required field and must have a value in order for the Zap to run.

- **Input**: Use this field to map the values of the data that you want to convert to line-items. You can either enter a static value, a dynamic value from previous steps, or a combination of both, to specify this value. Although this is not a required field, the formatter function will not return a result if there is no value.

- **Separator**: Use this field to enter the word, character, or syntax that you want to use as the splitting value from the **Input** field. You can either enter a static value, a dynamic value from previous steps, or a combination of both, to specify this value. This field supports special character syntax. For example, to split text separated by spaces, use the syntax [:space:]. Although this is not a required field, if left blank, the default is the character , .

An example is shown in the following screenshot:

Figure 17.12 – Using the Formatter by Zapier Utilities action event to change line-items to text and split them into separate fields

Click on the **Continue** button. You can then use the **Test action** section to transform line-items into comma-delimited text split into separate fields. The result from the scenario in *Figure 17.12* is shown in the following screenshot:

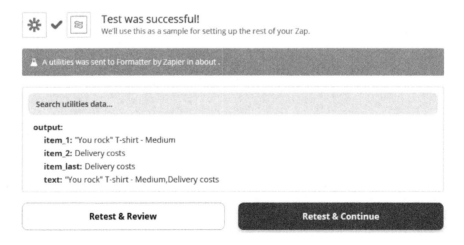

Figure 17.13 – An example of the data returned when transforming line-items to text split into fields

The output shown in *Figure 17.13* is separate field items (`item_1`, `item_2`, and `item_last`) as well as the full converted comma-separated `text`.

Proceed to add one or more action steps after your **Utilities** action step.

You should now have a better understanding of how and when to use the **Line-item to Text** transform function.

Next, let's explore creating, appending, and prepending line-items using the **Line Itemizer (Create/Append/Prepend)** transform function.

Using a line itemizer to create, append, or prepend line-items

Being able to create line-items, attach additional items to the end of a line-item grouping, or insert additional items at the start of a line-item grouping – and all in one action step – is very useful. This will be most commonly needed if you have variables in your data from your trigger app that you need to push into another app where there needs to be consistency. Alternatively, you might need to collate data from several different action steps and combine the data to form line-items. For example, you might sell your products through a shopping cart app such as ThriveCart and need to add the transaction information to QuickBooks Online. You might find that you need to use product searches to retrieve product IDs and combine order information from an upsell. You might also need to add on a quantity of 1 for a coupon and delivery costs, which may not be represented in the data from the shopping cart. You can do all of this using the Formatter by Zapier built-in app with the **Utilities** action event and the **Line Itemizer (Create/Append/Prepend)** transform option. It allows you to convert comma-delimited text to line-items, as well as to append or prepend to a group of existing line-items by adding them to the same field as comma-delimited text or as single values. You can also generate sub-totals with a specified number of decimal places if you include properties such as `Price` and `Quantity`.

Let's use this example to illustrate how to use and set up an action step with the **Line Itemizer (Create/Append/Prepend)** transform option.

Setting up the Utilities action event with the Line Itemizer (Create/Append/Prepend) transform option

Use the **Utilities** action event once you have set up your trigger step.

Once you have added an action step either by selecting the **Action** step or clicking on the + icon, and have chosen **Formatter by Zapier** as the app and **Utilities** as the action event, you can then edit the fields in the **Set up action** section as follows:

- **Transform**: From the drop-down menu, select the **Line Itemizer (Create/Append/Prepend)** option. This is a required field and must have a value in order for the Zap to run.

- **Line-item(s) Group Name**: Use this field to add an identifier for the group of line-items that you want to produce. For example, you could use Invoices, Orders, or Line-items for Invoice. You can either enter a static value, a dynamic value from previous steps, or a combination of both, to specify this value. The default is Line-Item(s).

- **Line-item Properties**: This table is comprised of two columns. In the left column, enter the line-item property name, such as Product code, Description, Price, Qty, and so on. The left column only accepts static text being entered. In the right column, enter the comma-separated text or single values when creating line-items. When appending or prepending, you can combine line-items with comma-separated text or single values. You can either enter a static value, a dynamic value from previous steps, or a combination of both, to specify the values in the right column. Add additional rows by clicking on the + button, and remove rows by clicking on the **X** button at the end of the row. Although this is not a required field, the formatter function will not return a result if there is no value.

- **Create Subtotal Property?**: Use this drop-down Boolean field to select **Yes** or **No** to creating a subtotal property. If you label your **Line-item Properties** as Price or Quantity (or Qty), these values can be multiplied together to create a Subtotal property. This is useful if the app you're sending data to requires Total values, which saves you having to add another Formatter action step to create these values. You can either enter a static value, a dynamic value from previous steps, or a combination of both, to specify this value. The default is **No**.

- **Decimal Places For Subtotal Values**: If you select **Yes** for the **Create Subtotal Property?** field, enter a numerical value for how many decimal places you want the subtotal to be displayed as. You can either enter a static value, a dynamic value from previous steps, or a combination of both, to specify this value.

An example is shown in the following screenshot:

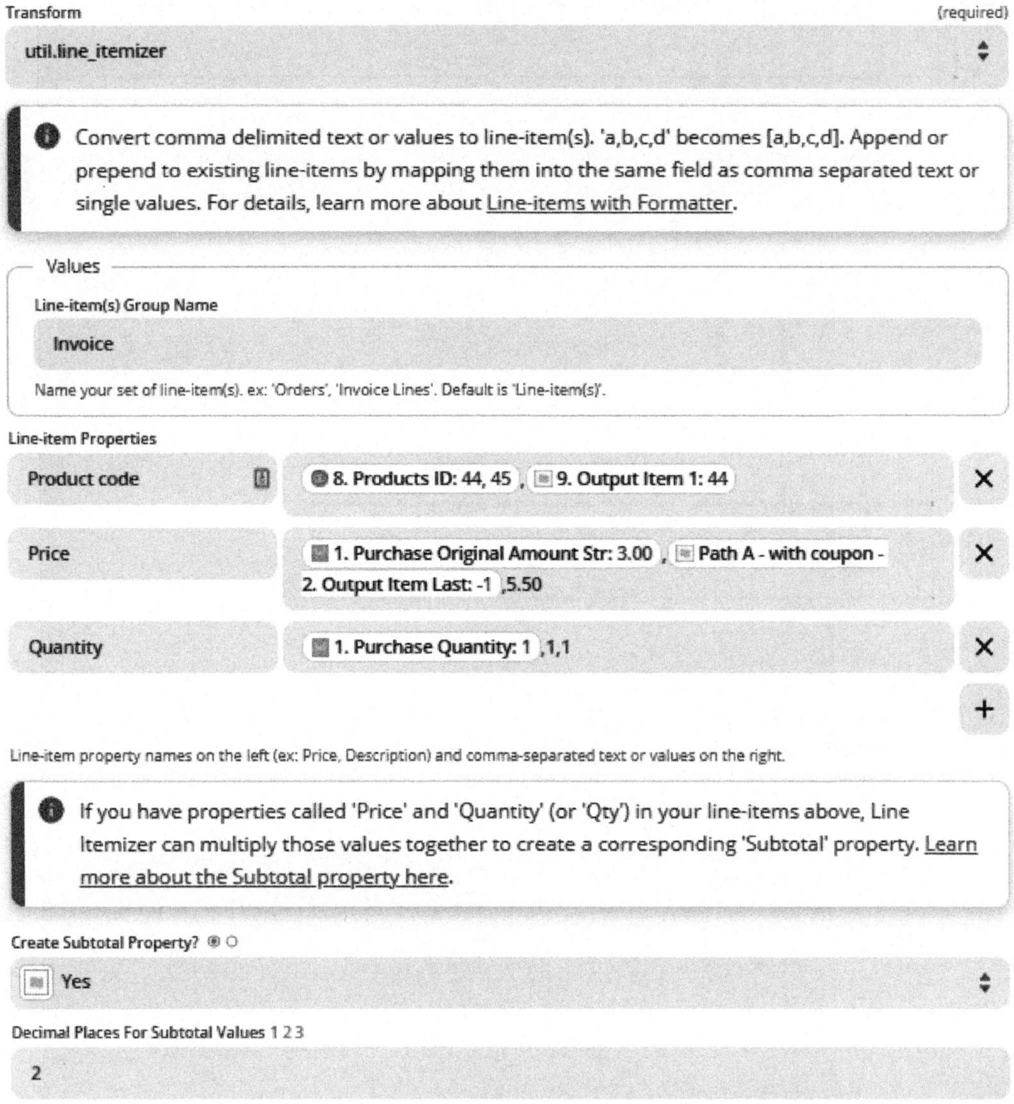

Transform (required)

util.line_itemizer

> ℹ Convert comma delimited text or values to line-item(s). 'a,b,c,d' becomes [a,b,c,d]. Append or prepend to existing line-items by mapping them into the same field as comma separated text or single values. For details, learn more about Line-items with Formatter.

Values

Line-item(s) Group Name

Invoice

Name your set of line-item(s). ex: 'Orders', 'Invoice Lines'. Default is 'Line-item(s)'.

Line-item Properties

| Product code | 📋 | ⊕ 8. Products ID: 44, 45 , 9. Output Item 1: 44 | ✕ |

| Price | 1. Purchase Original Amount Str: 3.00 , Path A - with coupon - 2. Output Item Last: -1 ,5.50 | ✕ |

| Quantity | 1. Purchase Quantity: 1 ,1,1 | ✕ |

| | | ✚ |

Line-item property names on the left (ex: Price, Description) and comma-separated text or values on the right.

> ℹ If you have properties called 'Price' and 'Quantity' (or 'Qty') in your line-items above, Line Itemizer can multiply those values together to create a corresponding 'Subtotal' property. Learn more about the Subtotal property here.

Create Subtotal Property? ⦿ ○

Yes

Decimal Places For Subtotal Values 1 2 3

2

Figure 17.14 – Using the Formatter by Zapier Utilities action event to create,
append, or prepend line-item data

Click on the **Continue** button. You can then use the **Test action** section to create, append, and prepend line-items. The result from the scenario in *Figure 17.14* is shown in the following screenshot:

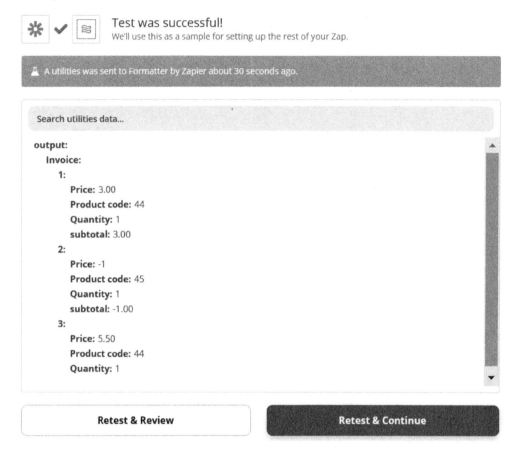

Figure 17.15 – An example of the data returned when creating, appending, and prepending line-item data

The output shown in *Figure 17.15* is separate line-items for `Price`, `Product code`, `Quantity`, and `subtotal`.

Proceed to add one or more action steps after your **Utilities** action step.

The following are a few useful resources created by Zapier that will help you further to use line-items with Formatter by Zapier:

`https://zapier.com/blog/formatter-line-item-automation/`

`https://zapier.com/help/doc/how-use-line-items-formatterv2`

You should now have a better understanding of how and when to use the **Text to Line-item**, **Line-item to Text**, and **Line Itemizer (Create/Append/Prepend)** transform functions to manipulate line-items.

Summary

In this chapter, we completed our exploration of the features of the Formatter by Zapier built-in app by covering the functionality of the Utilities action event. First, we introduced the Formatter by Zapier Utilities action event. Then, we discussed how to import CSV files, how to use lookup tables to store and help you find related data, and how to pick data from a list of values. Finally, we covered the various transform functions related to using line-items in your automations.

You now know how to use the Formatter by Zapier built-in app to transform a number of different functions, including importing CSV files, using lookup tables, picking data from lists, converting text to line-items, and vice versa, as well as line-item creation and customization.

In the next chapter, you will learn how to automate your marketing workflows. We will discuss the different types of marketing processes and give working examples of how these processes can be automated using Zapier. We will also provide practical tips on how to solve problems relating to marketing workflows.

Section 4: Getting the Most Out of Zapier – Business Automation Examples

In this section, you will gain an understanding of the different types of business processes that can be automated using Zapier. We will cover marketing, sales, operations, finance, and reporting processes and explore practical examples specific to commonly used digital tools. You will be able to test your knowledge with planned exercises.

This section comprises the following chapters:

- *Chapter 18, Automating Your Marketing Processes*
- *Chapter 19, Automating Your Sales Processes*
- *Chapter 20, Automating Your Operations Processes*
- *Chapter 21, Automating Your Finance and Reporting Processes*
- *Chapter 22, Tips, Tricks, and Best Practices to Enhance Your Productivity*
- *Chapter 23, Challenge Your Problem-Solving and Zap-Building Skills*

18
Automating Your Marketing Processes

So far in this book, we've reviewed how to get started with building workflow automations with Zapier and how to use the various built-in apps, including Formatter by Zapier, to boost your automations. Now that we've covered those topics, it will be useful to go into more detail regarding the different types of business processes that can be automated by using Zapier as a connector tool between thousands of business applications. Over the following few chapters, we will cover how to automate processes in five of the central business functions, namely marketing, sales, operations, finance, and analytics, and explore examples relating to some commonly used digital tools that integrate with Zapier. We will also go into more detail about how to use one specific integration related to each function.

To start off, marketing is generally the first part of the business cycle, and an important one at that. All businesses need marketing processes to varying degrees to ensure they have a way of attracting potential customers. In this chapter, we will discuss the different types of marketing processes that can be automated with Zapier, and we will provide examples of workflows used with some common marketing applications. First, we will take an overview of the types of marketing processes that can be automated with Zapier. Then, we will explore where to start with automating marketing processes with Zapier. Finally, we will dive into how to automate social media marketing with the Facebook Pages integration.

We will cover the following key topics in this chapter:

- An introduction to automating your marketing processes with Zapier

- Where to start with automating your marketing processes with Zapier

- Automating social media marketing processes with the Facebook Pages integration

Once you have worked through each of these topics, you will have a better understanding of the different marketing processes that can be automated with Zapier. You will know how to use Zapier to automate marketing processes with some of the most common marketing applications.

Technical requirements

To make the most of the content in this chapter, you will need access to a Zapier account. The Zapier Free plan will be required for you to create single-step workflows and use Zapier's pre-built templates. The Zapier Starter plan will be required for you to use Premium apps and to create multi-step workflows.

You can get access to the Zap template used in this chapter here: `https://bit.ly/3e5BUkn`. Using the template will help you to visualize how the process works.

An introduction to automating your marketing processes with Zapier

Every business needs some form of marketing to make sure they get the customers physically through the door or purchasing their products and services online. What every business strives for is lead generation by means of word of mouth or recommendation; in other words, getting your valued and happy customers to do the marketing work for you. However, when you're first starting out, the onus is on the business to get their name out there in one way or another. In the past, some of the most popular forms of marketing were newspaper and magazine ads, leaflet drops, radio ads, and, for those who could afford it, television ads, where customers were often limited to geographical areas. In this digital age, where we have the far reaches of the internet to attract everyone, businesses have more tools and services available for cost-effective marketing. However, with more options come more things that we need to do to stay ahead of the competition.

First of all, most businesses need some form of digital presence so that prospective buyers can find them, and that might be a website or a **Google My Business** page. Your website might have a blog so that you can improve your searchability on search engines such as Google. You might need to share your blog articles on your various social media channels, while engaging your followers with useful content, memes, and motivational posts, or strategic social media campaigns to drive traffic back to your website. You might embed forms on your website to allow people to subscribe to your newsletter. You might have landing pages to help you collect email addresses or prospects to add to your marketing campaigns. You might also use digital ads to increase traffic to these dedicated landing pages. All this effort, and all these tools being used, are purely for the purpose of getting an audience into your sales cycle and buying your product or service.

Understanding what marketing processes can be automated with Zapier

Zapier has several integrations with a range of marketing tools spanning numerous functions allowing you to automate your **marketing processes**. You can connect these apps with thousands of other apps, such as Slack, Google Drive, Airtable, and SMS by Zapier, to automate your social media marketing processes.

Here are a few examples of marketing processes that can be automated with Zapier:

- Online presence processes
- Social media marketing processes
- Social media scheduling processes
- Ad processes
- Email marketing and marketing automation processes

Let's explore each one of these and give some examples of marketing apps that can be used with Zapier to automate the processes that involve them.

Automating processes involving apps for online presence

Most businesses these days have some form of digital presence, and in most cases, that starts with a website. To help improve search engine optimization, it is generally recommended that you have a blog where you publish new and relevant content regularly. You might use **Tumblr**, WordPress, **Drupal**, or **Webflow** to manage your website and blog content.

Managing a blog can be a time-consuming activity, so you might find it useful to automate some of the related processes. One popular website builder and blog that integrates with Zapier is WordPress. You can use Zapier to automate your WordPress blog processes, such as creating, updating, and sharing new content, as well as managing comments and users. You can trigger workflows when you receive new comments, when a new user is added, when posts are added or updated, and when new media is added. Combine these trigger events with action events in notification apps such as Email by Zapier to get an email, social media apps such as Twitter or Medium to share new posts, or a Google Sheets spreadsheet to add new users to a list. You can also create new posts, update existing posts, upload media, create new users, and search for posts when, for example, new images are added to Google Drive or new users are added to your CRM, **Dubsado**, or task management app, Asana.

Many businesses that have a physical, bricks-and-mortar location, such as retail shops, dentists, or legal firms, may advertise their business on services such as Google My Business. With this type of service, you can advertise your opening hours and contact details, and collect customer reviews. Using Google My Business also increases your searchability on Google. As Google My Business integrates with Zapier, you can use Zapier to connect to other apps in your processes and automate your online presence. For example, you can trigger workflows when you receive a new review and get notifications such as a Slack message or SMS. You can respond to specific reviews, as soon as you receive a new review, or update a reply when a record appears in a view in Airtable.

There are many website builder apps that integrate with Zapier, which you can check out here: https://zapier.com/apps/categories/website-app-building.

Next, let's discuss how to automate social media marketing processes with Zapier.

Automating social media marketing processes

Most businesses use some form of social media to engage their prospects and existing customers. You might only be using one or perhaps several social media platforms, depending on the needs of your business. To name a few, these could be Facebook Groups, Twitter, Instagram for Business, and **Pinterest**, for example. Whatever your social media marketing processes are, there will be ways to connect your tools and automate those processes with Zapier.

With the Instagram for Business integration, you can trigger workflows when new videos or photos have been posted in your account or when your account is tagged in a photo or video. Combine these triggers with action events to share on your Facebook Page or on LinkedIn, or save the file in Google Drive. You can also publish a new photo to your feed when, for example, you publish new Shopify or WooCommerce products.

With the Pinterest integration, you can trigger workflows when new pins are added, a new board is created, or you get a new follower. Combine these with action events to post in Facebook Pages or notify your team in Slack. You can also create a new pin when, for example, you publish a new post on WordPress.

There are many social media marketing apps that integrate with Zapier, which you can check out here: `https://zapier.com/apps/categories/social`.

Next, let's explore how to automate social media scheduling processes with Zapier.

Automating social media scheduling processes

Posting content on social media is another time-consuming marketing activity. Writing the content, designing graphics, planning when to post it, and then actually doing the posting can take some time and be a very manual process. Using social media scheduling tools such as **Buffer**, **Meet Edgar**, and **Hootsuite** can make lighter work of part of that process by helping you post to multiple social media platforms at once on days and at times of your choosing. Being able to then automate processes involving these scheduling apps makes things even easier. You can, therefore, use Zapier to automate many social media scheduling workflows.

With the Meet Edgar integration, you can add new content to your library when new pins are added on Pinterest or when you release new videos on YouTube.

With the Buffer integration, you can trigger workflows when new items are added, and then share the new item on Wordpress as a new post, create Trello cards, or create Google Calendar events. You could also add new rows to a Google Sheets spreadsheet when a new profile is added. You might also want to add an item to your schedule for posting at a later date or send an immediate update when, for example, a new Instagram photo is posted, or a new Evernote note is created.

There are many social media scheduling apps that integrate with Zapier, which you can check out here: `https://zapier.com/apps/categories/social-marketing`.

Next, let's cover how to automate online advertising processes with Zapier.

Automating ad processes

Online paid advertising is a popular way of driving traffic to your website or to specific landing pages to promote your products and services. Facebook Lead Ads, Google Ads, and Instagram Lead Ads are popular apps used for online paid advertising, and you can use Zapier to automate ad workflows involving these three apps.

With the Facebook Lead Ads integration, for example, you can trigger workflows when a new lead is created, add new rows to a Google Sheets spreadsheet, or add the lead to your CRM.

With the **Google Ads** integration, you can trigger workflows when a new campaign is created or a lead form is created, and add new posts to LinkedIn or create events in Google Calendar. You can also create a customer list, add or remove contacts to and from a list, or set a status and send offline conversion information from your other apps. You can search for customer lists and campaigns and create a customer list if one does not exist.

There are several online advertising apps that integrate with Zapier, which you can check out here: `https://zapier.com/apps/categories/ads-conversion`.

Next, let's explore how to automate email marketing and marketing automation processes with Zapier.

Automating email marketing and marketing automation

Another popular way to nurture your leads and get your customer buying more from you is to use email marketing or marketing automation. In order to use these methods, once you've pushed new prospects to your website or specific landing pages using social media or ads, you first of all need to collect the email addresses of your contacts so that you can send them new free but valuable content, let them know of special offers, or introduce them to your team and services. You might do this by embedding forms on your website to allow people to subscribe to your newsletter, or setting up landing pages with free downloads such as cheat sheets, eBooks, or fun quizzes to help you collect email addresses so that you can add them to your marketing campaigns.

Email marketing processes

Email marketing apps such as **Constant Contact**, Mailchimp, and **Campaign Monitor** generally allow you to send one-off newsletter-style emails with some simple automations.

With the Constant Contact integration, you can trigger workflows when new contacts or lists are added and when an email is opened. You can combine these triggers with action events such as adding new contacts to Salesforce CRM and labeling them when they have opened an email. You can also create or update contacts in your account, find a contact or create one if it doesn't exist when, for example, new Gravity Forms or Typeform form submissions are made, or when you receive a new Facebook Lead Ad lead.

There are several email marketing apps that integrate with Zapier, which you can check out here: https://zapier.com/apps/categories/email-newsletters.

Marketing automation processes

Marketing automation apps such as ActiveCampaign, **Click Funnels**, and Keap allow you to set up automation sequences with conditional logic where you can remove and add contacts to different lists, segments, and automations based on their activity and behavior. They can often have additional functionality such as working as a CRM as well.

The ActiveCampaign integration has a long list of 15 trigger events, 12 action events, and 4 search action events. As ActiveCampaign also has CRM functionality such as contact management, deals, tasks, and notes, there are several CRM-specific events you can use, which we won't discuss here. However, for the marketing functionality, you can trigger workflows when a campaign starts sending emails, a campaign bounces, links in a campaign have been clicked, a contact unsubscribes from a campaign, or a campaign email is opened. You can combine these triggers with action events such as getting notifications in Slack or by email using Email by Zapier or posting new campaigns to your Facebook Page. You can also find a contact, create contacts, add them to automations, create and send a new campaign or add a tracked event when, for example, you have new Thinkific orders, get new form entries from Google Forms or **JotForm**, close a **ManyChat** chat, or receive a PayPal sale.

There are several marketing automation apps that integrate with Zapier, which you can check out here: https://zapier.com/apps/categories/marketing-automation.

> **Tip**
> If you're a business that serves the B2B market, then you can take advantage of the data extracted with the built-in Lead Score by Zapier app, which can then be used in lead qualification and scoring. This is especially useful for small companies and start-ups who don't have a large lead volume yet and may not be able to afford the fees associated with data insights platforms. The additional data you can retrieve about your prospects as they come in to your systems is invaluable, and at no extra cost for low volumes. You can explore the built-in Lead Score by Zapier app in more detail in *Chapter 10, Other Useful Built-In Apps by Zapier.*

You now understand what kind of marketing processes can be automated with Zapier.

Let's now take a look at the essential first steps to take to start automating your marketing processes.

Where to start with automating your marketing processes with Zapier

It is always good to do some pre-work before your start automating your processes. In *Chapter 2, Preparing to Automate Your Processes*, and *Chapter 3, Building Your First Automated Workflow (Zap)*, we covered a few important points that will help you when you are strategizing your marketing workflows, and they are as follows:

- *Map out your marketing processes*: You probably already have a marketing strategy in place and you have a clear idea of how your marketing processes work with all your tools. If you don't, however, follow the steps in the *Simplifying your processes and assessing what can be automated* section in *Chapter 2, Preparing to Automate Your Processes*, to visually map out your processes so that you have a high-level overview of how your tasks work with your existing software.

- *List your marketing tools*: Make a list of all the marketing tools and services that you use in your business to achieve your goals. Then, assess how these tools fit within your mapped out processes. You will then be able to simplify those processes and decide on what can be automated. Once you have this overview of your processes and tools, you will be better placed to understand where the holes are, and how Zapier can help you to close the gaps and automate your processes.

- *Review your app profile pages*: In *Chapter 2, Preparing to Automate Your Processes*, we also discussed reviewing your individual app profile pages as the best way to establish how your business apps integrate with Zapier. This will give you insights into the triggers, actions, and searches available to use in your workflows. Make a list of these for quick reference.

- *Use Zapier's pre-built guided workflow templates*: This is the easiest way to get started with automating your marketing processes. These templates are built from workflows that are commonly used by other users. They are perfect for inspiration, quick to set up, and will save you time immediately.

- *Customize your marketing workflows*: Get creative and start building multi-step workflows to achieve more in your automations. Use Zapier's built-in apps to help you do more and connect your marketing workflows to other parts of your business processes, such as your sales process.

You'll be well on your way to creating marketing automations for your business.

> **Tip**
>
> If you're looking for ideas of other marketing apps to use in your business, you can review the **Marketing** category in the app ecosystem directory to give you a list of public apps that integrate with Zapier here: `https://zapier.com/apps/categories/marketing`. Review the *A brief guide to choosing new apps for your business* section in *Chapter 2, Preparing to Automate Your Processes*, for guidance on choosing new apps.

You now know how to get started with automating your social media processes with Zapier.

Let's get more specific and discuss how social media marketing processes can be automated using Zapier's Facebook Pages integration.

Automating social media marketing processes with the Facebook Pages integration

Facebook is one of the most commonly used social media platforms, and it has two popular social media apps that integrate with Zapier, namely Facebook Pages and Facebook Groups. To give you some insight into how you can automate your social media marketing processes, we'll focus on the Facebook Pages integration with Zapier.

Most businesses don't use personal Facebook accounts for their social media marketing but will set up Facebook Pages. Facebook Pages are perfect for giving a business better online visibility, showcasing its products and services, opening hours, and customer recommendations, as well as sharing content, special offers, and news to engage prospects and customer.

You can use Zapier to automate your marketing processes if you use Facebook Pages in your business, and the Facebook Pages integration supports numerous trigger and action events. Let's review each of these.

Facebook Pages trigger events

The following is a list of supported trigger events that you can use with Facebook Pages with examples of when to use them:

- **New Post to Your Timeline**: This event triggers when a new post is added by you or someone else to the timeline of your Facebook Page. Among other things, you can use this trigger event in your automations when you want to be notified of a new post on your timeline. For example, combine this trigger event with a notification action event such as **Send SMS** with SMS by Zapier to send you an SMS, or the **Send Channel Message** action event with Slack to send a message to your team on a specified channel.

- **New Recommendation**: This event triggers when your Facebook Page receives a new recommendation. Among other things, you can use this trigger event in your automations when you want to assign a task to your team to review the recommendation. For example, combine this trigger event with the **Create Card** action event with Trello to add a new card to Trello and assign a member to it, or add a task to Clickup with the **Create Task** action event. You could also use it when you want to share the recommendation on other social media platforms.

- **New Post by You**: This event triggers when you post an update to the timeline of your Facebook Page. Among other things, you can use this trigger event in your automations when you want to reshare your post on other social media platforms. For example, combine this trigger event with an action event such as **Create Tweet** to post a tweet on Twitter. If you needed to make sure that your message is not over the maximum character length of 280 for a tweet, in a step prior to the action step, add the Formatter by Zapier **Text** action event with the **Truncate** transform option to truncate the character length.

Next, let's have a look at the Facebook Pages action events.

Facebook Pages action events

The following is a list of supported action events that you can use with Facebook Pages with examples of when to use them:

- **Create Page Photo**: You can use this action event to upload a photo to your Facebook Page, which then is posted on your Facebook Page stream. When setting up the action event, you must choose which Facebook Page you want to post to, bearing in mind that you must have been granted admin access to that page. You must add the file object or publicly accessible URL of the **Photo** you want to post and, optionally, add a **Description** for the photo. You could use this action event in combination with a trigger event such as **New File in Folder** in Google Drive to post new photos to your Facebook Page. Use the `File` field from your trigger to map in the file object. Photos should be smaller than 4 MB and saved as either `.JPG`, `.PNG`, `.GIF`, `.TIFF`, HEIF, or WebP files.

- **Create Page Post**: You can use this action event to create and post a new stream item to your Facebook Page. When setting up the action event, you must choose which Facebook Page you want to post to, bearing in mind that you must have been granted admin access to that page. You must add a **Message** in the form of static or dynamic text from previous steps. You can optionally add a **Link URL** to attach to the post. You could use this action event in combination with a trigger event such as **New Item in Feed** in RSS by Zapier to post new feed items from your favorite blog and share them with your Facebook audience, or **New Post** in Wordpress to share new posts from your blog. Add in a short static text message such as `Here's the latest from the Zapier blog...` in the **Message** field and the blog URL in the **Link URL** field. Prior to this action step, you could add a step with the Formatter by Zapier **Text** action event with the **Truncate** transform option to create a summary of the first few sentences of the blog description and map this output as dynamic data to the **Message** field.

- **Create Page Video**: You can use this action to upload a video to your Facebook Page, which then is posted on your Facebook Page stream. When setting up the action event, you must choose which Facebook Page you want to post to, bearing in mind that you must have been granted admin access to that page. You must add the file object or publicly accessible URL of the video you want to post and, optionally, add a title for the video and a message in the **Description** field for the video. You could use this action event in combination with a trigger event such as **New Video in Channel** in YouTube to post your latest videos to your Facebook Page. Use the `play_url` field from your trigger to map in the publicly accessible YouTube URL.

- **Change Page Profile Photo**: You can use this action event to change the profile picture on your Facebook Page. When setting up the action event, you must choose which Facebook Page you want to post to, bearing in mind that you must have been granted admin access to that page. You must add the file object or publicly accessible URL of the **Photo** you want to post. You could use this action event in combination with a trigger event such as **New Record** in Airtable to post new photos to your Facebook Page when a new record is created in Airtable with an image associated. Use the `File` field from your trigger to map in the file object. Photos should be smaller than 4 MB and saved as either `.JPG`, `.PNG`, `.GIF`, `.TIFF`, HEIF, or WebP files.

You can view common problems with the Facebook Pages integration by navigating to the **Help** tab of the app profile or following this link: `https://zapier.com/help/doc/common-problems-facebook-pages`.

Next, let's explore how to set up an example of a multi-step Zap using the Facebook Pages integration.

Setting up a multi-step Zap with the Facebook Pages integration

To illustrate this, we will use the example of creating a new page post on Facebook Pages when an RSS feed item is added to one of our favorite blogs, `https://zapier.com/blog/feeds/latest/`, where we truncate the blog description so that our message is more readable.

The Zap will involve three steps as follows:

1. *Trigger*: The **RSS by Zapier** app with the **New Item in Feed** trigger event
2. *Action*: The **Formatter by Zapier** app with the **Text** action event and the **Truncate** transform option.
3. *Action*: The **Facebook Pages** app with the **New Page Post** action event.

The following screenshot shows how your Zap should look once built, with some custom labeling:

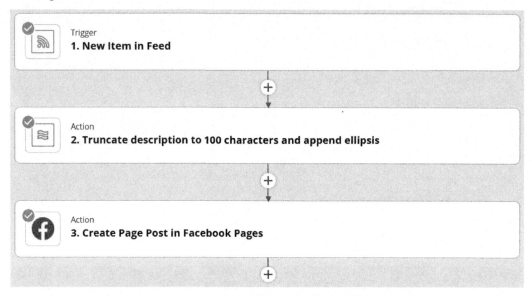

Figure 18.1 – A multi-step Zap using Facebook Pages as an action step

Let's walk through this step by step, starting with the trigger step.

Setting up step 1 – the trigger step

We will use the RSS by Zapier built-in app with the trigger event **New Item in Feed** as the trigger step. Follow the instructions in the *RSS by Zapier – Using RSS feed readers* section in *Chapter 9, Exploring Built-In Apps for Extracting and Compiling Data*, to add `https://zapier.com/blog/feeds/latest/` to the **Feed URL** field.

The following screenshot shows how this step should look:

Feed URL   (required)

> https://zapier.com/blog/feeds/latest/

Paste your publicly accessible RSS URL here.

Username

> Enter text...

If required to access the feed.

Password

> Type value...

If required to access the feed.

What Triggers A New Feed Item?

> 📄 Different Guid/URL (recommended)

This is an advanced option. Go with the recommended unless you're a total pro ;)

> ↻ **Refresh fields**

> **Continue**

Figure 18.2 – Using RSS by Zapier to trigger a workflow when there is a new item in a feed

Next, let's set up the first action step.

Setting up step 2 – the first action step

We will use the Formatter by Zapier app with the **Text** action event and the **Truncate** transform option. Follow the instructions in the *Truncating text to a specified character length* section in *Chapter 16, Text Formatting Functions in Zapier – Part 2*, to customize this action step so that we truncate the dynamic Description data from the trigger step by mapping it to the **Input** field, set to a **Maximum Length** of 100 characters without skipping characters and adding ... to the end by selecting **True** in the **Append Ellipsis?** field.

The following screenshot shows how this step should look:

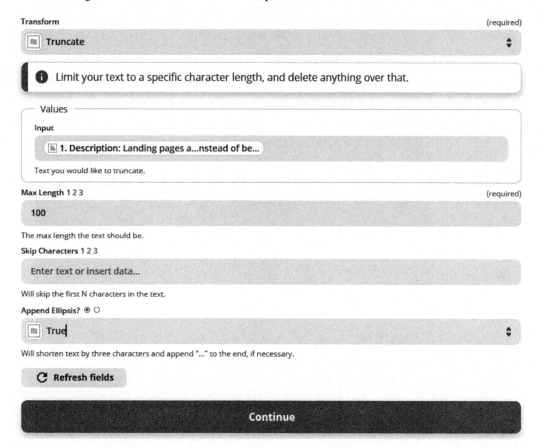

Figure 18.3 – Using the Formatter by Zapier Text action event to truncate the Description data

Click on the **Continue** button. You can then use the **Test action** section to truncate the text.

Next, let's set up the second and final action step.

Setting up step 3 – the second action step

We will use the Facebook Pages app with the **New Page Post** action event, and we will customize this action step by completing the fields as follows:

- **Page**: We will use this drop-down field to select a Facebook Page account that we have admin access to. In this case, we choose the option for **Solvaa – Zapier Experts**.

- **Message**: We will add static text `Here's the latest from the Zapier blog:`, the dynamic blog `Title` data from the step 1 trigger, and the formatted `Description` output from step 2.

- **Link URL**: We will map in the dynamic `Link` data from the step 1 trigger so that the reader can click on a link to take them to the actual blog post.

The following screenshot shows how this step should look:

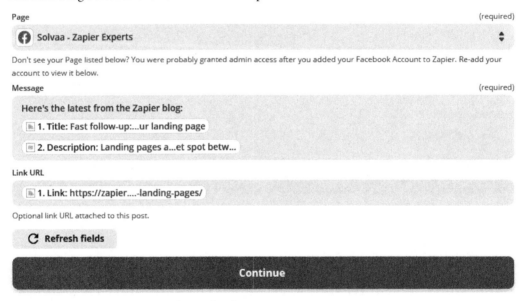

Figure 18.4 – Using the Facebook Pages integration to create a new page post

Click on the **Continue** button. You can then use the **Test action** section to create the post in Facebook Pages. The result from the scenario is shown in the following screenshot:

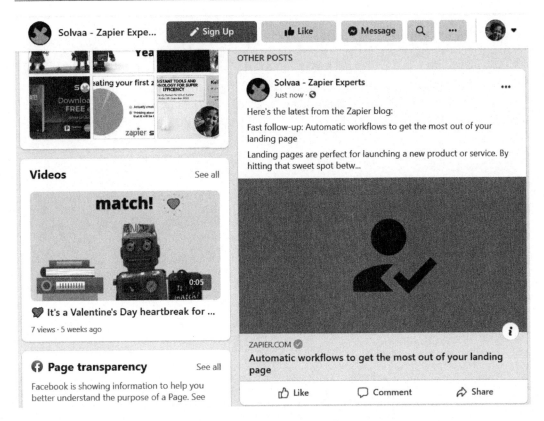

Figure 18.5 – The new page post created by Zapier in Facebook Pages

You can get access to a copy of this Zap template here: `https://bit.ly/3e5BUkn`.

You should now have a better understanding of how to automate social media marketing processes with the Facebook Pages integration.

Summary

In this chapter, we discussed the different types of marketing processes that can be automated with Zapier, and we explored some examples of workflows used with some common marketing applications. First, we gave an overview of the types of marketing processes that can be automated with Zapier. Then, we covered where to start with automating marketing processes with Zapier. Finally, we discussed how to automate social media marketing with the Facebook Pages integration.

You now know how to automate your marketing processes with Zapier and specifically with the Facebook Pages integration.

In the next chapter, you will learn how to automate your sales workflows. We will discuss the different types of sales processes and give working examples of how these processes can be automated using Zapier. We will also provide practical tips on how to solve problems relating to sales workflows.

19
Automating Your Sales Processes

Now that we've covered how to automate marketing processes with Zapier, the next important business function to explore is the sales cycle and how to automate its processes. Sales, of course, is one of the most important business functions. Once your marketing processes are working on autopilot to push new leads your way, you will need an efficient way of converting them into sales. No sales means no revenue, and a business without revenue will not survive long at all. Therefore, having a streamlined and automated sales process will most definitely help ensure business success.

In this chapter, we will discuss the different types of sales processes that can be automated with Zapier, and we will provide examples of workflows used with some common sales applications. First, we will give an overview of the types of sales processes that can be automated with Zapier, such as data collection, appointment scheduling, lead capture and management, getting digital signatures, and handling online sales transactions. Then, we will explore where to start with automating sales processes with Zapier. Finally, there are several different sales tools that integrate with Zapier, allowing you to automate your sales processes. To illustrate this, we will dive into how to automate lead management processes with the Pipedrive CRM integration.

We will cover the following key topics in this chapter:

- An introduction to automating your sales processes with Zapier

- Where to start with automating your sales processes with Zapier

- Automating lead management processes with CRM integrations illustrated with Pipedrive

Once you have worked through each of these topics, you will have a better understanding of the different sales processes that can be automated with Zapier. You will know how to use Zapier to automate sales processes with some of the most common sales applications.

Technical requirements

To make the most of the content in this chapter, you will need access to a Zapier account. The Zapier Free plan will be required for you to create single-step workflows and use Zapier's pre-built templates. The Zapier Starter plan will be required for you to use Premium apps and to create multi-step workflows.

You can get access to the Zap template used in this chapter here: `https://bit.ly/3e5BUkn`. Using the template will help you to visualize how the process works.

An introduction to automating your sales processes with Zapier

In days gone by, many businesses owned cash registers that made a "cha-ching" chime every time they received money from a sale. These days, it's not likely that many businesses have these antique cash registers, but many business owners might imagine that "cha-ching" sound when they make a sale and secretly do a little jig. Sales are what keep the business going and pay the employees, suppliers, and business owners.

Before the internet came along, companies often needed to have premises to trade from and made sales of their products or services when customers walked through the door. Some customers knew what they wanted, and others needed more information or a bit of convincing. The sales personnel worked the room and attended to potential buyers while having to answer the telephone, deal with inquiries, and book appointments. Customer details might have been recorded on a paper registration form, in a book or a spreadsheet, or not at all. Contracts were written out by hand or typed out, requiring a signature in person.

Things have moved on since then with the digital age, and companies now have many tools available to them to be able to run their sales cycle more efficiently and effectively. Salespeople now have better processes at their fingertips to be able to build stronger relationships with their prospective customers so that they buy and keep coming back for more without losing the personal touch.

Here is an example of how a sales process can be improved significantly by using connector tools such as Zapier to automate various tasks: `https://solvaa.co.uk/automate-dental-practice/`.

Understanding what sales processes can be automated with Zapier

Zapier has many integrations with a range of sales tools spanning numerous functions allowing you to automate your **sales processes**. You can connect these apps with thousands of other apps such as Microsoft Outlook, Asana, Dropbox, and Xero to automate your sales processes.

Here are a few examples of sales processes that can be automated with Zapier:

- Data collection processes with forms
- Appointment booking and scheduling processes
- Lead management processes
- Contract, proposal, and digital signature collection processes
- E-commerce processes

Let's explore each one and give some examples of sales apps that can be used with Zapier to automate processes that involve them.

Automating processes involving data collection

Many businesses use form builders to collect information from prospective customers. You might use Gravity Forms, Google Forms, JotForm, Typeform, or another form builder. These forms might be for the purpose of sending through an inquiry about the company's services and products when embedded on the company website or for marketing purposes so that people can sign up for the company's newsletter or fill out a survey.

It's common that you might receive an email notification when a form entry is made, but then it can be time-consuming and repetitive to process that data and add it to other systems. By automating the process, you can then add that form data to multiple tools in your app stack and kick off workflows accordingly. For example, when a new form entry has been made, you could notify your team with a Slack message, send an SMS to yourself, add the entry to Google Drive or Dropbox as a text tile, create a new issue in **Jira**, create a new contact and opportunity in **Close.io**, and more.

Gravity Forms is a popular WordPress plugin that allows you to create a custom form that you can embed on web pages so that you can collect data. With the Gravity Forms integration, you can trigger workflows when a form is submitted. You can combine this trigger with action events to add the form data to your CRM, add a new task to your project management app, or send an automated email with Gmail, for example. You can also create a form entry and additionally trigger rules associated with the form submission, such as notifications and feed add-ons.

When using Google Forms, you can create forms and then use them as stand-alone URLs or embed them on web pages. Form entries are also recorded on a Google Sheet. With the Google Forms integration, you can trigger workflows when a new form response is added to the bottom of the associated Google Sheet and, additionally, when a form response is modified. You can combine these triggers with action events to add or update data in your email marketing tool, such as **ConvertKit**, add events to Google Calendar, or send out an automated voicemail with Slybroadcast, for example. You can also create a new form response and row entry, find and create a new response, and look up a response row by column and value returning the data in that row.

There are many form and survey apps that integrate with Zapier, which you can check out here: https://zapier.com/apps/categories/forms.

Next, let's discuss how to automate appointment booking and scheduling processes with Zapier.

Automating appointment booking and scheduling processes

If you're a service business, getting appointments booked is a sure-fire way to get that revenue streaming in. Those appointments might be for free discovery or informative calls, charged consulting sessions, or other in-person services such as massages or therapy. The first step in improving your appointment booking and scheduling processes is to use either built-in booking functionality in your existing apps, such as with some CRMs such as Pipedrive, Dubsado, or HubSpot, or to use a dedicated scheduling app, such as Acuity Scheduling or Calendly. These apps allow you to create custom time slots that can be displayed on your website or shared using a URL. They integrate with your calendar so that your availability is displayed and events are automatically created in the calendar once a booking has been made. Some apps also allow you to take payments in advance. Once you're using this functionality, you can then automate processes accordingly by creating workflows that include these apps.

With the Acuity Scheduling integration, you can trigger workflows when new appointments are scheduled, canceled, or rescheduled, when appointments start, or when a new product order is completed. You can combine these triggers with action events to create new subscribers and deals in ActiveCampaign, create new Asana tasks, and add or update rows in a Google Sheet, for example. You can also add coupon and package codes, block off time in your Acuity schedule, and find existing appointments by client info or ID.

With the Calendly integration, you can trigger workflows when an invitee schedules an event or when an invitee cancels a scheduled event. Combine these triggers with action events to create meetings in **Zoom**, send Slack messages, and create or update contacts in your CRM, for example.

There are many scheduling apps that integrate with Zapier, which you can check out here: `https://zapier.com/apps/categories/scheduling`.

Next, let's explore how to automate lead management processes with Zapier.

Automating lead management processes

Many businesses use either a contact database or CRM app to centralize data so that they can manage their leads and customers. These tools quite often are the single source of truth about the contact and therefore hold all the information about the contact and communications with that contact. Most CRM apps allow you to classify contacts by the stage they are at in the buyer process, such as a lead, opportunity, or customer, and how warm a prospect they are based on their activities. You can create deals or opportunities to track your prospect's progress through your sales cycle and create activities or tasks to help manage your touchpoints with the prospect. In some cases, you can connect your email account, then send and record email communications, connect your calendar, and schedule appointments directly from the CRM. Some CRMs have product modules enabling you to add products and pricing to your deals, and some allow you to manage support tickets and perform email marketing functions.

There are hundreds of CRMs on the market, including popular apps such as HubSpot, Salesforce, Zoho CRM, Microsoft Dynamics 365 CRM, Capsule CRM, Dubsado, ActiveCampaign, and Pipedrive. Many of these integrate with Zapier, therefore allowing you to take your lead and contact management processes to the next level with automation. Most of the integrations have many triggers, actions, and searches available to use, allowing you to supercharge your lead management processes.

With the Salesforce integration, you can trigger workflows when new records such as Contact, Lead, and Opportunity records are added or updated, when a field within a record such as `email address` or `status` is updated, or when a new outbound message is received. Combine these triggers with action events such as creating new contacts and invoices in QuickBooks Online when an opportunity hits a certain stage, adding leads to Mailchimp or MailerLite, or adding new cards to Trello. You can also create new and update existing records, add contacts or leads to a campaign, create new attachments, find one or more records, and find or create a record if one does not exist (when, for example, you receive new Typeform entries, new Facebook Lead Ads leads, or new **Unbounce** leads).

Instead of using a CRM, you could use a customizable data table such as Airtable to manage your sales process, as well as other parts of your business such as social media planning, inventory management, staff vacation planning, and more. Airtable works similar to a spreadsheet; however, you have the additional benefits of using forms and displaying data in specific views as well, such as Kanban. With the Airtable integration, you can trigger workflows when new records are available, new records are available in a view, and records are created or updated.

Combine these triggers with action events such as sending an email with Gmail or Microsoft Outlook and creating Google Calendar events or ClickUp tasks. You can also create or update records, find records, and find or create records when, for example, you receive a new Google Forms submission or new contacts have been added to **Google Contacts**.

There are several lead management and CRM apps that integrate with Zapier, which you can check out here: `https://zapier.com/apps/categories/crm`.

Next, let's explore how to automate contract, proposal, and digital signature collection processes with Zapier.

Automating contract, proposal, and digital signature collection processes

Some businesses need to send client-facing documents such as proposals, quotes, or contracts. In some situations, these documents might need to be digitally signed by the client. Many businesses use a collection of tools to accomplish this, often involving manual processes of copying and pasting information into Microsoft Word or **PowerPoint** documents, or perhaps Google Docs or **Google Slides** documents. The documents are manually sent by email, and then, when a signature is required, customers often need to print, sign, and scan to sign the document or download software to use. We can make the whole process easier for ourselves and our clients by using digital proposal, quoting, and eSign tools, such as PandaDoc, **Proposify**, **HelloSign**, **DocuSign**, and **ZohoSign**, to streamline sales workflows. Users can create beautiful, branded templates, and as these tools quite often integrate with numerous CRM systems, they allow the user to create mail merge fields that pull in required information into the new document, such as name, email address, address, and products, for example. Some apps also allow you to take payments. Once you're using these tools, you can use Zapier to automate other processes.

With the PandaDoc integration, you can trigger workflows when a document has been sent, is completed, is paid, or when a status has changed to something such as `draft`, `sent`, `viewed`, `completed`, or `paid`. You can combine these triggers with action events such as uploading the completed PDF documents to Google Drive or Dropbox, creating contacts and invoices in Xero or FreshBooks, updating deal stages in ActiveCampaign or HubSpot, or sending notifications by email, SMS, or Slack. You can also create a new contact and a document from a template when, for example, new form submissions are made in **Ninja Forms**, opportunities move to a certain stage in Salesforce, or tasks are marked as complete in Google Tasks.

With the DocuSign integration, you can trigger workflows when a new folder is created and when an envelope is sent or completed. You can combine these triggers with action events such as uploading completed envelopes to Dropbox, creating tasks in Todoist, and adding new subscribers to Autopilot. You can also create a signature request when, for example, a Smartsheet row is updated or a new row is added to a Google Sheet.

There are several contract, proposal, and digital signature collection apps that integrate with Zapier, which you can check out here: `https://zapier.com/apps/categories/signatures`.

Next, let's explore how to automate e-commerce processes with Zapier.

Automating e-commerce processes

So far, we have mainly focused on sales processes that involve an element of human interaction and various touchpoints prior to a sale being made. Many businesses, however, already run their sales processes on autopilot by listing their physical or digital products, including online courses and subscriptions, on the internet using shopping carts such as ThriveCart or **SamCart**, e-commerce stores such as Shopify or WooCommerce, sales directories such as **eBay** or **Gumroad**, and online course platforms such as Kajabi or **Thinkific**. Many of these platforms integrate with Zapier, thereby allowing you to automate your processes further.

With the eBay integration, you can trigger workflows when a new order is made and then combine this with action events to create new Google Sheet rows, create new sales invoices in Xero, create new Airtable records, or create new Printful orders, for example. You can also create a shipping fulfillment to a line item and search for an order, when you receive a new Shopify order or for new ShipStation orders.

With the SamCart integration, you can trigger workflows when new orders are made, new prospect entries are created, recurring subscriptions are charged, new refunds are made, and new subscriptions are canceled. You can combine these triggers with action events such as granting or removing access to Kajabi offers, tagging Intercom users with their specific orders, adding new orders to ShipStation, or unenrolling Thinkific users from courses when payments are refunded.

There are many e-commerce apps that integrate with Zapier, which you can check out here: `https://zapier.com/apps/categories/ecommerce`.

You now understand what kind of sales processes can be automated with Zapier.

Let's now take a look at the essential first steps to take to start automating your sales processes.

Where to start with automating your sales processes with Zapier

It is always good to do some pre-work before you start automating your processes. In *Chapter 2, Preparing to Automate Your Processes,* and *Chapter 3, Building Your First Automated Workflow (Zap),* we covered a few important points that will help you when you are strategizing your sales workflows, and these are as follows:

- *Map out your sales processes*: If you don't have a clear idea of how your sales processes work with all your tools, follow the steps in the *Simplifying your processes and assessing what can be automated* section in *Chapter 2, Preparing to Automate Your Processes,* to visually map out your processes so that you have a high-level overview of how your tasks work with your existing software.

- *List your sales tools*: Make a list of all the sales tools and services that you use in your business to achieve your goals. Then, assess how these tools fit within your mapped-out processes. You will then be able to simplify those processes and decide on what can be automated. Once you have this overview of your processes and tools, you will be better placed to understand where the holes are, and how Zapier can help you to close the gaps and automate your processes.

- *Review your app profile pages*: In *Chapter 2, Preparing to Automate Your Processes,* we also discussed reviewing your individual app profile pages as the best way to establish how your business apps integrate with Zapier. This will give you insight into the triggers, actions, and searches available to use in your workflows. Make a list of these for quick reference.

- *Use Zapier's pre-built guided workflow templates*: This is the easiest way to get started with automating your sales processes. These templates are built from workflows that are commonly used by other users. They are perfect for inspiration, quick to set up, and will save you time immediately.

- *Customize your sales workflows*: Get creative and start building multi-step workflows to achieve more in your automation. Use Zapier's built-in apps to help you do more and connect your sales workflows to other parts of your business processes, such as your operations process.

You'll be well on your way to creating sales automation for your business.

> **Tip**
>
> If you're looking for ideas of other sales apps to use in your business, you can review the **Sales & CRM** category in the app ecosystem directory to give you a list of public apps that integrate with Zapier here: `https://zapier.com/apps/categories/sales-crm`. Review the *A brief guide to choosing new apps for your business* section in *Chapter 2, Preparing to Automate Your Processes*, for guidance on choosing new apps.

You now know how to get started with automating your sales processes with Zapier.

Let's get more specific and discuss how lead management processes can be automated using Zapier's integrations with CRMs, illustrated with Pipedrive.

Automating lead management processes with CRM integrations, illustrated with Pipedrive

As we've seen so far in this chapter, there are so many different sales tools that connect with Zapier allowing you to automate your sales processes. We specifically covered automating lead management processes and noted that there is a range of CRMs that integrate with Zapier. To further illustrate what the possibilities are, we're now going to focus on one of Zapier's most popular sales app integrations, which is Pipedrive.

This section will mostly help Pipedrive users who are considering automating their processes with Zapier to understand the options available to them. However, if you're not a Pipedrive user, this section will still be helpful for you as many similarities exist in the Zapier integrations with other well-known CRM tools such as Salesforce and HubSpot where the integrations are just as comprehensive and in some cases more extensive. This section may also be loosely useful for those users who are trying to assess whether a CRM might be appropriate for their business and how this fits with automating their sales processes.

Pipedrive is a popular CRM used by businesses that want to simply and effectively manage their sales process from lead capture, through sales cycle stages in pipelines, to integrating with other tools to connect other business functions such as calling and invoicing. Pipedrive is primarily built for B2B interactions but can be adapted to a B2C process. Pipedrive allows you to build forms to use standalone or to embed on your website so that you can automatically add new leads to the CRM. You can create and manage contacts in the form of Persons and associated Organizations, and you can create leads and then convert qualified leads to Deals to move them through your sales cycle in one or more pipelines. You can create activities or tasks set to certain dates and times to ensure that you and your sales team remember to work through various touchpoints to engage your prospects. You can connect your email account so that you can send and receive emails straight from within the platform, and emails are logged against the contact and associated Deals. You can also connect your calendar and schedule meetings. Pipedrive also has a products module, allowing you to create and manage line items with quantities and pricing that can be added to Deals. For reporting purposes, Pipedrive has dashboard reporting, and you can create custom filters for Activities, Persons, Organizations, Leads, and Deals, which can be used in Zapier automations. Pipedrive does allow you to create automation rules within the app, and it has several robust native integrations with other apps, such as calling apps, proposal and eSign tools, marketing apps, and invoicing apps. You can, however, use the Zapier integration to add power to your processes by connecting Pipedrive to thousands of other apps so that you can automate many parts of your sales processes. The Pipedrive integration is very comprehensive and currently supports 14 trigger events, 14 action events, and 7 search events. Let's review each of these.

Pipedrive trigger events

The following is a list of supported trigger events that you can use with Pipedrive with examples of when to use them:

- **New Person**: This event triggers when a new Person is added to Pipedrive. Among other things, you can use this trigger event in your automations when you want to add new contacts to other apps such as your email marketing app or invoicing platform as soon as they have been added to Pipedrive. For example, combine this trigger event with an action event such as **Create Contact** with Constant Contact or **Create Client** with FreshBooks Classic.

- **Updated Person**: This event triggers when an existing Person is updated in Pipedrive. You can use this trigger event in your automations when you want to update existing contacts in your other apps as soon as they have been added to Pipedrive. For example, combine this trigger event with action events to update a row in Google Sheets such as **Lookup Spreadsheet Row** first to find the ID for the row you want to update using a unique identifier such as the email address, and then use **Update Spreadsheet Row** to update the row.

- **Person Matching Filter**: This event triggers when a Person matches a filter. For this trigger to work, you must create an appropriate filter within Pipedrive. For example, you could create a filter that includes a Person when a Warm label is applied. When setting up this trigger event, select your filter from the **Filter** drop-down menu. Among other things, you can use this trigger event in your automations when you want to trigger workflows only when a Person matches a certain condition, without using Filter by Zapier, and then create a contact and add to an automation in marketing automation apps. For example, combine this trigger event with an action event such as **Add Contact to Automation** in ActiveCampaign to add the contact to a nurturing sequence.

- **New Organization**: This event triggers when a new Organization is added to Pipedrive. You can use this trigger event in your automations when you want to add new company details to other records such as spreadsheets or databases. For example, combine this trigger event with an action event such as **Add Row to Sheet** with Smartsheet or **Create Record** with Airtable.

- **Updated Organization**: This event triggers when an existing Organization is updated in Pipedrive. Use this trigger event in your automations similarly to the **Updated Person** trigger.

- **Organization Matching Filter**: This event triggers when an Organization matches a filter. For this trigger to work, you must create an appropriate filter within Pipedrive. For example, you could create a filter that includes an Organization when a Customer label is applied. When setting up this trigger event, select your filter from the **Filter** drop-down menu. You can use this trigger event in your automations when you want to trigger workflows only when an Organization matches a certain condition, without using Filter by Zapier, and then add these details in other apps. For example, combine this trigger event with an action event such as **Create Task List** in Google Tasks to perform customer onboarding tasks.

- **New Lead**: This event triggers when a new Lead is added to Pipedrive. Among other things, you can use this trigger event in your automations when you want to create new Deals in Pipedrive when new leads are added. For example, combine this trigger event with an action event such as **Create Deal** with Pipedrive.

- **New Deal**: This is an instant trigger event that triggers when a new Deal is added to Pipedrive. You can use this trigger event in your automations when you want to send out notifications to your team or send an email or SMS to your prospect. For example, combine this trigger event with an action event such as **Send Email** with Gmail or **Send SMS** with Twilio.

- **Updated Deal**: This is an instant trigger event that triggers when Deal components such as fields, followers, and Notes are updated in Pipedrive. As you cannot specify under which conditions this event will trigger, it is best used with a Filter by Zapier action step immediately following it. You can, for example, use this trigger event in your automations when you want to update existing elements in another app, such as updating a task in your task management app. Combine this trigger event and filter with an action event such as **Add Label to Card** with Trello or **Create Update** with monday.com.

- **Updated Deal Stage**: This is an instant trigger event that triggers when a Deal moves to a specified stage in a pipeline. Among other ways, you can use this trigger event in your automations when you want to create Deal stage-specific activities in Pipedrive or your other apps. For example, combine this trigger event with an action event such as **Create Checklist** with Process Street to create a detailed screening checklist when a Deal hits the "Screening" stage, or create a proposal in Proposify using **Create Proposal** when a Deal hits the "Proposal" stage.

- **Deal Matching Filter**: This event triggers when a Deal matches a filter. For this trigger to work, you must create an appropriate filter within Pipedrive. For example, you could create a filter that includes a Deal when the Deal moves to a certain stage, such as "Needs Defined," and the email count is more than 10. When setting up this trigger event, select your filter from the **Filter** drop-down menu. You can use this trigger event in your automations when you want to trigger workflows only when a Deal matches a certain condition, without using Filter by Zapier, and then add these details in other apps. For example, combine this trigger event with an action event such as **Find Person and Company Information** in Lead Score by Zapier to get lead scoring information for the Person and Organization.

- **New Activity**: This event triggers when a new Activity is added to Pipedrive to a Person, Organization, or Deal record. You can use this trigger event in your automations when you want to send out notifications to your team for new activities or assign tasks to your team to match the activities if not all of your team use Pipedrive. For example, combine this trigger event with an action event such as **Send Channel Message** with Slack or **Create Task** with Teamwork projects.

- **Activity Matching Filter**: This event triggers when an Activity matches a filter. For this trigger to work, you must create an appropriate filter within Pipedrive. For example, you could create a filter that includes an Activity with a due date of the next day, assigned to a specific user, and an "In-Person" meeting type. When setting up this trigger event, select your filter from the **Filter** drop-down menu. You can use this trigger event in your automations when you want to trigger workflows only when an Activity matches a certain condition, without using Filter by Zapier, and then add these details in other apps. For example, combine this trigger event with an action event such as **Get Tomorrow's Forecast** with Weather by Zapier to get the weather forecast for the next day and then send an email to the owner of the Activity using **Send Outbound Email** with Email by Zapier.

- **New Note**: This event triggers when a new Note is added to Pipedrive to a Person, Organization, or Deal record. Among other ways, you can use this trigger event in your automations when you want to add a follower to a Deal if a Note contains a certain word or phrase. For example, combine this trigger event with an action event **Only continue if...** with Filter by Zapier where the Content field is mapped, the condition is Text (Contains), and the value is the word or phrase you specify, and then another action event such as **Add Follower** with Pipedrive.

In comparison, the HubSpot integration has a similar trigger structure with contacts, companies tasks, and Deal creation and updates; however, it has a much more comprehensive range of trigger events covering other module components such as form submissions, products, tickets, line items, and email engagements, for example. Conversely, the Salesforce integration may have fewer triggers, but these generally are based on records being grouped together to allow the record type to be selected from a drop-down menu, such as **New Record**, **Updated Record**, and **Updated Field on Record**, allowing for significant flexibility covering most Salesforce module properties.

Next, let's have a look at the Pipedrive action events.

Pipedrive action events

The following is a list of supported action events that you can use with Pipedrive with examples of when to use them:

- **Create Person**: You can use this action event when you want to create a new Person record in Pipedrive. You must enter text or insert data from previous steps to add the name of the Person, and optionally fill in the standard fields, **Owner**, **Organization**, **Email**, **Phone**, **Label**, and **Visible To**, and any other Person-specific custom fields unique to your Pipedrive account. You could use this action event in combination with a trigger event such as **New Subscriber** with **AWeber** to add new email newsletter subscribers to Pipedrive and label them accordingly.

- **Update Person**: You can use this action event when you want to update an existing Person record in Pipedrive. You must specify the record of an existing Person by selecting from the drop-down menu, entering the Pipedrive record ID of the existing Person, not the name, into the **Person** field, or inserting the ID from previous steps. You can fill the standard fields of **Name**, **Owner**, **Organization**, **Email**, **Phone**, **Label**, and **Visible To**, and any other Person-specific custom fields unique to your Pipedrive account. You should fill in at least one other field to prevent this step from presenting an error. In order to find the Pipedrive record ID for the Person, you can use the **Find Person** search action event using a unique identifier for the record to search for data in a specific field, such as the contact's email address. You could use this action event and the search action event in combination with a trigger event such as **Appointment Start** with Acuity Scheduling to update custom fields in a Person record when a customer attends an appointment.

- **Create Organization**: You can use this action event when you want to create a new Organization record in Pipedrive. You must enter text or insert data from previous steps to add the name of the Organization, and optionally fill in the standard fields, **Owner**, **Address**, **Label**, and **Visible To**, and any other Organization-specific custom fields unique to your Pipedrive account. You could use this action event in combination with a trigger event such as **New Entry** with Typeform to add company details from new form entries to Pipedrive as Organizations.

- **Update Organization**: You can use this action event when you want to update an existing Organization record in Pipedrive. You must specify the record of an existing Organization by selecting from the drop-down menu, entering the Pipedrive record ID of the existing Organization, not the name, into the **Organization** field, or inserting the ID from previous steps. You can fill the standard fields, **Owner, Name, Address, Label,** and **Visible To,** and any other Organization-specific custom fields unique to your Pipedrive account. You should fill in at least one other field to prevent this step from presenting an error. In order to find the Pipedrive record ID for the Organization, you can use the **Find Organization** search action event using a unique identifier for the record to search for data in a specific field, such as the name. You could use this action event and the search action event in combination with a trigger event such as **New or Updated Spreadsheet Row** with Google Sheets to update custom fields in an Organization record when new details are added to company details in a spreadsheet row.

- **Create Lead**: You can use this action event when you want to create a new Lead record in Pipedrive. You must enter text or insert data from previous steps to add the title of the Lead and associate it with at least one existing Person or Organization. You can optionally fill in the standard fields, **Owner, Note, Label, Expected Close Date, Lead Value,** and **Lead Value Currency.** Lead- or Deal-specific custom fields unique to your Pipedrive account are not currently expressed in this action event. If the **Owner** field is left blank, the authorized user account associated with the Pipedrive – Zapier authenticated connection will be used. If **Lead Value** is filled in, **Lead Value Currency** must be set. You could use this action event in combination with a trigger event such as **New Form Response** with **LinkedIn Lead Gen Forms** to add new form submission contact details as a Lead. Prior to this step, you can use either the **New Person** or **New Organization** action events to create a record of an associated Person or Organization and then map the relevant ID values to the **Create Lead** action event accordingly.

- **Create Deal**: You can use this action event when you want to create a new Deal record in Pipedrive. You must enter text or insert data from previous steps to add the **title** of the Deal, and optionally fill in the standard fields of **Creation Date, Status, Stage, Owner, Organization, Person, Probability, Expected Close Date, Value, Currency, Visible To,** and **Label** and any other Deal-specific custom fields unique to your Pipedrive account. The **Creation Date** field can only be filled in if the authorized user account associated with the Pipedrive – Zapier authenticated connection has admin-level access in Pipedrive. If the **Owner** field is left blank, the authorized user account associated with the Pipedrive – Zapier authenticated connection will be used. You could use this action event in combination with a trigger event such as **New Email** with Email Parser by Zapier to add new parsed email details to Pipedrive as new Deals.

- **Update Deal**: You can use this action event when you want to update an existing Deal record in Pipedrive. You must specify the record of an existing Deal by selecting from the drop-down menu, entering the Pipedrive record ID of the existing Deal, not the title, into the **Deal** field, or inserting this ID from previous steps. You can fill the standard fields of **Title, Status, Stage, Owner, Organization, Person, Value, Currency, Visible To,** and **Label,** and any other Deal-specific custom fields unique to your Pipedrive account. You should fill in at least one other field to prevent this step from presenting an error. In order to find the Pipedrive record ID for the Deal, you can use the **Find Deal** search action event using a unique identifier for the record to search for data in a specified standard or custom field, such as an `Invoice Number` custom field. You could use this action event and the search action event in combination with a trigger event such as **New Payment** with QuickBooks Online to change the Deal status to `Won` when a new payment has been received for a sales invoice.

- **Create Note**: You can use this action event when you want to create a new Note in Pipedrive in a Person, Organization, or Deal record. You must enter text or insert data from previous steps to add details to the **Content** field and fill in at least one of the fields of **Deal, Person,** and **Organization** as their respective Pipedrive record ID, and if appropriate, the relevant fields of **Pin Note On Specified Deal?, Pin Note On Specified Person?,** and **Pin Note On Specified Organization?** to pin the Note to the top of the Activity history panel. The **Content** field supports some basic HTML for formatting purposes. You could use this action event in combination with a trigger event such as **Subscription Paused** or **Subscription Resumed** with ThriveCart to add Notes when changes are made to a customer's subscription.

- **Create Product**: You can use this action event when you want to create a new Product record in Pipedrive. You must enter text or insert data from previous steps to add the **name** of the Product and optionally fill in the standard fields of **Code, Unit, Tax Percentage, Is Active?, Owner, Currency, Price, Cost, Overhead Cost, Description,** and **Visible To,** and any other Product-specific custom fields unique to your Pipedrive account. The **Currency** field defaults to the currency settings in the Pipedrive account if not specified, and the **Price** field can only be filled in if a value has been specified in the **Currency** field. You could use this action event in combination with a trigger event such as **New Product** with Shopify to add new Products to Pipedrive when products are added to your Shopify e-commerce store.

- **Add Product to Deal**: You can use this action event when you want to add a Product to an existing Deal record in Pipedrive. You must specify the record of an existing Deal and Product in the **Deal** and **Product** fields respectively by selecting from the drop-down menu, entering the Pipedrive record ID, not the name or title, or inserting the ID from previous steps. You must also specify the **Price** and **Quantity**. You can fill the standard fields of **Discount Percentage**, **Comments**, and **Is Enabled?**. In order to find the Pipedrive record ID for the Deal and Product, if they are not recorded in your trigger or previous action steps, you can use the **Find Deal search action event**. Use a unique identifier for the record to search for data in a specified standard or custom field, such as `Title`, and **Find Product** using a search term such as the name. You could use this action event and the search action events in combination with a trigger event such as **New Submission** with JotForm to add new products to a Deal when a prospect fills out a survey form and selects a product.

- **Create Activity**: You can use this action event when you want to create a new Activity in Pipedrive in a Person, Organization, or Deal record. You must enter text or insert data from previous steps to add details to the **Subject** field and optionally fill in the standard fields of **Organization, Assign To, Person, Deal, Is Done?, Type, Due Date And Time, Duration**, and **Note**. When filling in the **Organization, Person**, or **Deal** fields, you can specify an existing record by selecting from the drop-down menu, entering the Pipedrive record ID, not the name or title, or inserting the ID from previous steps. If the **Assign To** field is left blank, the Activity will be assigned to the user account associated with the Pipedrive – Zapier authenticated connection. The **Duration** field must be in the format `HH:MM`, and the **Note** field supports some basic HTML for formatting purposes. You could use this action event in combination with a trigger event such as **Updated Deal Stage** with Pipedrive to add Activities to a Deal when it changes to a specific stage. In this case, there is no need to use search actions to find the record IDs; they can be mapped from the trigger step.

- **Update Activity**: You can use this action event when you want to update an existing Activity record in Pipedrive. You must specify the record of an existing Activity by selecting from the drop-down menu, entering the Pipedrive record ID of the existing Activity, not the subject, into the **Activity** field, or inserting the ID from previous steps. You can fill the standard fields of **Is Done?, Subject, Assign To, Deal, Person, Due Date And Time, Duration, Note, Type**, and **Organization**. You should fill in at least one other field to prevent this step from presenting an error. In order to find the Pipedrive record ID for the Activity, you can use the **Find Activity** search action event using the subject as the search term. You could use this action event and the search action event in combination with a trigger event such as **Completed Task** with Asana to mark an Activity status as `Done` when an Asana task is completed.

- **Attach File**: You can use this action event when you want to upload a file and attach it to a Person, Organization, Deal, Activity, Product, or Note record in Pipedrive. You must add the file object or publicly accessible URL of the document you want to upload to the **File** field and add a name to the **File Name** field. When filling in the **Deal**, **Person**, **Organization**, or **Product** fields, you can specify an existing record by selecting from the drop-down menu, entering the Pipedrive record ID, not the name or title, or inserting the ID from previous steps. You can also optionally fill in the **Activity ID** and **Note ID** fields to attach the document to an Activity or Note. In order to find the Pipedrive record ID for the Deal, Person, Organization, or Product, if they are not recorded in your trigger or previous action steps, you can use the **Find Deal**, **Find Person**, **Find Organization** or **Find Product** search action events. You could use this action event in combination with a trigger event such as **Document Completed** with PandaDoc to add completed PDF files to Pipedrive Deals.

- **Add Follower**: You can use this action event when you want to add a Follower file and attach it to a Person, Organization, Deal, or Product record in Pipedrive. You must specify the Pipedrive ID of the User you want to assign as a **Follower**. In the **What To Add Follower To?** field, you can choose a **deal**, **person**, **organization**, or **product** option from the drop-down menu, you can also enter the corresponding text, or map this from previous steps. Once selected, a new field will appear based on the option chosen to show **Deal**, **Person**, **Organization**, or **Product** where you must specify the record of an existing Deal, Person, Organization, or Product by selecting from the drop-down menu, entering the Pipedrive record ID, not the name or title, into that field, or inserting the ID from previous steps. In order to find the Pipedrive record ID for the User, Deal, Person, Organization, or Product, if they are not recorded in your trigger or previous action steps, you can use the **Find User**, **Find Deal**, **Find Person**, **Find Organization**, or **Find Product** search action events. You could use this action event in combination with a trigger event such as **Deal Matching Filter** with Pipedrive to add yourself as a follower when a Deal matches certain conditions.

Once again, in comparison, the HubSpot integration has a similar action event structure with contacts, companies, tasks, and Deal creation and updates; however, it has a much more comprehensive range of action events covering other module components, allowing for more flexibility in your automations. The Salesforce integration may have fewer actions; however, these generally are based on records being grouped together to allow the record type to be selected from a drop-down menu, allowing for significant flexibility covering most Salesforce module properties.

Next, let's have a look at the Pipedrive search action events.

Pipedrive search action events

Before we look at the individual search action events supported with the Pipedrive integration, let's explore the common fields used in most of the search actions:

- **Field To Search By**: This field is used to specify the Pipedrive field that you want to search by. In this field, you can choose a standard or custom field unique to your Pipedrive account from the drop-down menu; you can also enter the corresponding text for the field label, not the field name, or map it from previous steps. You should select a field that represents a unique identifier for the record to search for so that only one record is returned. For example, in the case of a Person record, a field that would represent a unique identifier could be the `Email` field name with a field label of `9041::Email::varchar::email`. This is a required field and must be entered in order for the step to work.

- **Term**: Once you have filled in the **Field To Search By** field, the **Term** field will remain with the field name, for example, **Email**. You must then enter text or insert data from previous steps to add the search, for example, the email address. This is a required field and must be entered for the step to work.

- **Search For An Exact Match?**: Use this Boolean field to select **Yes** or **No** from the drop-down menu; enter text or insert data from previous steps to search for an exact match. If you select **Yes**, a search will return results with the exact spelling of a word ignoring case-sensitive variations. If you select **No**, a search might return variations of the search term. For example, if the search term used is `Solvaa`, if **Yes** is selected, the search would return `Solvaa` or `solvaa` but not `Solvaa - Zapier Experts`, whereas selecting **No** would return `Solvaa - Zapier Experts`. The default for this field is **Yes**.

- **Should This Step Be Considered A "success" When Nothing Is Found**: Use this Boolean field to select **True** or **False** from the drop-down menu; enter text or insert data from previous steps for this step to be considered a "success" if nothing is found in the search. The default for this field is **False**, which you should choose if you want the Zap to stop running at this point if nothing is found, as this is the most common use case. This means that all subsequent steps will be skipped. Use the **True** option when you want to allow the Zap to continue and subsequent steps to run. You can then add more control to your workflows by using Filter by Zapier or Paths by Zapier conditional logic for more control and allowing those steps to pass or stop based on whether the search returned a result or not.

- **Create Pipedrive X if it doesn't exist yet?:** The "X" will be replaced by the entity you want to search for, for example, **Person**. Tick this checkbox if you want a new record to be created if the search does not return an existing record. Once ticked, the step will refresh and display fields, as with a **Create X** action event such as **Create Person**.

Now let's cover the supported search action events that you can use with Pipedrive:

- **Find Person**: You can use this search action event when you want to find a Person in Pipedrive. You must complete the required **Field To Search By** and **Term** fields, and optionally change the default options in the **Search For An Exact Match?** and **Should This Step Be Considered A "success" When Nothing Is Found** fields, and tick the **Create Pipedrive Person if it doesn't exist yet?** box if relevant. If the box is ticked, fill the fields as described in the **Create Person** action event.

- **Find Organization**: You can use this search action event when you want to find an Organization in Pipedrive. You must complete the required **Field To Search By** and **Term** fields, where the default is **Name**. Then, optionally change the default options in the **Search For An Exact Match?** and **Should This Step Be Considered A "success" When Nothing Is Found** fields, and tick the **Create Pipedrive Organization if it doesn't exist yet?** box if relevant. If the box is ticked, fill the fields as described in the **Create Organization** action event.

- **Find Deal**: You can use this search action event when you want to find a Deal in Pipedrive. You must complete the required **Field To Search By** and **Term** fields, where the default is **Title**. Then, optionally change the default options in the **Search For An Exact Match?** and **Should This Step Be Considered A "success" When Nothing Is Found** fields, and tick the **Create Pipedrive Deal if it doesn't exist yet?** box if relevant. If the box is ticked, fill the fields as described in the **Create Person** action event.

- **Find Product**: You can use this search action event when you want to find a Product in Pipedrive by product name or code. You must complete the required **Search Term** field by entering text or inserting data from previous steps. This field is not case-sensitive. Then optionally change the default option in the **Should This Step Be Considered A "success" When Nothing Is Found** field, and tick the **Create Pipedrive Product if it doesn't exist yet?** box if relevant. If the box is ticked, fill the fields as described in the **Create Product** action event.

- **Find Product(s)**: You can use this search action event when you want to find a Product in Pipedrive by Name, Code, or ID. You must complete the required **Field To Search By** and search value **Term(s)** fields, where the default is **Name**. The **Term(s)** field is not case-sensitive and supports line items so that you can search for and return multiple Pipedrive Products. Then, optionally change the default option in the **Should This Step Be Considered A "success" When Nothing Is Found** field.

- **Find Activity**: You can use this search action event when you want to find an Activity in Pipedrive by Subject. You must complete the required **Subject** field where partial sentences are okay to be entered, and Zapier will return the best match. Optionally, fill in the **Assigned To, Type, Filter**, and **Status** fields. Use the **Filter** field to have more control over your search by selecting a relevant Pipedrive Activity filter. The default for the **Status** field is **Not Done**. Then, optionally change the default option in the **Should This Step Be Considered A "success" When Nothing Is Found** field, and tick the **Create Pipedrive Deal if it doesn't exist yet?** box if relevant. If the box is ticked, fill the fields as described in the **Create Activity** action event.

- **Find User**: You can use this search action event when you want to find a User in Pipedrive by Name, Email, or ID. You must complete the required **Field To Search By** and **Term** fields. Then, optionally change the default option in the **Should This Step Be Considered A "success" When Nothing Is Found** field.

As with trigger and action events, in relation to search action events, the HubSpot integration has a much more comprehensive range of action events covering other module components. The Salesforce integration may have fewer search actions available, but they are based on records being grouped together to allow the record type to be selected from a drop-down menu.

Refer to the *Pipedrive action events* section for examples of how to use these search action events followed by Pipedrive action steps.

> Tip
> One of the most useful values that is used within searches, particularly in CRM integrations, is the record ID. For example, when searching for a contact, an email address is likely to be a unique value; however there might be a slight possibility of duplicate contacts within a system. The most reliable value for retrieving a record is the unique ID associated with that record. When assessing what CRM might be appropriate for use in your business, one thing to consider is how robust the API is. A good reference point is whether the integration allows you to retrieve information based on record ID and what range of information you can retrieve.

Next, let's review a few tips for the best use of the Pipedrive integration.

Tips for using the Pipedrive integration

Here are a few tips for successful use of the Pipedrive integration:

- Always check what type of field you are entering or mapping data to, and ensure your data is formatted accordingly. This will ensure data accuracy. You can review the *Understanding field data types* section in *Chapter 3, Building Your First Automated Workflow (Zap)*, for more information on field types.

- When using the **Custom** tab to type in or map data from previous steps into fields that display Pipedrive field options in drop-down menus, such as with **Field To Search By**, use the field label rather than the field name; for example, field name = Name, field label = 0.

- If you are using a combination of Pipedrive trigger and action events in your workflows, bear in mind that if you are mapping ID values, the name may vary between the steps. For example, in a trigger step of **New Note**, id is the Note ID, deal_id is the ID of the associated Deal, and org_id is the ID of the associated Organization. If you then use an action step such as **Create Deal**, the resulting ID would be the Deal ID.

- The Pipedrive integration does not have a specific trigger event that allows you to trigger a workflow when a field is updated, unlike the Salesforce **Updated Field on Record trigger**. A workaround for this involves using workflow automations in Pipedrive, only available on Advanced plans and higher, and filtered lists. You can create a workflow automation in Pipedrive that triggers a Deal being updated, with a filter on one or more fields being changed, and an action to create an activity marked as complete that is used in a filtered list. In the list filter, the specific activity would be already done but due on that day. You can then combine this with the Zapier – Pipedrive trigger **Activity Matching Filter** event to trigger a workflow as appropriate.

- To avoid using search action steps, display values for IDs for Pipedrive records in your other apps that you have connected in workflows, and vice versa. For example, if your Zap involves Pipedrive and Google Sheets, add Pipedrive record IDs to columns in your Google Sheet and Google Sheet row IDs to custom fields in Pipedrive. This allows for more reliability than using search actions.

- Review the Pipedrive API at `https://developers.pipedrive.com/docs/api/v1/#/` for information on other triggers and actions you can perform using Webhooks by Zapier and Code by Zapier. You can hire a Zapier Expert to help you with custom integration work here: `https://experts.zapier.com/`.

- You can view common problems with the Pipedrive integration by navigating to the **Help** tab of the app profile or following this link: `https://zapier.com/help/doc/common-problems-pipedrive`.

Next, let's explore how to set up an example of a multi-step Zap using the Pipedrive integration.

Setting up a multi-step Zap with the Pipedrive integration

To illustrate this, we will use the example of retrieving tomorrow's weather forecast, sending a reminder email to the Deal owner, and adding a Note to Pipedrive when an activity for an in-person meeting is due the next day.

The Zap will involve five steps as follows:

1. *Trigger*: Pipedrive app with the **Activity Matching Filter** trigger event

2. *Action*: Weather by Zapier app with the **Get Tomorrow's Forecast** action event

3. *Search Action*: Pipedrive app with the **Find User** search action event

4. *Action*: Email by Zapier app with the **Send Outbound Email** action event

5. *Action*: Pipedrive app with the **Create Note** action event

The following screenshot shows how your Zap should look once built:

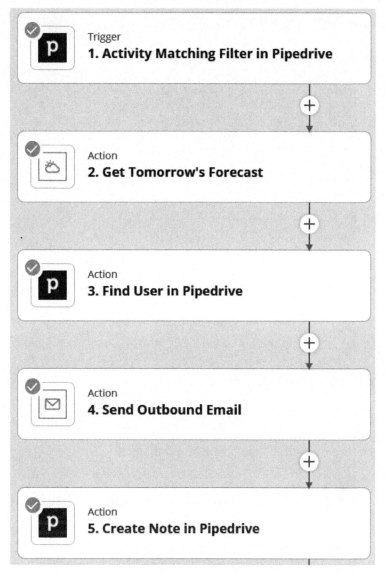

Figure 19.1 – A multi-step Zap using Pipedrive trigger and action events

The Pipedrive filter for this scenario is set up as shown in the following screenshot:

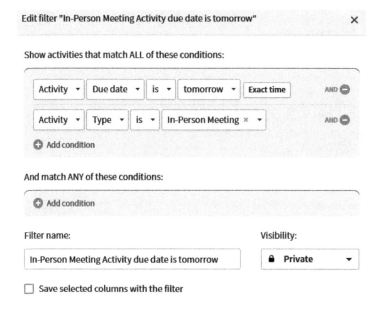

Figure 19.2 – A Pipedrive filter for in-person meetings due the next day (courtesy of Pipedrive)

Let's walk through setting up the Zap step by step, starting with the trigger step.

Setting up step 1 – the trigger step

We will use the Pipedrive app with the **Activity Matching Filter** trigger event as the trigger step. Select the relevant filter from the **Filter ID** drop-down menu.

The following screenshot shows how this step should look:

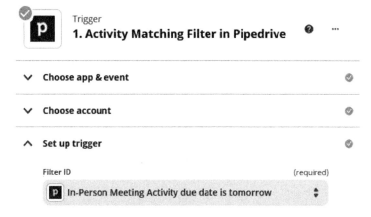

Figure 19.3 – Using Activity Matching Filter in Pipedrive to trigger a workflow

Click on the **Continue** button, then click on the **Test Trigger** button to pull through some sample data.

Next, let's set up the first action step.

Setting up step 2 – the first action step

We will use the Weather by Zapier app with the **Get Tomorrow's Forecast** action event. Follow the instructions in the *Weather by Zapier – using weather conditions in your Zaps* section in *Chapter 10, Other Useful Built-In Apps by Zapier*, to customize this action step to add **Latitude** and **Longitude** for New York, set **Units** as **Fahrenheit**, and leave **Should This Step Be Considered A "success" When Nothing Is Found?** as **False**.

The following screenshot shows how this step should look:

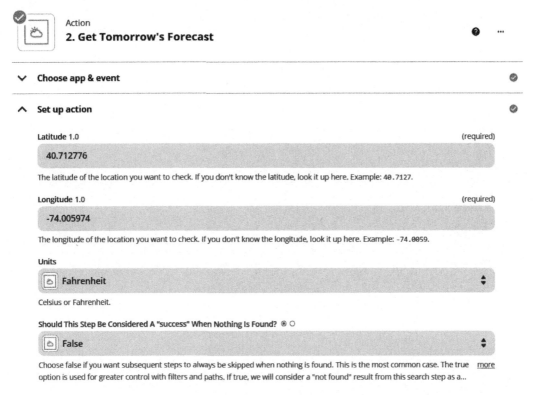

Figure 19.4 – Using the Get Tomorrow's Forecast in Weather by Zapier action event to retrieve the weather forecast for the next day

Click on the **Continue** button. You can then use the **Test action** section to get the forecast.

Next, let's set up the second action step.

Setting up step 3 – the second action step

As the **Activity Matching Filter** trigger step does not retrieve the email address of the user the activity is assigned to, we need to search for the user by name. We will use the Pipedrive app with the **Find User** action event, and we will customize this action step by using the **Name** field in **Field To Search By** and mapping Owner Name from the trigger step into the **Term** (or **Name**) field. Leave **Should This Step Be Considered A "success" When Nothing Is Found?** as **False**.

This is shown in the following screenshot:

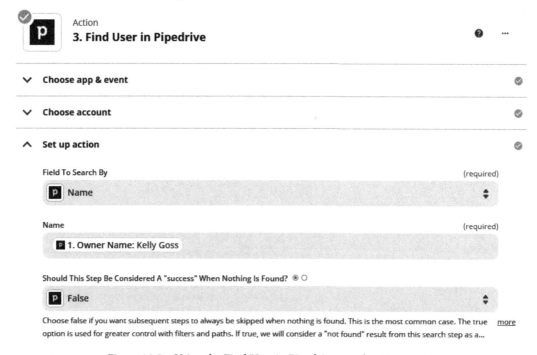

Figure 19.5 – Using the Find User in Pipedrive search action event

Click on the **Continue** button. You can then use the **Test action** section to retrieve the user data. The result from the scenario is shown in the following screenshot:

Figure 19.6 – Details of a user found using the Find User in Pipedrive search action event

Next, let's set up the third action step.

Setting up step 4 – the third action step

We will use the Email by Zapier app with the **Send Outbound Email** action event, and we will customize this action step by completing the **To** field with the User `Email` address from the search action in *step 3*, and customize the **Subject** and **Body (HTML Or Plain)** fields with relevant text and mapped dynamic data from previous steps, as shown in the following screenshot:

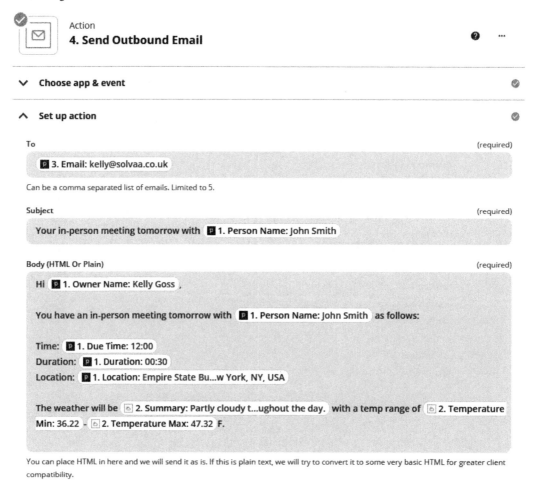

Figure 19.7 – Using the Email by Zapier integration to send a reminder email

Click on the **Continue** button. You can then use the **Test action** section to send the email.

Next, let's set up the final action step.

Setting up step 5 – the fourth action step

Finally, we will add a Note to Pipedrive to the associated Deal, Person, and Organization the Activity is linked to. We will use the Pipedrive app with **Create Note** with text and {{zap_meta_human_now}} to produce the time the Zap runs and add it to the Note. Map Deal ID into the **Deal** field, Person ID into the **Person** field, and Organization ID into the **Organization** field from *step 1*. This is shown in the following screenshot:

Figure 19.8 – Using the Create Note in Pipedrive action event

Click on the **Continue** button. You can then use the **Test action** section to create the Note. The result from the scenario is shown in the following screenshot:

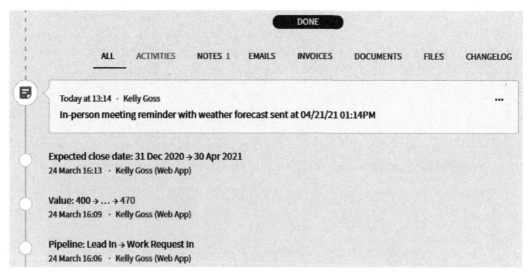

Figure 19.9 – A new Note created in Pipedrive (courtesy of Pipedrive)

You can get access to a copy of this Zap template here: `https://bit.ly/3e5BUkn`.

You should now have a better understanding of how to automate lead management processes with the Pipedrive integration.

Summary

In this chapter, we discussed the different types of sales processes that can be automated with Zapier, and we explored some examples of workflows used with some common sales applications. First, we gave an overview of the types of sales processes that can be automated with Zapier. Then, we covered where to start with automating sales processes with Zapier. Finally, we discussed how to automate contact management with the Pipedrive CRM integration.

You now know how to automate your sales processes with Zapier and specifically with the Pipedrive CRM integration.

In the next chapter, you will learn how to automate your operations workflows. We will discuss some of the different types of operations processes and give working examples of how these processes can be automated using Zapier. We will also provide practical tips on how to solve problems relating to operations workflows.

20
Automating Your Operations Processes

Once you've got the money rolling in with efficient marketing and sales processes, the next important topic to explore is how to automate various business operations processes. Having efficient operations processes will certainly help you and your team to keep things ticking along in the background on autopilot, giving you more time to focus on keeping your customers happy with better customer service and targeted retention activities.

In this chapter, we will discuss some of the different types of operations processes that can be automated with Zapier, and we will provide examples of workflows used with some common operations-focused applications. First, we will give an overview of the types of operations processes that can be automated with Zapier, such as task and project management, storage and organization, communication, and data handling with spreadsheets and databases. Then, we will explore where to start with automating operations processes with Zapier. Finally, we will dive into how to automate online Word document processes with the Google Docs integration to illustrate how operations processes can be automated.

We will cover the following key topics in this chapter:

- An introduction to automating your operations processes with Zapier
- Where to start with automating your operations processes with Zapier
- Automating online word processing processes with the Google Docs integration

Once you have worked through each of these topics, you will have a better understanding of the different operations processes that can be automated with Zapier. You will know how to use Zapier to automate operations processes with some of the most common operations-focused applications.

Technical requirements

To make the most of the content in this chapter, you will need access to a Zapier account. The Zapier Free plan will be required for you to create single-step workflows and use Zapier's pre-built templates. The Zapier Starter plan will be required for you to use Premium apps and to create multi-step workflows.

You can get access to the Zap template used in this chapter here: `https://bit.ly/3e5BUkn`. Using the template will help you to visualize how the process works.

An introduction to automating your operations processes with Zapier

Once you've made those ever-important sales, you need to provide your customers with the product or service that their well-earned money is paying for. Of course, in order for your business to succeed and be competitive, your product or service needs to fulfill a need or solve a problem, and it should be of exceptional quality to ensure your customers come back to buy more. While you can have the best processes in place to market and sell your products and services, and have exceptional offerings with good value for money, if the processes behind production and delivery are extremely manual, repetitive, and error-prone, delivery will be poor, and the customers you worked so hard to find will run a mile. Inefficient operations processes could cause you to have significant delays in responding to customer service queries, or you might forget to respond altogether. It could also mean that you experience order processing delays in stages such as manufacturing or shipping because someone forgot to order a crucial component. Having inefficient and poorly organized operations processes generally creates stress for the team, and ultimately results in more time and expense being spent recruiting new employees because staff leave when their jobs are too difficult.

Once you have the right cloud-based apps in place to help you stay organized and run your business better, being able to automate anything mundane and repetitive will increase productivity among members of the team. You will be able to automate task creation, project updates, document creation, communications internally and with customers or suppliers, document storage, and more with Zapier.

Here is an example of how operations processes can be improved significantly by using connector tools such as Zapier to automate various tasks: `https://solvaa.co.uk/how-iq-glass-saves-45-hours-per-week-with-zapier/`.

Understanding what operations processes can be automated with Zapier

Zapier has integrations with a range of different operations-focused tools spanning numerous functions, allowing you to automate your **business operations processes**. You can connect these apps with thousands of other apps, such as Google Drive, Microsoft 365, Asana, and Wrike to automate your operations processes.

Operations can span many facets of the business, including human resource functions such as recruitment and onboarding, as well as customer support. Although Zapier allows you to automate many operations processes, and we could go further to expand on this topic, we will only skim the surface with a few examples of ones that can be automated with Zapier:

- Task and project management processes
- Document storage processes
- Communication processes
- Word document and spreadsheet processes

Let's explore each one and give some examples of operations-focused apps that can be used with Zapier to automate processes that involve them.

Automating task and project management processes

Whether you're a service business or one that sells physical or digital products, at some point, someone in the business will be making a to-do list of some description. Most of us make lists of the things we need to accomplish, whether this is for personal use or for work. You might still like to record these items on paper or in your Notes app on your smartphone, or in a dedicated task management app. You might use Google Tasks, Todoist, or Microsoft To Do for your task recording and management. Many of these apps can help you with productivity by allowing you to create sub-tasks, set due dates and times, integrate with your calendar, and send yourself alerts. Once you have these apps set up, you can use Zapier to automate various other tasks based on triggers and actions.

With the Microsoft To Do integration, you can trigger workflows when new tasks or lists are created, a task is updated, or a task is completed. You can combine these triggers with action events to send an automated email with Microsoft Outlook, send an SMS with ClickSend SMS, or create tasks in Teamwork Projects, for example. You can also create a task or list, mark a task as complete, find a task, and if one is not found, optionally, create a task. Combine these actions with triggers to add new Facebook Lead Ads as tasks, add tasks when new messages are saved in Slack, or when new notes are added to OneNote.

Task management apps help you maintain individual productivity. However, when you need to manage simple or more complex projects with multiple tasks and categories, and if you need to assign tasks to different members of the team, to customers, or to contractors, it's better to use a dedicated project management app. Although many businesses handle their project management processes on spreadsheets, using a dedicated project management app can, in many scenarios, allow you to visualize your tasks and projects in lists or Kanban views, as well as Gantt charts. These apps also help you display team schedules and availability, manage timelines, and allow notifications, comments, and communications. Trello, Asana, `monday.com`, Teamwork Projects, Zoho Projects, Wrike, and ClickUp are a few examples of project management apps that integrate with Zapier.

With the ClickUp integration, you can trigger workflows when new tasks, folders, or lists are created, or a task changes. You can combine these triggers with action events to create and send an invoice in Xero or create and assign a new task within ClickUp itself. You can also create a task, subtask, folder, or list; add a new checklist to a task; post a comment or attachment to a task; and add time tracked to a task. Combine these actions with triggers such as new starred Gmail emails, new Google Form responses, or new GitHub issues.

There are several task and project management apps that integrate with Zapier, which you can check out at `https://zapier.com/apps/categories/todo-lists` and `https://zapier.com/apps/categories/project-management`.

Next, let's discuss how to automate document storage processes with Zapier.

Automating document storage processes

Every business will have either paper or online documents that they deal with from customers or suppliers, and potentially internally from employees. Organizing your documents in a dedicated storage location means that you will be able to locate documents easily once you have stored them. In days gone by, many businesses used folders and filing cabinet systems to store paper documents, and some businesses may still do this. Nowadays, with the digital age, it's common to store scanned versions of these paper documents or digital documents on a desktop computer or preferably in the cloud in a document storage app where those documents can be accessed from any location. Apps such as Google Drive, Dropbox, OneDrive, and Box are popular online storage solutions, which, once implemented, can be integrated with Zapier so that you can automate document storage. For example, you might receive documents by email that you need to then file in your online document storage app, you might need to store a PDF copy of a contract in a specific location once it has been signed, or you might want to save an image once it has been posted to Facebook Pages.

With OneDrive integration, you can trigger workflows when a new file is added in a folder or when a folder is added. You can combine these triggers with action events to copy new files to another storage app, such as Google Drive or Dropbox, or add new notes to Evernote with attachments, for example. You can also upload a file, create a folder or new text file, search for a file or folder, and if they are not found, optionally create a file or folder. Combine these actions with triggers to upload new Google Docs files, Gmail attachments, or YouTube videos.

With Google Drive integration, you can trigger workflows when a new file is added in any folder, a new file is added to a specific folder, a folder is added, or when a file is updated. You can combine this trigger with action events to send team notifications with Slack or create new Asana tasks, for example. You can also upload a file; create a folder; create a file from text; copy, move, or replace a file; or add file sharing preferences. You can also search for a file or folder, and if it is not found, optionally create a file or folder. Combine these actions with triggers to add new Instagram images, create folders when deals are marked as won in your CRM, or when new Google Calendar events are created in order to back them up.

There are several document storage apps that integrate with Zapier, which you can check out here: https://zapier.com/apps/categories/files.

Next, let's discuss how to automate communication processes with Zapier.

Automating communication processes

Communication is an essential part of any business. We need to be able to communicate with each other internally, communicate with prospective and existing customers, and with suppliers. Communication methods have changed significantly for businesses over the years, where perhaps some time ago the only method was by a face-to-face verbal conversation, by telegragh, telephone, or fax. Now many companies rely on other forms of communication such as email, SMS, telephone calls and voicemail drops, video conferencing, and online messaging tools. You might be using Gmail or Microsoft Outlook for your emails; Slack, Google Hangouts Chat, or Microsoft Teams for team collaboration; Zoom or GoToMeeting for video conferencing; RingCentral for voice calls, sending fax, and SMS; VoodooSMS for sending SMS; and Slybroadcast for voice drops. There is such a broad range of communication apps that integrate with Zapier, enabling you to automate many, if not all, of your communication processes.

Zoom is a video conferencing tool that has become extremely popular as businesses and teams embrace remote working and collaboration. The platform supports video and voice meetings, as well as webinars. With Zoom integration, you can trigger workflows when a new meeting or webinar is created, a new registrant is added to a webinar, or a new recording is completed for a meeting or webinar. You can combine these triggers with action events to add new registrants to ClickFunnels, create new Google Calendar events, or send a notification in Slack. You can also create a new meeting or webinar registrant. You can combine these action events with triggers such as when new Eventbrite orders are created, successful PayPal sales are made, or new Calendly events are created.

Slybroadcast allows you to send voice messages straight to voice mailboxes. This is perfect for sending appointment reminders or verbal company introductions to leads. With Slybroadcast integration, you can send a voicemail message to a person or group of people using an audio file uploaded to your Slybroadcast account or using an audio file URL. You can combine these action events with triggers such as when new contacts are added to Agile CRM, new orders are placed in WooCommerce, or when you enroll a new user on a Teachable course.

There are several communication apps that integrate with Zapier, which you can check out here: `https://zapier.com/apps/categories/communication`.

Next, let's discuss how to automate Word document and spreadsheet processes with Zapier.

Automating Word document and spreadsheet processes

For most businesses, gone are the days of handwriting letters, and using a typewriter or manual word processor to create documents that need to be faxed or posted. These days, companies generally use desktop word processing and presentation packages such as Microsoft Word and Microsoft PowerPoint. A lot more can be achieved by using cloud-based alternatives such as Google Docs or Zoho Writer, for example, as well as Google Slides. Zapier integrates with these cloud-based apps and many more, allowing you to automate your text and presentation document processes.

With Google Slides integration, you can trigger workflows when a new presentation is created. You can combine this trigger with action events such as posting presentations to a Slack channel or tweeting the presentation on Twitter. You can also search for an existing presentation, create a presentation from a template using mail merge placeholder variables, or refresh data for all charts in a presentation linked to a Google Sheets spreadsheet. You can combine these action events with triggers such as when data is parsed from PDFs in Docparser, when deals reach a certain stage in Zoho CRM, or when forms are submitted in Gravity Forms.

As with documents, many businesses have moved away from desktop versions of spreadsheets and databases, allowing them to access the data from anywhere if they are using a cloud-based app such as Google Sheets, Smartsheet, Airtable, Knack, or Microsoft Excel. Using Zapier with these apps allows you to automate processes involving recording, amending, sharing, and reporting on data in these online tools.

With Microsoft Excel integration, you can trigger workflows when a new row is added to a worksheet or table in a spreadsheet, when a row is added or updated, or when a new worksheet is added to a spreadsheet. You can combine these triggers with action events such as creating a new deal in your CRM, adding new rows to a Google spreadsheet, or adding new subscribers to ConvertKit. You can also add a new row to the end of a specific worksheet or table, update a row in a specific worksheet, create a new spreadsheet, search for an existing row by column or value, and optionally create a new row if one is not found. You can combine these action events with triggers such as when new **SurveyMonkey** responses are created, with new **Formstack** submissions, or when **Toggl** time entries are made.

> **Important note**
>
> One thing to bear in mind when using Microsoft Excel integration is that
> Zapier only works with the cloud-based Business Edition of Microsoft Excel
> Online. You can get more information here: `https://zapier.com/`
> `help/doc/how-get-started-microsoft-excel`.

There are many different text document and spreadsheet apps that integrate with Zapier, which you can check out here: `https://zapier.com/apps/categories/documents` and `https://zapier.com/apps/categories/spreadsheets`.

You now understand what kind of operations processes can be automated with Zapier.

Let's now take a look at the essential first steps to take to start automating your operations processes.

Where to start with automating your operations processes with Zapier

It is always good to do some pre-work before you start automating your processes. In *Chapter 2, Preparing to Automate Your Processes*, and *Chapter 3, Building Your First Automated Workflow (Zap)*, we covered a few important points that will help you when you are strategizing your operations workflows, and they are as follows:

1. *Map out your operations processes*: If you don't have a clear idea of how your operations processes work with all your tools, follow the steps in the *Simplifying your processes and assessing what can be automated* section in *Chapter 2, Preparing to Automate Your Processes*, to visually map out your processes so that you have a high-level overview of how your tasks work with your existing software.

2. *List your operations tools*: Make a list of all the operations tools and services that you use in your business to achieve your goals. Then, assess how these tools fit within your mapped-out processes. You will then be able to simplify those processes and decide on what can be automated. Once you have this overview of your processes and tools, you will be better placed to understand where the holes are, and how Zapier can help you to close the gaps and automate your processes.

3. *Review your app profile pages*: In *Chapter 2, Preparing to Automate Your Processes*, we also discussed reviewing your individual app profile pages as the best way to establish how your business apps integrate with Zapier. This will give you insight into the triggers, actions, and searches available to use in your workflows. Make a list of these for quick reference.

4. *Use Zapier's pre-built guided workflow templates*: This is the easiest way to get started with automating your operations processes. These templates are built from workflows that are commonly used by other users. They are perfect for inspiration, quick to set up, and will save you time immediately.

5. *Customize your operations workflows*: Get creative and start building multi-step workflows to achieve more in your automations. Use Zapier's built-in apps to help you do more and connect your operations workflows to other parts of your business processes, such as your invoicing process.

You'll be well on your way to creating operations automations for your business.

> **Tip**
> If you're looking for ideas of other operations-focused apps to use in your business, you can review the various categories in the app ecosystem library to give you a list of public apps that integrate with Zapier here: `https://zapier.com/apps/`. Review the *A brief guide to choosing new apps for your business* section in *Chapter 2, Preparing to Automate Your Processes*, for guidance on choosing new apps.

You now know how to get started with automating your operations processes with Zapier.

Let's get more specific and discuss how online Word document processes can be automated using Zapier's Google Docs integration.

Automating online Word document processes with the Google Docs integration

Zapier currently integrates with 20 apps in the Google suite of tools, including Google Sheets, Gmail, Google Drive, Google Docs, Google Analytics, and Google Ads. Google Docs is a popular online word processor app that allows you to create and edit text documents as well as to invite and collaborate with other people. Collaborators can make changes and add comments in real time. You can also upload a Word document and convert it to a Google Docs format, view your document's revision history, and translate the document into different languages. You can download documents in other file formats, such as Word, RTF, PDF, HTML, OpenOffice, or as a `.zip` file, or email documents as attachments. If you're a die-hard fan of Microsoft Word, but want a cloud-based word processor with similar features and functions with the added bonus of being able to collaborate in real time and integrate it with connector tools such as Zapier, you won't go wrong with Google Docs.

You can use Zapier's Google Docs integration to add power to your online Word document processes by connecting Google Docs to thousands of other apps so that you can automate many parts of your business processes. The Google Docs integration currently supports two trigger events, four action events, and one search action event. Let's review each of these.

Google Docs trigger events

The following is a list of supported trigger events that you can use with Google Docs with examples of when to use them:

- **New Document**: This event triggers when a new document is added inside any folder. There is a large amount of trigger data retrieved, such as the file `id` and `title`, file `ownerNames` and user details such as `emailAddress`, useful links for sharing or embedding the file such as with the `alternateLink` field, and the storage folder `parents_id`. The content of the file in plain text format is displayed in the `file_raw_plaintext_content` field or HTML format in the `file_raw_html_content` field. The document can be automatically downloaded using export fields such as `exportLinks__application/rtf` to download it as an RTF file. The document will also be available in several file formats, such as a PDF in the `file_pdf` field or as a text document in the `file_docx` field, allowing you to use these files in action steps when the field displays (`Exists but not shown`). You can use this trigger event in your automations when you want to forward a copy of the document, or extract the content of the document and add it to another app. For example, combine this trigger event with an action event such as **Send Email** with Gmail to send an email with a PDF of the document attached, or the **Update Record** with Salesforce to update a field in an opportunity with the direct URL for the document.

- **New Document in Folder**: This event triggers when a new document is added to a specified folder. In the **Folder** field, choose the folder from your connected account from the drop-down menu or insert data from previous steps matching the folder ID. Keep clicking the dropdown to go inside folders to select subfolders. This trigger does not work with documents being added to subfolders within the specified folder, therefore, it is important to be specific as to which folder you want the Zap to trigger on if new documents are added. If nothing is selected, the default will be the top-level `root` folder. The trigger data supplied is similar to the **New Document** trigger. You can use this trigger event in your automations similarly to the **New Document** trigger, but when you want to be specific about the document location. For example, combine this trigger event with an action event such as **Create Expense** with FreshBooks Classic when a new supplier bill is added to your **Expenses** folder.

Next, let's have a look at Google Docs action events.

Google Docs action events

The following is a list of supported action events that you can use with Google Docs with examples of when to use them:

- **Create Document from Text**: You can use this action event to create a new document from text or limited HTML. You must use the drop-down menu to select the document, or enter text or insert data from previous steps to specify what you want to name the document in the **Document Name** field. Then enter text or map data from previous steps to fill the **Document Content** field with the text you want to add to the document. You can use plain text and basic HTML to format the text and add links. Attempting to insert tables or images may not work. In the **Folder** field, choose the folder from your connected account from the drop-down menu or insert data from previous steps matching the folder ID to specify the storage location for the new document. Keep clicking the dropdown to go inside folders to select subfolders. If nothing is selected, the default will be the top-level `root` folder. You could use this action event in combination with a trigger event such as **New Email** with Microsoft Outlook to back up your emails by creating a Google Docs file, or **Meeting Stop** with **Solid** to add meeting notes to new Google Docs documents.

- **Upload Document**: You can use this action event to copy an existing file from another app and add it as a Google Docs file. Zapier will try to convert the file to Google Docs format where possible. You must add the file object of the file you want to upload by entering text or inserting data from previous steps in the **File** field. This field will not work with a publicly accessible file URL. By default, the new file will be named with the same name as the original file without the file extension. If you want to rename the document, then enter text or map data from previous steps to fill the **Specify Document Name** field. In the **Folder** field, choose the folder from your connected account from the drop-down menu or insert data from previous steps matching the folder ID to specify the storage location for the new document. Keep clicking the dropdown to go inside folders to select subfolders. If nothing is selected, the default will be the top-level `root` folder. You could use this action event in combination with a trigger event such as **New File in Folder** with Dropbox to copy new documents to Google Docs or **New Note** with Evernote to copy new note files to Google Docs.

- **Append Text to Document**: You can use this action event when you want to append text to the end of an existing Google Docs document. In the **Folder** field, choose the folder from your connected account from the drop-down menu or insert data from previous steps matching the folder ID. Keep clicking the dropdown to go inside folders to select subfolders. If nothing is selected, the default will be the top-level `root` folder. You must use the drop-down menu to select the document, or enter text or insert data from previous steps to specify the ID of the document in the **Document Name** field, not the actual name of the document. Then enter text or map data from previous steps to fill the **Text To Append** field. Use this action step in combination with the **Find Document** search action for greater accuracy of specifying the existing document. You could use this action event in combination with a trigger event such as **New Comment** with WordPress to add new comments to the end of a specified Google Docs document, or **New Entry** with **Cognito Forms** to back up form entries to a specified Google Docs document.

- **Create Document from Template**: You can use this action event when you want to create a new document from an existing template document. You can insert custom mail merge placeholder variables such as `{{name}}`, `{{email}}`, and `{{phone_number}}` into the template document, which you can specify to replace when the document is created. In the **Folder** field, choose the folder from your connected account from the drop-down menu or insert data from previous steps matching the folder ID to specify the storage location for the new document. Keep clicking the dropdown to go inside folders to select subfolders. If nothing is selected, the default will be the top-level `root` folder. Select this field first as the storage location for the new file must contain the template. In the **Template Document** field, use the drop-down menu, add text, or map data from previous fields to specify the ID of the template document, not the document name. Then, enter text or insert data from previous steps to specify what you want to name the new document in the **Document Name** field. Fill the **Sharing Preference** field using the drop-down menu, or enter text or map data from previous fields with the correct field labels to allow third parties to access the document as a `reader`, `writer`, or `commenter`, via direct links, exports, or embedded links. If left blank, the default will be that of your Google Drive default sharing preferences. Use the **Unused Fields Preference** field to specify whether you want to `keep` or `remove` any unused template fields. If you choose `keep`, they will remain unedited, for example, `{{name}}`, `remove` to leave no text, or replace them with a custom fallback value. You could use this action event in combination with a trigger event such as **Updated Deal Stage** with Pipedrive to create proposals, quotes, or invoices from templates when a deal reaches a certain stage, or **New Row** with Smartsheet to add details to a new document from a template.

Next, let's have a look at Google Docs search action events.

Google Docs search action events

Google Docs only has one supported search action event, which is **Find Document**. You can use this search action event when you want to find a Google Docs document. Complete the following fields to use this search action:

- **Folder**: Optionally, complete this field using the drop-down menu or enter text or map data from previous steps to specify the folder ID, not the name. If you specify a folder, subfolders within that folder will not be searched, only the main folder.

- **Document Name**: You must then enter text or insert data from previous steps to specify the name of the document you want to search for, and in this case, not the document ID. This is a required field and must be entered in order for the step to work.

- **Should This Step Be Considered A "success" When Nothing Is Found**: Use this Boolean field to select **True** or **False** from the drop-down menu, enter text, or insert data from previous steps for this step to be considered a "success" if nothing is found in the search. The default for this field is **False**, which you should choose if you want the Zap to stop running at this point if nothing is found, as this is the most common use case. This means that all subsequent steps will be skipped. Use the **True** option when you want to allow the Zap to continue and subsequent steps to run. You can then add more control to your workflows by adding Filter by Zapier or Paths by Zapier conditional logic for more control and allowing those steps to pass or stop based on whether the search returned a result or not.

- **Create Google Docs Document if it doesn't exist yet?**: Tick this checkbox if you want a new document to be created if the search does not return an existing record. Once ticked, the step will refresh and display a **Document Content** field.

- **Document Content**: Enter text or map data from previous steps to fill this field with the text you want to add to the document. You can use plain text and basic HTML to format the text and add links. Attempting to insert tables or images may not work.

You can use this search action event when you want to search for documents to use in other steps. It can be combined with Google Docs actions to make document specification more accurate as you can retrieve the document ID.

> **Tip**
> In Google Docs action steps, always use the ID of the file or folder when mapping dynamic data from previous steps or entering text into the **Document Name** or **Folder** fields respectively, rather than the name.

You can view common problems with the Google Docs integration by navigating to the **Help** tab of the app profile or following this link: `https://zapier.com/help/doc/common-problems-google-docs`.

Next, let's explore how to set up an example of a multi-step Zap using the Google Docs integration.

Setting up a multi-step Zap with the Google Docs integration

To illustrate this, we will use the example of creating a new onboarding document in Google Docs from a template when a row containing contact details is updated in a Google spreadsheet with the date the contact became a customer. Once the template has been created, an email with the document link and a PDF copy will be sent to the contact.

The Zap will involve five steps, as follows:

1. *Trigger*: The Google Sheets app with the **New or Updated Spreadsheet Row Filter** trigger event

2. *Action*: The Formatter by Zapier app with the **Text** action event and **Split** transform option

3. *Action*: The Google Docs app with the **Create Document from Template** action event

4. *Search Action*: The URL Shortener by Zapier app with the **Shorten URL** action event

5. *Action*: The Gmail app with the **Send Email** action event

The following screenshot shows how your Zap should look once built with some step title editing:

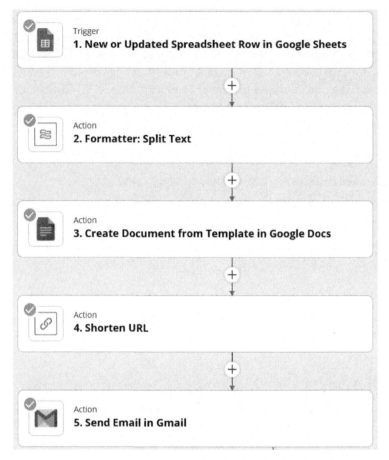

Figure 20.1 – A multi-step Zap using a Google Docs action event

Let's walk through setting up the Zap step by step, starting with the trigger step.

Setting up step 1 – the trigger step

The Google Sheet spreadsheet we are using as part of the trigger step looks as follows:

	A	B	C	D	E
1	Name	Email	Company Name	Products	Date signed
2	Freddie Mercury Jnr.	freddie@suppleleopardco.com	Supple Leopard Co.	Automation consulting and workflow building	04/25/2021
3					

Figure 20.2 – Using a Google spreadsheet to trigger when a field is updated

Once the `Date signed` column is updated with the date, the Zap will trigger. We will use the Google Sheets app with the **New or Updated Spreadsheet Row** trigger event as the trigger step. Select the relevant document and specify the worksheet in the **Spreadsheet** and **Worksheet** fields. We want the Zap to trigger only when the `Date signed` column is updated in the sheet and therefore, we will select that column from the drop-down menu of the **Trigger Column** field.

The following screenshot shows how this step should look:

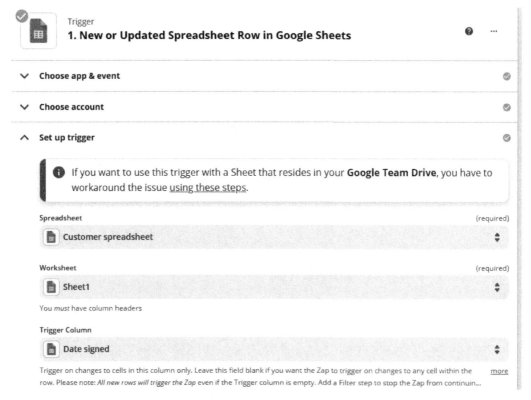

Figure 20.3 – Using the New or Updated Spreadsheet in Google Sheets trigger event

Click on the **Continue** button, then click on the **Test Trigger** button to pull through some test data.

Next, let's set up the first action step.

Setting up step 2 – the first action step

We want to extract the first name of the contact from the full name so that we can personalize the document and email with a less formal salutation. We will, therefore, use the Formatter by Zapier app with the **Text** action event and **Split Text** transform option to accomplish this. Follow the instructions in the *Splitting characters or words into segments* section in *Chapter 16, Text Formatting Functions in Zapier – Part 2*, to customize this action step to map the Name dynamic data from *step 1* to the **Input** field and select as First for **Segment Index**.

The following screenshot shows how this step should look:

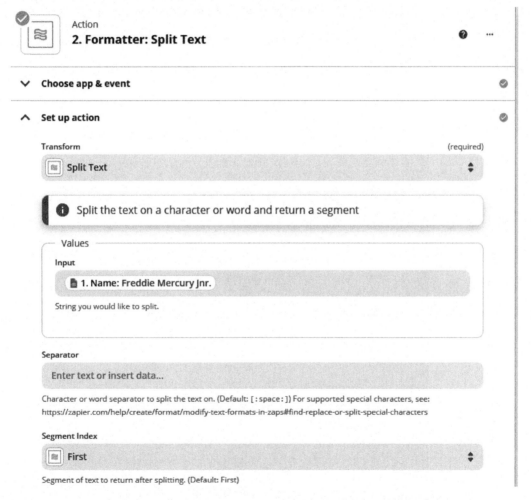

Figure 20.4 – Using the Text action event with the Split transform option
of Formatter by Zapier to split off the first name

Click on the **Continue** button. You can then use the **Test action** section to split out the first name.

Next, let's set up the second action step.

Setting up step 3 – the second action step

Firstly, we need to create and name the Google Docs template and store it in a specific folder location, which in this example, we will name `Templates`. Next, create custom mail merge fields as appropriate for the fields you want to add to the template. In this example, we will use `{{name}}`, `{{company}}`, `{{date}}`, and `{{products}}`, however, you can name them as you please. Our Google Docs template for this scenario is set up as shown in the following screenshot:

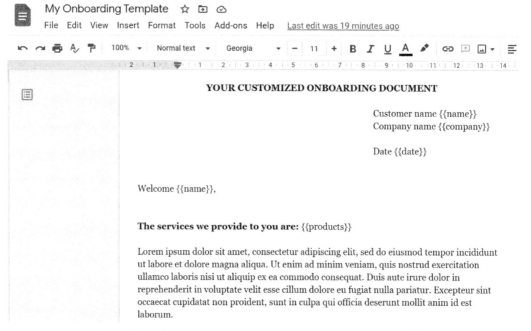

Figure 20.5 – A Google Docs template created with mail merge fields

Next, follow these steps to customize the action step:

1. Select the TEMPLATES folder from the drop-down menu in the **Folder For New Document** field so that we can locate the template we want to use. You can change this to a new location once your template document is retrieved if you want to store the new documents in another folder.

2. In the **Template Document** field, use the drop-down menu to select the template, in this case, My Onboarding Template.

3. Then map in the Company Name data from *step 1* and type the text onboarding plan into the **Document Name** field.

4. Select the **Anyone with link can view** option from the drop-down menu of the **Sharing Preference** field so that the contact can view the document.

5. Select the **Keep** option in the **Unused Fields Preference** field as the data will always be available.

6. Complete the custom mail merge fields by mapping dynamic data from *step 1* and the formatted text output from *step 2* accordingly, as shown in the following two screenshots:

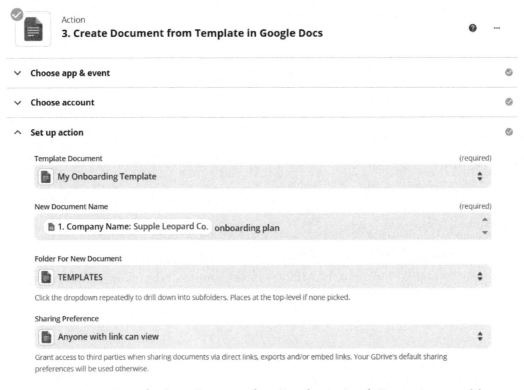

Figure 20.6 – Using the Create Document from Template in Google Docs action event (1)

The second part of the action step is shown in the following screenshot:

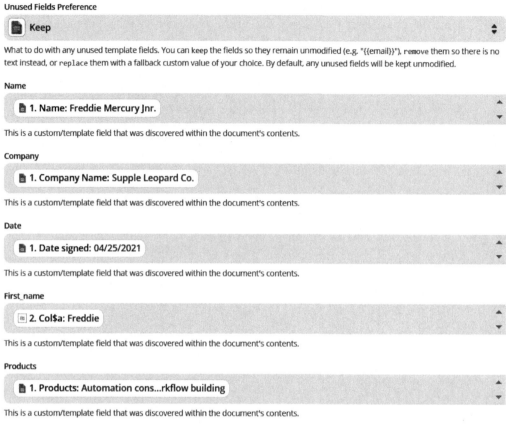

Unused Fields Preference

📄 Keep

What to do with any unused template fields. You can keep the fields so they remain unmodified (e.g. "{{email}}"), remove them so there is no text instead, or replace them with a fallback custom value of your choice. By default, any unused fields will be kept unmodified.

Name

📄 1. Name: Freddie Mercury Jnr.

This is a custom/template field that was discovered within the document's contents.

Company

📄 1. Company Name: Supple Leopard Co.

This is a custom/template field that was discovered within the document's contents.

Date

📄 1. Date signed: 04/25/2021

This is a custom/template field that was discovered within the document's contents.

First_name

🗔 2. Col$a: Freddie

This is a custom/template field that was discovered within the document's contents.

Products

📄 1. Products: Automation cons...rkflow building

This is a custom/template field that was discovered within the document's contents.

Figure 20.7 – Using the Create Document from Template in Google Docs action event (2)

7.   Click on the **Continue** button. You can then use the **Test action** section to create the document. The result from the scenario is shown in the following screenshot:

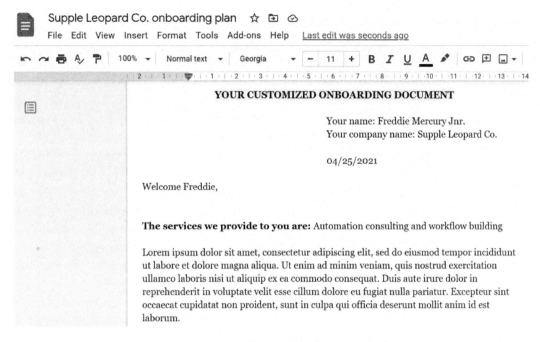

Figure 20.8 – A Google Doc created from a template

Next, let's set up the third action step.

Setting up step 4 – the third action step

We want to be able to share the document link with the customer, however, we want to make it shorter and more visually pleasing. We will, therefore, use the URL Shortener by Zapier app with the **Shorten URL** action event to accomplish this. Follow the instructions mentioned in the *URL Shortener by Zapier – Shortening URLs in your Zaps* section in *Chapter 10, Other Useful Built-In Apps by Zapier* to customize this action step to map the `Alternate Link` data from the action in *step 3*, which is a sharable link.

The following screenshot shows how this step should look:

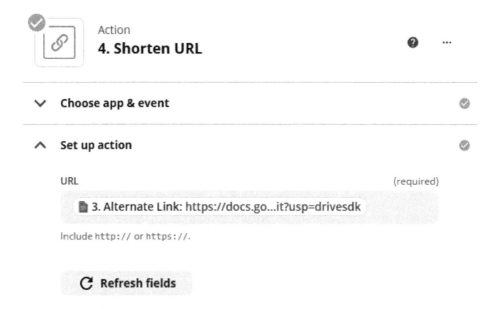

Figure 20.9 – Using the URL Shortener by Zapier integration to shorten a URL

Click on the **Continue** button. You can then use the **Test action** section to create the shortened URL.

Next, let's set up the final action step.

Setting up step 5 – the fourth action step

Finally, we want to send an email with the document URL and a PDF attachment to the contact. We will use the Gmail app with the **Send Email** action event, and we will customize this action step as follows:

1. Complete the **To** field by mapping the Email address dynamic data from *step 1* of your Zap.

2. Use the **From** and **Signature** drop-down fields to select the email address and signature to use from your Gmail account.

3. Customize the **Subject** and **Body (HTML or Plain)** fields with relevant text and mapped dynamic data for the first name from *step 2* and the shortened URL from *step 4* of your Zap.

4. Map the Export Links Application/pdf dynamic data from *step 3* to the **Attachments** field.

This is shown in the following three screenshots:

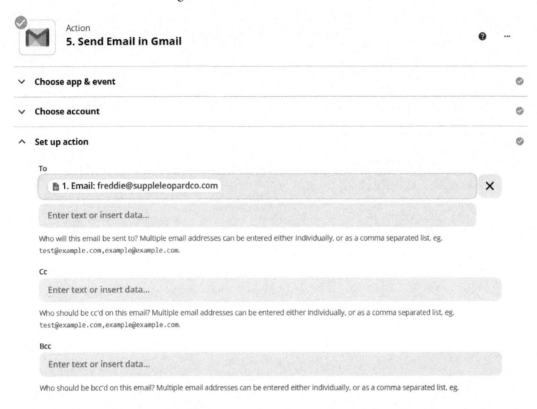

Figure 20.10 – Using Gmail integration to send an email with links and attachments (1)

The second part of the action step is shown in the following screenshot:

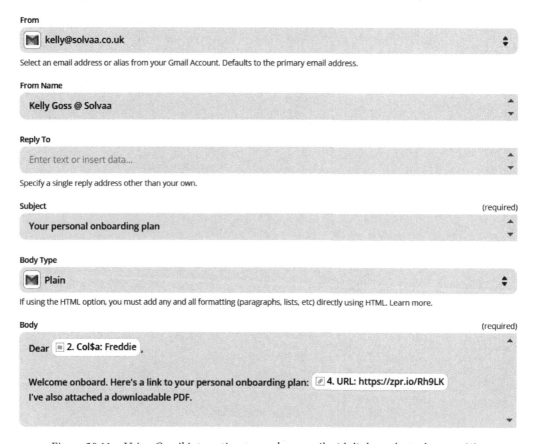

Figure 20.11 – Using Gmail integration to send an email with links and attachments (2)

The third part of the action step is shown in the following screenshot:

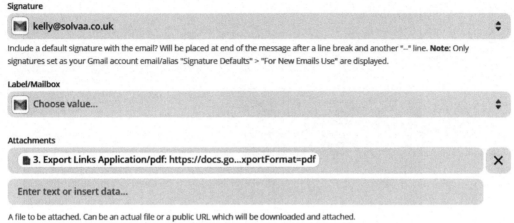

Figure 20.12 – Using Gmail integration to send an email with links and attachments (3)

5. Click on the **Continue** button. You can then use the **Test action** section to send the email.

The following are two screenshots of the resulting email:

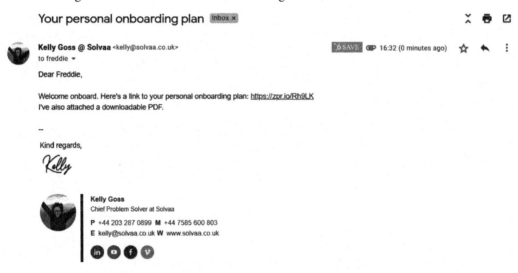

Figure 20.13 – The email sent to the contact showing the link (1)

The second part of the email with the attachment is shown in the following screenshot:

Figure 20.14 – The email sent to the contact showing the attachment (2)

If you are unable to view the file as a PDF, check and adjust your Google Drive sharing preferences. You can get access to a copy of this Zap template here: `https://bit.ly/3e5BUkn`.

You should now have a better understanding of how to automate online Word document processes with the Google Docs integration.

Summary

In this chapter, we discussed the different types of operations processes that can be automated with Zapier, and we covered some examples of workflows used with some common operations-focused applications. First, we gave an overview of some of the types of operations processes that can be automated with Zapier. Then, we explored where to start with automating operations processes with Zapier. Finally, we discussed how to automate online Word document processes with the Google Docs integration.

You now know how to automate your operations processes with Zapier, and specifically with the Google Docs integration.

In the next chapter, you will learn how to automate your finance and reporting workflows. We will discuss some of the different types of finance and reporting processes and give working examples of how these processes can be automated using Zapier. We will also provide practical tips on how to solve problems relating to finance and reporting workflows.

21
Automating Your Finance and Reporting Processes

So far, we've covered how to automate three essential business functions, namely, marketing, sales, and operations. Having efficient processes in those three areas directly impacts your finance processes as more leads are converted into sales, which are then smoothly served, which means that there are more accounting transactions to handle. Automating your finance processes therefore means that as you scale, you can handle larger volumes of transactions quicker and more accurately, thereby giving you access to real-time financial performance data.

Once you've got a better handle on your accounting processes, you can focus on getting better visibility of the higher-quality data coming from all aspects of your business by automating reporting processes. Having access to this up-to-date and accurate data allows you to proactively gain insights into business performance when you need to, without much manual intervention. You can easily produce management reports for key stakeholders and analyze the business for weaknesses and opportunities for improvement.

In this chapter, we will discuss the different types of finance and reporting processes that can be automated with Zapier, and we will provide examples of workflows used for some common applications. First, we will give an overview of the types of finance processes that can be automated with Zapier, such as handling sales and purchase invoices and managing online payment transactions. Then, we will give an overview of the types of reporting processes that can be automated with Zapier, such as creating datasets for reporting on and visualizing business performance data. After that, we will look at where to start with automating finance and reporting processes with Zapier. Finally, we will dive into how to automate accounting processes with the Xero integration.

We will cover the following key topics in this chapter:

- An introduction to automating your finance processes with Zapier

- An introduction to automating your reporting processes with Zapier

- Where to start with automating your finance and reporting processes with Zapier

- Automating accounting processes with the Xero integration

Once you have worked through each of these topics, you will have a better understanding of the different finance and reporting processes that can be automated with Zapier. You will know how to use Zapier to automate finance and reporting processes for some of the most common applications.

Technical requirements

To make the most of the content in this chapter, you will need access to a Zapier account. The Zapier Free plan will be required for you to create single-step workflows and use Zapier's pre-built templates. The Zapier Starter plan will be required for you to use Premium apps and to create multi-step workflows.

You can get access to the Zap templates used in this chapter here: `https://bit.ly/3e5BUkn`. Using the templates will help you to visualize how the process works.

An introduction to automating your finance processes with Zapier

Many businesses struggle with the drudgery of keeping their financial records up to date. In fact, bookkeeping is one of the tasks that many business owners leave to the last minute if they don't have a dedicated bookkeeper or accounting team. We would like to think that most businesses are now completely paperless in their approach to keeping their finances under control; however, sometimes you can't avoid having paper copies of purchases and expenses. And even when a business can move to a completely digital accounting management system by receiving all purchase invoices from suppliers by email, using expense management tools that allow you to take photographs of your expense purchases, and creating digital sales invoices and sending them to customers by email, the process of recording all of this data in one place can still be a manual, repetitive, time-consuming, and extremely error-prone process.

With advances in using native integrations between apps and using connector tools such as Zapier to connect other parts of your business processes to finance-specific tools, businesses are now able to quickly and accurately create purchase invoices and receipts, create and send sales invoices, and allocate payments to existing invoices – all this alongside attaching copies of the original transaction, if required. Improving these processes ultimately increases the efficiency and accuracy of real-time financial reporting.

Here is an example of how finance processes can be improved significantly by using native integrations and connector tools such as Zapier to automate various tasks: `https://solvaa.co.uk/optimising-xero-to-deliver-cost-and-time-savings/`.

Understanding what finance processes can be automated with Zapier

Zapier has many integrations, with a range of finance tools that allow you to automate your **finance processes** with ease and accuracy. You can connect these finance apps to thousands of other apps, such as Salesforce, Shopify, Google Drive, and Microsoft Excel, to automate all parts of your business processes, including your finance processes.

Here are a couple of examples of finance processes that can be automated with Zapier:

- Invoice management and accounting workflows
- Payment processing workflows

Let's explore each one and give some examples of finance apps that can be used with Zapier to automate the processes involved.

Automating invoice management and accounting processes

As a typical business, you will most likely need to deal with bills from suppliers and expense transactions, such as when you buy lunch at a restaurant for your clients, or when your sales teams travel and incur hotel and subsistence costs and collect receipts. You can automate the creation of these purchase invoices and expenses in your accounting app by automatically forwarding emails with attachments to **OCR** (short for **Optical Character Recognition**) apps such as **Dext** (previously called **ReceiptBank**) and **Hubdoc**. These OCR apps transcribe the details on the invoices and push the data straight into accounting apps such as Xero and QuickBooks Online.

Dext has an integration with Zapier, allowing you to trigger workflows when processed receipt data is available, receipt data is ready for export, and processed receipt notifications occur. You can combine these triggers with action events to create new invoices or bills in your accounting software or add the information to a Google Sheets spreadsheet. You can also submit receipts or sales invoices, check the number of process receipts, and create a new client account, if you're using a partner account. You can combine these actions with triggers such as new files being added to Google Drive or Box or new emails with attachments being received. Alternatively, if you are using an OCR app such as Hubdoc that doesn't have a Zapier integration, you can use the Gmail or Microsoft Outlook – Zapier integrations with the **New Labeled Email** or **New Email** trigger events, respectively, to forward emails with an attachment to an email address linked to the OCR app.

If you're using expense management apps such as **Expensify**, you can automate expense handling processes with Zapier by organizing receipts, creating reports, and exporting data to your accounting app. With the Expensify integration, you can trigger workflows when a new report is created. You can combine this trigger with action events to add or create purchase invoices for contractors in Xero or Quickbooks Online, or email copies of expense reports to a manager. You can also create a single expense item, create an expense report, export a report to PDF, and find a report. Combine these actions with triggers so as to create expense items from new Dropbox files or Google Sheets spreadsheet rows.

Dedicated invoice apps such as Zoho Invoice, **Invoice Ninja**, and **InvoiceBerry** allow you to create invoices on the fly and send them to customers. They also allow you to keep track of your accounts receivable processes with useful dashboards and analytics, often to take payments and send reminders. These apps integrate with Zapier, thereby allowing you to automate invoice creation and a number of other functions.

With Zoho Invoice integration, you can trigger workflows when a new contact, point of contact, estimate, item, invoice, or project is created. You can combine these triggers with action events to add invoice or estimate details to Smartsheet or send an invoice to a contact with Email by Zapier. You can also create a new contact, point of contact, estimate, item, or invoice, as well as search for an invoice. Combine these with trigger events so as to create contacts when a deal is won in ActiveCampaign or add invoices when new appointments are booked in Acuity Scheduling or Calendly.

If, on the other hand, you're using a dedicated accounting app such as Xero, Quickbooks Online, Freshbooks Classic, or Zoho Books to manage all of your accounts payable and receivable processes in one place, you can use Zapier to automate a large number of finance processes and then streamline other business processes that involve them. Each of these apps integrates with Zapier and offers many trigger, action, and search action events. The Zapier integrations with accounting apps generally have line-item support, allowing you to create multiple rows of data in sales invoices, bills, and expenses.

With the Quickbooks Online integration, you can use 13 trigger, 20 action, and 5 search action events. There are so many that we will only give a few examples of what you can do with this integration. You can trigger workflows when a new account, customer, estimate, invoice, sales receipt, payment, vendor, bill, or purchase order is added, a new payment is received, or when a customer record is updated. You can combine these triggers with action events to add new rows to a Microsoft Excel sheet, create new orders in Shipstation, or update a deal or opportunity in your CRM, for example. You can also create a new customer, estimate, invoice, sales receipt, refund receipt, credit memo, product or service, payment, vendor, bill, time activity, or purchase order, send an invoice or sales receipt, and update a customer or invoice. Combine these actions with triggers so as to create invoices and payments when new payments are confirmed in Stripe or Paypal, or to create new customers when form entries are submitted in Gravity Forms or **Wufoo**. You can also search for or create a customer or vendor, and you can find an account, invoice, product, or group of products.

The power of using automations in your finance processes is really highlighted if your business has a large volume of sales transactions – for example, if the business sells popular digital products and services such as courses and memberships through an e-commerce platform such as Shopify, Woocommerce, Kajabi, or Thinkific. Being able to automate the creation of sales invoices in your accounting app is literally a game-changer for many businesses, reducing bookkeeping time significantly. You can refer to the *Automating eCommerce processes* section in *Chapter 19, Automating Your Sales Processes*, for more information.

There are a few accounting and invoicing apps that integrate with Zapier, which you can check out at `https://zapier.com/apps/categories/accounting` and `https://zapier.com/apps/categories/invoices`.

Next, let's discuss how to automate payment processing processes with Zapier.

Automating payment processing processes

We've just touched on how you can use Zapier to automate the creation of sales invoices in your invoicing or accounting apps. Having accurate records of your sales is extremely important to any business, but what might be even more important is making sure that you're being paid as quickly as possible for your sales. Using online payment solutions to automatically take payments for invoices or allow customers to pay those invoices without having to do a bank transfer improves invoice payment times and cashflow in the business. Stripe and Paypal are two of the most popular online payment solutions that integrate with many invoicing and e-commerce apps.

With the Paypal integration, you can trigger workflows when a successful sale has been made, a sale is refunded, or any merchant transaction occurs. You can combine these triggers with action events to create new contacts in ActiveCampaign and add them to an automation, send post-sale or refund emails with Gmail, add new invoices or credit notes to Xero, or add records of sales to a Google Sheets spreadsheet.

Many businesses have embraced the opportunities for recurring revenue based on providing memberships, clubs, and product subscriptions. This might involve paying a monthly subscription for your favorite chocolate bar or health food products, or an annual subscription linked to an online course-support community. There are several subscription management tools, such as **Chargebee**, **Recurly**, and **Chargify**, that help you to manage recurring payments.

With the Chargify integration, you can trigger workflows when a new subscription or invoice is created, a new customer added, and when a subscription changes state or is updated. Combine these triggers with action events to get notifications in Slack or in Microsoft Outlook, update contacts in Mailchimp, or add tasks to Asana. You can also create a customer, coupon, and product price point and create or update a subscription. You can combine these actions with triggers so that you can create new subscriptions when a row is updated in SmartSheet or new contacts are added to Salesforce. You can add search actions to find a product, product family, or component, and optionally create a subscription or customer if one doesn't exist.

Using digital banking solutions such as **Revolut Business** can also improve efficiencies by allowing you to automate many finance-related processes. With the Revolut Business integration, you can trigger workflows when you exchange, send, or receive money. Combine this trigger with action steps such as sending notifications using Email by Zapier when you receive money. You can also search for an account, allowing you to retrieve information when, for example, you send money in Revolut Business and then add the details to a Google Sheets spreadsheet.

Once again, being able to automate payment notifications in your accounting app, especially where high volumes of transactions are concerned, increases productivity in bookkeeping processes significantly.

There are many payment processing apps that integrate with Zapier, which you can check out here: `https://zapier.com/apps/categories/payment-processing`.

You now understand what kind of finance processes can be automated with Zapier.

Let's now take a look at automating reporting processes with Zapier.

An introduction to automating your reporting processes with Zapier

Now that you have taken the time to simplify and automate your marketing, sales, operations, and finance processes, it's crucial to understand how all of these key areas perform against key performance indicators and metrics. Businesses can only make good decisions if they have up-to-date and accurate reporting information to hand. If this information is available instantly, you won't have to spend hours downloading and manipulating data to present it to key decision makers; they will have top-level critical data on demand.

With advances in technology, businesses no longer have to rely on hand-produced bar graphs and charts to visualize business performance data. Spreadsheet tools have become advanced reporting tools in themselves, allowing complex calculations and data manipulation. Many of the apps that we use for various business functions have their own reporting modules that enable the business to extract useful reports and visualize reporting data internally. The issue businesses then have is that their reporting exists in multiple systems and tools and still needs to be collated and condensed so that you have fewer places to log in to and view your important reporting data. Automation using tools such as Zapier can help you to get your key data into the right places for enhancing your reporting and metric visualization processes.

Understanding what reporting processes can be automated with Zapier

Zapier has integrations with a few reporting tools, allowing you to automate your **reporting processes**. You can connect these apps with thousands of other apps, such as Paypal, AgileCRM, **Quaderno**, and Google Sheets, to automate reporting from other business functions.

Here are a few examples of reporting processes that can be automated with Zapier:

- Spreadsheet reporting workflows
- Website analytics workflows
- Business intelligence and dashboard workflows

Let's explore each one and give some examples of reporting apps that can be used with Zapier to automate processes that involve them.

Automating spreadsheet reporting processes

In the *Understanding what operations processes can be automated with Zapier* section of *Chapter 20, Automating Your Operations Processes*, we covered using spreadsheet tools such as Microsoft Excel, Google Sheets, and Smartsheet in your various operations processes. These tools are widely used for recording and manipulating numerical data with simple or complex formulas, which can then be used for visual reporting in graphs and tables. You can also use add-ons with Google Sheets to extract data from other sources such as Google Analytics, or integrate Google Sheets with dashboard tools such as Infogram to display custom data in one place. By using Zapier, you can push key reporting data into your spreadsheet, which can be significantly manipulated and transformed to automatically display your data visually.

Next, let's discuss how to automate website analytics processes with Zapier.

Automating website analytics processes

Many businesses invest a vast amount of time and money in their online presence in creating a website and promoting their products, services, and reputation by pushing traffic from various sources to their website. As we discussed in *Chapter 18, Automating Your Marketing Processes*, businesses can use several methods to push traffic to their website, which could include paid ads, guest blog posting, and social media marketing. They also try to improve their online visibility in searches with **SEO** (short for **Search Engine Optimization**). With all this happening, a business needs to have a way to see the results of their marketing efforts at a glance, and both Google Analytics, an industry-standard tool for analyzing and visualizing website traffic, and **Hotjar**, an app that allows you to analyze your website traffic data, are examples of apps that enable you to do so. By using tools such as this, you will have better insights into your website visitors, such as their source and geographical location, and understand behaviors such as how long they spend on your website and on which pages. Then, by using automation tools such as Zapier, you can boost your productivity by automating your reporting processes, such as scheduling reports to run at a specific time each week and delivering the report by email, and tracking offline conversions for completed calls from your calling app, Twilio.

When using Google Analytics, you can create goals and measurements against those goals to track data from various sources. With the Google Analytics integration, you can trigger workflows when new goals are added, and then combine this with an action to send notifications by SMS. You can also create a measurement, update a goal, and run a report, as well as search for a goal. You can combine these actions with triggers so as to create new measurements from Typeform responses or Calendly bookings, or schedule a report to run every week on a Friday at 9 A.M. using Schedule by Zapier.

There are several analytics apps that integrate with Zapier, which you can check out here: `https://zapier.com/apps/categories/analytics`.

Next, let's discuss how to automate business intelligence and dashboard processes with Zapier.

Automating business intelligence and dashboard processes

Aside from website analytics, most of the tools in your tech stack probably have some kind of reporting functionality. However, when you have multiple tools, that means you have many places that you need to extract reporting data from. Wouldn't it be fantastic if we could collate all of the key reporting from our various apps on one dashboard or on a few key dashboards, but all in one place where the data is refreshed automatically? That's where business intelligence and dashboard tools come in. These apps allow you to collate all your important reporting data in one place, create **KPIs** (short for **Key Performance Indicators**) to measure your collected data against, and represent this data in graphical forms that suit your needs. Many of these tools have integrations with popular apps such as Facebook and Salesforce, but often integrations don't exist. Automation tools such as Zapier increase the efficiency of your reporting processes by extracting key segments of data and pushing the exact data you want to change metrics in these dashboard tools. This is especially handy if integrations don't exist between your apps and the chosen dashboard tool. **Databox**, **Geckoboard**, **Klipfolio**, **Dasheroo**, and **Zoho Analytics** are examples of business intelligence and dashboard reporting tools that integrate with Zapier.

With the Klipfolio integration, for example, you can add data to a source, update data in a data source, and refresh a data source. You can combine these action events with triggers involving other apps, allowing you to update insights without you having to manually import data. You could track the growth of a specific segment of your subscriber list in Klaviyo or Autopilot, or track unsubscribes and campaign clicks in ActiveCampaign. You could also monitor Twitter follower numbers, SurveyMonkey responses, Toky calls, or closed Asana tasks.

There are several business intelligence and dashboard apps that integrate with Zapier, which you can check out here: `https://zapier.com/apps/categories/dashboards`.

> **Tip**
> You can use business intelligence and dashboard processes to link in with other key areas such as marketing analytics from Google Analytics and YouTube, for example, to get better visibility of how your business is performing in all of your business functions.

You have now learned what kind of reporting processes can be automated with Zapier.

Let's take a look at the essential first steps to take to start automating your finance and reporting processes.

Where to start with automating your finance and reporting processes with Zapier

It is always good to do some pre-work before your start automating your processes. In *Chapter 2, Preparing to Automate Your Processes*, and *Chapter 3, Building Your First Automated Workflow (Zap)*, we covered a few important points that will help you when you are strategizing your finance and reporting workflows; they are as follows:

1. *Map out your finance and reporting processes*: If you don't have a clear idea of how your finance and reporting processes work with all your tools, follow the steps in the *Simplifying your processes and assessing what can be automated* section in *Chapter 2, Preparing to Automate Your Processes*, to visually map out your processes so that you have a high-level overview of how your tasks work with your existing software.

2. *List your finance and reporting tools*: Make a list of all the finance and reporting tools and services that you use in your business to achieve your goals. Then, assess how these tools fit within your mapped-out processes. You will then be able to simplify those processes and decide on what can be automated. Once you have this overview of your processes and tools, you will be better placed to understand where the holes are and how Zapier can help you to close the gaps and automate your processes.

3. *List your finance and reporting tools*: Follow the steps in *Chapter 2, Preparing to Automate Your Processes*, to simplify your processes and make a list of all the tools that you use in your business to achieve your goals, so that you can assess what can be automated.

4. *Review your app profile pages*: In *Chapter 2, Preparing to Automate Your Processes*, we also discussed reviewing your individual app profile pages as the best way to establish how your business apps integrate with Zapier. This will give you an insight into the triggers, actions, and searches available to use in your workflows. Make a list of these for quick reference.

5. *Use Zapier's pre-built guided workflow templates*: This is the easiest way to get started with automating your finance and reporting processes. These templates are built from workflows that are commonly used by other users. They are perfect for inspiration, quick to set up, and will save you time immediately.

6. *Customize your finance and reporting workflows*: Get creative and start building multi-step workflows to achieve more in your automations. Use Zapier's built-in apps to help you do more and connect your finance and reporting workflows to other parts of your business processes, such as your operations process.

You'll be well on your way to creating finance and reporting automations for your business.

> **Tip**
>
> If you're looking for ideas of other finance and reporting apps to use in your business, you can review the **Commerce** and **Business Intelligence** categories in the app ecosystem directory to give you a list of public apps that integrate with Zapier at `https://zapier.com/apps/categories/commerce` and `https://zapier.com/apps/categories/business-intelligence`. Review the *A brief guide to choosing new apps for your business* section in *Chapter 2, Preparing to Automate Your Processes,* for guidance on choosing new apps.

You now know how to get started with automating your finance and reporting processes with Zapier.

Let's get more specific and discuss how accounting processes can be automated using Zapier's Xero integration.

Automating accounting processes with the Xero integration

Xero is a popular cloud-based accounting package used by small and medium-sized businesses. With Xero, you can manage your accounts payable and accounts receivable processes, as well as manage expense claims and payroll and track inventory projects. You can create and send quotes, sales invoices, and purchase orders, and you can comprehensively report on your financials. You can also connect payment processing solutions such as PayPal, **GoCardless**, and **Stripe** to help you get paid faster by your customers. The ability to connect bank feeds to Xero automates part of the transaction reconciliation process, removing the need to manually import bank statements and transaction line entries. Depending on your location, you can submit tax returns and pay bills straight from Xero. Xero also allows you to handle multiple currencies.

Xero natively integrates with hundreds of other apps to allow you to connect other parts of your business to your finance system. You can, however, use the Zapier integration to add power to your processes by connecting Xero to thousands of other apps so that you can automate many parts of your accounting processes. The Xero integration is very comprehensive and currently supports 8 trigger events, 11 action events, and 3 search events. Let's review each of them.

Common fields in Xero trigger, action, and search action events

Before we look at the individual trigger events supported with the Xero integration, let's explore a common field used in most of the search actions:

- **Organization**: As you may be invited to access multiple Xero organizations with your login details, you must specify the Xero organization in every trigger, action, and search action event. You can do this by selecting the relevant organization from the drop-down menu and entering the record ID of the Xero organization, not the name, into this field, or you can insert this ID from previous steps in the case of action and search action events. The Xero organizations displayed will depend on the user access level that has been granted to you for each organization based on the module in Xero you are trying to view data from trigger and search action steps or post data in action steps. For example, **Read Only** users will not be able to use the integration, whereas **Standard** and **Advisor** users will be able to view and post depending on the modules they have access to. This is a required field and must be entered in order for the step to work.

- **Status**: Many trigger events allow you to specify the status for which want the Zap to trigger on. This field is a drop-down menu with options that may differ between trigger events. The field name might also vary slightly between trigger events, for example, **Quote Status**, as well as the options associated with it. This is an optional field.

- **Contact**: Some action events have this field specified as a required field that must be filled in in order for the step to work. You can do this by selecting the relevant contact from the drop-down menu and entering the record ID or name of an existing Xero contact into this field, or you can insert this ID or name from previous steps. Xero uses the contact's name as the unique identifier for the contact record.

- **Contact Name** or **Name**: These fields are specifically used in action events, allowing you to search for contacts by name or create contacts. In this case, the fields are not drop-down menus with lists of the organization's contacts, but you must enter text into this field or insert data from previous steps. These are required fields and must be filled in in order for the step to work.

- **Invoice Number** or **Invoice**: Some action events have this field specified as a required field and must be filled in in order for the step to work. You can do this by selecting the relevant invoice from the drop-down menu and entering the record ID of an existing Xero invoice into this field, or you can insert this ID from previous steps.

Now, let's review Xero trigger events.

Xero trigger events

The following is a list of supported trigger events that you can use with Xero with examples of when to use them:

- **New Contact**: This event triggers when a new contact is added to Xero. You must specify the Xero organization in the **Organization** field. Among other things, you can use this trigger event in your automations when you want to add new contacts to other apps such as your email marketing app or inventory management app as soon as they have been added to Xero. For example, combine this trigger event with an action event such as **Create Subscriber** with Klaviyo, or combine **Create Customer** with Dear Inventory.

- **New Quote**: This event triggers when a new quote is created in Xero. You must specify the Xero organization in the **Organization** field. You can also specify which status you want the Zap to trigger on by selecting **Draft** (DRAFT), **Sent** (SENT), **Declined** (DECLINED), **Accepted** (ACCEPTED), **Invoiced** (INVOICED), or **Deleted** (DELETED) from the **Quote Status** field drop-down menu. If this field is left empty, the Zap will trigger on any new quote, regardless of its status. Among other things, you can use this trigger event in your automations when you want to set a reminder in your CRM to follow up with the recipient when a quote has been sent or if you want to send a notification to your team if a quote is accepted. For example, combine this trigger event with an action event such as **Create Task** with AgileCRM, or combine **Create Post** with **Ryver**.

- **New Sales Invoice**: This event triggers when a new sales invoice (accounts receivable) is created in Xero. You must specify the Xero organization in the **Organization** field. You can also specify which status you want the Zap to trigger on by selecting **All** (all), **Draft** (draft), **Awaiting Approval** (submitted), **Awaiting Payment** (authorised), **Paid** (paid), or **Voided** (voided) from the **Status** field drop-down menu. You can use this trigger event in your automations when you want to add details of new submitted sales invoices to a spreadsheet or send a fax to your client for all authorized sales invoices. For example, combine this trigger event with an action event such as **Add Row** with Microsoft Excel, or combine **Send Fax** with ClickSend SMS.

- **New Purchase Order:** This event triggers when a new purchase order is added to Xero. You must specify the Xero organization in the **Organization** field. You can also specify which status you want the Zap to trigger on by selecting **Draft** (DRAFT), **Submitted** (SUBMITTED), **Authorized** (AUTHORISED), **Billed** (BILLED), or **Deleted** (DELETED) from the **Purchase Order Status** field drop-down menu. Among other things, you can use this trigger event in your automations when you want to add details of new purchase orders to a database or notify your team depending on the status of the purchase order. For example, combine this trigger event with an action event such as **Create Record** with Knack or combine **Send Channel Message** with Microsoft Teams.

- **New Bill:** This event triggers when a new bill (accounts payable) is created in Xero. You must specify the Xero organization in the **Organization** field. You can also specify which status you want the Zap to trigger on by selecting **All** (all), **Draft** (draft), **Awaiting Approval** (submitted), **Awaiting Payment** (authorised), **Paid** (paid), or **Voided** (voided) from the **Status** field drop-down menu. You can use this trigger event in your automations when you want to add a new calendar event on the bill due date or add a task to your task management app to pay the bill on the due date. For example, combine this trigger event with an action event such as **Create Event** with Microsoft Outlook, or combine **Create Task** with **Any.Do**.

- **New Expense Claim Receipt:** This event triggers when a new draft expense claim receipt is created in Xero. You must specify the Xero organization in the **Organization** field. Among other things, you can use this trigger event in your automations when you want to notify an approver that a new expense claim is ready to be reviewed or add a task to your to-do list. For example, combine this trigger event with an action event such as **Send Outbound Email** with Email by Zapier, or combine **Create Task** with Teamwork Projects.

- **New Bank Transaction:** This event triggers when a new bank transaction is made in Xero. Spend, Receive, and Transfer transactions are recognized. You must specify the Xero organization in the **Organization** field. Among other ways, you can use this trigger event in your automations when you want to keep track of what transactions are being processed by adding them to a spreadsheet. For example, combine this trigger event with an action event such as **Create Spreadsheet Row** with Google Sheets.

- **New Payment**: This event triggers when a new payment is made in Xero. You must specify the Xero organization in the **Organization** field. From the **Payment Type** field drop-down menu, you can specify which status you want the Zap to trigger on by selecting from a long list of options, for example, **Accounts Receivable** (ACCRECPAYMENT), **Accounts Payable** (ACCPAYPAYMENT), or **Accounts Payable Overpayment (Refund)** (APOVERPAYMENTPAYMENT). The default is **Accounts Receivable** (ACCRECPAYMENT). You can use this trigger event in your automations when you want to send a thank you email to your customer for paying your invoices or send a summary to your team of all paid invoices that day. For example, combine this trigger event with an action event such as **Send Email** with Gmail or **Append Entry and Schedule Digest** with Digest by Zapier and **Send Channel Message** with Slack. You can download the Zap template here: https://bit.ly/3e5BUkn.

Next, let's have a look at the Xero action events.

Xero action events

The following is a list of supported action events that you can use with Xero with examples of when to use them:

- **Create/Update Contact**: You can use this action event when you want to create a new contact or update an existing contact in Xero. You must specify the Xero organization in the **Organization** field and the name of the contact in the **Contact Name** field. Xero uses the contact's name as the unique identifier for the record. You can then optionally enter text or insert data from previous steps in a number of fields, including **Account Number**, **Primary Person – First Name**, **Primary Person - Last Name**, **Primary Person – Email**, **Tax Number**, and **Bank Account Number**, as well as several different mobile, telephone, and address fields. You should fill in at least one other field to prevent this step from presenting an error. Completing the **Account Number** field can be useful as you can use this field as search criteria in the **Find or Create Contact** search action. You will only be able to add or edit details in the **Bank Account Number** field if you have user permission to do so. In the **Groups** field, you can add the contact to one or more groups by using the drop-down menu; subsequent dropdowns appear as this field is added. When updating a contact, specifying data in the **Groups** field will not replace the contact's existing groups but add to it. You could use this action event in combination with a trigger event such as **Updated Deal Stage** with Pipedrive to add contacts to Xero when a deal reaches a certain stage in your CRM or in combination with **Link Clicked** in Mailchimp to update contacts in Xero when a link is clicked in a campaign email.

- **Create New Quote Draft**: You can use this action event when you want to create a new draft quote in Xero. You must specify the Xero organization in the **Organization** field and the name of the contact in the **Contact** field. You can then optionally complete the **Date, Expiry, Quote Number, Reference, Theme, Title, Summary, Currency, Amount Are**, and **Terms** fields with drop-down menu values in some cases, enter text or insert data from previous steps. The **Date** field will default to the date the Zap runs if not specified, and Xero will autogenerate a number if the **Quote Number** field is left blank. The **Amounts Are** field will default to **Tax Exclusive** (`Exclusive`) if not specified. For the **Line Items** section, you must enter a **Description**, and then optionally enter **Item Code, Quantity, Unit Price, Discount %, Account**, and **Tax Rate**, and any tracking categories unique to the organization. Note that if you specify a **Quantity** value, you must specify a **Unit Price** value and vice versa, to prevent an error from being presented. You could use this action event in combination with a trigger event such as **New Form Submission** with Hubspot to create new draft quotes when a contact requests a quote via a Hubspot form, or combine **New Contact** with Xero to create a draft quote when new contacts are added to Xero.

- **Create Sales Invoice**: You can use this action event when you want to create a new sales invoice (account receivable) in Xero. You must specify the Xero organization in the **Organization** field and the name of the contact in the **Contact Name** field. You can then optionally complete the **Email Address, Status, Date, Due Date, Currency, URL, Attachment, Branding Theme, Number, Reference, Send To Contact, Title, Summary, Currency, Amount Are,** and **Terms** fields, with drop-down menu values in some cases, text, or data from previous steps. The **Status** field defaults to **Draft** (draft) if not specified, the **Date** field will default to the date the Zap runs if not specified, and the **Due Date** field must be specified if **Status** is **Approved** (authorised). The default currency for the organization will be used if the **Currency** field is not specified. Xero will autogenerate an invoice number if the **Number** field is left blank; otherwise, enter an alphanumeric code. Note that selecting the **True** option in the **Sent To Contact** field does not send the invoice but marks it as "sent" and can only be set when the **Status** field is **Approved** (authorised). For the **Line Items** section, you must fill in **Quantity**, and then optionally fill in **Line Items Type, Item Code, Description, Quantity, Unit Price, Discount %, Account, Tax Rate,** and **Tracking**. Note that you must either specify an **Item Code** value, or both a **Description** value and **Unit Price** value, to prevent an error from being presented. Complete the **Tracking** field by adding the tracking category name on the left with the category option on the right. You could use this action event in combination with a trigger event when, for example, a deal moves to the **Invoicing** stage in your CRM and you only want to add a detailed contact to Xero if that contact does not exist and then create a sales invoice in Xero associated with that contact. You can use the **New Deal in Stage** trigger event in Hubspot with the **Find Contact** search action with Xero, and the **Create Sales Invoice** action event with Xero. You can watch a video about a working example using a Pipedrive CRM trigger event and download the Zap template here: https://bit.ly/3e5BUkn.

- **Add Items to Existing Sales Invoice**: You can use this action event when you want to update an existing sales invoice in Xero with new items. You must specify the Xero organization in the **Organization** field and the specific invoice in the **Invoice** field. Then, in the **Line Items** section, you must fill in **Quantity**, and then optionally fill in **Item Code, Description, Quantity, Unit Price, Discount %, Account,** and **Tax Rate**, and enter any tracking categories unique to the organization. Note that you must either specify an **Item Code** value, or both a **Description** value and **Unit Price** value, to prevent an error from being presented. You could use this action event in combination with a trigger event such as **Updated Order** with Shopify to add additional items to an existing invoice in Xero, and you could use the Xero **Find Invoice** search action to find the invoice when the invoice number or reference has been filled out with an appropriate reference from Shopify.

- **Send Sales Invoice by Email**: You can use this action event when you want to send an existing sales invoice in Xero. You must specify the Xero organization in the **Organization** field and the specific invoice in the **Invoice Number** field. The email will be sent from Xero to the email address of the primary contact specified in your Xero contact settings and any other contacts marked as **include in emails**. It will include the subject and body based on your default email template in Xero. Invoices must have a status of **Awaiting Approval**, **Awaiting Payment**, or **Paid**. You could use this action event in combination with a Xero **Create Invoice** action event when you want to create a new invoice and then send it to the contact from Xero.

- **Create Purchase Order**: You can use this action event when you want to create a new purchase order in Xero. You must specify the Xero organization in the **Organization** field and the name of the supplier contact in the **Contact (Supplier)** field. You can then optionally complete the **Date**, **Delivery Date**, **Order Number**, **Reference**, **Theme**, **Currency**, and **Tax Type** fields with drop-down menu values, text, or data from previous steps. The **Date** field will default to the date the Zap runs if not specified and Xero will autogenerate a bill number if the **Order Number** field is left blank; otherwise, enter an alphanumeric code. For the **Line Items** section, you must fill in **Quantity**, and then optionally fill in **Line Items Type**, **Item Code**, **Description**, **Quantity**, **Unit Price**, **Discount %**, **Account**, **Tax Rate**, and **Tracking**. Note that you must either specify an **Item Code** value, or both a **Description** value and **Unit Price** value, to prevent an error from being presented. You could use this action event in combination with a trigger event with the **New or Updated Record** with Airtable to create a purchase order when a field is filled in Airtable.

- **Create Bill**: You can use this action event when you want to create a new bill (account payable) in Xero. You must specify the Xero organization in the **Organization** field and the name of the contact in the **Contact Name** field. You can then optionally complete the **Email Address, Status, Date, Due Date, Currency, URL, Attachment, Branding Theme**, and **Reference** fields with drop-down menu values in some cases, text, or data from previous steps. The **Status** field defaults to **Draft** (draft) if not specified, the **Date** field will default to the date the Zap runs if not specified, and the **Due Date** field must be specified if **Status** is **Approved** (authorised). The default currency for the organization will be used in the **Currency** field if nothing is specified. The alphanumeric code entered into the **Reference** field does not need to be unique. For the **Line Items** section, you must fill in **Quantity**, and then optionally fill in **Line Items Type, Item Code, Description, Quantity, Unit Price, Account, Tax Rate**, and **Tracking**. Note that you must either specify an **Item Code** value, or both a **Description** value and **Unit Price** value, to prevent an error from being presented. Complete the **Tracking** field by adding the tracking category name on the left with the category option on the right. You could use this action event in combination with a trigger event such as **Parsed Document Data Available** with Docparser when you want to parse bill details using Docparser and then create the corresponding bill in Xero.

- **Create Credit Note**: You can use this action event when you want to create a new accounts payable or accounts receivable credit note associated with a contact in Xero. You must specify the Xero organization in the **Organization** field, whether you want **Bill Credit Note (Accounts Payable)** (ACCPAYCREDIT) or **Sales Credit Note (Accounts Receivable)** (ACCRECCREDIT) in the **Type** field, and the name of the contact in the **Contact** field. You can then optionally complete the **Date, Attachments, Currency, Tax Type**, and **Credit Note Status** fields with drop-down menu values in some cases, text, or data from previous steps. The **Date** field will default to the date the Zap runs if not specified, you can upload up to 10 attachments of up to 3 MB each in size using the **Attachments** field, and the **Credit Note Status** field defaults to **Draft** (draft) if not specified. The default currency for the organization will be used if the **Currency** field is not filled in. For the **Line Items** section, you must fill in **Quantity**, and then optionally fill in **Item Code, Description, Quantity, Unit Price, Account, Tax Rate**, and any tracking categories unique to the organization. Note that you must either specify an **Item Code** value, or both a **Description** value and **Unit Price** value, to prevent an error from being presented. You could use this action event in combination with a trigger event such as **New Sales Order Credit Memo** with Magento and **Find Invoice** with Xero to create credit notes in Xero against the associated invoice when a credit memo is raised in Magento.

- **Create Bank Transaction**: You can use this action event when you want to create a new spend of receive money transaction in Xero. You must specify the Xero organization in the **Organization** field, the name of the contact in the **Contact** field, and the Xero bank account in the **Bank Account** field. Also specify the type of bank transaction you want to create in the **Transaction Type** field, with options for **Spend Money (Direct Payment)** (SPEND), **Spend Money (Prepayment)** (SPEND-PREPAYMENT), **Spend Money (Overpayment)** (SPEND-OVERPAYMENT), **Receive Money (Direct Payment)** (RECEIVE), **Receive Money (Prepayment)** (RECEIVE-PREPAYMENT), and **Receive Money (Overpayment)** (RECEIVE-OVERPAYMENT). Optionally, fill in the **Date** field. Once the **Transaction Type** field has been filled, depending on the option chosen, an additional field will appear. For **Direct Payments**, optionally fill in the **Reference** field, and in the **Line Items** section, you must fill in **Quantity**, and then optionally fill in **Item Code**, **Description**, **Quantity**, **Unit Price**, **Discount %**, **Account**, **Tax Rate**, and any tracking categories from your Xero organization. For **Prepayments**, the **Item Code** value will not be presented. Note that you must either specify an **Item Code** value, or both a **Description** value and **Unit Price** value, to prevent an error from being presented. For **Overpayments**, you must fill in **Description** and **Unit Price**, and then optionally enter tracking categories from your Xero organization. You could use this action event in combination with a trigger event such as **New Charge** or **New Refund** in Stripe to create, receive, or spend money direct payments when new payments or refunds are made with Stripe.

- **Create Bank Transfer**: You can use this action event when you want to transfer money between your different bank accounts in a specified Xero organization. You must specify the Xero organization in the **Organization** field, the bank account the payment is being made from in the **From Account** field, the bank account the payment is being made to in **To Account**, and the amount in **Amount**. Optionally, complete the **Date** field. You could use this action event in combination with a trigger event such as **Successful Sale** in Paypal when you routinely transfer funds from your Paypal bank account to your current bank account in Xero whenever a sale is made.

- **Create Payment**: You can use this action event when you want to create a new payment against an invoice, credit note, prepayment, or overpayment in Xero. You must specify the Xero organization in the **Organization** field, the ID or number in the **Document ID or Number** field, the bank account or clearing account the payment is being made to in the **Paid To** field, and the payment amount in the **Amount** field. Optionally, change the default option in the **Document Type** field from **Invoice (default)** (`Invoice`), **Credit Note** (`CreditNote`), **Prepayment** (`Prepayment`), or **Overpayment** (`Overpayment`). You can then optionally complete the **Date**, **Currency Rate**, and **Reference** fields by entering text or inserting data from previous steps. Only use the **Currency Rate** field for invoices where the currency is not the Xero account base currency, entering the exchange rate when the payment is received. The **Date** field will default to the date the Zap runs if not specified. You could use this action event in combination with a trigger event such as **New Transaction** with Square and **Find Invoice** with Xero to create payments against Xero invoices when transactions are completed in Square.

Next, let's have a look at the Xero search action events.

Xero search action events

Before we look at the individual search action events supported with the Xero integration, let's explore the common fields used in both of the Xero search action events:

- **Organization**: Refer to the notes in the *Common fields in Xero trigger, action, and search action events* section for details on how to use this field.

- **Search By**: This field is used to specify the Xero field that you want to search by. You can choose between identifiers in the records from the drop-down menu, you can also enter the corresponding text for the field label, not the field name, or map this from previous steps. You should select a field that represents a unique identifier for the record to search for so that only one record is returned. For example, in the case of an invoice record, a field that would represent a unique identifier could be the **Invoice Number** field name with a field label of Number. This is a required field and must be entered in order for the step to work. Once selected, the relevant data entry field will appear for you to either enter text or map data from previous fields. This must be entered exactly as it appears in Xero. For example, if **Invoice Reference** is selected in the **Search By** field, the new field that appears is the **Reference** field.

- **Should This Step Be Considered A "success" When Nothing Is Found**: Use this Boolean field to select **True** or **False** from the drop-down menu, or enter text or insert data from previous steps, for this step to be considered a **success** if nothing is found in the search. The default for this field is **False**, which you should choose if you want the Zap to stop running if nothing is found, as this is the most common use case. This means that all subsequent steps will be skipped. Use the **True** option when you want to allow the Zap to continue and subsequent steps to run. You can then add more control to your workflows by adding Filter by Zapier or Paths by Zapier conditional logic and allowing those steps to pass or stop based on whether the search returned a result.

- **Create Xero Contact if it doesn't exist yet?**: This field is specific to the **Find Contact** search action. Tick this checkbox if you want a new record to be created if the search does not return an existing record. Once ticked, the step will refresh and display fields as with the **Create/Update Contact** action event.

Now let's cover the two supported search action events that you can use with Xero:

- **Find Contact**: You can use this search action event when you want to find a contact in Xero. You must complete the **Organization** and **Search By** fields. In the **Search By** field, choose from **Name** (Name) or **Account Number** (AccountNumber), and once selected, the relevant field will appear for you to either enter text or map data from previous fields for the contact's name or account number. This must be entered exactly as it appears in Xero. You can then optionally change the default option in the **Should This Step Be Considered A "success" When Nothing Is Found** fields and tick the **Create Xero Contact if it doesn't exist yet?** box if relevant. If the box is ticked, fill in the fields as described in the **Create/Update Contact** action event. You can use this search action in combination with other Xero trigger or action events in your automations. Refer to the *Xero action events* section for an example of how to use this search action event followed by Xero **Create Sales Invoice** action steps.

- **Find Invoice**: You can use this search action event when you want to find an Invoice in Xero. You must complete the **Organization** and **Search By** fields. In the **Search By** field, choose from **Invoice Number** (Number) or **Invoice Reference** (Reference), and once selected, the relevant field will appear for you to either enter text or map data from previous fields for the invoice number or reference. You can optionally change the default option in the **Should This Step Be Considered A "success" When Nothing Is Found** fields. You can use this search action in combination with other Xero trigger or action events in your automations. For example, when you want to send a thank you email to your customer for paying your invoices and you want to attach a PDF copy of the invoice, you can use the **New Payment** trigger event with the **Find Invoice** search action and the **Send Email** with Gmail action event. You can download the Zap template here: https://bit.ly/3e5BUkn.

Next, let's review a few tips for the best use of the Xero integration.

Tips for using the Xero integration

Here are a few tips for the successful use of the Xero integration:

1. **Read Only**, **Invoice Only**, and **Cashbook Client** users will not be able to use the integration. You must have *Standard* or *Advisor* access, and the triggers and actions you will be able to use will depend on your access rights to certain modules.

2. Only connect your Xero account to one Zapier account. This will prevent disconnection issues.

3. Always check what type of field you are entering or mapping data to, and ensure your data is formatted accordingly. This will ensure data accuracy. You can review the *Understanding field data types* section in *Chapter 3, Building Your First Automated Workflow (Zap)*, for more information on field types.

4. When using the **Custom** tab to type in or map data from previous steps into fields that display Xero field options in drop-down menus, such as with **Status**, use the field label rather than the field name. For example, field name = **Awaiting Payment**, field label = authorised.

5. The Xero integration supports the use of line-items. To optimize using this integration in your workflows, you can review the *Manipulating line-items* section in *Chapter 17, Zapier's Utilities Functions*, for more information on transforming line item data. If your trigger and action steps both support line-items, you will not need to transform the data.

6. You can create connections between your different apps by displaying clickable URL links to Xero records by using the Xero record ID plus the view URL. For example, when you create a sales invoice in Xero, update a custom field in the deal or opportunity record in your CRM with the invoice URL so other Xero users in the organization can view the invoice. The URL + ID combination in this case would be `https://go.xero.com/AccountsReceivable/View.aspx?InvoiceID=b2f9e6df-73ab-4ccd-9978-258f22ef4665`, where `b2f9e6df-73ab-4ccd-9978-258f22ef4665` is the sales invoice ID.

7. Review the Xero API at `https://developer.xero.com/documentation/` for information on other triggers and actions you can perform using Webhooks by Zapier and Code by Zapier. You can hire a Zapier expert to help you with custom integration work here: `https://experts.zapier.com/`.

8. You can view common problems with the Xero integration by navigating to the **Help** tab of the app profile or following this link: `https://zapier.com/help/doc/common-problems-xero`.

Next, let's explore how to set up an example of a multi-step Zap using the Xero integration.

Setting up a multi-step Zap with the Xero integration

To illustrate this, we will use the example of creating a sales invoice and bill for associated Stripe transaction fees in Xero when a new charge is made in Stripe. We also want to correctly allocate the Xero tax code based on the buyer's country location.

The Zap will involve four steps as follows:

1. *Trigger*: Stripe app with the **New Charge** trigger event

2. *Action*: Formatter by Zapier app with the **Utilities** action event with the **Lookup Table** transform function

3. *Action*: Xero app with the **Create Sales Invoice** action event

4. *Action*: Xero app with the **Create Bill** action event

The following screenshot shows how your Zap should look once built with some step name customization:

Figure 21.1 – A multi-step Zap using Xero action events

Let's walk through setting up the Zap step by step, starting with the trigger step.

Setting up step 1 – the trigger step

We will use the Stripe app with the **New Charge** trigger event as the trigger step. In the **Include Failed Charges?** field, choose **False** as we do not want the Zap to trigger on failed charges.

The following screenshot shows how this step should look:

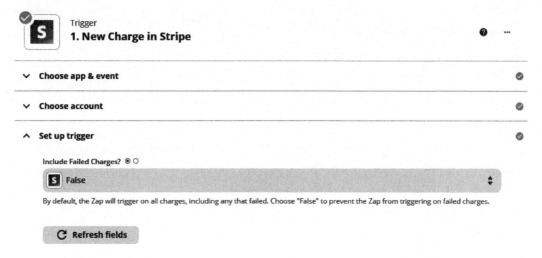

Figure 21.2 – Customizing the New Charge in Stripe trigger event to trigger a workflow

Click on the **Continue** button and then use the **Test Trigger** button to pull through some test data.

Next, let's set up the first action step.

Setting up step 2 – the first action step

We want to customize the sales invoice tax to match the country that the customer's card is linked to. In this scenario, we want all European customer locations to have **20% VAT (on Income)** (OUTPUT2) and all other countries to have **No VAT** (NONE). Your tax settings will be different based on your Xero region. We will use the Formatter by Zapier app with the **Utilities** action event and the **Lookup Table** transform option. Follow the instructions in the *Using lookup tables* section in *Chapter 17, Zapier's Utilities Functions*, to customize this action step to add the **Lookup Key** value as the Payment Method Details Card Country, and the **Lookup Table** fields will contain the Stripe European country codes on the left and Xero tax code (OUTPUT) on the right. We will set **Fallback Value** as NONE for all other countries.

The following screenshot shows how this step should look:

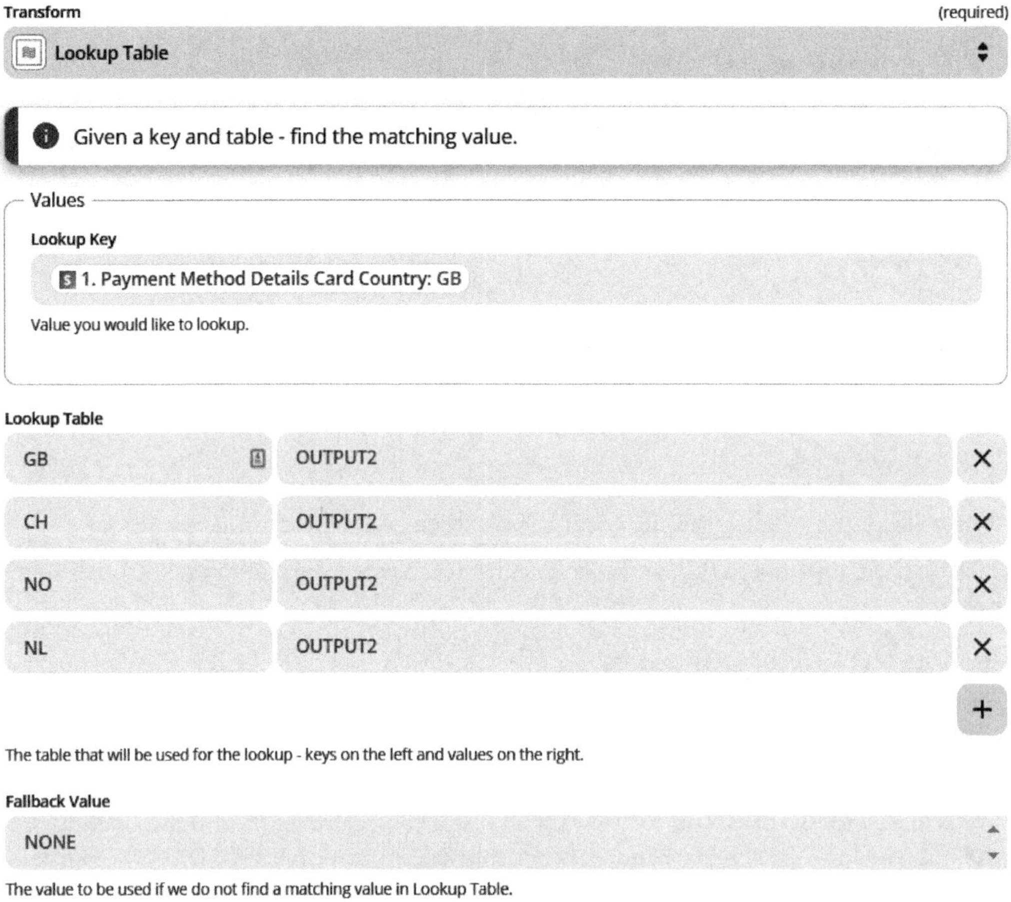

Transform (required)

📄 Lookup Table	⬍

> ℹ️ Given a key and table - find the matching value.

Values

Lookup Key

> 🔢 1. Payment Method Details Card Country: GB

Value you would like to lookup.

Lookup Table

GB	🔢	OUTPUT2	✕
CH		OUTPUT2	✕
NO		OUTPUT2	✕
NL		OUTPUT2	✕
			➕

The table that will be used for the lookup - keys on the left and values on the right.

Fallback Value

NONE	⬍

The value to be used if we do not find a matching value in Lookup Table.

Figure 21.3 – Using the Utilities action event with the Lookup Table transform option in a Formatter by Zapier action event to look up a tax code

Click on the **Continue** button. You can then use the **Test action** section to get the tax code. In this case, the step output will be OUTPUT for the GB country code.

Next, let's set up the second action step.

Setting up step 3 – the second action step

We will use the Xero app with the **Create Sales Invoice** action event, and we will customize this action step by completing the **Organization, Contact Name, Email Address, Status, Date, Due Date, Currency, Branding Theme, Reference, Description, Quantity, Unit Price, Account,** and **Tax Rate** fields by using the drop-down menu options or mapping dynamic data from previous steps. Importantly, we can enter the contact's name and email address and create a new contact straight from this step, and then map the **Tax Rate** field with the output from *step 2*. Use the following three screenshots to complete the step:

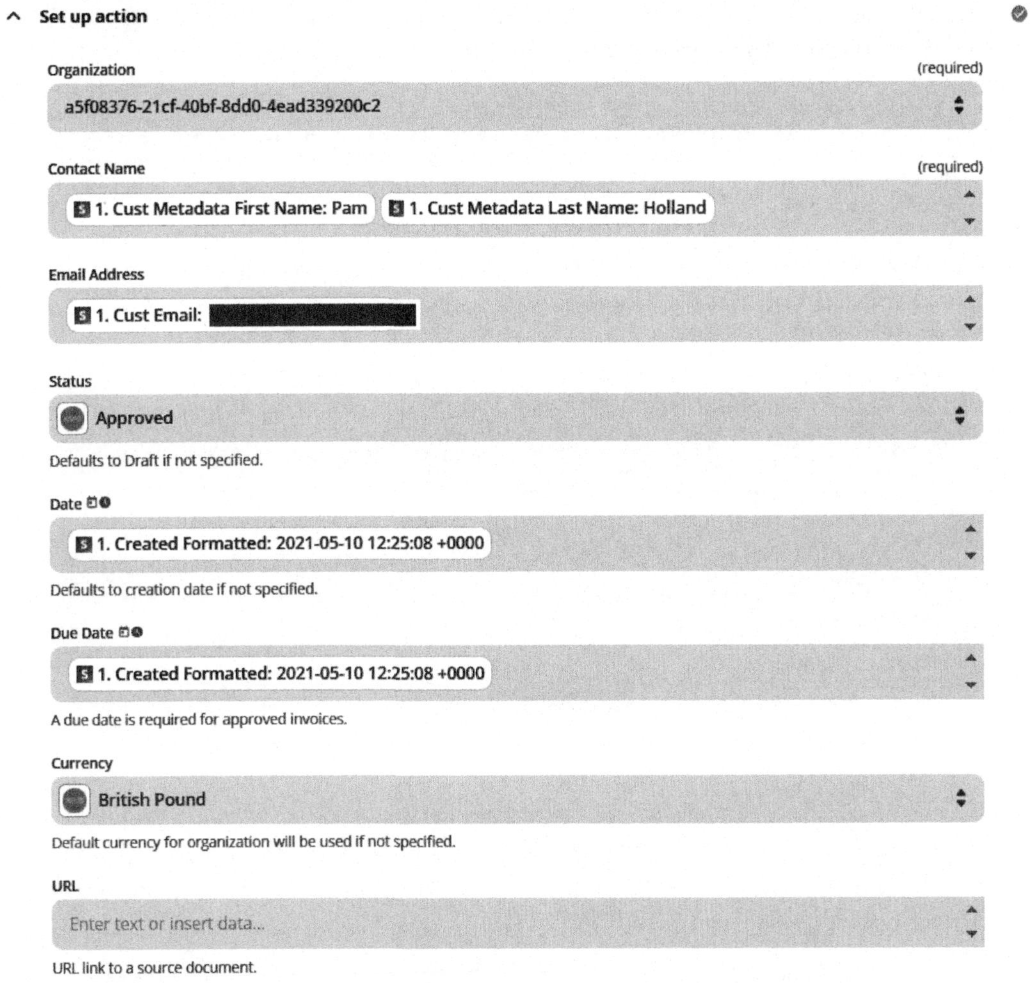

Figure 21.4 – Using the Xero app integration to create a sale invoice (1)

The second part of the action step is shown in the following screenshot:

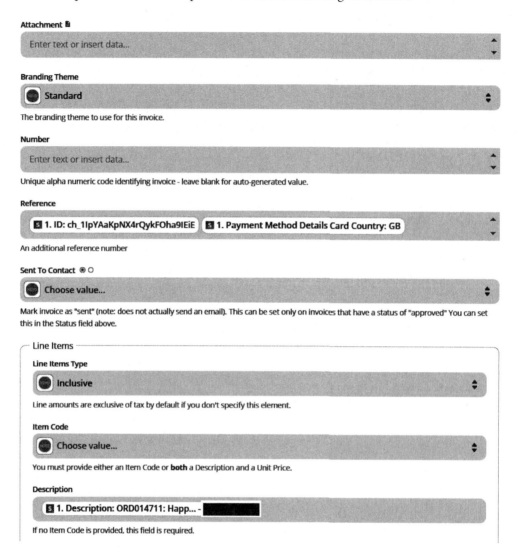

Figure 21.5 – Using the Xero app integration to create a sale invoice (2)

The third part of the action step is shown in the following screenshot:

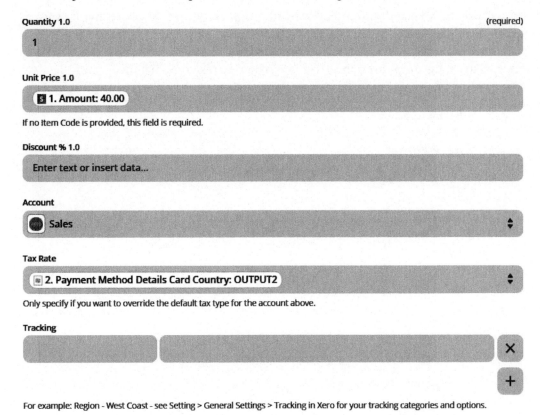

Quantity 1.0   (required)

> 1

Unit Price 1.0

> **$ 1. Amount: 40.00**

If no Item Code is provided, this field is required.

Discount % 1.0

> Enter text or insert data...

Account

> ⬤ Sales   ⬍

Tax Rate

> ▣ 2. Payment Method Details Card Country: OUTPUT2   ⬍

Only specify if you want to override the default tax type for the account above.

Tracking

> [   ] [   ]   ✕

                                                                              +

For example: Region - West Coast - see Setting > General Settings > Tracking in Xero for your tracking categories and options.

Figure 21.6 – Using the Xero app integration to create a sale invoice (3)

Click on the **Continue** button. You can then use the **Test action** section to send the email.

Next, let's set up the final action step.

Setting up step 4 – the third action step

We will use the Xero app with the **Create Bill** action event, and we will customize this action step by completing the **Organization, Contact Name, Status, Date, Due Date, Reference, Line Items Type, Description, Quantity, Unit Price, Account,** and **Tax Rate** fields by using the drop-down menu options, entering text, or mapping dynamic data from previous steps. Use the following three screenshots to complete the step:

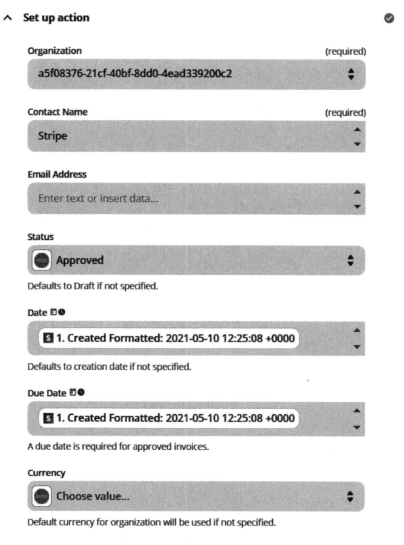

Figure 21.7 – Using the Xero app integration to create a sale invoice (1)

The second part of the action step is shown in the following screenshot:

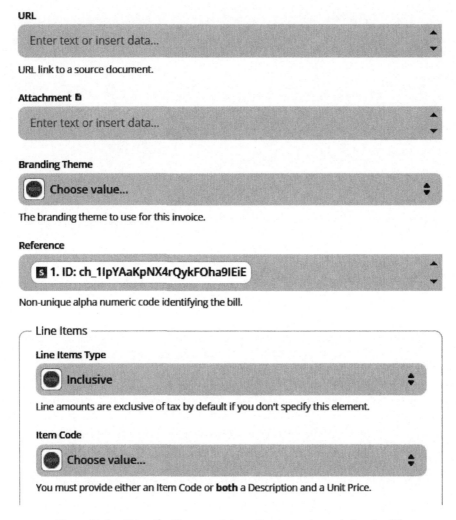

Figure 21.8 – Using the Xero app integration to create a sale invoice (2)

The third part of the action step is shown in the following screenshot:

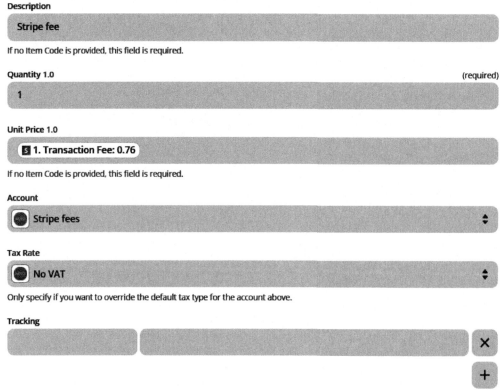

Figure 21.9 – Using the Xero app integration to create a sale invoice (3)

Click on the **Continue** button. You can then use the **Test action** section to create the note.

You can get access to a copy of this Zap template here: https://bit.ly/3e5BUkn.

You should now have a better understanding of how to automate finance processes with the Xero integration.

Summary

In this chapter, we discussed the different types of finance and reporting processes that can be automated with Zapier, and we explored some examples of workflows used with some common applications. First, we gave an overview of the types of finance processes that can be automated with Zapier. Then, we covered the types of reporting processes that can be automated with Zapier. After that, we explored where to start with automating finance and reporting processes with Zapier. Finally, we discussed how to automate accounting processes with the Xero integration.

You now know how to automate your finance and reporting processes with Zapier and, specifically, finance processes involving the Xero integration.

In the next chapter, you will learn some practical tips, tricks, and best practices to enhance your success when using Zapier in your business.

22
Tips, Tricks, and Best Practices to Enhance Your Productivity

We'll soon be coming to the end of our Zapier coaching journey. We have covered many topics that will help you to create effective workflow automations in your business or for your clients using Zapier. In this chapter, we will discuss the best practices for utilizing Zapier effectively and build on the tips and tricks we learned in each chapter. First, we will recap the steps covered throughout this book to help you with your Zap building. We will also explore a range of tips and tricks that you can use to effectively create workflows in Zapier for top performance.

We will cover the following key topics in this chapter:

- Best practices for using Zapier effectively
- Tips and tricks to enhance your use of Zapier

Once you have worked through each of these topics, you will have a better understanding of the best practices to use when building workflow automations in Zapier.

Technical requirements

To get the most out of the content in this chapter, you will need access to a Zapier account. The Zapier Free plan will be adequate for you to create single-step workflows and use Zapier's pre-built templates. The Zapier Starter plan will be required for you to use Premium apps and to create multi-step workflows.

Best practices for using Zapier effectively

The best way to understand how to optimize using Zapier in your business is to review the content we explored in each chapter of this book so that you have a point for quick reference. Let's briefly explore the content we covered in this book as an overview of the best practices to use when building workflows in Zapier.

Start with the basics

Getting the groundwork done at the beginning will prepare you for success. Once you've chosen the best Zapier plan for you and created a Zapier account, the next step is to familiarize yourself with navigation on the Zapier platform and then edit your settings and preferences to suit. Make sure you've also grasped the terminology used on the Zapier platform as this will help you when troubleshooting. We covered these topics in *Chapter 1, Introduction to Business Process Automation with Zapier*.

Prepare before you automate

Preparation is the key to success and will save you a lot of time from the start. A large part of implementing effective automations is ensuring you have identified your manual and repetitive processes, documented them, and simplified them first. Once you've done that, you should establish how your business apps fit into those processes and how those apps integrate with Zapier. Make the most of the information provided in the Zapier app ecosystem directory to help you do this. We covered these topics in *Chapter 2, Preparing to Automate Your Processes*.

When you're ready to start building your Zaps, strategize the best flow structure first. As you can't drag and drop your steps around in the Zap editor, planning out the steps in advance of building your Zaps will save you time. We covered this topic in *Chapter 3, Building Your First Automated Workflow (Zap)*.

Get to grips with steps, fields, and data mapping

A crucial first step in your Zap building is understanding how to trigger, action, and search action steps work together. It's also important to have a firm grasp on how to enter data into fields in your action steps using dropdowns, data mapping from the previous steps of your Zap, and by entering text. You will also need to know about the different field types used in action steps and what kind of data is accepted in these fields. We covered these topics in *Chapter 3, Building Your First Automated Workflow (Zap)*.

Manage your Zaps effectively

Having a well-organized Zapier account will help you maintain structure the more Zaps you build and the more you automate in your business. Keeping your Zaps organized with appropriate naming and storage in specific folders helps maintain a tidy account. It's also useful to know how to individually manage your Zaps and connected apps, as well as understanding statuses, to save you time with troubleshooting. You might also want to share Zaps with other Zapier users, and Zaps, app connections, and folders with team members. We covered these topics in *Chapter 4, Managing Your Zaps*.

Stay on top of your task usage

While you're getting to grips with Zapier, you will want to keep an eye on your task usage. It may not seem obvious from the start; however, it is easy to make a mistake in your Zaps that can cause your Zaps to trigger excessively, resulting in high task usage. This is even more important when you're using the lower-priced plans with less task allocation. The solution is often adding a Filter by Zapier step in soon after the trigger step to allow your Zap to run only if the trigger data satisfies certain conditions. Now, to ensure you are able to monitor your task usage, you can set up a Zap using the Zapier Manager built-in app and turn off a specific Zap if required. We covered this topic in *Chapter 12, Managing Your Zapier Account with Built-In Apps*.

Set up alerts and understand how to troubleshoot

At some point, you will experience errors and issues with your Zaps. A key tip for success is having a well-monitored Zapier account so that you can address these problems swiftly. Make sure that you have adjusted your account settings accordingly and have created Zap error and app status alerts to notify you of problems with your Zaps and your Zapier account. Once you've done that, knowing how to troubleshoot when you see errors or things don't go according to plan with workflows is critical to success with Zapier. When you can't solve the problem yourself, you'll also need to know where to go to find assistance. We covered these topics in *Chapter 5, Troubleshooting and Handling Zap Errors*, and *Chapter 12, Managing Your Zapier Account with Built-In Apps*.

Understand the different built-in Zapier apps

You don't need to know how to use all of the built-in apps by Zapier at once, but having a good understanding of what they all do and how they can help you when you're building your Zaps is extremely useful.

We started with a handy overview of all the approved built-in apps (those not in the beta phase) in *Chapter 6*, *Creating Multi-Step Zaps and Using Built-In Apps*, then discussed each one in detail from *Chapter 7*, *Getting Started with Built-In Apps*, onward.

The most useful built-in apps to start with are Filter by Zapier, which we covered in *Chapter 7*, *Getting Started with Built-In Apps*, and the versatile Formatter by Zapier built-in app, which we covered from *Chapter 13*, *Formatting Date and Time*, to *Chapter 17*, *Zapier's Utilities Functions*.

You can get access to a comprehensive cheat sheet to all the Zapier built-in apps here: `https://bit.ly/3e5BUkn`.

Get inspired

Having a good idea of what you can automate in your business is an important starting point in your Zap-building process. If you need some inspiration and examples of ways in which you can automate your different business function processes with Zapier, you can check out the content from *Chapter 18*, *Automating Your Marketing Processes*, to *Chapter 21*, *Automating Your Finance and Reporting Processes*.

Review your processes and automations regularly

Continuous improvement is another key factor in maintaining successful automated processes. Once you have built your first few Zaps, make sure that you review them regularly and adjust them accordingly based on errors and changes in your processes. Reviewing your Zaps regularly and ensuring they have the minimum number of required steps will also help reduce task usage and prevent you from paying more than you need to. We covered this topic in *Chapter 3*, *Building Your First Automated Workflow (Zap)*.

You should now have a better understanding of the best practices for using Zapier effectively. Next, let's review a few tips and tricks that will further optimize your Zapier usage.

Tips and tricks to enhance your use of Zapier

Now that you've learned how to build your first few Zaps and you're on your way to supercharging your business and running it on autopilot, there might be times that you come across pain points that can be solved relatively easily if you know what to do next. Let's go over a few tips and tricks that will help you.

Trigger data not pulling through

Some app integrations may have issues pulling through real trigger data for you to use when building your Zap and you try to test your trigger. In many cases, if no trigger data can be found, Zapier will pull through dummy data that you can use in your action step mapping. Sometimes Zapier doesn't produce any dummy data, and if you click on the **Skip Test** button, you should be able to use placeholders in your action steps that will fill with data once the Zap is turned on and running. Rest assured that your Zap will run with the correct mappings once you have turned it on.

Extra Fields alerts

You might find that once you have built your steps, when you change the app or folder within an action step, you will be presented with an **Extra Fields** warning. This means that fields that you had previously filled in no longer exist. This is shown in the following screenshot:

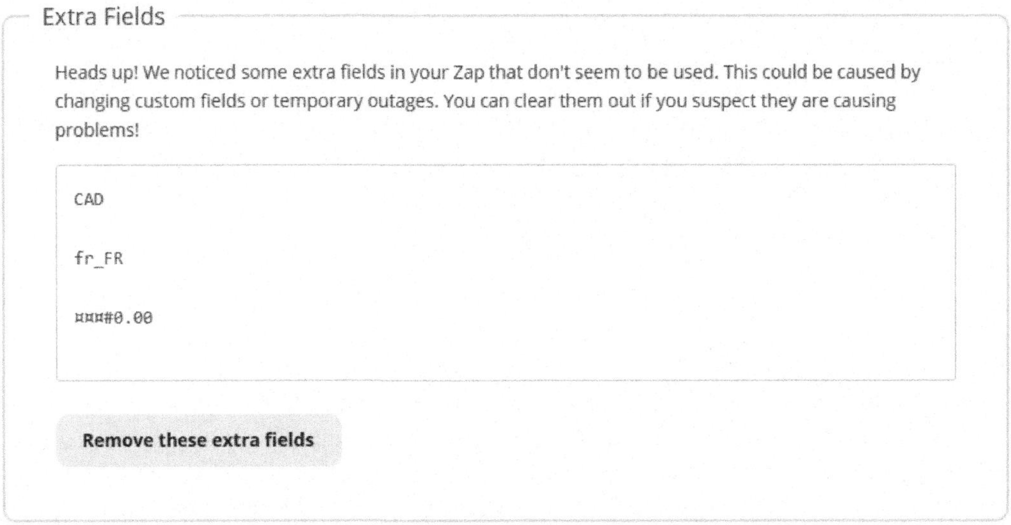

Figure 22.1 – An Extra Fields warning message

It is best to ensure that you always clear unused field data, or this can cause errors when your Zaps run. Just click on the **Remove these extra fields** button to do so.

Refresh fields when you make adjustments in your app

When you add new custom fields to your apps, make sure that you refresh the fields in any steps involving this change. This is important as often that data in old fields may remap against newer fields, causing inaccuracies when your Zap is turned on. This is shown in the following screenshot:

Figure 22.2 – Using the Refresh fields button to bring through new field information

This is quite common, for example, if you add additional columns in a Google Sheets spreadsheet, particularly between existing columns, or new merge fields in a Google Docs template. Click on the **Refresh fields** button to bring in new field information.

Improving the Zapier integration

You might find that the Zapier integration with one or more apps that you use in your business is tailored for common use cases. You, however, might want to achieve more with the integration, with different triggers, actions, or searches, or you might want certain fields to be added and data to be restructured in a more usable way. Often, you can achieve more with the data you're presented using Formatter by Zapier, using webhooks if they are available, or with code. You can also approach Zapier Support to find out who built the integration, be it a **Software-as-a-Service (SaaS)** app vendor or Zapier, and discuss whether improvements can be made to the integration. When app integrations are in the beta phase, this is usually a good opportunity to give feedback and suggest improvements.

Think outside of the box

When you're creating your workflows, be creative. If you can't achieve something with the Zapier integration with your app and you've explored all avenues, think about using a free tool as a stepping stone. You don't have to stick to conventional uses of the app. For example, you can use the Formatter by Zapier **Utilities** action event with the **Lookup Table** transform function to look up one value matching a key. If, however, you want to search for numerous values related to one key, you could use a Google Sheets spreadsheet as the lookup table instead.

Use the Zapier community as a resource

If you run into a problem, chances are that other Zapier users will have experienced it too. The Zapier Community forum, which can be found at `https://community.zapier.com/`, holds a log of searchable questions and answers to problems experienced by other users. The forum is also frequented by the Zapier Support team, several Zapier Experts, and other advanced users who will happily help with your issue if you find it hasn't been addressed previously.

You should now have a better understanding of the tips and tricks for enhancing your use of Zapier.

Summary

In this chapter, we discussed the best practices to adopt to enhance your success with using Zapier in your business. First, we did a recap of the topics that were covered in this book, which will help you use Zapier effectively. Then, we explored some practical tips and tricks for optimum Zap building.

You now know the best practices to follow to enhance your success with Zapier while implementing and using it in your business.

In the next chapter, we'll look at various scenarios that will help you assess your problem-solving and Zapier workflow-building skills. We will look into a specific problem that can be solved using Zapier and work through each example practically, with tips being given along the way. The scenarios are classified by skill level, and you will have the opportunity to put your knowledge to the test and adapt your problem-solving and Zap-building skills.

23
Challenge Your Problem-Solving and Zap-Building Skills

In this chapter, we will take a look at three scenarios that will help you assess your problem-solving and Zapier workflow-building skills. The chapter will first describe a specific problem that can be solved by using Zapier and work through each example with a suggested solution, with tips being given along the way. The scenarios are classified by skill level, and you will have the opportunity to put your knowledge to the test and adapt your problem-solving and Zap-building skills.

We will cover the following key topics in this chapter:

- Introduction and guidance

- Scenario 1 – novice

- Scenario 2 – intermediate

- Scenario 3 – advanced

- Guidance on suggested solutions for each scenario

Once you have worked through each of these topics, you will be able to build complex Zaps from scratch.

Technical requirements

To get the most out of the content in this chapter, you will need access to a Zapier account. The Zapier Starter plan will be required for you to use Premium apps and to create multi-step workflows. The Professional plan will be required for you to create Zaps with Paths by Zapier.

Introduction and guidance

We've suggested three different scenarios with increasing difficulty to test your problem-solving and workflow-building skills. When formulating your solutions, try to use the built-in apps by Zapier in your problem-solving where possible. This will optimize your Zap building without having to use other apps. Also, try to use as few steps as possible to reduce the task usage.

Remember, there are many ways that you can create a workflow. Just like the apps that you're using in your business are likely to be different from someone else's, the logic that you use for your Zaps is likely to be different from someone else's. The aim is to create Zapier workflows for repeatable processes with as few steps as possible and no errors. There are no wrong answers if the Zap achieves the objective. You can do this by designing a process that makes the most of the available features and integrations in the apps that are being used, and balance this with Zapier workflows to achieve the ultimate automation goal.

Now that you have a better understanding of how to tackle the three scenarios and get the best results from the challenge, let's dive into the first challenge.

Scenario 1 – novice

Dave runs an online business selling courses and membership programs. He uses Kajabi, a popular course platform, to host multiple courses and memberships. However, he wants to implement a highly converted standalone sales page app with a payment solution that gives him more flexibility with offers, discounts, and upsells. Kajabi does not integrate with many third-party apps, so whatever solution Dave chooses might not integrate with the course platform. Dave wants to streamline and automate his processes to reduce the time he spends manually granting access to the relevant course or membership program once the person has purchased the product through the sales page app. The problem Dave is likely to have when creating his workflow is that the product IDs in the two apps may not match. As the Kajabi integration with Zapier does not have any search actions, he is not able to use the product name to find the course product. Dave would also like to incorporate upsells and downsells, as well as account for access being removed after a refund is processed.

Can you suggest a better process for Dave by introducing a sales page app to his business and connecting this to Kajabi with Zapier?

Remember, be creative and think outside the box.

Now, go ahead and try to build out the Zap. If you need some inspiration, you can review a suggested solution in the *Guidance on suggested solutions for each scenario* section.

You should now be able to solve a problem requiring novice Zap building skills. Now, let's have a look at a more complex scenario.

Scenario 2 – intermediate

Winnie runs a small gardening and landscaping service with a team member, Eugene. Winnie receives inquiries for quotations via a contact form on her website. These inquiries include the lead's name, email address, contact number, job location address, budget, preferred project date, and inquiry notes. She then creates a quotation by email and once a customer has accepted a quotation for a job with a response, Winnie adds the new customer details to her Rolodex and writes the agreed project dates in her diary. She then emails her colleague, Eugene, with the date, start time, number of hours, and location of the project. She does not book more than one project in a day to allow for travel time, all projects start at 09:00, and they never leave for the job before 07:00. On the day, the project starts, both she and Eugene check the weather separately to decide whether they need to take waterproof clothing just in case it rains. They both also have to double-check the start time and location in the diary or the email Winnie sent. Once the job is complete, Winnie writes out an invoice for the number of hours Eugene and she have worked on the job and posts it through the letterbox for the customer with payment instructions.

With this current process, Winnie spends a lot of time manually writing out details for her quotation, in her Rolodex, diary, and invoice book, as well as typing out emails to Eugene and checking the weather. The process is not scalable, and as Winnie would like to grow the business, she would like to migrate to a digital process using appropriate apps and automations that will make her job much more efficient. Both Winnie and Eugene use Gmail for their emails, all their jobs are localized to San Diego, and the customer's invoice address is always the same as the project location.

Can you suggest a better process for Winnie by introducing other apps to her business that are more fit for purpose and connect her processes with Zapier? For this challenge, you must stick to a monthly app subscription budget of $50 per month for any additional apps and limit the additional apps you introduce to three new paid apps (including Zapier). There is no limit to the number of built-in apps by Zapier that you can use in your workflows.

Remember, be creative and think outside the box.

Now, go ahead and try to build out the Zap. If you need some inspiration, you can review a suggested solution in the *Guidance on suggested solutions for each scenario* section.

You should now be able to solve problems requiring intermediate Zap-building skills. Next, let's have a look at the last scenario to test your advanced problem-solving skills.

Scenario 3 – advanced

Liv is a career coach who runs a small firm with two other team members. The firm offers three types of coaching services with different prices and each team member is responsible for one of them. She currently receives inquiries via contact form submissions on her website. The contact form collects the lead's name, email address, and mobile number, the requested service, and additional inquiry notes. She then responds to the inquiry by pasting a response template into an email from a document and customizing it to the inquiry, asking the contact the best time for them to have a Zoom call. Once she has responded, she then manually adds the leads to a spreadsheet to track their progress through her sales cycle. The sheet has columns for each touchpoint in the sales cycle and Liv fills in each column once it is complete.

If the lead does not respond to the email, Liv manually follows this up with two further emails and a text message from her mobile over a period of 3 days. If the lead does not respond after 5 days, she updates the spreadsheet to mark the lead as **Dead**.

If the lead responds to the emails or text message, after some back-and-forth communication to arrange a meeting time, Liv meets with the lead on a Zoom call to discuss the inquiry. Once she has met with the lead, and if the project is not appropriate, Liv updates the spreadsheet to mark the lead as **Lost**.

If the project is appropriate, depending on the service the lead has requested, Liv chooses from three templates based on the service that has been selected, then manually creates a proposal in a document and sends the lead a PDF of the proposal by email. She then manually follows up the proposal with two emails spread over 4 days if the lead has not responded by email to accept the proposal. If she is unable to contact the lead or the lead does not respond, she updates the spreadsheet to mark the lead as **Dead**. If the lead accepts the terms and conditions in her proposal with a response to the email, she assigns the project to the relevant service owner in the team for them to start the onboarding process using another spreadsheet. The first step in the process is for the team member to send an email to the customer to book the coaching session with them.

With this current process, Liv spends a lot of time manually pasting templates into emails, following up on email responses, and updating the spreadsheet. Sometimes, she forgets to perform part of the process, doesn't respond to leads, and forgets to record the progress on the spreadsheet and her precious leads fall through the cracks. She uses Microsoft Outlook for her emails, WordPress for her website, a Microsoft Excel spreadsheet to record her leads, and a Microsoft Word document to record her email and proposal templates.

Can you suggest a better process for Liv by introducing other apps to her business that are more fit for purpose, and connecting her processes with Zapier? For this challenge, you must stick to a monthly app subscription budget of $150 per month for any additional apps and limit the additional apps you introduce to five new apps (including Zapier). There is no limit to the number of built-in apps by Zapier that you use in your workflows.

Remember, be creative and think out of the box.

Now, go ahead and try to build out the Zap. If you need some inspiration, you can review a suggested solution in the *Guidance on suggested solutions for each scenario* section.

You should now be able to solve a problem requiring advanced problem-solving and Zap-building skills. Let's explore some suggested solutions for the three scenarios we have just presented.

Guidance on suggested solutions for each scenario

Now that you've given it a go and tried to build out your Zaps to solve the problems in each of the three scenarios, let's go over a few suggested solutions to solve each of the problems. Remember, there are many ways to solve these problems, and the suggested solutions may offer you the opportunity to broaden your thought process.

Scenario 1 – one possible solution

There may be several ways to solve the problem that Dave has. To give you a hint at how you can potentially solve this problem, we will suggest that Dave uses ThriveCart as the sales page. You could suggest to Dave that he change from Kajabi to another course platform with more native integrations; however, in this case, it's more practical to use Zapier to join the dots. To address the problem of product IDs not matching, the most important step to include is a lookup table, using the ThriveCart product ID as the key and the Kajabi offer ID as the lookup value.

If you haven't done so already, go ahead and try to build out the Zap.

You can then proceed to create other Zaps to perform similar actions for upsells and downsells, as well as accounting for access being removed after a refund.

> **Tip**
> If you have multiple apps that you need to add as action steps and you consistently need to find data IDs to perform actions in the other apps, it is better to use a spreadsheet or database that can return multiple field values for one lookup key as opposed to adding multiple Formatter by Zapier Utilities Lookup Table steps.

Next, let's have a look at a possible solution to the second scenario.

Scenario 2 – one possible solution

There will be many ways to make Winnie's processes more efficient. To give you a hint at how you can potentially solve this problem, I would suggest that, first of all, Winnie implements a quoting and invoicing tool that can hold her customer details. It might be useful if this is an accounting app, such as Xero, that allows her to keep track of her payments and expenses too.

When Winnie receives a contact form submission, she will use Email Parser by Zapier to extract the inquiry information. This will trigger a workflow in Zapier to create a new contact with their name, email address, phone number, and address in Xero, and create a quote with the standard description `Gardening services`, noting the budget. In the quote, Winnie could specify the preferred project date in the **Reference** field or if she has no other place to add it, then she can put it as the last variable in the string of text in the line-item in the quote. She will also use the **Quantity** field for the number of hours that they will work on the project.

When the quote is accepted digitally, it will trigger a workflow in Zapier to split the project date from the quote line item (if she is not using the **Reference** field) using Formatter by Zapier and create a new event in her and Eugene's Google Calendars. The new event will be created with a start time of 09:00 and the number of hours from the quote will be used for the duration, as well as the customer's address as the location. As Winnie and Eugene use their calendars for other events, the new event will be created with the description **Job** to identify it.

At 17:00, the day before the Google Calendar event starts (16 hours prior), a workflow will be triggered in Zapier that will use Filter by Zapier to continue only if the event description is **Job**, then Zapier will check the weather forecast in San Diego for the next day with Weather by Zapier, and send an email using Email by Zapier to Winnie and Eugene with the weather forecast and job location. As Winnie forgets to check her emails regularly, she also needs an SMS to be sent to her using SMS by Zapier.

When the job is complete, Winnie converts the quote into an invoice and emails it to the customer from Xero, giving them the option to pay online using Stripe.

Winnie's additional app costs are $20 per month for the Xero Starter Plan and $29.99 per month for the Zapier Starter Plan. Google Calendar is included in Winnie and Eugene's Google Workspace subscriptions. That's a total of two new apps at $49.99 per month.

If you haven't done so already, go ahead and try to build out the Zaps involved in the improvements.

Next, let's have a look at a possible solution to the final scenario.

Scenario 3 – one possible solution

There will be many ways to make Liv's processes more efficient. To give you a hint at how you can potentially solve this problem, I suggest that, first of all, Liv consolidates her lead management processes by introducing an app such as a CRM. A CRM such as HubSpot will help Liv to visualize her sales cycle in a pipeline with different stages that will mirror her touchpoints. It will also allow her to use email templates, use embeddable forms, and send emails straight from the CRM, among other features.

In HubSpot, Liv could set up her sales pipeline to have five stages as follows: New lead, Call booked, Proposal Sent, Closed lost, Closed won. She will also create a contact form that she will embed into her WordPress website. Liv will now have no need for the spreadsheet.

We would also suggest that Liv sets up a Calendly account with three users that allows customers to book and pay for their coaching sessions via Stripe and integrates with their Outlook calendars. For each team member, Liv would create coaching session events for each of the services.

When a contact form is submitted, the workflow will be triggered in Zapier to use Formatter by Zapier to look up the project price of the service from a **Lookup Table** action step. Then, Zapier will create a new deal in the New lead stage with the contact association that was created when the form was submitted and the project price as the deal value, and noting the requested service and inquiry notes in custom fields within the deal. We will use Delay by Zapier to wait for 10 minutes before sending out an email using Microsoft Outlook. The email will be customized from a template including Liv's Calendly meeting booking link and personalized with the contact's first name and inquiry notes. The next steps in the Zap will involve a sequence that includes delays, checkpoints to establish which stage the deal is in, filters, and follow-up emails or SMS messages. For example, once the email has been sent, we will use Delay by Zapier to delay the workflow for 1 day, then after the delay, search for the deal details in HubSpot. Using Filter by Zapier, if the deal is still in the New lead stage, then Zapier will send the first follow-up email using Microsoft Outlook. This can be repeated for the next follow-up email and the follow-up SMS message, which could be sent by a service such as Voodoo SMS. After the SMS has been sent, delay the workflow for another 2 days, search for the deal, and if the deal is still in the New lead stage, update the deal to Closed lost.

If during this time the lead books a Zoom meeting through Calendly, this will trigger a workflow in Zapier to update the deal to the Call booked stage. The Calendly integration with Liv's calendar and Zoom will create the relevant events.

Once Liv has had the call, if the project is not appropriate, Liv will update the deal to `Closed lost`. If it is appropriate, Liv will update the deal to `Proposal sent`. We could suggest Liv uses a proposal or e-signature tool but as Liv does not require a signature for her service to be accepted, to keep the costs of additional apps down, we will suggest Liv creates a free Google account and uses Google Slides to create customizable branded templates. She will have one template for each of her services with `{{proposal date}}`, `{{name}}`, and `{{price}}` placeholder variables to prefill the lead's inquiry details.

The deal being moved to `Proposal sent` will trigger a new Zapier workflow that will involve a Formatter by Zapier step to format the date the proposal is created (when the Zap runs) from `{{zap_meta_human_now}}` or `today` to a prettier format. We will use Paths by Zapier to create a path for each service, where the filter will only allow the path to continue if the `Service` from the HubSpot custom field matches the text of the relevant service name. Then, we will create the Google Slides document from the template and send the PDF attached to a personalized email using Microsoft Outlook. Liv would also add the relevant team member's Calendly link to each of the proposals indicating that if they book a coaching call, they are agreeing to their terms and conditions and accepting the proposal. The next steps in the Zap will involve a sequence of steps that includes delays, checkpoints to establish which stage the deal is in, filters, and follow-up emails over a period of 4 days.

To manage the rest of the onboarding process, we could suggest Liv creates a free Trello account and invites her team members to a "Coaching Onboarding" board. Once the lead books and pays for the call through Calendly, a workflow will be triggered in Zapier to search for a deal associated with the contact, update the deal to `Closed won`, and create a new card in Trello. The rest of the onboarding process can then be followed.

Liv's additional app costs are $0 per month for HubSpot's free CRM, $0 for Google Slides, $15 per month for the Calendly Pro plan, plus $8 per month per additional user, $0 per month for the Trello Free plan, and $73.50 per month for the Zapier Professional plan. That's a total of five new apps at $104.50 per month.

If you haven't done so already, go ahead and try to build out the Zaps involved in these improvements.

You should now be able to solve a variety of problems requiring different levels of problem-solving and Zap-building skills.

Summary

In this chapter, you saw three scenarios ranging from novice to intermediate to advanced skill levels to give you the opportunity to put your knowledge to the test and adapt your problem-solving and Zap-building skills. We described specific problems classified by skill level that can be solved using Zapier in combination with introducing new apps to a business to make the process more efficient. We also worked through each example to demonstrate how it could be solved.

You now know how to use Zapier to build complex workflow automations that will help you to make your business, or your clients' businesses, more efficient.

Congratulations! You've completed the book and you're now well on your way to becoming a Zapier pro. You can get access to all the resources used in this book here: `https://bit.ly/3e5BUkn`.

Packt.com

Subscribe to our online digital library for full access to over 7,000 books and videos, as well as industry leading tools to help you plan your personal development and advance your career. For more information, please visit our website.

Why subscribe?

- Spend less time learning and more time coding with practical eBooks and Videos from over 4,000 industry professionals

- Improve your learning with Skill Plans built especially for you

- Get a free eBook or video every month

- Fully searchable for easy access to vital information

- Copy and paste, print, and bookmark content

Did you know that Packt offers eBook versions of every book published, with PDF and ePub files available? You can upgrade to the eBook version at packt.com and as a print book customer, you are entitled to a discount on the eBook copy. Get in touch with us at customercare@packtpub.com for more details.

At www.packt.com, you can also read a collection of free technical articles, sign up for a range of free newsletters, and receive exclusive discounts and offers on Packt books and eBooks.

Other Books You May Enjoy

If you enjoyed this book, you may be interested in these other books by Packt:

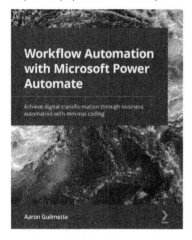

Workflow Automation with Microsoft Power Automate

Aaron Guilmette

ISBN: 978-1-83921-379-3

- Get to grips with the building blocks of Power Automate, its services, and core capabilities

- Explore connectors in Power Automate to automate email workflows

- Discover how to create a flow for copying files between two cloud services

- Understand the business process, connectors, and actions for creating approval flows

- Use flows to save responses submitted to a database through Microsoft Forms

- Find out how to integrate Power Automate with Microsoft Teams

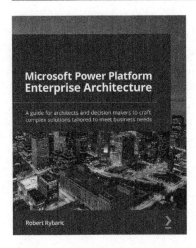

Microsoft Power Platform Enterprise Architecture

Robert Rybaric

ISBN: 978-1-80020-457-7

- Understand various Dynamics 365 CRM, ERP, and AI modules for creating Power Platform solutions

- Enhance Power Platform with Microsoft 365 and Azure

- Find out which regions, staging environments, and user licensing groups need to be employed when creating enterprise solutions

- Implement sophisticated security by using various authentication and authorization techniques

- Extend Power Apps, Power BI, and Power Automate to create custom applications

- Integrate your solution with various in-house Microsoft components or third-party systems using integration patterns

Packt is searching for authors like you

If you're interested in becoming an author for Packt, please visit authors.packtpub.com and apply today. We have worked with thousands of developers and tech professionals, just like you, to help them share their insight with the global tech community. You can make a general application, apply for a specific hot topic that we are recruiting an author for, or submit your own idea.

Hi!

I am Kelly Goss, author of *Automate It with Zapier*. I really hope you enjoyed reading this book and found it useful for increasing your productivity and efficiency in Zapier.

It would really help me (and other potential readers!) if you could leave a review on Amazon sharing your thoughts on *Automate It With Zapier*.

Go to the link below or scan the QR code to leave your review:

`https://packt.link/r/1800208979`

Your review will help me to understand what's worked well in this book, and what could be improved upon for future editions, so it really is appreciated.

Best Wishes,

Index

Symbols

5W1H method
  about 33
  reference link 33

A

accounting processes
  automating, with Xero integration 524
action 11
action descriptions
  used, for labeling Zaps 95
Acuity Scheduling 415
Add/Subtract Time transform option
  Date/Time action event, setting
    up with 329-331
advanced problem-solving skills
  scenarios, tackling for best
    results 560, 561
advanced text formatting features
  about 407
  options 407, 408
American Standard Code for Information
    Interchange (ASCII) 408
API integrations 7

Append Entry and Schedule
    Digest action event
  about 248
  Frequency field options 249
  setting up 248
application programming
    interface (API) 7
appointment booking and
    scheduling processes
  automating, with Zapier 459
apps
  connecting, in My Apps 67-69
  connecting, to Zapier 66
apps, selecting for business
  about 54
  app directories, searching 56
  app ecosystems, searching 55
  core app, defining 55
  feedback, reviewing 56
  key features and requirements listing 55
  options, exploring 54
  product demonstrations and testing
    support resources, arranging 56
  shortlist of apps, trailing 57
  transition to new app, planning 57

Zapier app ecosystem directory,
    searching 55
App Status by Zapier built-in app
  about 298
  error alert action, setting up 135
  pre-built workflow, selecting 133
  trigger event, customizing 134, 135
  used, for setting up Zap app
      status alerts workflow 133
  use cases 318
  using 299
App Status tab 132
array of objects 421
Asana API
  reference link 290
Autoreplay
  about 13
  feature, using 148
Autoreplay function
  tasks, replaying 149
  working 148

B

best practices, for using Zapier
  about 550
  automations, regulating 552
  built-in Zapier apps, using 552
  grips, obtaining with data mapping 551
  grips, obtaining with fields 551
  grips, obtaining with steps 551
  inspiration, obtaining 552
  preparing, before automations 550
  processes, reviewing 552
  task usage, monitoring 551
  troubleshoot alerts, setting up 551
  Zaps, managing 551
Bitly 266

blocks of text
  data, extracting with Extract
      transform functions 397, 398
  email address, extracting from 398
  HTML, removing with Remove
      HTML transform function 392
  numbers, extracting from 400
  phone numbers, extracting from 404
  URLs, extracting from 402
Boolean filters
  about 186
  options 186
Boolean (true/false) field type 89, 90
Box 491
Buffer 441
business applications
  communicating with 7
business apps, integrating with Zapier
  about 42
  apps, assessing to use with Zapier 48, 49
  app, searching 42, 43
  information, reviewing on app
      profile page 43, 44
business intelligence and
    dashboard processes
  automating, with Zapier 522
business operations processes 489
business process automation (BPA)
  about 4-6, 32
  examples 5
business process automation
    (BPA), exercise
  processes, analyzing 37, 38
  processes, brainstorming 34-36
  processes, documenting 40, 41
  processes, prioritizing 34-36
  processes, simplifying 37, 38
  team, involving 34

top-level management
    goals, assessing 33
    automation list and steps,
        identifying 39, 40
business tools
    options 8

C

Calendly 44
Campaign Monitor 442
Capitalize transform option
    Text action event, setting
        up with 359, 360
Capsule CRM 460
carriage-return characters 372
characters
    replacing 372
characters, in string of text
    converting, to lowercase 365
    converting, to uppercase 363
characters or words, into segments
    splitting, with Split Text transform
        function 386, 387
Chargebee 518
child values 292
Click Funnels 443
cloud-based Business Edition of
        Microsoft Excel Online
    reference link 494
Code by Zapier
    about 291
    reference link 292
    trigger and action events 291
    using, examples 291
comma-delimited text 424
comma-separated text 424

communication processes
    automating 492
conditional logic 12
conditional logic, in Zaps
    examples 180, 181
connected app accounts
    sharing 114-116
    sharing, stopping 116
connected apps
    managing 111-113
    sharing 114
Constant Contact 442
contract signature collection processes
    automating, with Zapier 461, 462
ConvertKit 458
country locales 341
Create Item in Feed action event
    about 243
    setting up 243-247
Create Team Invitation action event
    about 316
    setting up 317
CSV files
    data, importing from 411
currencies
    formatting, with Formatter
        by Zapier 340, 341
    working with 341
Customer Relationship Management
        (CRM) 55, 147

D

data
    importing, from CSV files 411
    picking, from list 418
Databox 176

data collection processes
   automating, with Zapier 457, 458
Data In information 145
Data Out information 145
data privacy and security, Zapier
   reference link 66
date and time
   formatting 331, 332
   manipulating, with Formatter
      by Zapier app 327
   used, for executing Formatter by
      Zapier app in fields 325-327
   values, adjusting with Formatter
      by Zapier app 323-325
Date/Time action event
   setting up, with Add/Subtract Time
      transform option 329-331
   setting up, with Format transform
      option 332-334
Date/time field type
   about 88
   supported formats 88
   timezone settings 88, 89
date/time filters
   about 186
   options 186
Decimal field type 91
default value
   assigning 394, 395
Default Value transform option
   Text action event, setting
      up with 395-397
Delay After Queue action event
   about 196
   setting up 196, 197
Delay by Zapier app
   about 192
   Delay After Queue action event 196

Delay For action event 193
Delay Until action event 194
Delay For action event
   about 193
   setting up 193
Delay Until action event
   about 194
   setting up 195, 196
detailed Zap run information
   Data In and Data Out information 145
   page, navigating 143, 144
   step data, assessing 145
   viewing 143
Detect Language action event
   about 270
   setting up 270
Dext 516
Digest by Zapier app
   Append Entry and Schedule
      Digest action event 248
   data, compiling 247, 248
   Find Digest search action event 257
   Release Existing Digest action event 256
digital signature collection processes
   automating, with Zapier 461, 462
digital transformation 54
Docparser 236
document storage processes
   automating 491
DocuSign 461
Draw.io 40
Drupal 439

E

Eastern Standard Time (EST) 326
e-commerce processes
   automating, with Zapier 462

effective workflow automation
   implementing, in business 92
email address
   extracting, from blocks of text 398
Email by Zapier
   about 212
   New Inbound Email trigger event 212
   New Read Receipt trigger event 217
   Send Outbound Email action event 214
   trigger and actions events 212
email marketing and marketing
         automation processes
   automating, with Zapier 442
email marketing processes
   automating, with Zapier 442
email notification
   settings 127
Email Parser by Zapier account
   mailbox, setting up 233-235
Email Parser by Zapier app
   data, extracting 230
   New Email trigger event 231
   New Mailbox trigger event 237
Email Parser mailbox templates
   adjusting 235, 236
error alert action
   setting up 129
Every Day trigger event
   about 200
   setting up 200, 201
Every Hour trigger event
   about 198
   setting up 199
Every Month trigger event
   about 202
   setting up 203

Every Week trigger event
   about 201
   setting up 201, 202
Expensify 516
Extract Email Address transform option
   Text action event, setting
      up with 399, 400
Extract Number transform option
   Text action event, setting
      up with 400-402
Extract Phone Number transform option
   Text action event, setting
      up with 405-407
Extract transform functions
   used, for extracting data from
      blocks of text 397, 398
Extract URL transform option
   Text action event, setting
      up with 403, 404

F

Facebook Pages action events
   about 447
   usage, examples 447
Facebook Pages integration
   multi-step Zap, setting up with 448
   social media marketing processes,
      automating with 445
Facebook Pages trigger events
   about 446
   usage, examples 446
FastField Mobile Forms 348
field data types
   about 87
   Boolean (true/false) 89, 90
   Date/time field type 88
   Decimal 91

File 90
Number (integer) 89
File field type 90
filter 12
Filter by Zapier
  about 163
  conditional logic, applying 180, 181
  filter conditions 184
  rules, customizing 181, 182
  setting up 181
  step, adding 181, 182
  testing 182-184
filter conditions, Filter by Zapier
  about 184
  Boolean filters 186
  date/time filters 186
  generic filters 187
  number filters 185, 186
  text filters 185
finance and reporting processes
  automating, with Zapier 523, 524
finance processes
  automating, with Zapier 515
finance processes, automated with Zapier
  about 515
  invoice management and accounting
    processes, automating 516-518
  payment processing processes,
    automating 518, 519
Find App search action event
  about 303
  setting up 303, 304
Find Digest search action event
  about 257
  setting up 257, 258
Find Person and Company Information
    search action event
  about 272

setting up 272-275
Find transform option
  Text action event, setting
    up with 370-372
Find Zap search action event
  about 310
  setting up 310
folders
  creating 99
  managing 100
  naming 99
  selecting, to view content 99
  shared folders, managing 121
  sharing, in Team or Company
    plan account 120
  sharing, with team 120
  using, in Zap management area 96-98
Format Currency transform option
  Numbers action event, setting
    up with 342-344
Format Number transform option
  Numbers action event, setting
    up with 338-340
Format Phone Number transform option
  Numbers action event, setting
    up with 345, 347
formatter 12
Formatter by Zapier
  about 176, 177, 322, 323
  custom date formats, using 327-329
  dates and times, formatting 331, 332
  executing, in fields with date
    and time 325-327
  mathematical operations,
    performing with 348
  phone numbers, formatting
    with 344, 345

spreadsheet-style formulas,
    using with 350, 351
time, adding 329
time, subtracting 329
used, for adjusting date and
    time values 323-325
used, for formatting currencies 340, 341
used, for formatting numbers 337
used, for manipulating dates
    and times 327
Formatter by Zapier, format
dates and times 176
numbers 177
text 177
utilities 177
Formatter by Zapier Utilities
    action event 410, 411
Format transform option
    Date/Time action event, setting
        up with 332-334
Frequency field options, Append Entry
    and Schedule Digest action event
    Daily option 249, 250
    Manual option 255
    Monthly option 252, 253
    Threshold option 254, 255
    Weekly option 251, 252

G

generic filters
    about 187
    options 187
Get App
    URL 56
Get Current Weather search action event
    about 278

setting up 279-281
using, examples 278
GitHub 490
Google Calendar 208
Google Docs action events
    about 497
    Append Text to Document 498
    Create Document from Template 498
    Create Document from Text 497
    Upload Document 497
Google Docs integration
    Google Docs action events 497, 498
    Google Docs search action events 499
    Google Docs trigger events 496
    multi-step Zap, setting up 500, 501
    online Word document processes,
        automating 495
Google Docs integration, issues
    reference link 500
Google Docs search action events 499
Google Docs trigger events
    about 496
    New Document 496
    New Document in Folder 496
Google Forms 348
Greenwich Mean Time (GMT) 326
guidance
    about 558
    on suggested solutions, for scenario 562

H

HelloSign 461
Hootsuite 441
Hubdoc 516
HubSpot 271

HyperText Markup Language (HTML)
  about 214, 392, 408
  removing, from blocks of
    text with Remove HTML
    transform function 392
Hypertext Transfer Protocol (HTTP) 288

I

IMAP by Zapier
  about 223
  setting up 224, 225
  trigger events 224
Import CSV File transform function
  using, examples 411
  Utilities action event, setting up 412-415
Incident History tab
  about 133
  reference link 133
information, reviewing on app profile page
  Help tab 48
  Integrations tab 45-47
integration automation 10
intermediate skill level
  scenarios, tackling for best
    results 559, 560
Internet Message Access Protocol (IMAP)
  about 173, 223
  reference link 223
InvoiceBerry 516
invoice management and
    accounting processes
  automating, with Zapier 516-518
Invoice Ninja 516

J

JavaScript 175

K

Key Performance Indicators (KPI) 522

L

latitude
  reference link 276-279
lead management processes
  automating, using Zapiers integrations
    with CRM illustrated 464, 465
  automating, using Zapier's with
    CRM Pipedrive 464, 465
  automating, with Zapier 460
Lead Score by Zapier
  about 271
  using, examples 271
Length transform option
  Text action event, setting
    up with 376, 377
line itemizer
  used, for appending line-items 429
  used, for creating line-items 429
  used, for prepending line-items 429
Line Itemizer (Create/Append/
    Prepend) transform option
  Utilities action event, setting up 430-433
line-items
  about 421-424
  appending, with line itemizer 429
  converting, to text 426, 427
  creating, with line itemizer 429
  manipulating 421
  prepending, with line itemizer 429
  text, converting to 424
line-item support
  apps 423

line-items, with Formatter by Zapier
   reference link 432
Line-item to Text transform option
   Utilities action event, setting up 427-429
list
   data, picking from 418
longitude
   reference link 276-279
lookup tables
   using 415
Lookup Table transform option
   using, examples 415
   Utilities action event, setting up 416-418
Lowercase transform option
   Text action event, setting
      up with 366, 367

M

MadKudu
   URL 271
mailbox
   setting up, in Email Parser by
      Zapier account 233-235
   setting up, in mapping
      templates 233-235
Mailchimp 166
Mailparser 236
mail servers
   reference link 218
mapping templates
   mailbox, setting up 233-235
Markdown 408
marketing processes
   about 439
   automating, with Zapier 438-443

marketing processes, with Zapier
   ad processes, automating 441
   automating, first steps 444, 445
   email marketing and marketing
      automation processes,
      automating 442
   email marketing processes,
      automating 442
   online presence processes,
      automating 439, 440
   social media marketing processes,
      automating 440, 441
   social media scheduling
      processes, automating 441
mathematical operations
   performing, with Formatter
      by Zapier 348
Meet Edgar 441
Mercury enters Retrograde trigger event
   data, retrieving for 284
Mercury in Retrograde trigger event
   data, retrieving for 284
Mercury leaves Retrograde trigger event
   data, retrieving for 285
Microsoft Dynamics 365 CRM 460
Microsoft Visio 40
Miro
   URL 34
multiple action and search
   used, for creating Zaps 158, 159
multi-step Zap
   about 13
   creating, with delay 204, 205
   creating, with filter 204, 205
   creating, with path 204, 205
   creating, with RSS feed digest 259
   creating, with scheduled trigger 204, 205

creating, with search action 204, 205
setting up, with Facebook
    Pages integration 448
setting up, with Pipedrive
    integration 478-486
setting up, with Xero
    integration 537-546
multi-step Zap, setting up with
    Google Docs integration
  about 500, 501
  first action step 503, 504
  fourth action step 508-512
  second action step 504-506
  third action step 507, 508
  trigger step 501, 502
multi-step Zap, with Facebook
    Pages integration
  first action step, setting up 450, 451
  second action step, setting up 452, 453
  trigger step, setting up 449
Mural
  URL 34
My Apps
  apps, connecting 67-69
my profile settings, Zapier platform
  email address, validating 26
  role, adding 26
  timezone, adding 26

N

name
  converting, into superhero name 384
native integrations 8
New Email trigger event
  about 231
  customizing 226
  setting up 231, 232

setup, completing 237
using 226, 231
New Folder trigger event
  about 304
  setting up 305
New Inbound Email trigger event
  about 212
  setting up 213
  using, examples 212
New Invoice trigger event
  about 314
  setting up 314, 315
New Item in Feed trigger event
  about 239
  setting up 239, 240
New Items in Multiple Feeds trigger event
  about 241
  setting up 241, 242
newline characters 372
New Mailbox trigger event
  about 237
  customizing 226
  setting up 238
New Public App trigger event
  about 301
  setting up 302
New Push trigger event
  about 264
  setting up 264-266
New Read Receipt trigger event
  about 217
  setting up 217, 218
  using, examples 217
New Team Member trigger event
  about 315
  setting up 315, 316
New Zap trigger event
  about 306

setting up 306, 307
no-code revolution
    about 9
    with Zapier 9
novice skill level
    scenarios, tackling for best results 559
number filters
    about 185
    options 186
Number (integer) field type 89
numbers
    extracting, from blocks of text 400
    formatting, with Formatter
        by Zapier 337
Numbers action event
    setting up, with Format Currency
        transform option 342-344
    setting up, with Format Number
        transform option 338-340
    setting up, with Format Phone Number
        transform option 345-347
    setting up, with Spreadsheet-Style
        Formula transform option 351-353
    setting up, with Perform Math
        Operation transform option 349, 350

O

OneDrive 491
online advertising processes
    automating, with Zapier 441
online presence processes
    automating, with Zapier 439, 440
online Word document processes
    automating, with Google
        Docs integration 495

operations processes, automating
        with Zapier
    about 488, 489
    communication processes 492
    document storage processes 491
    initiating, workflows 494, 495
    task and project management
        processes 490
    Word document and spreadsheet
        processes 493
Optical Character Recognition (OCR) 516

P

Pandadoc 52
paths 12
Paths by Zapier
    about 163
    branching logic, adding 187-189
    customizing 190
    navigating, within 191
    setting up 190
    step, customizing 192
payment processing processes
    automating, with Zapier 518, 519
Perform Math Operation transform option
    Numbers action event, setting
        up with 348-350
phone numbers
    extracting, from blocks of text 404
    formatting, with Formatter
        by Zapier 344, 345
phrases
    replacing 372
Pick from List transform option
    using, examples 418
    Utilities action event, setting up 419-421

Pipedrive action events
  about 469-473
  usage, examples 469-473
Pipedrive CRM 159
Pipedrive integration
  multi-step Zap, setting up with 478-486
  using, tips 477, 478
Pipedrive search action events
  about 474-476
  search action 475, 476
Pipedrive trigger events
  about 465-468
  usage, examples 465-468
Pluralize transform option
  Text action event, setting
    up with 368, 369
polling method 7
Process Bliss 40
processes
  automating 32
  simplifying 32
process mapping 32
Process Street 40
Product Hunt
  URL 56
proposal signature collection processes
  automating, with Zapier 461, 462
Proposify 461
Push by Zapier 262
Python 175

R

Really Simple Syndication (RSS) 174, 238
ReceiptBank 516
Recurly 518
Reddit
  URL 56

Release Existing Digest action event
  about 256
  setting up 256, 257
Remove HTML transform function
  used, for removing HTML
    from blocks to text 392
Remove HTML transform option
  Text action event, setting
    up with 393, 394
Replace transform function 372
Replace transform option
  Text action event, setting
    up with 373-375
reporting processes
  automating, with Zapier 519
reporting processes, automated
    with Zapier
  about 520
  business intelligence and dashboard
    processes, automating 522
  spreadsheet reporting processes,
    automating 520
  website analytics processes,
    automating 521
Retrograde by Zapier
  about 283
  trigger event options 283
Retrograde by Zapier trigger event
  Mercury enters Retrograde trigger
    event, data retrieving for 284
  Mercury in Retrograde trigger
    event, data retrieving for 284
  Mercury leaves Retrograde trigger
    event, data retrieving for 285
  setting up 283
Revolut Business 519
RSS by Zapier app
  about 238

Create Item in Feed action event 243
New Item in Feed trigger event 239
New Items in Multiple Feeds
    trigger event 241
RSS feed digest
    used, for creating multi-step Zap 259

S

sales processes
  about 457
  automating, with Zapier 456
sales processes, with Zapier
  about 457
  appointment booking and scheduling
      processes, automating 459
  automating, first steps 463, 464
  contract signature collection
      processes, automating 461
  data collection processes,
      automating 457, 458
  digital signature collection
      processes, automating 461
  e-commerce processes, automating 462
  lead management processes,
      automating 460
  proposal signature collection
      processes, automating 461
scenario
  challenge 558
  suggested solutions, guidance 562
scenarios, tackling for best results
  advanced skill level 560, 561
  intermediate skill level 559, 560
  novice skill level 559
Schedule by Zapier app
  about 198
  Every Day trigger event 200

Every Hour trigger event 198
Every Month trigger event 202
Every Week trigger event 201
Search Engine Optimization
    (SEO) 370, 521
searches 11
Secret Storage Key 292
Send Outbound Email action event
  about 214
  setting up 214-217
Shorten URL action event
  setting up 267, 268
Short Message Service (SMS) 208
Simple Mail Transfer Protocol (SMTP)
  about 173, 218
  reference link 218
Single Sign-On (SSO) 17
single-step Zap 13
Slack 45
Slybroadcast 345
SMS by Zapier
  about 208, 209
  setting up 210-212
  using, examples 208
SMTP and IMAP server
  reference link 219, 224
SMTP by Zapier
  about 218
  setting up 220-222
  using, examples 219
social media marketing processes
  automating, with Facebook
      Pages integration 445
  automating, with Zapier 440, 441
social media scheduling processes
  automating, with Zapier 441
Software as a Service (SaaS) 54, 554

space characters 372
Split Text transform function
    characters or words, splitting into
        segments with 386, 387
Split transform option
    Text action event, setting
        up with 387-389
spreadsheet reporting processes
    automating, with Zapier 520
spreadsheet-style formulas
    using, with Formatter by
        Zapier 350, 351
Spreadsheet-Style Formula
        transform option
    Numbers action event, setting
        up with 351-353
Standard Operating Procedures (SOPs) 40
Storage by Zapier
    about 292
    action and search action events 293, 294
    reference link 294
    using, examples 294
string of words
    title case, applying to 360, 361
suggested solutions
    guidance, for scenario 562-565
superhero name
    name, converting into 384
Superhero Name transform option
    Text action event, setting
        up with 385, 386
syncing interval 12
System Metrics tab 131, 132

T

tab characters 372
task 11

task statuses
    about 141, 142
    detailed Zap run information,
        viewing 143
    Holding reasons 142
Task Usage Limit Reached trigger event
    about 312
    setting up 312, 313
Task usage tab 138, 139
Team and Company account
        user management
    events 315
text
    converting, to line-items 424
    first position, finding of
        specified text 369, 370
    line items, converting to 426, 427
    number of characters, counting
        in string of text 375
    number of words, counting in
        string of text 377, 378
Text action event
    setting up, with Capitalize
        transform option 359, 360
    setting up, with Default Value
        transform option 395-397
    setting up, with Extract Email Address
        transform option 399, 400
    setting up, with Extract Number
        transform option 400-402
    setting up, with Extract Phone Number
        transform option 405-407
    setting up, with Extract URL
        transform option 403, 404
    setting up, with Find transform
        option 370-372
    setting up, with Length transform
        option 376, 377

setting up, with Lowercase
transform option 366, 367

setting up, with Pluralize
transform option 368, 369

setting up, with Remove HTML
transform option 393, 394

setting up, with Replace
transform option 373-375

setting up, with Split transform
option 387, 389

setting up, with Superhero Name
transform option 385, 386

setting up, with Titlecase
transform option 361-363

setting up, with Trim Whitespace
transform option 380-382

setting up, with Truncate
transform option 390-392

setting up, with Uppercase
transform option 363-365

setting up, with Word Count
transform option 378, 379

text filters
about 185
options 185

Text to Line-item transform option
using, examples 424, 425
Utilities action event, setting up 425, 426

text, to specified character length
truncating, with Truncate
transform function 389, 390

text values
transforming, with Zapier 356-358

tips and tricks, for enhancing use of Zapier
about 553
community, using as resource 555
Extra Fields alerts 553
outside of box thinking 555

refresh fields, when making
adjustments in app 554

trigger data, not pulling through 553

Zapier integration, improving 554

title case
applying, to string of words 360, 361

Titlecase transform option
Text action event, setting
up with 361-363

Today's Forecast trigger event
about 277
setting up 278
using, examples 277

Tomorrow's Forecast search action event
about 282
setting up 282
using, examples 282

Top-Level Domain (TLD) 402

top navigation bar
used, for managing Zaps 101, 102

transform numerical values
Zapier, using to 336

Translate by Zapier
about 268
action events 268
Detect Language action event 270
Translate Text action event 268

Translate Text action event
about 268
setting up 268, 269

Transport Layer Security (TLS) 220

Trello 38

Trello's API documentation
reference link 289

trigger
about 11
used, for labeling Zaps 95

trigger event
   customizing 129
   selecting 128
trigger event, options
   New Halted Task 128
   New Zap Error 128
   Zap Turned Off 128
Trim Whitespace transform option
   Text action event, setting
      up with 380-382
Truncate transform function
   used, for truncating text to specified
      character length 389, 390
Truncate transform option
   Text action event, setting
      up with 390-392
Trustpilot
   URL 56
Tumblr 439
Turn Zap On/Off action event
   about 308
   setting up 308, 309
Twitter 46
Two-Factor Authentication (2FA) 28
Typeform webform 372

U

Uniform Resource Locator (URL)
   about 174
   encoding, reference link 408
   extracting, from blocks of text 402
unique identifier
   about 76
   used, for labeling Zaps 95
Universally Unique Identifier
   (UUID4) 292

Universal Time Coordinated (UTC) 325
update time 12
Uppercase transform option
   Text action event, setting
      up with 363-365
URL Shortener by Zapier
   about 266
   Shorten URL action event,
      setting up 267, 268
User Interface (UI) 17
UTC (Coordinated Universal Time) 26
Utilities action event
   setting up, with Import CSV File
      transform function 412-415
   setting up, with Line Itemizer
      (Create/Append/Prepend)
      transform option 430-433
   setting up, with Line-item to Text
      transform option 427-429
   setting up, with Lookup Table
      transform option 416-418
   setting up, with Pick from List
      transform option 419-421
   setting up, with Text to Line-item
      transform option 425, 426

W

Weather by Zapier
   about 275
   Get Current Weather search
      action event 278
   Today's Forecast trigger event 277
   Tomorrow's Forecast search
      action event 282
   Will It Rain Today? trigger event 276
Webflow 439

webhooks
    reference link 290
    using, in Zaps 288-290
Webhooks by Zapier
    about 288-290
    reference link 290
    trigger and action events 289
    using, examples 290
webhooks method 7
website analytics processes
    automating, with Zapier 521
whitespace
    removing 380
Will It Rain Today? trigger event
    about 276
    setting up 276
    using, examples 276
WooCommerce 209
word
    first letter, capitalizing 358
Word Count transform option
    Text action event, setting
        up with 378, 379
Word document and
        spreadsheet processes
    automating 493
words
    pluralizing 367
    replacing 372
workflow automation
    about 6
    with Zapier 9
workflow events, filter options
    app 141
    data range 140
    folder 141
    status 141
    Zap 141

workflow, strategizing
    about 60
    app information, reviewing 61
    process, reviewing 61
    step-by-step workflow plan,
        creating 61-66

X

Xero action events
    about 528
    common fields 525
    usage, examples 528-534
Xero integration
    accounting processes,
        automating with 524
    used, for setting up multi-
        step Zap 537-546
    using, tips 536, 537
Xero search action events
    about 534-536
    common fields 525
    fields 534
Xero trigger events
    about 526
    common fields 525
    usage, examples 526-528

Z

Zap
    about 10
    creating, in Zap editor 70
    enabling 84
    naming 84
Zap app status alerts
    managing 130

workflow, setting up with App Status
    by Zapier built-in app 133
Zapier Status page, monitoring 130, 131
Zap editor
    about 11
    action step, setting up 77-84
    navigating 70
    right-side panel 71, 72
    top bar 71
    trigger step, setting up 73-76
    visual editor 72, 73
Zap error alerts
    email notification, settings 127
    managing 126
    workflow, setting up with Zapier
        Manager built-in app 127
Zap error alerts, workflow
    error alert action, setting up 129
    trigger event, customizing 129
    trigger event, selecting 128
Zap history 13
Zap history data
    Autoreplay feature, using 148
    managing 146, 147
Zap history information
    task statuses 141
    utilizing, for troubleshoot 136
Zap history page
    about 136, 137
    navigating 137
    Task usage tab 138, 139
    workflow events, viewing
        as filter 140, 141
    workflow events, viewing as list 140, 141
    workflow events, viewing
        as search 140, 141
    Zap runs tab 139, 140

Zapier
    about 9
    appointment booking and scheduling
        processes, automating with 459
    apps, connecting to 66
    business apps, integrating with 42
    business intelligence and dashboard
        processes, automating with 522
    contract signature collection processes,
        automating with 461, 462
    data collection processes,
        automating with 457, 458
    digital signature collection processes,
        automating with 461, 462
    e-commerce processes,
        automating with 462
    email marketing and marketing
        automation processes,
        automating with 442
    email marketing processes,
        automating with 442
    finance and reporting processes,
        automating with 523, 524
    finance processes, automating with 515
    guided workflows, using 84-86
    invoice management and accounting
        processes, automating with 516-518
    lead management processes,
        automating with 460
    marketing processes, automating
        with 438-443
    online advertising processes,
        automating with 441
    online presence processes,
        automating with 439, 440
    operations processes, automating
        with 488, 489

payment processing processes,
  automating with 518, 519
proposal signature collection processes,
  automating with 461, 462
reporting processes,
  automating with 519
sales processes, automating with 456
social media marketing processes,
  automating with 440, 441
social media scheduling processes,
  automating with 441
spreadsheet reporting processes,
  automating with 520
used, for workflow automation 9
using, best practices 550
using, tips and tricks 553
using, to transform text values 356-358
website analytics processes,
  automating with 521
Zapier account
  creating 17-19
Zapier account administration
  events 311
Zapier app ecosystem directory
  about 49
  app profile summary popup 52
  central navigation pane 50
  left navigation sidebar 51, 52
  navigating 50
Zapier app ecosystem directory,
    profile summary popup
  about 52
  central navigation pane 53
  left sidebar 53
Zapier apps
  about 171, 172
  account, managing 176
  advanced features 175, 176

data, compiling 174
data, extracting 174
Formatter by Zapier app, using 176, 177
functions 174, 175
logic, using 172, 173
run conditions, setting 172, 173
using, for communication 173
Zapier built-in apps, comprehensive
    cheat sheet
  reference link 552
Zapier Certified Expert 152
Zapier Chrome extension
  about 262
  setting up, on browser 263
Zapier, communication apps
  reference link 492
Zapier community
  about 151
  URL 151
Zapier Community forum
  reference link 555
Zapier Expert Directory
  about 152
  reference link 152
Zapier help document
  reference link 294
Zapier, key terms
  about 10
  action 11
  application (app) 10
  Autoreplay 13
  filter 12
  formatter 12
  multi-step Zap 13
  paths 12
  syncing interval 12
  task 11
  trigger 11

update time 12

Zap 10

Zap editor 11

Zap history 13

Zapier Manager built-in app

  account changes, managing 299, 300

  Create Team Invitation action event 316

  errors and alerts, managing 300

  errors, managing 299, 300

  events, for Team and Company
    account user management 315

  events, for Zapier account
    administration 311

  Find App search action event 303

  Find Zap search action event 310

  managing 301

  New Folder trigger event 304

  New Invoice trigger event 314

  New Public App trigger event 301

  New Team Member trigger event 315

  New Zap trigger event 306

  sorting, in folders 301

  Task Usage Limit Reached
    trigger event 312

  Turn Zap On/Off action event 308

  used, for setting up Zap error
    alerts workflow 127

  Zaps, naming 301

Zapier plan

  selecting 13-15

Zapier plan, for business

  company plan 17

  free plan 16

  professional plan 16

  starter plan 16

  team plan 16

  using 15

Zapier platform

  app-specific help, finding
    in app profiles 150

  community, engaging with 151

  customer support 152

  help center, utilizing 150, 151

  implementing 149

Zapier platform, navigation

  about 20

  footer menu 23

  left sidebar icon 21, 22

  top right icon 23

Zapier platform, settings and preferences

  account 29

  advanced area 28

  billing and usage 29

  data management 28

  email notifications 26-28

  members area 29

  modifying 23

  my profile 24, 25

  my profile settings, customizing 25

Zapier Status page

  App Status tab 132

  Incident History tab 133

  monitoring 130, 131

  System Metrics tab 131, 132

  URL 130

Zapier, storage apps

  reference link 491

Zapier, task and project management apps

  reference link 490

Zapier to automate tasks

  reference link 489

Zapier, Word document and
    spreadsheet apps

  reference link 494

Zapier workflows
  sharing 117
Zap management area
  folders, using 96, 97
Zap runs tab 139
Zaps
  copy of Zap, sharing 117-120
  creating, with multiple action
      and search 158, 159
  labeling 94
  labeling, with action descriptions 95
  labeling, with trigger 95
  labeling, with unique identifiers 95
  letters, adding 96
  link sharing, disabling 120
  managing 100, 101
  managing, from within specific
      Zap boxes 102-106
  managing, with top navigation
      bar 101, 102
  moving, between personal and
      team accounts 122, 123
  multi-step Zap, creating with
      search action 171
  numbers, adding 96
  organizing 94
  ownership, transferring 122
  restoring, from Trash folder 106, 107
  roman numerals, adding 96
  search actions 159
  search actions, adding in Choose
      value field 167-170
  search actions, adding with
      + icon 160-167
  sharing, in Team or Company
      plan account 120
  statuses 109, 110

Zap Settings tab
  utilizing, in Zap editor 107, 108
Zap template
  reference link 512
ZohoSign 461

Printed in Great Britain
by Amazon